Human Enhancement

Human Enhancement

Edited by Julian Savulescu and Nick Bostrom

OXFORD
UNIVERSITY PRESS

OXFORD
UNIVERSITY PRESS

Great Clarendon Street, Oxford OX2 6DP

Oxford University Press is a department of the University of Oxford.
It furthers the University's objective of excellence in research, scholarship,
and education by publishing worldwide in

Oxford New York

Auckland Cape Town Dar es Salaam Hong Kong Karachi
Kuala Lumpur Madrid Melbourne Mexico City Nairobi
New Delhi Shanghai Taipei Toronto

With offices in

Argentina Austria Brazil Chile Czech Republic France Greece
Guatemala Hungary Italy Japan Poland Portugal Singapore
South Korea Switzerland Thailand Turkey Ukraine Vietnam

Oxford is a registered trade mark of Oxford University Press
in the UK and in certain other countries

Published in the United States
by Oxford University Press Inc., New York

British Library Cataloguing in Publication Data

Data available

Library of Congress Cataloging in Publication Data

Human enhancement/edited by Julian Savulescu and Nick Bostrom.
      p.; cm.
   Includes bibliographical references and index.
   ISBN 978–0–19–929972–0 (alk. paper)
 1. Medical innovations—Social aspects. 2. Medical ethics. 3. Prenatal diagnosis. 4. Genetic
engineering. I. Savulescu, Julian. II. Bostrom, Nick, 1973-
   [DNLM: 1. Biomedical Enhancement—ethics. 2. Genetic Engineering—ethics. 3. Prenatal
diagnosis—ethics. W 82 H918 2008]
   RA418.5.M4H86 2008
   610.1'9—dc22   2008031138

Typeset by Laserwords Private Limited, Chennai, India
Printed in Great Britain
on acid-free paper by
CPI Antony Rowe, Chippenham, Wiltshire

ISBN 978–0–19–929972–0

10 9 8 7 6 5 4 3 2 1

Contents

Acknowledgements

The Editors would like to gratefully acknowledge the support of the Uehiro Foundation on Ethics and Education and the Carnegie Council on Ethics and International Affairs for their support. Much of this book began as the 2004 Oxford-Uehiro-Carnegie Council Conference held at the Carnegie Council in New York on November 18–19, 2004. The theme of that conference was "How Can Human Nature Be Ethically Improved ?"

We would also like to thank Heather Bradshaw, Christine Gowing, Ruth Coster, and Miriam Wood for assistance with preparation of the manuscript.

Introduction

Human Enhancement Ethics: The State of the Debate

Nick Bostrom and Julian Savulescu

Background

Are we good enough? If not, how may we improve ourselves? Must we restrict ourselves to traditional methods like study and training? Or should we also use science to enhance some of our mental and physical capacities more directly?

Over the last decade, human enhancement has grown into a major topic of debate in applied ethics. Interest has been stimulated by advances in the biomedical sciences, advances which to many suggest that it will become increasingly feasible to use medicine and technology to reshape, manipulate, and enhance many aspects of human biology even in healthy individuals. To the extent that such interventions are on the horizon (or already available) there is an obvious practical dimension to these debates. This practical dimension is underscored by an outcrop of think tanks and activist organizations devoted to the *biopolitics* of enhancement. Already one can detect a biopolitical fault line developing between pro-enhancement and anti-enhancement groupings: transhumanists on one side, who believe that a wide range of enhancements should be developed and that people should be free to use them to transform themselves in quite radical ways; and bioconservatives on the other, who believe that we should not substantially alter human biology or the human condition.[1] There are also miscellaneous groups who try to position themselves in

---

[1] See e.g. Bostrom, N. 2006. 'A Short History of Transhumanist Thought', *Analysis and Metaphysics*, 5: 63–95 (http://www.nickbostrom.com/papers/history.pdf).

between these poles, as the golden mean. While the terms of this emerging political disagreement are still being negotiated, there might be a window of opportunity open for academic bioethicists to influence the shape and direction of this debate before it settles into a fixedly linear ideological tug-of-war.[2]

Beyond this practical relevance, the topic of enhancement also holds theoretical interest. Many of the ethical issues that arise in the examination of human enhancement prospects hook into concepts and problems of more general philosophical significance—concepts such as human nature, personal identity, moral status, well-being, and problems in normative ethics, political philosophy, philosophy of mind, and epistemology. In addition to these philosophical linkages, human enhancement also offers thought-fodder for several other disciplines, including medicine, law, psychology, economics, and sociology.

The degree to which human enhancements constitute a distinctive cluster of phenomena for which it would be appropriate to have a (multidisciplinary) academic subfield is debatable, however. One common argumentative strategy, used predominantly to buttress pro-enhancement positions, is to highlight the continuities between new controversial enhancement methods and old accepted ways of enhancing human capacities. How is taking modafinil fundamentally different from imbibing a good cup of tea? How is either morally different from getting a full night's sleep? Are not shoes a kind of foot enhancement, clothes an enhancement of our skin? A notepad, similarly, can be viewed as a memory enhancement—it being far from obvious how the fact that a phone number is stored in our pocket instead of our brain is supposed to matter once we abstract from contingent factors such as cost and convenience. In one sense, *all* technology can be viewed as an enhancement of our native human capacities, enabling us to achieve certain effects that would otherwise require more effort or be altogether beyond our power.

Pushing this thought further, one could argue that even mental algorithms such as we use to perform basic arithmetic in our heads, and learned skills such as literacy, are a kind of enhancement of our mental software. When we learn to calculate and read we are literally reprogramming the

---

[2] For one early discussion, see Glover, J. 1984. *What Sort of People Should There Be?* (Harmondsworth: Penguin).

micro-structure of our nervous system, with physiological effects just as real as those resulting from the ingestion of a psychoactive drug, and often more durable and with more profound consequences for our lives. At the limit of this line of reasoning, *all* learning could be viewed as physiological enhancement, and *all* physical and organizational capital could be viewed as external enhancements. Stripped of all such "enhancements" it would be impossible for us to survive, and maybe we would not even be fully human in the few short days before we perished.

If the concept of human enhancement is stretched to this extent, it becomes manifestly unfit for service as an organizing idea for a new and distinctive field of ethical inquiry. This need not trouble enhancement advocates who maintain that there is no morally significant difference between novel biomedical enhancements and all the other more familiar ways of enhancing. Those who object to human enhancement, however, must resist this inflationary interpretation of what enhancement is, drawing a line somewhere to distinguish the problematic new types of enhancements from the unobjectionable use of shoes, clothes, tea, sleep, PDAs, literacy, forklifts, and the bulk of contemporary medicine.

Such a line need not be sharp. Many important and useful philosophical terms are vague. Nevertheless, two challenges must be met. First, some account needs to be given of what counts as an enhancement—an account that must be reasonably intelligible and non-arbitrary, capturing something that might plausibly be thought of as a kind. Second, given such an account, it needs to be shown that it tracks a morally relevant distinction. Unless these two challenges can be met, it would appear misguided to organize our ethical thinking in this area around the concept of enhancement. "Enhancement" might still be useful to flag a patch of territory consisting of a variety of loosely related practices, techniques, and prospects. But it would hardly make sense either to pledge allegiance to such a flag, or to devote oneself to opposing what it stands for. Instead, our ethical judgments would have to track different and finer distinctions that would reflect the concrete circumstances and consequences of particular enhancement practices: Precisely what capacity is being enhanced in what ways? Who has access? Who makes the decisions? Within what cultural and sociopolitical context? At what cost to competing priorities? With what externalities? Justifiable ethical verdicts may only be attainable following a specification of these and other similarly contextual variables. To accept this conclusion is to accept a kind of *normalization* of enhancement. That is, at a fundamental normative level, there is nothing special about human enhancement interventions: they should be evaluated, sans prejudice and bias, on a case-by-case basis using the same messy criteria that we employ in other areas of practical ethics.[3]

The contributors to this volume bring to the table a variety of perspectives, from both sides of the debate and from both Eastern and Western, secular and religious traditions. We have organized the chapters into two roughly distinguishable groups. First, those dealing with the ethics of enhancement more or less in general, and with associated issues such as the normative significance of human nature. Second, those focusing on the ethics of some particular type of enhancement. This is followed by a final chapter that addresses enhancement medicine as a practical (scientific) challenge.

Enhancement in general

NORMAL DANIELS asks what it would take to change *human nature*. He argues that this is a taller order than might at first appear to be the case. Human nature, says Daniels, is a dispositional selective population concept. It is *dispositional* in the sense that the same human nature will manifest as very different phenotypes depending on the environment in which it is placed. It is a *population* concept in the sense that to characterize human nature we must aggregate across individual variation. And it is *selective* in the sense that some traits (e.g., rationality) are often claimed to be more central to human nature than others (e.g., nasal hair). On this account, we cannot modify human nature unless we act on a population level. Furthermore, the intervention must affect traits central to that nature. To Daniels, this suggests that "genetic interventions are less likely to be threats than environmental interventions that undermine our human capabilities or nature."

It has been argued that human germ-line engineering must be opposed on grounds that it would change human nature. George Annas, in particular, has been promoting the need for a new U.N. "Convention on the Preservation of the Human Species", which would realize itself in an

---

[3] Even ethical theories that are simple in their structure—such as hedonism—become complex and messy in their application to many real-world predicaments.

international treaty to ban "species altering" research. Annas claims that "cloning and inheritable genetic alterations can be seen as crimes against humanity of a unique sort: they are techniques that can alter the essence of humanity itself." The chapter by ERIC JUENGST offers a critique of this view.

Juengst notes that species are not "static collections of organisms that can be 'preserved' against change like a can of fruit; they wax and wane with every birth and death and their genetic complexions shift across time and space." Interpreted strictly, a ban on altering the human species would cover too much since almost everything we do as humans might affect the genetic composition of the next generation. (Taken literally, such a ban would seem to require the universal adoption of cloning as the sole method of reproduction.) Yet if the proposed ban on "species altering" is given a more relaxed reading—as, say, a proscription of interventions that would alter our "taxonomically defining" traits or that would significantly alter human nature—then it would fail to serve its intended purpose. For under this interpretation, even most germ-line modifications, genetic enhancements, and reproductive manipulations, like cloning, would not be species altering.

RYUICHI IDA presents an Asian bioconservative perspective on human enhancement. Ida tells us that, "in Japan,"

ethical theories culturally specific.

> we respect the view of 'As it stands'... This attitude expresses respect for Nature and for the natural state of the baby... Ethical appeals to the human welfare or individual happiness to justify the use of science of technology may have intuitive force in the West, but may seem alien to a non-Western audience.

Ida distinguishes between "natural improvement" such as may come about through training and study, and "unnatural improvement" such as may result from taking anabolic steroids. The latter kind of improvement, he believes, may not be permissible because it depends on and fosters an instrumentalist or dualistic view of human beings. On this view, as Ida points out, it is not only newfangled enhancement interventions such as memory enhancing drugs or genetic engineering that are morally suspect. Much of what Westerners now consider to be normal therapeutic medicine is also problematic:

> Oriental medicine has as its basic principle the reestablishment of the balance of body and soul. All the diseases come from the imbalance of the patient. It is true that this type of medicine does not practice big operations, like organ transplants, or brain operations. Oriental medicine sees the conditions that might call for

such interventions as natural, simply a consequence of human mortality, and it accordingly sees such a patient as entering a stage of returning to nature, i.e. dying.

Ida notes that in East and South East Asia, Buddhism and Confucianism often have a dominant role in daily life, and the life style and social practices are still rooted in agricultural traditions.

While the sensibilities that Ida describes may seem somewhat alien to Western bioethicists—especially the idea that there are any kind of *ethical* grounds for recoiling from "big operations" and organ transplantations—a position quite close to that of Ida has recently been articulated by MICHAEL SANDEL, an American political philosopher who has served on the President's Council on Bioethics during the George W. Bush administration. Sandel warns that enhancement and genetic engineering represent a kind of "hyperagency"—a dark Promethean aspiration to remake nature to serve our purposes and satisfy our desires. We are at risk, Sandel believes, of losing our "openness to the unbidden":

The problem is not the drift to mechanism but the drive to mastery. And what the drive to mastery misses and may even destroy is an appreciation of the gifted character of human powers and achievements . . . To acknowledge the giftedness of life is to recognize that our talents and powers are not wholly our own doing, despite the effort we expend to develop and to exercise them.

When put in this way, however, the objection becomes a concern about a contingent and speculative psychological effect of the practice of enhancement. One could imagine an enhancement user who is under no illusion that her talents and powers are wholly her own doing, understanding clearly that without the contributions from Nature, God, or Fortune she would be literally nothing.

Perhaps one solution would be for the FDA to require appropriate labeling of enhancement products. A bottle of memory-boosting pills could come with the inscription:

MAY CAUSE CONSTIPATION, DRY MOUTH, SKIN RASHES, AND LOSS OF OPENNESS TO THE UNBIDDEN. IF SYMPTOMS PERSIST AFTER 48 HRS, CONSULT YOUR PHYSICIAN AND/OR YOUR SPIRITUAL ADVISOR.

A more philosophically sophisticated response to Sandel's argument is on offer in the chapter by FRANCES KAMM. She considers whether, as Sandel claims, the desire for mastery motivates enhancement and whether such a desire could be a ground for its impermissibility. Kamm also examines Sandel's views about parent/child relations, and how enhancement would affect distributive justice and the duty to aid. She also discusses the therapy/enhancement distinction and criticizes some recent attempts to explicate this distinction in a way that would allow it to carry normative weight, including attempts by Sandel and by P. H. Schwartz.

The therapy/enhancement distinction comes in for further scrutiny in the chapter by JOHN HARRIS. He critiques the idea, developed by Norman Daniels and others, of using the notion of normal or "species typical" functioning as the dividing line separating morally high-priority interventions (those aimed at preserving or restoring normal functioning) from morally low-priority interventions (those aimed at enhancing normal functioning). Arguing from a consequentialist position, Harris concludes that

[t]he overwhelming moral imperative for both therapy and enhancement is to prevent harm and confer benefit. Bathed in that moral light it is unimportant whether the protection or benefit conferred is classified as enhancement or improvement, protection or therapy. *enhancement / therapy distinction dissolves.*

Harris also briefly touches on some other objections to enhancement, including the "playing God" objection, which he gives short shrift. This objection is treated in more detail in the chapter by TONY COADY. The objection may, but need not, rely on theological assumptions. Coady distinguishes three traditions in Christian theology regarding the relationship between human beings and the natural order: domination, stewardship, and co-creation. According to the domination model, humans were created to lord it over nature. According to the stewardship model, the role of humans is to act to preserve the natural order. And in the metaphor of co-creation, God has called human beings into a creative partnership in the ongoing creation of the world. The domination model has been criticized as insensitive to ecological concerns; the stewardship model for according an unduly passive role to a species endowed with as much initiative and creativity as ours; and the co-creation for downplaying the distance between God and creatures. Coady thinks that all three models have an element of truth in them, and that "the dialogue between them exhibits the tensions that need to be kept in view by believers in negotiating the mystery of humanity's place in the created order".

In its secular interpretation, the critique of playing God seems primarily a criticism of an attitude (hubris) and only derivatively of a program or proposal. Coady suggests that when people worry about the application of the latest scientific and technological discoveries and put this worry in terms of "playing God", they are concerned that these applications may embody an unjustified confidence in knowledge, power, and virtue beyond what can reasonably be allowed to human beings. Overzealous transhumanists do not have a monopoly on this vice, as Coady writes:

The temptation to act in ways that ignore or make light of the in-built constraints on human knowledge, power and benevolence is certainly one to which all humans are prone, including bishops, theologians and priests. Indeed, those who believe that they are privy to God's purposes through revelation, inspiration or tradition or all combined are perhaps especially open to the temptation. We should recall in this connection the sad history of religious wars, crusades, inquisitions, the preaching of erroneous doctrines and the failure to preach important truths. I am a Catholic, and my own Church has its blemishes in all these regards.

ERIK PARENS, in a similarly conciliatory spirit, suggests that proponents and critics of enhancement technologies, while often talking past one another, have more in common than they realize. Parens believes that both groups proceed from a "moral ideal of authenticity", although they differ in how they understand this ideal, and he believes that these different understandings of authenticity "grow out of two different but equally worthy ethical frameworks, which stand in a fertile tension with each other".

It may be apropos to mention a recent psychological study, which found that people are much more reluctant to enhance traits believed to be fundamental to self-identity (e.g., social comfort) than traits considered less fundamental (e.g., concentration ability)—consistent with the idea that beliefs about authenticity may be an important shaper of attitudes towards enhancement.[4] However, the same paper also found that perceptions about authenticity could be easily manipulated. Advertisement taglines that framed enhancements as enabling ("Become Who You Are") rather

---

[4] Riis, J., Simmons, J. P. and Goodwin, G. P. Forthcoming. 'Preferences for Enhancement Pharmaceuticals: The Reluctance to Enhance Fundamental Traits', *Journal of Consumer Research* (http://papers.ssrn.com/sol3/papers.cfm?abstract_id=967676). For one attempt to leverage psychological findings to draw philosophical conclusions for the enhancement debate, see Bostrom, N. and Ord, T. 2006. 'The Reversal Test: Eliminating Status Quo Bias in Bioethics', *Ethics*, 116: 656–80 (http://www.nickbostrom.com/ethics/statusquo.pdf).

than enhancing ("Become More Than Who You Are") eliminated the preference for non-fundamental over fundamental trait enhancements. We can rely on big pharmaceutical companies for our drugs, and on marketing firms for our authenticity.

The chapter by ARTHUR CAPLAN considers some general arguments against enhancement made by bioconservatives ("anti-meliorists" in Caplan's terminology), including concerns about authenticity and the worry that the happiness and satisfaction achieved though engineering is seductive and will lead to a deformation of our character and spirit. Caplan argues that neither of these arguments provides a sufficient reason for opposing enhancement or optimization either of ourselves or our children. He concludes that what we must do is "take each proposed enhancement technology under consideration and decide whether what it can do is worth whatever price it might exact".

Minor enhancements, such as a nootropic giving us a temporary 10 or 20 per cent boost in our ability to memorize facts when studying for a medical exam, is one thing; but what about more radical forms of enhancement? What of enhancements that would give us some significant non-human characteristics? Or ones that could make us "post-human"? These questions are addressed in a chapter by JULIAN SAVULESCU. In particular, Savulescu discusses the views put forward in "The human prejudice", a posthumously published paper by the late philosopher Bernard Williams. Williams argued that a prejudice in favor of our human conspecifics is morally acceptable, by contrast to certain other prejudices such as racism and sexism. Savulescu argues that Williams' defense of speciesism fails. Savulescu also shows how the issues raised in this debate connect to fundamental problems in normative ethics and in metaethics—such as internalism vs. externalism about normative reasons; the criteria for moral status; submaximization vs. satisficing; and the role of partiality and special relations in determining our moral duties.

Enhancements of certain kinds

Even if there is no moral reason to forgo enhancement in general, there might still be aspects of some particular types of enhancement that are morally problematic.

One morally charged context of enhancement is reproduction. There are many methods, low- and high-tech, by which we influence the character of new persons being brought into the world. At one end of the spectrum, mate choice has an obvious effect on what our children will be like, and the quality of prospective offspring is one factor that can influence our choice of romantic partners. According to evolutionary psychology, sexual attraction is often keyed to a subconscious assessment of the genetic quality of a potential mate (along with other factors). These factors can also be taken into account when we consciously deliberate to select among romantic prospects. We can also achieve "eugenic" objectives by exerting choice over the timing of conception—for example, by taking into account the increasing risk of birth defects associated with conceiving at an older age. Further, maternal nutrition and drug use can affect the fetus, and abortion can be used to terminate pregnancies when chromosomal abnormalities or other serious defects are detected. For couples undergoing in vitro fertilization, preimplantation genetic diagnoses can be used to select embryos without the need for abortion. The number of genetic conditions that can be assayed will increase with advancing technology; it will likely become possible to select not only *against* genetic defects but also *for* gene combinations correlating with positive desirable traits. It is also likely that more active forms of genetic interventions will become feasible, such as gene therapy either on zygotes, gametes, or even on the reproductive systems of adults, which could increase the likelihood that resulting embryos will have genetic endowments correlating with desirable attributes. After birth, parents and society continue to shape the character and capacities of children through means including education, nutrition, and rearing.[5]

The context of reproduction involves making choices that directly and intimately affect not only the decision-maker but also the resulting children. This introduces distinctive moral elements that are not usually present to the same extent in cases where a competent adult makes a free and informed decision to enhance herself. Another complicating moral element in reproduction is that our choices may determine which of several possible persons come into existence. According to many ethical theories, there are fundamental moral differences between cases in which our actions affect

---

[5] Savulescu, J. 2006. 'Genetic Interventions and the Ethics of Enhancement of Human Beings'. In *The Oxford Handbook on Bioethics*, ed. B. Steinbock (Oxford: Oxford University Press), 516–35.

some person who already exists or will come to exist independently of our actions, and cases in which our actions result in the creation of a new person who would not otherwise have existed.

Negative selection—selection against disability—has come under criticism, especially from some members of the disability community. Positive selection—selection for some desired trait in our offspring other than absence of disability or disease—has generated even broader unease in the public at large. DAN BROCK examines a series of arguments for the claim that selection of children is morally wrong, including expressivist concerns, the "playing God" objection, the worry that selection might undermine our unconditional acceptance of children, the critique of the notion of "perfection", and the allegation that selection is in a bad sense eugenics. Brock argues that selection of our children is not in itself morally problematic, and concludes that "If negative or positive selection should be rejected, it will have to be for other reasons, not simply because selection of our children is wrong."

Some other moral considerations relating to genetic selection and genetic engineering of offspring are evaluated in the chapter by PETER SINGER. The objection that genetic selection would be bad for the child does not work, Singer argues. Of greater concern are some of the potential societal effects that such enhancement could have. If Robert Nozick's proposal to establish a "genetic supermarket" (i.e. letting prospective parents make their own reproductive choices, within wide moral limits) were adopted, it could lead to resources being squandered in a competitive pursuit of positional goods.[6] Positional goods, such as height, are ones whose goodness for those who have them depends on other subjects not possessing them. An enhancement that had no effect other than making the user six inches taller would provide no net benefit if universally applied. It might, on the contrary, result in net losses inasmuch as food consumption would increase, vehicles would need to be redesigned, etc. But as Singer notes, many enhancements would provide benefits that are not merely positional. A related concern is that genetic selection might aggravate inequality. In principle there are many ways in which this concern could be assuaged: the technology could be made available to all, or only to the worst off; or other compensating social policies could be put in place. (In practice, whether

(handwritten margin note: individual vs. society)

---

[6] Nozick, R. 1974. *Anarchy, State and Utopia* (New York: Basic Books), 315 n.

any such measures were implemented would depend on the outcome of political struggles.) Singer points out that bans on genetic enhancement would have limited effect if couples wishing to avail themselves of such opportunities could simply travel to another state or another country in order to do so. Moreover, nations that prohibit their citizens from using genetic enhancement might lose out in terms of economic competitiveness and fall behind countries that embrace enhancement.

Susumu Shimazono discusses attitudes to prenatal selection in Japan, where screening is less accepted and less widely practiced than it is in many Western countries such as France, the United States, and the United Kingdom. In the mid-nineties, approximately 90 per cent of fetuses with Down's syndrome were aborted in these countries, while less than 10 per cent of affected Japanese fetuses were aborted.[7] This is not because Japanese culture is especially averse to abortion: some 350,000 abortions are performed there annually. So what is the explanation? Shimazono suggests several factors. In Japan, acceptance of abortion was historically driven not so much by women's rights as by a concern to control population growth for Malthusian reasons. To the extent that screening and selective abortion is a manifestation of women's rights and reproductive freedom, the practice might therefore have less historical backing than in the West. Shimazono also notes that while Westerners place great confidence in "reasoning power that has become independent from nature and body" and stress self-determination of sovereign selves as indispensable for the value of freedom, Japanese culture places less weight on individual autonomy and is more critical of the arrogance typically associated with modernization and modern scientific technology. "Differences in the perceptions of prenatal genetic diagnosis among different nations", Shimazono concludes, "suggest that the culture and historical background of each nation affect people's bioethics."

It would be a mistake to suppose that there exists a unified Asian outlook or Eastern set of values that is opposed to genetic selection. Consider, for example, the situation in Singapore, whose former Prime Minister Lee Kuan Yew spoke frequently about the heritability of intelligence and its

---

[7] The exact figures vary between studies; for a review see Caroline Mansfield, Suellen Hopfer, Theresa M. Marteau, "Termination rates after prenatal diagnosis of Down syndrome, spina bifida, anencephaly, and Turner and Klinefelter syndromes: a systematic literature review", *Prenatal Diagnosis*, 19(9): 808–12.

importance for the country's future, and whose government introduced measures explicitly designed to encourage university graduates to have more children.[8] And of course, attitudes can vary sharply even within a country, as anyone familiar with public bioethics in the United States is well aware.

One context in which enhancement is already in use and with proven efficacy is sports. This makes it an interesting case study. One should, however, be careful not unduly to generalize conclusions based on the model of athletic performance enhancement, because competitive sport is characterized by certain features that are not present in many other enhancement contexts. The advantage that an athlete gets from doping is a purely positional: he might win the race, but this benefit comes at the expense of all the other athletes who rank lower as a result. Moreover, a sport (or a game more generally) is a peculiar kind of activity that is essentially constituted by more or less arbitrary conventions.[9] In golf, the goal is not simply to get the ball down in the hole—*that* could be achieved easily by picking up the ball and placing it in the hole by hand—rather, the goal is to sink the ball while following a set of rules whose justification may be a combination of tradition, entertainment value, and fairness; but not (narrowly construed) instrumental utility. These and other factors combine to make sports ethics a distinct subfield of practical ethics.

TORBJÖRN TÄNNSJÖ draws a tristinction between "negative" interventions, aimed at curing a disease or eliminating a disability; "positive" interventions, aimed at improving the functioning of a human organism within the range of natural variation; and "enhancement", by which he means an intervention aiming to take an individual beyond normal functioning of a human organism. In medicine in general, he says, we can accept both positive measures and enhancement. In sports medicine, however, both positive measures and enhancement are viewed with suspicion. Tännsjö believes that the rationale behind this suspicion

has to do with a very special aspect of the ethos of elite sport, the idea that in elite sport we search for the limits of what a human being can do, together with

---

[8] Chan, C. K. and Chee, H. L. 1984. 'Singapore 1984: Breeding for Big Brother'. In *Designer Genes: I.Q., Ideology and Biology, Institute for Social Analysis (Insan)*. Chan, C. K. and Chee, H. L. (eds.), (Malaysia: Selangor), 4–13. (Reference from Singer, this volume.)

[9] Cf. Suits, B. 2005: *The Grasshopper: Games, Life and Utopia* (Ontario: Broadview Press).

a very special notion of justice according to which we are allowed to admire the individual who has drawn a winning ticket in the natural genetic lottery and excels.

Tännsjö himself, however, does not accept this special notion of justice, so he is unwilling to embrace the ethos of elite sport. Without this ethos, he thinks, there is no need for a special medical ethics for sports medicine. It is enough if elite sport "provides us with good entertainment: fierce, fair, and unpredictable competition—a sweet tension of uncertainty of outcome." However, he suggests that if we do want to add something to this, it could be the following:

In elite sport we can test out the results of such enhancements and see, not where the limits are of the (given) human nature, but how far we can push them. We can enjoy what we see at the competition, and we can feel admiration for all the scientific achievements that have rendered possible the performances. And we can thank the athletes for taking the inconvenience to test them out before us.

CHRISTINE OVERALL, focusing particularly on life extension, argues that social category identities are relevant for the ethics of enhancement. One's membership in social categories such as sex, race, and socioeconomic class, she says, largely determines whether or not one has access to the benefits of life enhancement and whether or not one can pay the costs of these enhancements, making questions of access and exclusion important. It would also be a mistake to ignore the ways in which various enhancement practices could affect social attitudes towards various groups. Overall makes the point that enhancement could be used in equality-promoting ways by giving opportunities to disadvantaged groups that they could not otherwise have had. She criticizes bioconservative bioethicist Daniel Callahan's view that older patients should be denied life-saving treatments on grounds that the normal human life cycle is already enough for a full life. Overall points out that the fullness of a life is not a simple function of age; since, for example, people living in disadvantaged circumstances might have been deprived of important experiences even if they have lived for a long time. Life extension could be the only way in which an old person who has lived a deprived life could get a fair shot at having a full life. One might also add that even for somebody who is living a rich and flourishing life, there may not be any point at which the life becomes "full" in the sense that it could not possibly become better still if it were continued; and even if there were such a point there is no guarantee that it would coincide with one's seventieth birthday or whatever the "natural lifespan" is taken to be. (Even a tree-life takes much more than three score and ten to complete, so why not a human life?[10])

Francis Fukuyama, who in a widely-cited article nominated transhumanism as "the world's most dangerous idea", believes that liberal democracy depends on the fact that all human beings share the same essence, which in Fukuyama's view consists in some undefined "factor X".[11] Were we to engage in enhancement we might unwittingly alter this factor X and thereby destroy the basis of human dignity and the idea of equality underpinning the liberal democratic ideal. In this volume, DANIEL WIKLER, building on his own earlier work, considers specifically the prospect of cognitive enhancement and asks whether civil liberties presuppose roughly equal mental abilities.

Wikler begins by noting that egalitarians need not, and do not, assume that everybody has the same cognitive capacities, or even the same genetic predisposition to intelligence. One must distinguish the empirical claim of human equality of capacities (which is false) from the normative claim that all competent human persons should have the same civic status (which might well be true). Wikler then draws our attention to the paternalism with which we treat human beings with severe or moderate cognitive impairments. Mentally incompetent adults may be barred from voting and from making certain financial decisions, and may even be denied freedom of movement. Now, suppose that cognitive enhancement produced a sizeable population of human beings as intellectually superior to what is now a normally-intelligent person as the latter is to someone who is now regarded as mentally incompetent. In this situation, could we remaining "normals" be rightfully subjected to similar kinds of paternalistic restriction that in the present world are uncontroversially imposed on humans who are mentally incompetent? After distinguishing between a relativistic view and

---

[10] For arguments for the radical extension of the human lifespan, see Bostrom, N. 2008. 'Letter from Utopia', *Studies in Ethics, Law, and Technology*, 1 (http://www.nickbostrom.com/utopia.pdf), and Bostrom, N. 2005: 'The Fable of the Dragon-Tyrant', *Journal of Medical Ethics*, 31: 273–7 (http://www.nickbostrom.com/fable/dragon.pdf).

[11] Fukuyama, F. 2002. *Our Posthuman Future* (New York: Farrar, Straus and Giroux), 149. For a critique of Fukuyama's view, see Bostrom, N. 2004: 'Transhumanism: The World's Most Dangerous Idea?', *Foreign Policy*, September/October (http://www.nickbostrom.com/papers/dangerous.html), Bostrom, N. 2005: 'In Defence of Posthuman Dignity', *Bioethics*, 19: 202–14 (http://www. nickbostrom.com/ethics/dignity.pdf), and Bailey, R. 2005: *Libertarian Biology* (New York: Prometheus Books).

a threshold view of what qualifies an individual for full civic status, Wikler answers his own question with a tentative *yes*: under certain circumstances at least, a future population of cognitively superior agents might have a duty to treat remaining normals paternalistically.

ROBIN HANSON addresses one particular intellectual attribute: truth-orientation. He reviews three types of enhancement that might strengthen our truth-orientation: more recording and standardized statistics on our lives, prediction markets on major disputed topics, and techniques or modifications that could render our minds more transparent. Trends towards these kinds of enhancement, he suggests, could reduce the epistemic vice of self-deception and bias—a vice that can be especially dangerous in a modern world with nuclear weapons and other powerful technologies. Yet, as Hanson notes, self-deception and bias are quite central features of our present psyches, their prevalence having been demonstrated in many studies as well as, according to Hanson, by the ubiquity of persistent disagreements even among agents who have mutual knowledge of each other's opinion. We might balk at the prospect of living without illusions when we realize how jarringly different such lives would be from our accustomed condition. If so, we might also be tempted to seek to regulate the behavior of others, including our distant descendants, for example by trying to prevent the development of the technologies that would make an illusion-deprived condition feasible.

Hanson warns against the danger of moral arrogance. Aside from the moral importance of autonomy, he adduces also an epistemic reason for why we should be wary of imposing our moral views on others. Just as we can be, and frequently are, overconfident in our beliefs regarding empirical questions, we can also be, and no doubt frequently are, overconfident in our moral beliefs. We often deceive ourselves into thinking that our moral convictions are better supported by reason than they really are, and better supported than the moral convictions of those who disagree with us. This warning applies particularly when we are tempted to regulate the behavior of future generations of people:

We should also be especially wary of moral arrogance regarding the moral behavior of our distant descendants, as those descendants will have a clear information advant-age over us; we cannot listen to them as we could when arguing with a contempor-ary. Our descendants will know of our advice, and also of many other things we do not know. In addition . . . they may well have a stronger truth orientation than us.

The argument from moral arrogance, Hanson suggests, might cut especially against those who think we should limit truth-orientation enhancements:

The warning to beware of our self-deception regarding our moral abilities would seem to apply with a special force to those who argue the virtues of self-deception. After all, does not the pro-self-deception side in a debate seem more likely to be self-deceived in this matter?

Enhancement as practical challenge

Several of the authors represented in this book, including Francis Kamm and Norman Daniels, express concerns about the difficulty of succeeding and ensuring sufficient safety when attempting to enhance complex systems. In the final chapter of the book, NICK BOSTROM and ANDERS SANDBERG tackle this practical challenge of enhancement heads on.

Bostrom and Sandberg observe that there is a widespread popular belief in the "wisdom of nature", which we ignore at our peril. Many people prefer "natural" remedies and "natural" food supplements, and willingly embrace "natural" ways of improving human capacities such as training, diet, and grooming. Interventions seen as "unnatural" or "artificial", by contrast, are commonly viewed with suspicion—at least until they become familiar enough to become assimilated into the category of the natural. This attitude seems to be especially pronounced in relation to unnatural ways of enhancing human capacities, which are viewed as unwise, short-sighted, and hubristic. The belief in the wisdom of nature, Bostrom and Sandberg suggest, can also manifest as diffusely moral objections against enhancement.

Bostrom and Sandberg then propose that the belief in the wisdom of nature is partially true. A human being is a marvel of evolved complexity, and when we manipulate complex evolved systems which are poorly understood, our interventions often fail or backfire. Bostrom and Sandberg seek to encapsulate the grain of truth contained in the belief in the wisdom of nature in form of the Evolutionary Optimality Challenge. When somebody proposes an intervention alleged to enhance some biological function of capacity, we should pose ourselves the following challenge: "Why, if this intervention is such a good thing, have we not already evolved to be that way?". Developing this evolutionary heuristic, Bostrom and Sandberg go on to explain and exemplify three categories of potential answers to the challenge question: changed tradeoffs, value discordance, and evolutionary restrictions. For some proposed enhancement interventions, a satisfactory answer to the evolutionary optimality challenge can be found in one of these categories, giving us a green light to proceed: we can see precisely why in the particular case at hand we can reasonably hope to improve on nature. For other proposed interventions, the heuristic gives a red light, suggesting that the intervention may not work, or may have long-term and perhaps subtle side-effects. In such cases, we may need to rethink our enhancement idea or at least proceed with extreme caution.

The heuristic that Bostrom and Sandberg develop (inspired by the field of evolutionary medicine) is primarily empirical and practical in nature: it is intended to help researchers and enhancement users identify and evaluate promising enhancement interventions by providing a method for thinking through what evolutionary considerations can tell us about their likely effects on our minds and bodies. As such, the heuristic has no moral content. Yet if Bostrom and Sandberg are correct in surmising that anti-enhancement intuitions which surface as moral sentiments are sometimes rooted in an implicit belief in nature's wisdom, then the heuristic can also contribute to ethical discourse by allowing for a more transparent and constructive way of acknowledging and taking into account these hidden and subtle prudential concerns.

Conclusion

Human enhancement has moved from the realm of science fiction to that of practical ethics. There are now effective physical, cognitive, mood, cosmetic, and sexual enhancers—drugs and interventions that can enhance at least some aspects of some capacities in at least some individuals some of the time. The rapid advances currently taking place in the biomedical sciences and related technological areas make it clear that a lot more will become possible over the coming years and decades. The question has shifted from "Is this science fiction?" to "Should we do it?".[12]

---

[12] It remains important, however, to distinguish between what is possible today, what may become feasible soon, and what would require radical new technological capabilities to achieve. And in answering the question of what is possible today, it is also important to distinguish proof-of-concept in a laboratory study from applications that are ready to be rolled out for widespread use.

This book presents a wide variety of perspectives relevant to answering this question. Christine Overall, in an assessment which seems to be supported by many of our authors, opines that given the enormous variation, moral generalizations about all enhancement processes and technologies are unwise, and they should instead be evaluated individually. Whether we should employ a particular enhancement depends on the reasons for and against that particular enhancement. Creating superimmunity to all known biological and viral insults is very different from practicing sports doping; choosing the personality traits of our offspring through genetic selection is very different from taking a pill that temporarily boosts our ability to concentrate. On this line of reasoning, it is time to take a further step, from asking "Should we do it?" to analyzing the "it" and asking a number of much more specific questions about concrete actions and policy options related to particular enhancement issues within a given sociopolitical-cultural context. The result of this will not be a yes or no to enhancement in general, but a more contextualized and particularized set of ideas and recommendations for how individuals, organizations, and states should move forward in an enhancement era.[13]

Where do we go from here? We believe that the enhancement debate needs to be developed simultaneously in two directions: both, as we might say, downwards and upwards. The "downwards" direction is the one just suggested: zooming in on issues of more limited scale by disaggregating and contextualizing enhancements, and addressing the particularities of the choices faced by various stakeholders and decision-makers. The "upwards" direction is to address ethical and pragmatic challenges that emerge when we zoom out and consider the roles that enhancement of various types of capacity could play in the long term and big-picture future of humanity. This would require discussing how enhancement—including the prospect of future more radical enhancement—might interact with other macro-trends and global problems and prospects such as economic growth and inequality, existential risks and global catastrophic risks, molecular nanotechnology, artificial intelligence, space colonization, virtual reality, surveillance technology, democracy and global governance, along with the deep epistemological, methodological, and moral questions that arise

---

[13] Savulescu, J. 2003. 'Human–animal transgenesis and chimeras might be an expression of our humanity', *Am J Bioethics*. Summer, 3(3): 22–5.

when one attempts to think about these interlocking issues in a serious and critical manner.[14] These two directions may seem to be in tension to one another, but in fact they simply point to two coexisting intellectual frontiers, each with important and worthy problems to be addressed. A danger we see for enhancement ethics is its getting stuck in the middle. An uncritical acceptance of "enhancement" as an analytical category and as a organizing idea for our inquiries risks obscuring the heterogeneity of potential enhancement applications and the need to situate them within the micro-context of particular policy decisions, as well as within the macro-context constituted by other big-picture challenges for humanity in the twenty-first century. In some circumstances, regulated access may be fairer and safer than prohibition.[15] In other cases, enhancements could be selected to address inequality or social injustice,[16] or deployed at a population level for societal benefit. One spokesperson for the US Military, which is actively exploring the potential of human enhancement technology, said

The world contains approximately 4.2 billion people over the age of twenty. Even a small enhancement of cognitive capacity in these individuals would probably have an impact on the world economy rivaling that of the internet.[17]

It seems likely that this century will herald unprecedented advances in nanotechnology, biotechnology, information technology, cognitive science, and other related areas. These advances will provide the opportunity

[14] See e.g. Bostrom, N. 2007. 'Technological Revolutions and the Problem of Prediction'. In *Nano-ethics: The Ethical and Social Implications of Nanotechnology*. Allhoff, F., Lin, P., Moor, J. and Weckert, J. (eds.), Wiley-Interscience (http://www.nickbostrom.com/revolutions.pdf), and Bostrom, N. 2007. 'The Future of Humanity'. In *New Waves in Philosophy of Technology*. Berg Olsen, J. K., Selinger, E. and Aldershot, S. R. (eds.) (Basingstoke: Palgrave Macmillan).

[15] Savulescu, J., 'It Is Time to Allow Doping at the Tour de France', *The Telegraph*, 30 Jul. 2007. http://www.telegraph.co.uk/sport/main.jhtml?view=DETAILS&grid=A1YourView&xml=/sport/2007/07/30/sodrug130.xml, accessed 8 February 2008. 'Doping true to the Spirit of Sport', Julian Savulescu, *Sydney Morning Herald*, Aug. 8, http://www.smh.com.au/news/opinion/doping-true-to-the-spirit-of-sport/2007/08/07/1186252704241.html, accessed 8 Feb. 2008. J Savulescu, B Foddy, and M Clayton, 'Why we should allow performance enhancing drugs in sport', in *British Journal of Sports Medicine*, Dec. 2004; 38: 666–70. Savulescu, J., and Foddy, B., 2007. 'Ethics of Performance Enhancement in Sport: Drugs and Gene Doping', in *Principles of Health Care Ethics*, Second Edition, Ashcroft, R E., Dawson, A., Draper, H. and McMillan, J. R (eds.) (London: John Wiley & Sons, Ltd), 511–20.

[16] Savulescu, J. 2006. 'Justice, Fairness and Enhancement'. In *Progress in Convergence: Technologies for Human Wellbeing*, eds. Sims Bainbridge, W. and Roco, M. C. *Annals of the New York Academy of Sciences* vol. 1093 doi: 10.1196/annals.1382.021, Ann. N.Y. Acad. Sci. 1093: 321–38.

[17] Army: Proposal Submission, at http://www.dodsbir.net/solicitation/sttr08A/army08A.htm, accessed 8 Feb. 2008.

fundamentally to change the human condition. This presents both great risks and enormous potential benefits. Our fate is, to a greater degree than ever before in human history, in our own hands.

To decide whether we have reason to promote a particular enhancement will require wisdom, dialogue, good scientific research, good public policy, and academic debate. This book represents one of the first steps to advancing academic discussion of enhancement from a variety of analytic philosophical perspectives. It is neither our expectation nor our primary objective that readers will be persuaded either to support or oppose enhancement. Rather, our hope is that the book will cause its readers to reflect more deeply on one of the most important and challenging issues of the new century.[18]

References

Bailey, R. 2005: *Libertarian Biology* (New York: Prometheus Books).

Bostrom, N. 2004: 'Transhumanism: The World's Most Dangerous Idea?', *Foreign Policy*, September/October.

———2005: 'The Fable of the Dragon-Tyrant', *Journal of Medical Ethics*, 31: 273–7.

———2005: 'In Defence of Posthuman Dignity', *Bioethics*, 19: 202–14.

———2006: 'A Short History of Transhumanist Thought', *Analysis and Metaphysics*, 5: 63–95.

———2007: 'The Future of Humanity'. In *New Waves in Philosophy of Technology.*, Berg Olsen, J. K., Selinger, E. and Aldershot, S. R. (eds.) (Basingstoke: Palgrave Macmillan).

———2007: 'Technological Revolutions and the Problem of Prediction'. In *Nanoethics: The Ethical and Social Implications of Nanotechnology*. Allhoff, F., Lin, P., Moor, J., and Weckert, J. (eds.) (New York: Wiley-Interscience).

———2008: 'Letter from Utopia', *Studies in Ethics, Law, and Technology*, 1.

———and Ord, T. 2006: 'The Reversal Test: Eliminating Status Quo Bias in Bioethics', *Ethics*, 116: 656–80.

Chan, C. K. and Chee, H. L. 1984: 'Singapore 1984: Breeding for Big Brother'. In *Designer Genes: I.Q., Ideology and Biology, Institute for Social Analysis (Insan)*. Chan, C. K. and Chee, H. L. (eds.) (Malaysia: Selangor), 4–13.

Fukuyama, F. 2002: *Our Posthuman Future* (New York: Farrar, Straus and Giroux).

---

[18] We are grateful to Rebecca Roache for valuable comments on an earlier version of this introduction.

Glover, J. 1984: *What Sort of People Should There Be?* (Harmondsworth: Penguin).

Mansfield, C., Hopfer, S., and Marteau, T. M. 1999: 'Termination rates after prenatal diagnosis of Down syndrome, spina bifida, anencephaly, and Turner and Klinefelter syndromes: a systematic literature review', *Prenatal Diagnosis*, 19: 9, 808−12.

Nozick, R. 1974: *Anarchy, State and Utopia* (New York: Basic Books).

Riis, J., Simmons, J. P. and Goodwin, G. P. Forthcoming: 'Preferences for Enhancement Pharmaceuticals: The Reluctance to Enhance Fundamental Traits', *Journal of Consumer Research*.

Selinger, E. and Aldershot, S. R. (eds.), (Basingstoke: Palgrave Macmillan).

Suits, B. 2005: *The Grasshopper: Games, Life and Utopia* (Ontario: Broadview Press).

PART I
Human Enhancement in General

1

Can Anyone Really Be Talking About Ethically Modifying Human Nature?

*Norman Daniels**

Abstract

Threats to human nature?

[handwritten margin note: generally, we see our obligation to enhance]

The discussion of human enhancement remains, in my view, confounded by a failure to distinguish important concepts, issues, and cases. Improving specific individuals phenotypically, including with regard to important cognitive and behavioral traits, is something we do all the time. Indeed, we see doing so as our obligation as parents, teachers, health care providers, managers, and citizens through environmental manipulation (sometimes biological, sometimes social) that affects gene-environment interactions. Yet many novel biological and especially genetic interventions, including embryonic selection, are feared as threats to human nature. The suggestion made by some, that we might ethically improve human nature, presupposes we have a clear idea what that means, let alone that it may become feasible. I suspect the very concept of human nature is confused in ways that contribute both to the alarm many feel about some of these novel interventions, and to the optimism others feel about solving social and political problems by improving human nature biologically. Some of the confusion is traceable to forms of genetic determinism that underestimate the plasticity of human capabilities; some is due to confusion about the traits people fear or hope can be modified. What is a threat to human nature? After clarifying the concept of human nature, I specify some conditions that would have to be met if we were to think seriously about intervening with individuals to modify biologically key cognitive or behavioral traits.

[handwritten margin note: no idea what human nature is]

* Harvard School of Public Health.

The organizers of a conference I was recently invited to asked speakers to examine what is involved ethically in modifying human nature through genetics. One possibility is that their invitation deliberately engaged in hyperbole in order to stimulate more interesting papers. The premise of that hyperbole is that we might truly modify human nature with such interventions. In what follows I propose to take that premise seriously. Doing so requires being clear about what the key term, "human nature," means. Only then can we tell when it is modified, and only then can we ethically assess the prospect of such modification. Nothing in my analysis suggests that modifying human nature is impossible, but I do believe that much that is envisioned in the realm of genetic intervention does not involve modifying human nature (even if it sometimes modifies an individual's nature). After spending much of my time on the analytic task of saying what is plausibly meant by modifying human nature, I turn briefly to some ethical issues raise by the prospect of modifying otherwise normal human traits.

1. Fruit fly nature

Let us start with a somewhat simpler idea before we take on the more controversial concept of human nature. Consider Figure 1, which shows the viability at different temperatures of fruit flies that have different alleles for a particular gene. Each line graphs what is called a "norm of reaction." The phenotypic, or manifest, trait, in this instance viability, that is expressed by each fruit fly variant depends on temperature as well as its genes. Viability is the result of this interaction. Specifically, although some variants tend to be less viable than others at any temperature, and one seems to be more viable across the range of environments, more generally, norms of reaction cross. Which variant has superior viability will depend, in this case, on temperature.

This variability in norms of reaction is not a special case. It is the general rule for allelic variation in all species. Though some alleles confer dominant advantage or disadvantage in a broad range of environments (as in the norms for one or two variants at the top and bottom of Figure 1, see opposite), in general advantage or disadvantage depends on the combination of environment and genes and not just genes. Notice that if our dominant

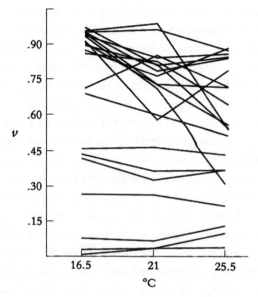

Figure 1. Actual reaction norms for viability of fourth chromosome homozygotes of *Drosophilia pseudoobscura*. Figure provided by Richard Lewontin. Data from Dobzhansky, Th., and Spasky, B., *Genetics*, 29 (1944): 270–90.

mode of thinking about the effect of genes were in terms of norms of reaction, then we would be far less tempted to think or speak as if genes determine traits. We would be inclined to think about interactions and we would look to environmental modification as much as genetic modification when we were motivated to alter phenotype.

In this sense, the norm of reaction is an antidote not just to genetic determinism but to pure forms of environmental determinism as well. Of course, environmental determinism has as its excuse the fact that our main way of modifying phenotype for humans—leave animal and plant breeding aside—has always been environmental. Parents are obliged, and generally believe they are, to provide the best environment they can for their children. That is all they know how to do to improve phenotype. Indeed, that is all they or anyone can do post conception.

Figure 1 may mislead the reader into thinking we can easily pick out the "superior" or "inferior" alleles and select for or against them, thus improving fruit fly nature. But this inclination rests on an oversimplification. Figure 1, focusing on but one environmental variation and on one allele and its variants, leaves aside the additional complexity, common in the real world, that some allelic variations may be superior or inferior with regard to viability in response to temperature and may not be so superior or inferior when other environmental variables are included. Figure 1 also leaves aside the association of some apparently superior or inferior genes with other genes that may be inferior or superior with regard to other environmental variables. Leaving these matters aside should not encourage the reader to assume that it is apparent from Figure 1 just what allele to select for, all things considered. Indeed, the survival of a population of fruit flies through temperature variations in their standard environment may depend on retaining much of this allelic diversity, not selecting for what we may think, given Figure 1, is the "obviously" superior variant.

What can we learn about fruit fly nature from the simple case of the norms of reactions for fruit flies? One obvious point is that fruit flies are diverse in their response to temperature. They are diverse in any given environment (across allelic variation) and they are diverse in their response to environmental change. If we want to attribute fruit fly nature to them, we must understand it to be a *population* concept, not primarily a concept applied to individuals. Fruit fly nature is not captured by any one norm of reaction, any more than it is captured by some one degree of viability. Indeed, fruit fly nature is a many splendored thing. The nature of fruit flies—in this population sense—is to vary widely in viability in their response to temperature. We may for some purposes be tempted to specify the range in which one or another variant is viable, and we may say the nature of this or that variant is to have this or that viability response to temperature change. But if we are motivated to think more loftily about the nature of fruit flies, and not just of one variant of fruit flies, we should think of the composite of ranges of the variants as the range of viability across temperature variation.

We might want to insist that fruit fly nature must be given by a set of traits all fruit flies share, despite this variation. In that case, we need to refer to the trait in a very general way. We might say, for example, that fruit flies are temperature-sensitive: their viability always depends on temperature, even if in different ways. This point brings out another key feature of the concept of fruit fly nature: the phenotypic traits that are part of the nature of fruit flies are dispositional. It is the "nature" of water to solidify at 32° F at one atmosphere pressure, and it is the nature of water to solidify at other temperatures at other pressures. Water is disposed to become ice under certain combinations of temperature and pressure (and vapor under others). Fruit flies are disposed to be more or less viable under certain temperature conditions. Water is not always ice any more than fruit flies are always viable to such and such a degree.

Is every trait that fruit flies are disposed to manifest under some condition or other part of fruit fly nature? Here I am at a bit of a loss, since I do not know fruit flies well—none of my best friends are fruit flies—and I do not have a reason for getting to do so. If I were to generalize from my own experience and what is salient to (the non-expert) me, I might suppose it is part of their nature to end up in glasses of wine or juice, especially my glass of wine or juice. That is how I most frequently encounter them. I could easily be persuaded, however, that the drownings are just a frequent accident, predictable from their true nature. I might not be so easily persuaded that having one or three or no bars on their wings or bodies is part of their nature—that might seem more like hair color for humans. But this is just guessing. I am inclined to say that only some traits should be seen as part of fruit fly nature, because I extrapolate from other cases where I know more about what counts as the nature of the beast.

In many cases where we talk about the "nature" of a species—dogs, horses, and humans—come to mind we are using the concept of their nature in an explanatory way. We are trying to explain some important set of behaviors or features they have that are of special interest to us. So dog breeders or exhibitors might be intensely interested in the length of the rough on a specific breed or their posture or manner in walking, but most of us would not think of hair length or posture in walking as part of the nature of dogs. We might, however, think that loyalty or willingness to please were elements of dog nature, for that is what usually interests us in dogs, even if we also have to admit that some dogs behave more like cats. This is not to say, of course, that specific breeds of dogs have not been bred to exhibit particular traits that are important to the nature of the breed—say herding capabilities in Border Collies or tracking abilities in Bloodhounds or Beagles. The qualification makes the point: what we emphasize as the nature of the breed answers to a specific purpose we have, herding or hunting, and thus breed nature emphasizes only a selection among traits. For the sake of brevity, I shall affirm a generalization without real argument, that the concept of "X nature" involves a theory-laden

What interests us is what we perceive to be 'natural'

selection of traits of X's. I will test the generalization briefly when I return to humans.

To summarize the lessons from my excursion into fruit fly nature: fruit fly nature is a **population** concept: to characterize the nature of fruit flies we must aggregate phenotypic variations across allelic variations among fruit flies. It is a **dispositional** concept, since the phenotypic traits we take to be the "nature" of fruit flies vary within some range under different conditions. Finally it is a **selective**, theory-laden concept: not every trait of fruit flies is likely to be considered part of their nature, but only those that we use to explain something of importance to us about them. Putting these points together, the concept of fruit fly nature applies to what we consider the central explanatory features of the **phenotype** fruit flies manifest under some range of conditions.

We can draw several important inferences from these analytic points. First, whatever role the genotype of fruit flies plays in explaining fruit fly nature, it is a concept with different properties: it is not dispositional and it is not selective, even if it may be populational. Accordingly, I resist the idea that the nature of a type of creature is the specifically genetic contribution to the key traits characterizing it. Rather, its nature is some set of traits (or rather the ranges of those traits) that we take to be explanatory of what interests us about it. The ranges and distributions of those traits that interest us are the results of the range of environments and the genetic variations we find in those creatures. Genes, like environments, contribute to that nature, but they do not constitute it. Indeed, they are made of different stuff: the natures we pick out are neither genes nor environments, but are affected and shaped by both.

Second, if we intervene in a fruit fly population and produce an allelic variation of a known sort in a fly or a group of flies, then we are not changing fruit fly nature. We might be changing the particular nature of those individuals: for example, we might be changing the gene that affects temperature sensitivity in the complex ways Figure 1 reveals are possible, perhaps moving the individuals from one norm of reaction to another. But that is not a change in fruit fly nature, which reflects the full range of norms of reaction. When we just move the manipulated flies within the range of known variations in traits or dispositions to exhibit traits under certain conditions, we do not change that range and thus we do not change fruit fly nature.

Third, in some cases, if we introduce a completely novel allele, one whose norm of reaction is so different from others found in the species that it produces a novel capability under certain conditions, then we might say we had modified fruit fly nature. For example, let us suppose that fruit flies are stealth fliers, unlike some mosquitoes: you just can't hear them until they climb into your wine glass. But now a genetic scientist has produced a noisy, whining flier, easily avoided before it drowns in your wine. If stealth had been an important trait of fruit flies, then we might think the intervention was a threat to fruit fly nature; if enough were saved from drowning in wine glasses, it might be an improvement in their nature. But not just any change in any trait would do, and most would simply involve manipulating the variants' expression of a trait somewhere within the natural range for the species.

This example brings out another point, however. Producing isolated examples of non-stealth fruit flies does not do anything significant to the fruit fly population, at least not by itself. Since it does not affect the fruit fly population as a whole, and fruit fly nature is a population concept, it does not alter fruit fly nature. Perhaps over time these noisy flies would interbreed with the quiet fliers, and if their new capability conferred advantage rather than disadvantage, they might multiply and flourish, perhaps shifting the range of flying styles among fruit flies accordingly. Eventually, they might drive out the quiet fliers through selective advantage. In that dramatic case, we might say we had changed fruit fly nature—assuming that we viewed the decibel level of flying a part of fruit fly nature and not just an uninteresting incidental trait. A significant change in the frequency of a trait central to fruit fly nature would constitute a change in that nature. Nothing in my analysis says we cannot change fruit fly or human nature—only that it takes a massive intervention to do that.

2. Human nature

Do the points we have abstracted from our casual and brief examination of fruit fly nature apply to human nature? I believe they do.

First, human nature is also a population concept. Consider a trait that some theories of human nature (notice we have different theories!) take to be very central to it, such as self-interest or aggressiveness or reciprocity (leave aside the controversy about the theories). A point that jumps out is that we see great variation in the degree of self-interest or aggressiveness or reciprocity that different people (different genotypes?) manifest. Some people are as timid as voles, others as aggressive as a startled black rhinoceros. Some can be as self-effacing as Mother Theresa, others as self-serving and self-promoting as George Bush. Some tally up every favor and slight; others are forgiving team players. The claim that humans are by nature aggressive or selfish or cooperative must somehow be compatible with the diversity we see in these traits among all humans. Thus the view that says humans are by nature selfish must explain away Mother Theresa's behavior ("deep down, she is doing only what makes her happy"). And the view that says it is human nature to be aggressive must focus on some part of the range of environments and on some subset of the variants to make its case that aggressiveness is the salient feature.

Suppose we were able to isolate allelic variations among people that correlated with their manifesting different degrees of aggressiveness under some similar environmental conditions. For example, we discovered that people with pattern A of these alleles tend to be more aggressive than those with patterns B or C when encountering threats from people they do not know in otherwise non-threatening settings. We might be tempted to say we had uncovered a biological determinant of aggressiveness, and we might think we had evidence about which allelic variation produced more aggressiveness.

Remember, however, the general point we uncovered when we looked at norms of reaction for fruit flies. People with these different allelic patterns might manifest different degrees of aggressiveness under different conditions; people aggressive under some conditions (Pattern A) might be less aggressive than others (Patterns B or C) under different conditions. In effect, their norms of reaction might vary and even cross. There may be genetic factors affecting aggressiveness, for all we know, but if there are, they most likely will depend on interaction with the environment. Consequently, we won't be able to extrapolate from position on one vertical "slice" of the norm of reaction graph to conclusions about position on another vertical slice of that graph. I take it these remarks also establish that human nature is a dispositional concept: the traits that characterize it (assuming they do) are ones people are disposed to exhibit under specific conditions, but not always. (I also return to an implication of this point when I discuss later attempts to modify some such important behavioral trait.)

Suppose we intervened genetically to modify "aggression" genes by making the beneficiaries of the intervention "nicer" (less aggressive) under some particular environmental stressor or trigger. Would we be changing human nature? Most likely the answer is "no." The story is the same as for the fruit fly intervention that produced noisy fliers. Even supposing this trait is a central one for a true story about human nature, we at best would have changed the position of these beneficiaries within the broad distribution of aggression we see among humans in that environment. We may be changing this or that individual's particular nature (here we have the relevant concept of temperament), but we did not change human nature. It is human nature to exhibit a broad range of temperaments under a broad range of conditions. Of course, if we altered to a significant degree the frequency of some salient traits, that might well alter human nature since it alters the explanatory value of the appeal to those traits, but that requires a massive intervention. Again, I am not claiming we cannot change human nature, only trying to clarify what is involved.

Indeed, many parents, teachers, and playmates intervene environmentally all the time with their children, students, and peers aiming to modify the manifestation of aggression or other behaviorally important traits. We try in many contexts to make the phenotypic change by pulling a different lever in the interaction, the environmental one. Yet we do not really think of what we do, even if it has the same outcome as the supposed genetic intervention, as changing human nature. Presumably, our everyday interactions presuppose that we think our human nature is sufficiently plastic—our dispositions to manifest traits are sufficiently malleable—that we can shape it through good parenting, teaching, and friendship. If we produce similar outcomes by biological interventions, we should not be misled by genetic determinism into thinking we are changing human nature as opposed to merely bringing out traits compatible with it that we prefer to see.

Human nature is also a selective, theory-laden concept, as is fruit fly nature (I asserted). Suppose we develop a genetic intervention that works to make all future people three inches taller (assuming we intervene widely enough). I doubt we would conclude we had altered human nature. Indeed, population height increased nearly that much over the nineteenth and twentieth centuries, presumably a result of improved nutrition. (I hope I am not stretching the example.) But no one thinks that changed human nature. Presumably, we found a different environmental point on the norms of reaction of most human variants.

The point is worth emphasizing with another example. Suppose we could intervene with the entire human population by giving it a super-vaccine. It would have the effect of reducing morbidity for a broad range of diseases to which humans are now susceptible. Suppose further it need only be given once, for the offspring of all who have had it are also protected, and so on, although there is no modification of germ plasm. I doubt we would think human nature was modified (or threatened) any more than we now think it is modified because all children get vaccinated against polio. Nor would we think so if the intervention were genetic. In short only some human modifications even begin to count as candidates for being modifications of human nature, even when done on a population level.[1]

So the concept of human nature is in these three ways like the concept of fly nature: it is a concept that applies to populations, it is dispositional, and it is selective. The various (conflicting) theories that have purported to describe human nature are about the *phenotypic* traits thought to be central in explaining human behavior and social structure. Knowledge of the human variations that compose our genotype and of the myriad norms of reaction that they exhibit would further help us explain how

---

[1] In one sense, providing people with a vaccine "enhances" their otherwise normal resistance to a disease, which might be low. In another sense, providing the vaccine stimulates a normal immune system to produce antibodies it is capable of producing, so that individuals and a population are protected against serious diseases. I have generally characterized vaccines as part of the array of "treatments" for departures from normal functioning—although this is stretching the idea of treatment to include preventive measures, a stretch I have made explicit in my writings. In effect, anything to do with maintaining normal function falls under the scope of "treatment" as opposed to enhancement. Harris in his contribution to this volume objects to this classification, but I view the issue as largely semantic and not central to the distinction between treatment and enhancement. Indeed, had we no vaccine for HIV/AIDS, and no genetic modification providing protection, but instead found a diet that included dandelion leaves gave protection, we would hardly say we had enhanced human nature. Harris also objects that we might have good reason to enhance some otherwise normal conditions, such as very low intelligence, if they imposed significant disadvantages on people. In Buchanan et al. 2000, I suggest some such interventions may not only be permissible but obligatory, but not for the same reason we standardly justify the provision of health care. It would take a careful discussion of the case, however, to persuade me to weaken the conclusion I draw about the difficulty of justifying experiments where the risks are significant and the benefits less significant: low intelligence may be coupled with many other traits that make life well worth living and not worth risking, a point that may be hard for academics to digest. Obviously the argument from experimental risk depends for its scope on what we can do to change the risks.

that human nature is produced through complex interactions of genes and environment.

3. Changing human nature

Nothing about the concept of human nature means it cannot be changed with certain kinds of interventions, as I have already said. The interventions need not be genetic. Consider typical science fiction examples, usually dystopic ones, such as zombies.

I have in mind the following type of case. Suppose some island population discovered a mind-altering drug of great power. Developed to relieve tension, which it does initially, it also eventually flattens all emotional response. People carry on with business, at least some of it, but without any affect of any kind. The content of all their relationships is different, and consequently social interaction is deeply affected. They are like no people we have ever encountered. Unfortunately, the effect is permanent. It cannot be reversed. What is worse, the drug not only works its effect on adults, but on all their offspring—not through a modification of germ plasm, but through some chemical effect on fetal brains in utero. When these effects were understood, unaffected islanders tried to dispose of the compound by burying it in a deep salt mine. Because of faulty engineering, it quickly leaked out into the water supply, with the effect that the island population all became zombie-like. Forgive the sci-fi environmentalist story, when we are supposed to be concentrating on genetic sci-fi, but I think you get the message.

I am inclined to say that these islanders have inadvertently modified human nature. Emotionality is a central human trait. Variability in emotions under the same environmental stimulus is also what we expect of human nature. We further expect variation in the variability of emotion across people and the environments they encounter. Presumably many different norms of reaction are at work for this trait. But having no emotional response at all is beyond even human pathology (except for persistent vegetative state). It is beyond human experience. It is beyond being human. Of course, my story only involves the islanders, but let us suppose the compound is produced in large quantity when the ozone layer thins. Now you can fill in the end of the story (but please include in it Bush's walking away from the Kyoto treaty).

Suppose we modify my example slightly. The drug we are talking about does not produce zombies but extremely shy people. By extremely shy, I mean in the lowest 3 per cent of shyness we tend to find among people in the normal range of environments in Boston or New York. The drug has the same properties: it is permanent in its effects and it affects all offspring, and suppose through an environmental disaster, all are affected by it. I still am inclined to say we have altered human nature because the trait, although not strictly speaking novel has such a profound impact on society and culture when it is distributed in this new way. We would not be speaking metaphorically if we said the nature of humans had changed.

So we can modify human nature, but it takes a very tall tale. We must affect the (or at least a) whole population of humans, and we must do so with a trait central to that nature. Had the drug worked on only one or two islanders, or even on 5 per cent of them, we might have been more inclined to say they were seriously ill. The illness sadly destroyed a central feature of their human capabilities. The intervention has to work on the *population* concept of human nature. It is also important that we did not modify just a minority of them in ways that simply moved them from one level of human emotionality to another. That would not alter human nature, even if it altered their individual natures. It might simply replicate the effect of some cultural change—perhaps the change in inquisitiveness that may have resulted from literacy becoming a mass phenomenon, or the electronic media substituting for reading for many people.

Let me take stock before moving on. If human nature is a dispositional, selective population concept, then interventions, whether genetic or not, cannot alter human nature simply by moving some individuals within the range of traits already thought part of human nature. If, however, the prevalence of those select traits shifted so dramatically that the explanatory role of that trait had to be modified, even though the range of the new distribution fell within the extreme tails of the old one, then we might be inclined to view this as a change of human nature. To alter human nature, the analysis so far suggests, we must really act at a population level.

4. Novel capabilities

Suppose we modify pigs so that their organs contain surface proteins that are typical of humans and will not be rejected if transplanted into humans. I do not think we have changed pig nature in doing so, despite the new capability of pig organs to serve human needs in a new way. Presumably, the pig with these new proteins will walk like a pig, feed like a pig, and oink like one. What we commonly think of as pig nature will remain. If the pig could talk, of course, we would think differently. But that is the point: it matters what changes.

Suppose we give select humans a new capability, one not found in other humans, even if it is sometimes imagined to be present. For example, suppose we give some humans some form of extra-sensory perception or the ability to read other minds (the modification need not be genetic). Would this constitute a modification of human nature?

Again, I think the answer, even for the individual case, depends on the trait. If we suddenly enabled (environmentally or genetically) an individual to jump over houses in a single bound through a novel steroid or genetic intervention—or if we suddenly encountered a mutation in various alleles that let the mutant jump so high—we would not be inclined to consider the super-human power a change in human nature (or so my intuitions run; if many other traits regarding physical powers were altered and we produced Superman, then I might agree we had modified human nature). The ability to read minds may be different: it would profoundly affect all human interactions and would be central to the individual's social life. There would be no privacy of thought, no point to politeness, to being indirect, or to lying. Politics as we know it would be impossible.

Still, what the modification does at most is change the particular individual's nature into something beyond human (or it could be beneath human, remember the zombie). By itself, this does not alter human nature. It creates freaks. If it operated on a population level, we might well, as we have seen, count it as a change in human nature. A world full of mind readers instead of liars would be one in which we would not encounter human nature as we know it. Not many traits fit this description, I suspect.

5. The ethics of genetically modifying human nature

What are the ethical implications of the analysis I have so far offered? I shall be brief, perhaps frustratingly or annoyingly so, largely because I think we are facing that line from the old joke about the Maine farmer. When asked by the tourist how to get to the gas station, the farmer offered several suggestions, rejecting each, and finally concluded "you can't get there from here."

One sense in which we can't get there from here is a commonplace in the ethics literature on genetic enhancement. If we are to engage in experiments on human subjects, for example, on embryos that will be carried to term, there must be a reasonable risk-benefit ratio. For example, if we are trying to ameliorate or eliminate a serious genetic disease, or disease for which there may be some genetic or other medical remedy, the probability of potential benefit from the experimental intervention may plausibly outweigh the certainty of catastrophic illness. But if we are trying to improve on an otherwise normal trait, the risks of a bad outcome, even if small, outweigh the acceptable outcome of normality. So we cannot ethically get there from here.

I believe this argument has great force, and I shall shortly suggest how it more directly applies to the modification of central cognitive or behavioral traits. I also observe in passing that we do not act on the principle underlying it in some other medical interventions, though perhaps we should. For example, cosmetic surgeons frequently "innovate"—in effect conduct experiments on human subjects who are otherwise normal and who might suffer worse outcomes than they would from the ordinary procedure if the idea or its execution is a bad one. In general, standard ethical constraints on research are not applied to many forms of clinical innovation. Nor are they applied to many forms of health system reforms of delivery or financing policies, even though these may involve significant changes in the risks and benefits faced by patients.[2] Still, our incomplete adherence to appropriate patient-protection concerns should not count as an argument in favor of ignoring them in the case of medical—genetic or not—interventions to improve on otherwise normal human cognitive or behavioral traits.

---

[2] Daniels N. 2006. 'Toward Ethical Review of Health System Transformations', *Am. J. Public Health*, 96: 447–51.

Let us imagine, for a moment, a proposal to improve on some cognitive or behavioral trait through a biological (genetic, pharmacological, or other medical) intervention. I shall briefly look at one cognitive and one behavioral target. In light of my previous discussion, I scale the proposal back from one aimed at modifying human nature to one aimed at enhancing a particular phenotypic trait that is relevant to human nature, though we are at most concerned with changing the particular nature of some individuals.

Suppose we are interested in improving (otherwise normal) cognitive performance on some range of tasks, say reading performance or reasoning from presented evidence. Suppose we hypothesize, based on some inform- ation processing theory regarding these tasks, that improving short-term memory could enhance performance on the more complex cognitive task. Suppose we then found an association or modest correlation between better performance on some tasks measuring short-term memory and some pattern of alleles. Suppose further (I am assuming a high toleration for science fiction) that we can modify embryos we plan to carry to term so that they have the preferred pattern of alleles (the issues are different if we are simply selecting from among some array of embryos already having different alleles, as in pre-implantation genetic diagnosis).

What else might we have to know to proceed ethically with the modification? We would have to know a lot more. We would have to know that the increased short-term memory involved here actually plays a role in enhancing the more complex cognitive task rather than interfering with it. Perhaps it creates too much noise that interferes with the complex task, or does so in some range of environments not tracked in the original finding of the association. Keeping our earlier lesson about norms of reaction in mind, we would have to be sure the association we found was not specific to a poor sampling of environments, so that in some other range of environments, say after drinking orange juice or listening for an hour to an Ipod, short-term memory might be worse for these alleles. Without some clear sense of these complex issues, we could not have any confidence that improving the component capability has the intended or desired effect on the more complex one. And all of this information goes well beyond the standard worry that the intervention itself carries with it risks that non-interference lacks. In short, a careful human research protocol would most likely stop this experiment in its tracks.

Consider now a complex behavioral trait or complex of traits. I limit my discussion to one point (drawing directly on a passage I contributed to *From Chance to Choice*): most virtues of interest to us because they make people "better," whether prudential or moral virtues, are exceedingly complex traits.[3] They are contextually highly sensitive and specific, they require considerable perception and discrimination for their exercise, their exercise often requires balancing their appeal with other virtues. Many underlying capabilities or dispositions that might enhance virtues, for example, sensitivity to the feelings of others, intelligence, ability to modulate emotional response, capabilities that we might think have some significant genetic basis, can just as easily be put into the service of vice as well as virtue. Consider Cynthia, for example.

Cynthia has great intuition about the feelings of others. She can read their emotions well, she knows how to feel their pain and anxiety. Indeed, people find her empathetic: they see that she resonates with their pain. At the same time, she does not lapse into pity, and she is not incapacitated by her emotions. She keeps a level head. She puts people at ease, and is able to say the right things to them. Without being condescending or pandering—which would put people off if they too were perceptive—she judiciously exhibits her responsiveness. Cynthia is blessed in other ways: she is extremely good at planning a detailed but flexible course of action. She is willing to make sacrifices, even painful ones, in the short term to improve her situation—or that of others she is advising—in the long run. She knows how others will respond to the steps she takes and to anticipate their reactions. Like a good chess player, she thinks her way through several courses of action, but she does not seem calculating or cunning to others so much as careful and thoughtful. She does not seem calculating because she seems responsive to the wishes of others in her planning: she builds on their intentions and encourages their desires to do well for themselves. She incorporates their desires and goals into her own planning.

Cynthia exhibits many of the dispositions and traits that would make her an excellent social worker. She might even win an award for excellence: Virtuous Social Worker of the Year. But, alas, Cynthia is a very successful con artist, not a social worker: she sells phoney real estate to unsuspecting

---

[3] Buchanan, A., Brock, D., Daniels, N., and Wikler, D. 2000. *From Chance to Choice: Genetics and Justice* (New York: Cambridge University Press).

retirees. Or at least she was successful until she met an equally successful former con artist who ran a sting operation for the FBI. She clearly lacks the direct concern for the well-being of others that would make her many capabilities serve as components of a moral virtue.

Moral: *we should be leery of any promises that a genetic intervention (or an environmental one) that enhances a trait or disposition that is merely a necessary condition for having a virtue will help us produce morally "better" offspring.* If we could genetically enhance the various capabilities that contribute to Cynthia's arsenal, it does not follow she will be morally virtuous. These are component capabilities, the mechanical underpinnings as it were, not the virtue itself. How could we then reassure a human subjects Institutional Review Board that we were not producing more con artists rather than social workers?

Consider a more specific implication of my discussion that has something of the character of "you can't get there from here." We cannot modify human nature unless we act on a population level. Further, the action must affect traits we think central to that nature. This suggests that genetic interventions are less likely to be threats than environmental interventions that undermine our human capabilities or nature. Even if it were true that it would always or generally be bad to modify human nature, the inference that we should be wary of genetics as a threat to human nature does not follow. It does not follow because it is hard to conceive how such interventions would operate on a population level rather than on selected individuals. My earlier discussion undermines a premise of most arguments that would point to the potential danger of genetics to human nature. If "ought" implies "can," then so does "ought not" imply "can." But it is hard to see how we can, at least genetically.

What about action on part of the population? The kind of case that has typically been discussed is the private marketing of a genetic technology that would enhance some trait considered valuable—beauty, intelligence (or its component capabilities), strength. Typically, the threat here is not to human nature, since the traits being modified simply improve them within the range we find among humans, though if there were modification of population frequencies on a large enough scale, we might conclude we had modified human nature. The prospect creates problems of fairness—will wealth lead to ramified competitive advantages—and possibly of coordination. Making a trait valued for its positional advantage common may make it less valuable. I leave these points aside since they have been discussed elsewhere.[4]

What if the trait involves a sub- or super-human capability? Are we not threatening human nature in the sense that the individual might no longer exhibit what we agree to be human nature? I see no general answer to this question, and I am not quite sure it is just one question. As soon as we are aware we are not talking about creating a musical genius (another Mozart still has a nature we recognize as human), we must first try to describe what the life of this organism would be like. I leave this exercise to those who engage in similar tasks—say novelists or at least the best science fiction writers. But the complexities are obvious: It might be terrible if we created only one such creature, since its nature requires it to live as a social animal, but it might be wonderful, from some cosmic perspective, if there were many of them, for by any measure there might be more good in the world and no harm to anyone. But then I am cognizant of my earlier warning about how far we are from knowing how to improve either cognitive or behavioral performance when we restrict ourselves to tampering with component capabilities or traits.

I should stop because I want to leave the ethics of science fiction to others.

---

[4] I note that the argument in Buchanan et al. 2000, far from prohibiting all enhancing interventions, suggests that some may be obligatory, though not for the same reasons given to justify standard obligations to provide medical treatments.

2

What's Taxonomy Got to Do with It? 'Species Integrity', Human Rights, and Science Policy

Eric T. Juengst

I. Inheritable Genetic Modification as a Science Policy Issue

For the last 25 years, human gene transfer research has been bounded by two simple lines: the line between using gene transfer techniques to cure disease or improve the human design, on one hand, and the line between applying gene transfer techniques to somatic cells or germ-line cells, on the other.[1] The dominant view, received as wisdom in both formal sciences policies and in the rhetoric of scientists, has been that enhancement applications of gene transfer would be too morally problematic, and germ-line applications would be too risky to prospective offspring, at least until the practice of safe and effective somatic cell therapy could be perfected.[2]

Today, both of these lines are being challenged, in unexpected ways. 'Enhancement' turns out to be a matter of definition, and the relevant definitions all move the discussion away from objective description and into competing accounts of the values at stake.[3] Inheritable genetic modifications, moreover, can be accomplished without using recombinant

---

[1] Eric Juengst and L. Walters, 'Ethical issues in gene transfer research', in T. Friedman, ed., *The Development of Human Gene Therapy* (NY: Cold Spring Harbor Press, 1999), pp. 691–713.

[2] Leroy Walters and Julie Palmer, *the Ethics of Human Gene Therapy* (Oxford University Press, 1997).

[3] Erik Parens, ed., *Enhancing Human Traits: Ethical and Social Implications* (Washington DC: Georgetown University Press, 1998).

DNA gene transfer techniques, and are thereby escaping scrutiny as 'germ-line gene therapy'.[4] Moreover, even the anticipated modes of both enhancement and germ-line modification have public advocates within the scientific and bioethical communities that would have been very surprising in 1985: mainstream theologians, prominent molecular biologists, distinguished philosophers and senior bioethicists.[5,6,7] In short, the dykes against human genetic engineering are bulging against the tide of the 'post-human', and much of the intellectual establishment on these matters seems to be leaning in the direction of letting them go.

This leaves a set of very strange bedfellows striving to maintain the science policy status quo. On the right are natural law theorists, both religious and secular, who continue to maintain that human nature would be corrupted by such change, sacrificing important human values to selfish desires.[8,9] Most of the new apologists for genetic modification have felt compelled to address the challenge of the natural lawyers, and there are now a number of good critiques of the essentialism to which their views fall prey.[10,11]

On the left, however, are a collection of environmentalists, human rights activists, and communitarians, for whom attempting to 'direct evolution' is willful hubris, with consequences already foreshadowed in the eugenics movements of the past.[12,13,14] In this essay, I offer a sympathetic critique of their views. This camp has been active in attempting to influence

---

[4] Erik Parens and Eric Juengst, 'Inadvertently crossing the germ line', *Science* 292 (2001): 397.

[5] Ted Peters, For *the Love of Children: Genetic Technologies and the Future of the Family* (Louisville, KY: Westminster/John Knox, 1996).

[6] Cf. Gregory Stock and John Campbell, eds., *Engineering the Human Germ-line* (New York: Oxford University Press, 2000).

[7] Philip Kitcher, the *Lives to Come: The Genetic Revolution and Human Possibilities* (New York: Simon and Schuster, 1997).

[8] Leon Kass, *Life, Liberty and the Pursuit of Dignity* (San Francisco: Encounter Books, 2002).

[9] Francis Fukuyama, *Our Posthuman Future: Consequences of the Biotechnology Revolution* (New York: Profile Books, 2002).

[10] Allen Buchanan, Dan Brock, Norman Daniels, and Daniel Wikler, *From Chance to Choice: Genetics and Justice* (New York: Cambridge University Press, 2002).

[11] Kurt Bayertz, 'Human nature: how normative might it be?' *Journal of Philosophy and Medicine* 28 (2003): 131–50.

[12] Bill McKibben, *Enough: Staying Human in an Engineered Age* (NY: Henry Holt & Co., 2003).

[13] Council for Responsible Genetics, 'Position statement on human germ-line manipulation', *Human Gene Therapy* 4 (1993): 35–9.

[14] Bruce Jennings, 'The liberalism of life: Bioethics in the face of biopower', *Raritan* 22: 4 (Spring, 2003): 132–46.

international science policy, and their policy arguments are attractive to many who consider themselves progressive thinkers on social and environmental matters. But the price they pay for their rhetoric is a reliance on a set of morally idolatrous assumptions about biological taxonomy that are ultimately more mistaken than the naturalist's essentialism, and unnecessary to boot. Or so I shall argue below.

II. Preserving the Species

Signs and samples of the kind of views I have in mind appear in science policy arguments that range from an advocacy group's proposal for an international 'Genetic Heritage Safeguard Treaty' designed to 'repudiate eugenic political ideologies and deepen our commitment to the integrity of the human species',[15] to US Senator Brownback's bill to defend 'the dignity and integrity of the species' against the creation of stem cell chimeras,[16] and the European Union's explanation that its 'Convention on Human Rights and Biomedicine' prohibits inherited genetic modification in humans because of concerns that 'misuse of these developments may endanger not only the individual but the species itself'.[17] As these tokens indicate, a common theme is a concern for the welfare of humanity as a whole and the dangers that biomedicine poses to our 'integrity' as a biological species. In most policy proposals, this concern is left relatively unexplained, as if it were self-evident. One particularly articulate expression of it however is provided by work of the human rights lawyer George Annas and his collaborators. They promote the need for a new UN 'Convention on the Preservation of the Human Species', which would realize itself in an international treaty to ban 'species altering' research (at least, where the species involved is ours).[18] The language of this proposed

[15] Richard Hayes, 'The science and politics of genetically modified humans', Worldwatch 15: 4(July/August, 2002), at http://www.geneticsandsociety.org/article.php?id=1962

[16] Samuel Brownback, Senate Bill 1373 [109th] Human Chimera Prohibition Act of 2005, at http://www.govtrack.us/congress/billtext.xpd?bill=s109-1373

[17] Convention for the Protection of Human Rights and Dignity of the Human Being with regard to the Application of Biology and Medicine: Convention on Human Rights and Biomedicine. Oviedo4.IV.1997, at http://conventions.coe.int/treaty/en/treaties/html/164.htm

[18] George Annas, Lori Andrews, and Rosario Isasi, 'Protecting the endangered human: toward an international treaty prohibiting cloning and inheritable alterations', American Journal of Law and Medicine 28 (2002): 151–78.

convention bears scrutiny, since it betrays assumptions that seem to lie behind much of this genre of policy argument, and in doing so helps suggest how its efforts might be better directed.

Annas defines the class of 'species altering' research as encompassing 'any experimental interventions aimed at altering a fundamental beneficial characteristic of being human'. He elaborates with a distinction:

> There are at least two ways to change such characteristics. The first is to make a necessary beneficial human trait optional. Changing it in one member (who continues to be seen as a member of the species) would change the definition for everyone. . . . A second way to change a characteristic of being human is any alteration that would make the resulting person someone we (homo sapiens) would no longer identify as a member of our species, or who could not sexually reproduce with a human.[19]

Under this rubric, the proposed treaty targets two kinds of research for prohibition: research involving human reproductive cloning, and research aimed at effecting inheritable genetic modifications in humans. As Annas and his colleagues argue: 'cloning and inheritable genetic alterations can be seen as crimes against humanity of a unique sort: they are techniques that can alter the essence of humanity itself (and thus threaten to change the foundation of human rights) by taking human evolution into our own hands and directing it toward the development of a new species sometimes termed the "posthuman"'.[20]

The core provisions of the proposed Convention expand on the dangers of such hubris:

The Parties to this Convention,

. . . *Noting* the increased power of genetic science, which opens up vast prospects for improving health, but also has the power to diminish humanity fundamentally by producing a child through human cloning or by intentionally producing an inheritable genetic change;

Concerned that experiments which for the first time would produce children with predetermined genotypes, rather than novel genotypes, might cause these children to be deprived of their human rights;

---

[19] George Annas, 'The man on the moon, immortality and other millennial myths: the prospects and perils of human genetic engineering', *Emory Law Journal* 49: 3 (Summer 2000): 753–82, at 779.

[20] Annas, Andrews, and Isasi, 'Protecting the endangered human', p. 153.

Concerned that by altering fundamental human characteristics to the extent of possibly producing a new human species or subspecies, genetic science will cause the resulting people to be treated unequally or deprived of their human rights;. . .

Have agreed on the following:

Parties shall take all reasonable action, including the adoption of criminal laws, to prohibit anyone from initiating or attempting to initiate a human pregnancy or other form of gestation using embryos or reproductive cells which have undergone intentional inheritable genetic modification.[21]

Annas's proposed convention is a good example of the left-leaning concern to preserve and formalize the existing moratorium on human germ-line genetic interventions because it neatly folds together a number of important themes from that literature. On one hand, by framing the major danger of such interventions as the loss of *human rights*, the Convention puts species altering interventions on a par with slavery, terrorism, and genocide as a legitimate topic for cross-cultural, international legislation. The argument is that since 'membership in the human species is central to the meaning and enforcement of human rights',[22] the post-human progeny of genetic engineering may find themselves disqualified by definition. Annas writes that:

There are limits to how far we can go in changing our human nature without changing our humanity and our basic human values. Because it is the meaning of humanness (our distinctness from other animals) that has given birth to our concepts of both human dignity and human rights, altering our nature necessarily threatens to undermine both human dignity and human rights. With their loss, the fundamental belief in human equality would also be lost. . . . If history is a guide, either the normal humans will view the 'better' humans as 'the other' and seek to control or destroy them, or vice-versa. The better human will become, at least in the absence of a universal concept of human dignity, either the oppressor or the oppressed.[23]

The proposed draft convention's text focuses on the political plight of the engineered as a potentially oppressed minority. What human rights advocates could be for the undermining of human dignity through taxo-nomical terrorism? On the other hand, the Convention's title—'On the

---

[21] Ibid., p. 154.   [22] Ibid., p. 153.
[23] Annas, 'The man on the moon', p. 773.

Preservation of the Human Species'—clearly alludes to the alternative: that the engineered would be our oppressors. As Annas writes:

...Ultimately, it almost seems inevitable that genetic engineering would move *homo sapiens* into two separable species: the standard-issue human beings would be seen by the new, genetically enhanced neo-humans as heathens who can properly be slaughtered and subjugated. It is this genocidal potential that makes species-altering genetic engineering a potential weapon of mass destruction and the unaccountable genetic engineer a potential bioterrorist.[24]

Raising this specter allows Annas et al. to play two other attractive international policy cards in promoting his views: *arms control concerns* to forestall the extinction of our species at the hands of our own weapons, and the *environmentalist concerns* about the extinction of endangered species through the careless human introduction of eco-destabilizing, genetically modified, biological competitors. These are clever gambits: what humanitarians could be against additional curbs on humanity's reckless self-destruction? What environmentalists could resist extending their concerns about endangered species and genetically modified organisms to ourselves? What better place to invoke, as Annas does, the environmental movement's 'precautionary principle', and change the burden of proof by 'outlawing potentially lethal activities, thus requiring proponents to change the law before proceeding'.[25]

A third theme captured in the convention is that interventions like inheritable genetic modifications, because they might expand or transgress the current biological boundaries of our species, involve decisions in which the whole species has a stake. As Annas and his colleagues say,

As a baseline, if we take human rights and democracy seriously, a decision to alter a fundamental characteristic in the definition of 'human' should not be made by any individual or corporation without wide discussion among all members of the affected populations.... Altering the human species is an issue that directly concerns all of us, and should only be decided democratically, by a body that is representative of everyone on the planet.[26]

This position resonates well with the popular European view that the human genome is, like the sea-bed, a part of humanity's 'common heritage',

---

[24] Annas, 'The man on the moon', p.773.
[25] Annas, Andrews, and Isasi, 'Protecting the endangered human', p. 154.   [26] Ibid., p. 153.

and should be explored and exploited only under the auspices of global agreements informed by what Vaclav Havel calls 'species consciousness'.[27] For Annas, private genetic decisions that affect the larger human gene pool 'could all fit into a new category of "crimes against humanity" in the strict sense, as actions that threaten the integrity of the human species itself'.[28] This concern for the corporate human control of our species' boundaries provides common ground with both those who fear the consequences of disregarding 'evolution's wisdom' in crafting our inheritance, and those who would seek to protect the rights of future generations by defending their 'right to an untampered genome'.[29] Thus, Annas et al. conclude that:

Opposition to cloning and inheritable genetic alteration is 'conservative' in the strict sense of the word: it seeks to conserve the human species. But it is also liberal in the strict sense of the world: it seeks to preserve democracy, freedom and universal human rights for all members of the human species.[30]

Casting human germ-line modification research as 'species-altering' experimentation is a clever strategy for international science policy-making. It enables policy-makers to invoke concern over the political oppression of minorities, human extinction, and ecological recklessness, private exploitation of public resources, species integrity, the wisdom of nature, and the rights of future generations. But it is, as they say, too clever by half. I will argue that, as an international science policy approach to germ-line modification research, banning 'species-altering procedures' either does much too much or much too little, and on either interpretation sends much too muddled a message about the nature and grounding of the human values at issue in this research. The real moral concerns with the creation of neohumans still lie far ahead of the science, but, sadly enough, they are not at all futuristic. Ultimately, what is at stake in genetic modification is our tolerance for human genetic diversity. Appeals to 'species integrity' are about as helpful in that context as appeals to 'racial purity' are in designing population genetic research.

---

[27] Annas, Andrews, and Isasi, 'Protecting the endangered human', p. 152.

[28] Annas, 'The man on the moon', p. 778.

[29] Council of Europe (Parliamentary Assembly), 'Recommendation 934 (1982) On Genetic Engineering', Council of Europe, Strasbourg, France, 1982.

[30] Annas, Andrews, and Isasi, 'Protecting the endangered human', p. 173.

III. 'Altar-ing' the Species

Annas says that he draws his line at the nature of our species, because he thinks that of all the morally problematic uses of genetic technologies, interventions that go beyond 'therapy', and beyond 'enhancement', to 'the extent of possibly producing a new human species or subspecies' will be seen by the widest range of cultures and countries as clearly 'inhuman' or 'de-humanizing'. However, there are two different ways to interpret this, neither of which will be terribly helpful for international science policy.

First of all, this convention cannot literally seek to preserve our species from all genetic change, or even from the changes for which we are responsible. Species are not static collections of organisms that can be 'preserved' against change like a can of fruit; they wax and wane with every birth and death and their genetic complexions shift across time and space.[31,32] In our case, almost everything we do as humans affects that process. To argue, as some Europeans have, that everyone has the right to inherit 'an untampered genome' only makes sense if we are willing to take a snap-shot of the human gene pool at some given instant, and reify it as the sacred 'genetic patrimony of humankind'—which some come close to doing.[33] But putting some particular genetic version of our species on an altar and attempting to police human behavior in order to protect it is, from a human rights point of view, no better than the eugenicists' attempts to sanctify and promote a particular genetic ideal for our species: even if it were possible to do, it could not be done without widespread violations of basic human rights and liberties.[34] Under this interpretation, the draft convention's ban on 'species altering procedures' would cover much too much, laying groundwork for the very kind of human rights abuses history has warned us of already. Even limiting prohibited alterations to changes in

[31] Ronald De Sousa, 'The natural shiftiness of natural kinds', *Canadian Journal of Philosophy* 14 (1984): 561–81.

[32] David Hull, 'On the plurality of species: questioning the party line', in RA Wilson, ed., *Species: New Interdisciplinary Essays* (Cambridge: MIT Press, 1999).

[33] Emmanuel Agius, 'Germ-line cells: our responsibilities for future generations', in E. Agius, P. S. Inglott, and T. Macelli, eds., *Our Responsibilities Toward Future Generations* (Valleta, Malta: Foundation for International Studies, 1990), pp. 133–43.

[34] Eric Juengst, 'Should we treat the human germ-line as a global human resource?' in E. Agius and S. Busutill, eds, *Germ-Line Intervention and Our Responsibilities to Future Generations* (Boston: Kluwer Academic Publishers, 1998), pp. 85–102.

'fundamental beneficial characteristics of being human' doesn't help, since it merely shifts the problem to defining those characteristics. (Why, for example, is two-parent sexual reproduction a more fundamentally beneficial human characteristic than having two-parent sexual reproduction involving coitus, or having two rearing parents of different genders?)

But if it is not simply the genetic complexion of our species that is the true concern of this Convention, what does 'species altering' mean? Some language in the Convention suggests that 'altering' is being used here not just to convey 'modifying', but in the strong sense of 'transforming' or 'replacing'. In other words, we are worried about interventions and experiments that might change the biological classification of their subjects entirely: procedures that can produce what evolutionary biologists would call 'speciation events'.

Indeed, this is the only interpretation that allows the Convention's title to read as an environmentalist might, as referring to saving the species from extinction. The human species is not endangered by mere genetic change: but if a new species was generated that exterminated us, we might be endangered by a speciation event. If 'fundamentally beneficial' traits are to be read as 'taxonomically defining', then this interpretation might work. But then our treaty would cover only the most dramatic of genetic interventions: interventions that rendered the subjects biologically incapable of reproducing with human beings, but compatible with each other. Under this interpretation, even most germ-line modifications, genetic enhancements, and reproductive manipulations, like cloning, would be unproblematic, since their subjects are uncontroversially still taxonomically human. Since concerns over cloning and germ-line modifications are at the heart of this treaty, however, this interpretation would mean that banning 'species altering procedures' would not allow this convention to achieve its own goals.

IV. What's species membership got to do with it, anyway?

Moreover, these definitional problems suggest a fundamental moral question about the 'preservation of the human species' approach. What does our taxonomic designation have to do with our moral status and fundamental rights? There is a risk here of confusing the biological sense of 'human' as an taxonomic term (like 'canine' or 'simian') and the word's use in 'human rights', where it serves as a synonym for 'natural', 'inalienable' or 'fundamental' to distinguish that class of moral claims from other conferred, negotiated or legislated rights.[35] Obviously it is not enough to be taxonomically human to enjoy human rights: human tissue cultures and human cadavers show us that. Is it even necessary to be taxonomically human to enjoy human rights?

There are many candidates for the qualities that serve to give us our inalienable rights (the Convention singles out reason and conscience), but none hinge on a taxonomic designation.[36] So how is it that species altering procedures 'might cause the children to be deprived of their human rights'? As the draft convention tellingly says, from most moral points of view on the derivation of human rights, even genetic speciation events would produce 'new **human** species or subspecies'. In fact, framing our concern about genetic threats to human rights in terms of 'species-altering', makes the same mistake that others make when they seek to defend our 'species integrity': it suggests that taxonomy might determine a creature's moral status, and that it is conceivable only those with creatures that display the motley collection of genes human beings share (at some instant) warrant basic rights. Again, this it is a form of 'altar-ing' our gene pool that we should spurn as moral idolatry.

In this context, it is worth noting just how porous the integrity of the human species might be at the genetic level. For example, consider what we are learning about the critical role of lowly microbial 'flora' in underpinning our lives as human organisms.[37] We know that on and in the healthy human body microbial cells outnumber human cells ten to one, and play an active role in maintaining our normal physiology. Advances in microbial genomics are now underlining the significance of that role by suggesting that it may involve interactions at the genetic level as well, between human and bacterial cells.[38] Our commensual bacteria, in

---

[35] Alisdair Campbell, K. G. Glass, and L. C. Charland, 'Describing our humanness; Can genetic science alter what it means to be human?' *Science and Engineering Ethics* 4 (1998): 413–26.

[36] Jason Scott Robert and Francoise Baylis, 'Crossing species boundaries', The *American Journal of Bioethics* 3: 3 (2003): 1–14.

[37] R. T. J. Clarke, and T. Bauchop, *Microbial ecology of the gut* (London; New York: Academic Press, 1977).

[38] L. V. Hooper, M. H. Wong, A. Thelin, et. al.. 'Molecular analysis of commensal host-microbial relationships in the intestine', *Science*, 291 (2001): 881–84.

essence, serve as crucial genomic extenders, much as they do in termites (whom they allow to digest wood). If so, the microbiologists argue, our basic concept of the human organism should be expanded to include our normal symbionts.[39] Rather than single organisms, human individuals, like termites, are in fact super-organismic eco-systems, involving multiple species' genomes in complex interaction.[40] Moreover, since those genomic profiles will vary between individuals and wax and wane over time, this science suggests that a canonical set of 'human genes' will never be available as a ground for human rights, or for determining when humans' 'species integrity' has been breached.[41]

No one seems much concerned that we are all mixtures of many indigenous bacterial species and human cell lines. It neither undermines our fundamental rights, nor confers special moral status on bacteria. But it does seem as if concerns about the moral implications of blurring boundaries between the human species and non-human organisms are animating those who are striving to protect our species' 'dignity and integrity'. Perhaps taking a closer look at this concern might suggest where the real science policy issues in this domain might lie.

V. Crossing Species Boundaries

The normative importance of 'species integrity' has been posited before within bioethics, to critique biomedical practices as varied as the fertilization of hamster ova with human spermatozoa, the transplantation of porcine organs into humans, and the propagation of human stem cell lines in mice and the transfer of human genes into bacteria. 'Crossing species barriers' sounds like trespassing, and the qualms it provokes have been explained in a variety of ways, from invocations of essentialistic or theological visions of human (and animal!) nature to fears about risks of creating new forms of disease or ecological disruptions. Common across these claims, however, is

[39] Michael J. Blaser, 'Who are we? Indigenous microbes and the ecology of human diseases', *EMBO Rep.* 7 (10) (Oct. 2006): 956–60.

[40] Jeff I. Gordon, R. E. Ley, R. Wilson, et al., 'Extending our view of self: The Human Gut Microbiome Initiative (HGMI)'. http://www.genome.gov/Pages/Research/Sequencing/SeqProposals/HGMI seq.pdf. Accessed 24 June 2007.

[41] J. Wilson, *Biological Individuality: The Identity and Persistence of Living Entities* (Cambridge and New York: Cambridge University Press, 1999).

the worry that biomedicine will undermine a given stability in the world by violating the categories that order it. Drawing in equal measure from Aristotelean essentialism and nineteenth-century Romantic sensibilities, this concern gives high normative weight to the biological kinds produced by the 'Wisdom of Evolution', and their relative ranking in a hierarchical 'great chain of being'. On this view, 'splicing life' in the creation of transgenic organisms, or interspecies tissue chimeras, or hybridized embryos—like importing alien species into an established ecosystem—is always dangerous enough to justify the use of the 'precautionary principle'.[42] For some, as Jeffrey Stout has pointed out, the creation of such 'abominations' is also morally suspect, simply in its willful disregard for the natural order it crosses.[43]

Anthropologists suggest that these concerns are often animated by the tacit roles that concepts of 'purity' and 'pollution' play in our cultural definitions of human bodily boundaries, health and disease.[44] In situations that involve the integrity of the human species, like xenotransplantation, or the creation of man–machine 'cyborgs', this moral hazard can be explained as the danger of dehumanization: that polluting the constellation of traits that humans have inherited from our ancestors—our given 'human nature'—with nonhuman attributes we will inevitably degrade the elements of human identity we find morally important, like human dignity, autonomy, and vulnerability. As Jurgen Habermas puts it,

What is at stake is a dedifferentiation, through biotechnology, of deep rooted categorical distinctions which we have as yet, the description we give of ourselves, assumed to be invariant. This dedifferentiation might change our ethical self-understanding as a species in a way that could also affect our moral consciousness.[45]

Moreover, it is not just the blurring of human/nonhuman lines that can be abominable: conflating the natural kinds of humans—as men and women, for example, or children and adults—can evoke the same repugnance. For example, sports ethicists report that:

---

[42] William Wright, 'Germ-line genetic engineering and the Precautionary Principle', *Chrestomathy* 5 (2006): 333–46.

[43] Jeffrey Stout, *Ethics after Babel: The Languages of Morals and their Discontents* (Princeton: Princeton University Press, 1988).

[44] Mary Douglas. *Purity and Danger: An Analysis of the Concepts of Pollution and Taboo* (London: Routledge, 1994 [1966]).

[45] Jurgen Habermas, *The Future of Human Nature* (Cambridge, UK: Polity Press, 2003), p. 42.

While anecdotal, the members of our undergraduate Sport Ethics class were generally revulsed at the sight of the Chinese women swimmers. These swimmers displayed a body type that did not fit into the socially constructed category of female. . . . They looked like men, but were labeled 'women'. Interestingly, the class was not similarly disgusted with Ben Johnson. . . . His sin was against a lesser god: he merely cheated. The problem with the Chinese swimmers was that they were gender freaks first, and cheaters a distant second.[46]

Unfortunately, even female athletes who look like women experience similar reactions when they simply attempt to compete with men, and mixed gender sports remain rarer than our bodies necessarily dictate.[47] In the past, competitions between athletes from different racial groups—or even different social classes—raised similar concerns about disturbing the natural order and its degrading effects on the most privileged players, dehumanizing the underprivileged in the process.[48]

As the allusions above to the history of sexism, racism and social class bias in sport suggest, there are dangers to beware in giving biological categories moral force. The notion that nature is normatively ordered into a hierarchy of natural kinds, each with their inviolable essence and fixed moral status, is a distinctly premodern view, increasingly rejected over the last two centuries by the natural sciences as a matter of fact and by the political sciences as a guide to human rights, and by theology, as an adequate vision of Creation. Maintaining this worldview for science policy in the face of the history of oppression and intolerance that is fueling its rejection in other spheres of human activity would be an uphill challenge that most would rather avoid, particularly if there are alternatives.

But perhaps I'm taking the language of 'species integrity' too literally. Perhaps that metaphor is simply intended to warn us that, despite their evident moral status, the victims of species-altering procedures might be (wrongly) perceived by others to be 'inhuman' and have their rights abused as a consequence. That interpretation would make sense of George Annas' Convention's opening appeals to our convictions about 'rights based on the dignity and worth of the human person', the 'equal rights of all persons'

[46] Michael Burke and Terrance Roberts, 'Drugs in sport: An issue of morality or sentimentality?' *Journal of the Philosophy of Sport* 24 (1994): 99–113 (at 103).

[47] Laurel Davis and Linda Delano, 'Fixing the boundaries of physical gender: Side effects of anti-drug campaigns in athletics', *Sociology of Sport Journal* 9: 1 (1992): 1–19.

[48] John Hoberman, *Mortal Engines: The Science of Performance and the Dehumanization of Sport* (Caldwell, NJ: The Blackburn Press, 1992).

and 'the inadmissibility of discrimination'. But if it is actually genetic prejudice, or, in Annas' own felicitous terminology, 'genism' that is the real problem here, then his proposed Convention and its kin have a real problem. By focusing on 'species integrity' and the genetic interventions that might qualify as 'species-altering procedures', like radical germ-line modifications, these proposals actually distract us from the vast bulk of real and imminent threats to human rights that genetic research can pose.

If we are worried about the threats of 'genism', the most dangerous products of human genetic research are not gene-splicing techniques: they are changes in what people think they know about each other that exacerbate existing prejudices between them. It is the social perception of genetic difference, not the actual biological differences that fuel human rights abuses. These perceptions, the prejudices they bolster, and the abuses they feed, will be coming for the foreseeable future not from the lunatic fringes of genetic research, but from its brightest hopes: from the new work in human genetic variation research, 'public health genetics', and Pharmacogenomics. To the extent that this wave of post-genomic work accentuates perceived genetic differences between human groups already socially sorted by their mutual power relations (like the 'races'), it will be the primary engine for human rights threats, because it is what will feed draconian 'public health' infringements on reproductive freedoms, oppressive DNA identification and data banking programs, neo-eugenic immigration policies, economic discrimination practices, and, at the extreme, biological warfare strategies. These are the problems that international policy makers should be worried about long before they concern themselves with the moral merits of sexual reproduction. To the extent that the convention's focus on 'species altering procedures' distracts us from the distinctly intra-species issues of genetic oppression, it is likely to be accused by the oppressed of being simply another smokescreen thrown up to hide the real, and more difficult issues of how to keep manifestly beneficial research from being abused.

VI. Conclusion: the alternative

So how *should* we frame a convention designed to protect human rights in an age of genetic technology? One approach would be to address the danger of genism directly, and present the initiative as simply a 'Convention on Human Rights Abuses of Human Genetic Research'. Here the word 'abuses' does intentional double duty: we are worried about the ways in which (otherwise laudable) human genetic research can be abused to create social perceptions and practices that provoke human rights abuses. This reframing would take us back to the drawing board, admittedly. In addition to trying to prevent the genism that might attend reproductive cloning or germ-line modification, the initiative would pay more attention to the messier and more mundane matters of limiting law enforcement and political uses of genetic profiling, defining appropriate public health uses of genetic screening tools, and combating genetic discrimination in insurance and employment.[49] Framed explicitly as a human rights initiative, the Convention would direct international attention more directly on the social and political assumptions about race, class, and group membership that continue to infect mainstream 'normal science' in human population genetics, genetic epidemiology and comparative genomics. In doing so, the real reasons why prohibitions against particular reproductive or germ-line genetic interventions might be warranted could be articulated in a cogent way: not because they alter the blend of humanity's gene pool or create new taxons within the genus *homo*, but because they diminish the range of opportunities that human rights are designed to protect.

Of course, some inheritable genetic modifications might also *expand* the range of opportunities available to their human recipients, whom a regulatory framework based on human rights protections would not condemn, in and of it. As advocates for people with disabilities increasingly point out, to the extent that genetic interventions can be used to enhance strengths and compensate for weaknesses in creative ways that expand opportunity without 'normalizing' their recipients, they could be a social force in improving tolerance for human diversity.[50] In other words, it is the opportunities for creativity that the human genome makes possible, not the genes themselves that we should strive to preserve. In the long run, that means that in contemplating inheritable genetic modifications,

---

[49] Cf. Anita Silvers and Michael Stein, 'Human rights and genetic discrimination: protecting genomics' promise for public health', *Journal of Law, Medicine and Ethics* 31 (2003): 377–89.

[50] Anita Silvers, 'Meliorism at the millennium: positive molecular eugenics and the promise of progress without excess', in Lisa Parker and Rachel Ankeny, eds., *Mutating Concepts, Evolving Disciplines: Genetics, Medicine and Society* (Boston: Kluwer Academic Publishers, 2002), pp. 215–35.

the international community should focus on the promises we would like to make to our children, rather than fret about what we have (or have not) inherited from our parents. The human gene pool, unlike the sea, has no top, bottom, or shores: it cannot be 'preserved'. The reservoir of human mutual respect, good will and tolerance for difference, however, seems perennially in danger of running dry. That is the truly fragile heritage that we should work to preserve in monitoring genetic research on behalf of the future.

3

Should We Improve Human Nature? An Interrogation from an Asian Perspective

*Ryuichi Ida**

Introduction: setting the tone

Advances in the life sciences and in associated technologies has tremendously increased the possibilities offered by medicine. Today we have the capacity to replace parts of the human body and to increase its functions beyond normal levels. We call this "improvement" or "enhancement" of the human body and of nature.

However, consideration of the attitudes of Japanese and other Asian people may lead to a different understanding of human nature to that common in the West, in particular with respect to the relation of human beings to the natural world. The very idea of improving human nature may thus appear incoherent or incongruous to people in those parts of the world. Moreover, in non-Western countries the idea of modifying human nature is associated with Utilitarianism, a Western doctrine that is not especially popular in Asia.

This paper will discuss the topic of improving human nature from a Japanese perspective, using as an example bioethical discussions in the standard ethical setting found in Japan and Asia.

* Kyoto University Graduate School of Law Oxford-Uehiro-Carnegie Conference on Bioethics 18–19/11/2004 Carnegie Council on Bioethics, NY.

I. "Improvement"

It is true that today's life sciences and technologies give us a wide variety of possibilities for increasing human welfare. Such technologies are now put to use not only for medical purposes, but also for non-therapeutic aims.

An embryo, which previously could be examined only after birth, can now be tested at the pre-implantation stage in order to identify genetic defects. It is possible to eliminate or select the embryo for implantation depending on the results of the test. Another possibility is that a young man or woman, apparently in good health, can be conclusively diagnosed, using genetic testing, as having a condition such as Huntington's disease, even though no effective treatment for this condition exists as of yet. The genetic data of each individual may also be used for so-called individualized medicine, and information about genetic particularities might be abused in various forms of discrimination. The expected clinical use of human embryonic stem cells requires the therapeutic cloning of embryos, which puts us on the risky road towards reproductive cloning.

These are only some examples showing the light and the shadow of the life sciences and their associated technologies. They show us how vague the distinction is now between life and death, between the normal and the abnormal, between the just and the unjust, etc. That is to say that as the life sciences advance further, the greater the challenge to our understanding of life itself.

(1) The basic question

If we start with the assumption that improvement or enhancement of human nature is morally permissible, the question becomes 'What are ethically reasonable means of enhancing human beings, given that enhancement itself is morally permitted or even recommended?' This assumption, however, is not universally accepted. It is true that medical and pharmaceutical care, thanks to advances realized by today's bioscience and technology, saves the lives of, or gives relief to, a tremendous number of diseased people. However, beyond such medical or pharmaceutical purposes, an overall authorization, permission, or even affirmation of the use of these techno-scientific advances for non-therapeutic purposes is still very much in question.

The ethical issue to be considered, therefore, is whether we should improve ourselves with scientific or technological means, rather than by forging on with our existing physical and intellectual endowment. If the answer to this question is affirmative, then we may take the next question, the question of proper means and constraints. However, if the answer is negative, or at least is not clearly affirmative, then this further question become irrelevant. This chapter asks whether we really ought to take this further step.

(2) Two senses of improvement

We can distinguish two relevant senses of "improvement". One is to obtain better results through physical or intellectual exercise. Here one makes use of one's naturally given talents and capabilities in the same way an athlete trains to improve her record. Thus, for example, the athlete chooses her exercise in different ways, like muscle training or sprinting, etc. according to her particular talents. Or a candidate for a demanding examination might study continuously every day until midnight and be rewarded by coming top of the class. Improvement in this sense uses or realizes naturally given capabilities. We may call this "natural improvement".

The other sense of improvement is to obtain better results by using biological means that directly affect the human body or some aspect of it. In a wider social context this sort of improvement may even amount to the elimination of those who have "lesser capabilities, intellectually or physically", leading to greater overall levels. Or it may use biological measures to replace, add or remove some parts of the human body. Such replacement, addition or removal is achieved artificially. Examples include taking steroids that strengthen the muscles, or applying a genetic test in order to detect genetic abnormalities, so that an embryo bearing such abnormalities can be terminated (to be replaced in the mother's uterus by an embryo without significant abnormalities).

The latter case implies the selection of a potential human being. It may naturally happen that such abnormalities would cause the embryo to be rejected before implantation, or cause a miscarriage in the process of implantation or of development after implantation. However, since such a rejection or miscarriage is not assured in the natural state, one might use a biological method for these purposes in order to ensure that such an embryo does not develop. The result is that the parents or mother may have a life without the hardship of raising a disabled child. This would not be an improvement in a proper sense of the term, but one might pretend that it is an improvement of the mother's life. Thus the second improvement may be called "artificial improvement".

Before turning to critically assess the ethics of artificial improvement, it is also worth noting that there are risks of an unknown nature for a body "improved" in these and other ways. The safety of such procedures is not totally assured, even if we accept this type of so-called improvement in principle.

(3) A philosophical standpoint on artificial improvement

I want to suggest that the ideology behind this second type of improvement has its roots in Western philosophical thought. Western philosophy often conceives of human beings as consisting of a body and a soul, with the soul being the essential of the two. Descartes argued that "Cogito, ergo sum". A human being exists because he thinks. A human being cannot exist without thinking. Therefore, a human body is nothing but a material case for the soul. Modern medical science grew from this thought, so that medicine aims at analyzing the mechanical principles of the human body, elucidating the causes of diseases, and curing the patient with medical treatment or pharmaceutical products or by surgical operations.

From this standpoint, it seems permissible to use any available scientific and technological tool to enable the human body to survive or function better. The idea of improvement seems, at least in part, to come from such a philosophical construction.

Another explanation may be possible. Modern Western civilization is closely aligned with *science*, where science is understood as a system of reflection and action through which Nature is objectively cognized and controlled. Science has as its objective the control and management of nature through knowledge and technology. Modern society is thus a society where the human being governs nature.

Thus the human body is also to be controlled by human reason, and science is the means for such control. The benefits of science and technology are to be used to the full to promote a better human life. So unless somehow constrained, we should aim to maximize the use of science and technology.

The ideology of improvement seems to have been derived from this background. It is true that modern Western philosophy has been dominant in the world. However, conceptions of the human body and of life are different from one country to another and from one religion to another. This Western conception is not the only one available.

Thus, although the idea of "artificial improvement" is usually discussed from a largely Western standpoint, there should also be room for examining it from a non-Western perspective.

II. Interrogation from another standpoint: a Japanese and Asian perspective

(1) Nature and human beings

In Japan and in some other Asian countries, we, human beings, are understood as a part of Nature. The human being is simply one particular component among all living beings: fauna and flora. The human species is a kind of animal living in nature. Human beings are not taken to be superior or as having a supreme moral status compared to other living beings.

In Japanese thought, there is a tendency to deny any deep distinction between human beings and the other fauna and flora. The life of all living beings is a kind of a wheel, and the life of human beings and of fauna and flora is in the same circle, and follows an infinite cycle of life. Therefore, every living being stands in a circle of whole life. Moreover, just as each human being, as one of the entities living in such a circle, has its own spirit, each of the other living beings has its own spirit too. People often recognize that a tree has its life, or a small insect has its own spirit. It is in light of this view of life that people speak of the omnipresence of Gods: the God of the mountains, God of the rivers, God of the flowers, God of the trees, etc.

Evolution takes place within this cycle of life. It is unimaginable that a human being could evolve artificially at her ease. Human beings do not control Nature, but must recognize the principle of "living together": since the wheel of life is common to all the members of the cycle of living, we should aim to live *together* with nature. Otherwise, human beings will destroy nature, as we have already experienced in the framework of the current approach to the protection of the environment.

Paradoxically enough, the advancement of life science, in particular of genome science, has provided fresh evidence for the view that human beings are only a part of nature. Biologically speaking, according to the results of research on the human genome and other animals' genomes, the difference between human beings and chimpanzees at the genomic level is only a few percent of the whole genome of each. Genomic science also demonstrates to us that the genome of the human being is the heritage of all living beings in the process of biological evolution since the first living being (unicellular organism) emerged on our Planet. Thus, biologically speaking too, the human being is very much a part of nature.

(2) "Improvement" in the Japanese spiritual context

A human being may be improved in two ways, extrinsic and intrinsic. The first is by way of scientific or technological means. This improvement is extrinsic and artificial. The body of the human being is just an object of change. Such improvement, if this counts as improvement, generates a materialistic attitude to human beings, because, here the body is granted only instrumental value. A dualism of body and soul is assumed, with the soul seen as the core of the value human existence, and the body as merely a kind of material.

Another way of improvement is improvement through daily effort and training. This improvement is intrinsic. Here the body and the soul are integrated in the existence of the human person. The body is trained by the will to improve in the case of physical improvement, and in the case of intellectual improvement, the will itself is the most important factor. There is no intervention from outside.

Needless to say, the former conception of improvement is not easily accepted by the Japanese people and some other Asians. Japanese people and some Asian peoples have a long history of a lifestyle dominated by agriculture which is always conditioned by Nature. Climate, soil, water, and minding the plants, these elements are associated in their life. Crops are deemed as presents or grace from Nature. People believe that humans are *allowed* to live, and do not live only by themselves. From the standpoint of such a conception of life, it is hard to think that humans could change or improve nature. The natural world is not simply a material for manipulation or an object for domination. Rather, the natural world dominates human beings.

There is an objection. If we cannot change nature, what about the role of the medicine, which, in fact, changes the state of health of a diseased person? It should be remembered that oriental medicine does not stand on the same footing as Western medicine. Oriental medicine has as its basic principle the re-establishment of the balance of body and soul. All the diseases come from the imbalance of the patient. It is true that this type of medicine does not practice big operations, like organ transplants, or brain operations. Oriental medicine sees the conditions that might call for such interventions as natural, simply a consequence of human mortality, and it accordingly sees such a patient as entering a stage of returning to nature, i.e. dying.

Nevertheless, it can't be denied that many Japanese as well as other Asian people receive the benefits of modern (Western) medicine based on modern scientific principles. However, this does not mean that the above-mentioned Asian understanding of the relationship between human beings and nature is no longer present. It is often pointed out, for example, that Japanese people are reluctant to undergo organ transplantation, although Japanese techniques in this field are at the very top level. They might explain this choice by noting that organ transplantation is unnatural. And aged people, at the time of death, are said to be honoured to have lived their whole natural lives.

These remarks do not mean that the Japanese people ignore or reject the development of life science and technology. Japan competes at the highest level of life sciences in the world with the US and Europe. The Japanese government gives top priority to progress in the life sciences. What then is medicine in the Japanese spiritual context? Medicine has as its objective the removal of unreasonable handicaps derived from disease in order to let the patient recover and live a normal daily life, and no more than that. Available science and technology are used only for that purpose. Seen from this standpoint, a human person fortified with artificial parts might not even be considered a human being, and might be called instead a "humanoid", "android", or even "robot".

Thus we arrive at the main question proposed in the title of this paper: "Should we improve human nature?" This question is misleading. We might modify the question to "Is it permissible to improve human nature?" And if the answer is "Yes", then we must ask "What will be the limits?"

In the Japanese and Asian context, this last question amounts to a new question—"How far can we depart from nature?"

(3) "How far can we depart from nature?"

The scene we face is one where we have available to use scientific or technological knowledge which would enable us to artificially improve ourselves, and we are ready to use them. We all know the benefits and the risks of today's science and technology, and the benefits are in many cases apparently predominant. The ethical questions, then, are, first, "Is it morally permissible to use this knowledge for whatever purpose some of us would want to use them for?" and, second, "Is there any limit on our use of these sciences and technologies, even if such use would lead to significantly greater benefit than harm?" and finally, "Is the predominance of benefits sufficient to justify the use of these sciences and technologies, even contrary to nature?"

We have already discussed the distinctive outlook on nature that shapes Japanese thought. We will now turn to consider some concrete examples, all of which involve cutting-edge life sciences and technologies. In each case these sciences and technologies offer us something we do not yet have. These examples will illustrate how the Asian perspective of nature leads to very different ethical conclusions than those typically reached in the West.

(a) The ideology of "As it stands" and the case of children with Down's syndrome

Nowadays, it's possible to use prenatal diagnosis to determine with a relatively high degree of confidence whether a pregnancy will produce a child with Down's syndrome. Although this information is merely probabilistic, many pregnant women who take the test act on it, so as to avoid, by abortion, any chance of having a child with this syndrome. It is often claimed that abortion in such cases is justified. The Japanese Law on the Protection of Motherhood allows abortion only if one of three possible conditions is met, namely, (1) the pregnancy is due to rape, (2) the pregnancy seriously threatens the mother's health or life, and (3) the mother suffers from adverse economic and social conditions. The third condition is a very flexible one and in many cases abortion is practised for this reason. So it is in the case of Down's syndrome babies.

However, there are mothers and parents, who have already had such a baby, who say there is much happiness and joy in bringing up the child as he/she stands. They explain that to have such a child reveals the happiness and joy of human life. Every smile of their son or daughter makes the mother happy. This is why it is important for them to protect life "as it stands." If they had used pre-natal diagnosis and then aborted these babies, they could not have found the joy in having such an "angel" child. They say that the babies give them a reason to keep living. Consequently, the Ministry of Health produced a report to recommend that doctors should not tell parents about the possibility of a pre-natal test for Down's syndrome, because the advice of doctors is often mistakenly interpreted as recommending abortion.

These attitudes of Japanese parents who have a Down's syndrome child, and this directive of the Japanese Health Ministry, seem to me to illustrate that in Japan we respect the view of "As it stands." What does it mean to treat something "As it stands"? This attitude expresses respect for Nature and for the natural state of the baby.

It is nevertheless true that there are also many couples who find out about the possibility of such a prenatal test from other different sources, and who ask their doctors to test for Down's syndrome with the intention of choosing abortion should the test return positive. However, the existence of the kind of attitude favourable for the survival of the child represents symbolically the inseparability of the existence of human beings from the natural world, and that the improvement of the mother's life is not always taken as justified, because this way of using the results of scientific and technological research strays too far from nature.

(b) The concept of death and organ transplantation   Death in humans in society had been marked by heart death until the possibility of organ transplantation from brain-dead donors was developed. We have known since the 1950s that the brain "dies", or stops functioning in some cases. However, the term brain–death is not so popular in Japanese society, even among medical doctors. Traditionally, death for human beings has been heart death. The concept of brain death gained popularity once the first human organ transplant was realized in South Africa. We found a new medical method for those who suffer because of their organs. If we wish to transplant an organ into a patient and if we hope for a successful operation and the survival of the patient, the organ to be transplanted should be as fresh as possible. Organs taken from the body of a dead person are known

to increase the risks of failure. There are thus advantages to removing organs before the heart of the dying patient stops beating. For the purpose of promoting successful organ transplantation, and in order to satisfy the recipients on the long waiting lists, it seemed necessary to develop the concept of brain death.

This brief history illustrates how science and necessity might encourage the development of a new concept for a particular purpose, with the aim of using new technology to save lives. But although we can celebrate the discovery of a new method for saving the life of a patient, we should not forget that this is achieved by removing organs from the body of a human being that had previously been deemed still living. This change in the definition of death is not driven by some new scientific discovery or innovation. The necessity of procuring fresh organs came first and the concept of brain death second. Although I do not want to suggest that it is morally wrong to use organ transplantation from brain-dead patients, I do wish to point out the ethical complexity of such a choice. Indeed, even if we accept the use of brain-dead donors, it remains the case that the number of patients waiting for transplantation is too big to manage. Jacques Atali once made the criticism, in his excellent book on the "Order of Cannibalism", that organ transplantation today is close to cannibalism in the primitive ages.

(c) Pre-implantation diagnosis In addition to pre-natal diagnosis, there has recently appeared a new kind of genetic testing, which is called "Pre-implantation genetic diagnosis (PGD)". PGD is practiced after IVF (in vitrofertilization) and before the implantation of the embryo in the uterus of a woman. PGD can be used to identify genetic anomalies in an embryo. If the embryo exhibits the genetic particularities of a disease of an incurable kind—a disease likely to cause heavy handicap and with a high probability of early death—then in common practice this embryo will be eliminated.

It is true that the lives of the prospective parents might benefit from the elimination of a genetically defective embryo. However, PGD treatment is located on the very edge of the abuse that is the selection of future human lives on the basis of deliberate and artificial criteria. Some people believe that such selection is morally permissible so long as it is based on fair, just, reasonable, and objective criteria. But this, and the supposed benefits for the prospective parents, does not yet give us sufficient reason to permit the destruction of an embryo which is the germ of a human life. It is scientifically possible, but ethically questionable. One day, someone is likely to abuse this constraint on the use of PGD and use it to create a "designer baby".

It could of course be argued that PGD can be used to prevent the inheritance of serious diseases, thus cutting the chain which transmits them and that it thus offers parents the prospects of a better life. This point however does not change the fact that PGD is being used here to destroy human embryos, embryos which would normally develop to become human beings through the birth process. There thus remains a serious risk that the massive employment of PGD will lead us to discount the value and dignity of such embryonic human lives, and ultimately to discount the dignity of human life itself, by treating it as an object for selection and destruction. It is thus essential to impose a strict system of control on the use of pre-natal diagnosis. In my opinion, these methods of diagnoses should never be recommended by medical doctors.

(d) Human reproductive cloning   The last example relates to the concept of "human dignity", which is quite a popular term in Western civilization. However, this concept is not totally universal. In this section I would like to very briefly explain how the concept of human dignity is understood in Japan in the context of questions about human reproductive cloning.

Human dignity is sometimes cited as a universally recognized reason for the prohibition of reproduction of human beings by cloning techniques. However, when an act is to be punished, the reason for punishment must be clear and precise. That is one of the requirements in criminal law. Is the concept "human dignity" clear and precise enough?

It should be noted that the concept of human dignity is not as self-evident as it is sometimes presented. Although something like this concept is taken for granted in the Western world, it is not always as familiar to members of other civilizations. In the Japanese context, this meant that an explicit account of the concept of human dignity had to be given in the context of discussion of the ethics of human reproductive cloning. According to the Japanese Bioethics Committee, which undertook the preparatory work for the prohibition of human reproductive cloning by legislation, the violation of the concept of "human dignity" in this case is composed of the following three elements:

1) instrumentalization of human beings for a particular purpose;
2) violation of individuality through presetting of genetic particularities;
3) parthenogenesis which leads to family and social disorder.

The conjunction of these three elements defines human dignity on this account, although it defines it only in a negative way. (In reverse, like the negative on the film of an old fashioned camera.)

This example is only intended to show that many central concepts commonly used in Western bioethics are not immediately recognized or endorsed by members of non-Western cultures. Ethical appeals to human welfare or individual happiness to justify the use of science of technology may have intuitive force in the West, but may seem alien to a non-Western audience.

Conclusion

The Utilitarian approach to the use of advances in the life sciences and associated technologies is not widely accepted in many non-Western countries, in particular in Japan and in other Asian countries. In East and South East Asia, Buddhism and Confucianism often have a dominant role in daily life, and the lifestyle and social practices are still rooted in agricultural traditions. The doctrine of Utilitarianism might still find some adherents in Japan and in Asian countries, but only if it was revised and adapted to this very different cultural and ethical setting.

4

The Case Against Perfection: What's Wrong with Designer Children, Bionic Athletes, and Genetic Engineering

*Michael J. Sandel**

Breakthroughs in genetics present us with a promise and a predicament. The promise is that we may soon be able to treat and prevent a host of debilitating diseases. The predicament is that our newfound genetic knowledge may also enable us to manipulate our own nature—to enhance our muscles, memories, and moods; to choose the sex, height, and other genetic traits of our children; to make ourselves "better than well." When science moves faster than moral understanding, as it does today, men and women struggle to articulate their unease. In liberal societies they reach first for the language of autonomy, fairness, and individual rights. But this part of our moral vocabulary is ill equipped to address the hardest questions posed by genetic engineering. The genomic revolution has induced a kind of moral vertigo.

Consider cloning. The birth of Dolly the cloned sheep, in 1997, brought a torrent of concern about the prospect of cloned human beings. There are good medical reasons to worry. Most scientists agree that cloning is unsafe, likely to produce offspring with serious abnormalities (Dolly recently died a premature death). But suppose technology improved to the point where clones were at no greater risk than naturally conceived offspring. Would

* Originally appeared in *The Atlantic*, April 2004. For a considerably extended version of this essay, see Michael J. Sandel, *The Case against Perfection: Ethics in the Age of Genetic Engineering* (Harvard University Press, 2007).

human cloning still be objectionable? Should our hesitation be moral as well as medical? What, exactly, is wrong with creating a child who is a genetic twin of one parent, or of an older sibling who has tragically died—or, for that matter, of an admired scientist, sports star, or celebrity?

Some say cloning is wrong because it violates the right to autonomy: by choosing a child's genetic makeup in advance, parents deny the child's right to an open future. A similar objection can be raised against any form of bioengineering that allows parents to select or reject genetic characteristics. According to this argument, genetic enhancements for musical talent, say, or athletic prowess, would point children toward particular choices, and so designer children would never be fully free.

At first glance the autonomy argument seems to capture what is troubling about human cloning and other forms of genetic engineering. It is not persuasive, for two reasons. First, it wrongly implies that absent a designing parent, and children are free to choose their characteristics for themselves. But none of us chooses his genetic inheritance. The alternative to a cloned or genetically enhanced child is not one whose future is unbound by particular talents but one at the mercy of the genetic lottery.

Second, even if a concern for autonomy explains some of our worries about made-to-order children, it cannot explain our moral hesitation about people who seek genetic remedies or enhancements for themselves. Gene therapy on somatic (that is, nonreproductive) cells, such as muscle cells and brain cells, repairs or replaces defective genes. The moral quandary arises when people use such therapy not to cure a disease but to reach beyond health, to enhance their physical or cognitive capacities, to lift themselves above the norm.

Like cosmetic surgery, genetic enhancement employs medical means for nonmedical ends—ends unrelated to curing or preventing disease or repairing injury. But unlike cosmetic surgery, genetic enhancement is more than skin-deep. If we are ambivalent about surgery or Botox injections for sagging chins and furrowed brows, we are all the more troubled by genetic engineering for stronger bodies, sharper memories, greater intelligence, and happier moods. The question is whether we are right to be troubled, and if so, on what grounds.

In order to grapple with the ethics of enhancement, we need to confront questions largely lost from view—questions about the moral status of nature, and about the proper stance of human beings toward the given world. Since these questions verge on theology, modern philosophers and political theorists tend to shrink from them. But our new powers of biotechnology make them unavoidable. To see why this is so, consider four examples already on the horizon: muscle enhancement, memory enhancement, growth-hormone treatment, and reproductive technologies that enable parents to choose the sex and some genetic traits of their children. In each case what began as an attempt to treat a disease or prevent a genetic disorder now beckons as an instrument of improvement and consumer choice.

Muscles

Everyone would welcome a gene therapy to alleviate muscular dystrophy and to reverse the debilitating muscle loss that comes with old age. But what if the same therapy were used to improve athletic performance? Researchers have developed a synthetic gene that, when injected into the muscle cells of mice, prevents and even reverses natural muscle deterioration. The gene not only repairs wasted or injured muscles but also strengthens healthy ones. This success bodes well for human applications. H. Lee Sweeney, of the University of Pennsylvania, who leads the research, hopes his discovery will cure the immobility that afflicts the elderly. But Sweeney's bulked-up mice have already attracted the attention of athletes seeking a competitive edge. Although the therapy is not yet approved for human use, the prospect of genetically enhanced weightlifters, home-run sluggers, linebackers, and sprinters is easy to imagine. The widespread use of steroids and other performance-improving drugs in professional sports suggests that many athletes will be eager to avail themselves of genetic enhancement.

Suppose for the sake of argument that muscle-enhancing gene therapy, unlike steroids, turned out to be safe—or at least no riskier than a rigorous weight-training regimen. Would there be a reason to ban its use in sports? There is something unsettling about the image of genetically altered athletes lifting SUVs or hitting 650-foot home runs or running a three-minute mile. But what, exactly, is troubling about it? Is it simply that we find such superhuman spectacles too bizarre to contemplate? Or does our unease point to something of ethical significance?

It might be argued that a genetically enhanced athlete, like a drug-enhanced athlete, would have an unfair advantage over his unenhanced competitors. But the fairness argument against enhancement has a fatal flaw: it has always been the case that some athletes are better endowed genetically than others, and yet we do not consider this to undermine the fairness of competitive sports. From the standpoint of fairness, enhanced genetic differences would be no worse than natural ones, assuming they were safe and made available to all. If genetic enhancement in sports is morally objectionable, it must be for reasons other than fairness.

Memory

Genetic enhancement is possible for brains as well as brawn. In the mid-1990s scientists managed to manipulate a memory-linked gene in fruit flies, creating flies with photographic memories. More recently researchers have produced smart mice by inserting extra copies of a memory-related gene into mouse embryos. The altered mice learn more quickly and remember things longer than normal mice. The extra copies were programmed to remain active even in old age, and the improvement was passed on to offspring.

Human memory is more complicated, but biotech companies, including Memory Pharmaceuticals, are in hot pursuit of memory-enhancing drugs, or "cognition enhancers," for human beings. The obvious market for such drugs consists of those who suffer from Alzheimer's and other serious memory disorders. The companies also have their sights on a bigger market: the 81 million Americans over fifty, who are beginning to encounter the memory loss that comes naturally with age. A drug that reversed age-related memory loss would be a bonanza for the pharmaceutical industry: a Viagra for the brain. Such use would straddle the line between remedy and enhancement. Unlike a treatment for Alzheimer's, it would cure no disease; but insofar as it restored capacities a person once possessed, it would have a remedial aspect. It could also have purely nonmedical uses: for example, by a lawyer cramming to memorize facts for an upcoming trial, or by a business executive eager to learn Mandarin on the eve of his departure for Shanghai.

Some who worry about the ethics of cognitive enhancement point to the danger of creating two classes of human beings: those with access to enhancement technologies, and those who must make do with their natural capacities. And if the enhancements could be passed down the generations, the two classes might eventually become subspecies—the enhanced and the merely natural. But worry about access ignores the moral status of enhancement itself. Is the scenario troubling because the unenhanced poor would be denied the benefits of bioengineering, or because the enhanced affluent would somehow be dehumanized? As with muscles, so with memory: the fundamental question is not how to ensure equal access to enhancement but whether we should aspire to it in the first place.

Height

Pediatricians already struggle with the ethics of enhancement when confronted by parents who want to make their children taller. Since the 1980s human-growth hormone has been approved for children with a hormone deficiency that makes them much shorter than average. But the treatment also increases the height of healthy children. Some parents of healthy children who are unhappy with their stature (typically boys) ask why it should make a difference whether a child is short because of a hormone deficiency or because his parents happen to be short. Whatever the cause, the social consequences are the same.

In the face of this argument some doctors began prescribing hormone treatments for children whose short stature was unrelated to any medical problem. By 1996 such "off-label" use accounted for 40 percent of human-growth-hormone prescriptions. Although it is legal to prescribe drugs for purposes not approved by the Food and Drug Administration, pharmaceutical companies cannot promote such use. Seeking to expand its market, Eli Lilly & Co. recently persuaded the FDA to approve its human-growth hormone for healthy children whose projected adult height is in the bottom one percentile—under five feet three inches for boys and four feet eleven inches for girls. This concession raises a large question about the ethics of enhancement: If hormone treatments need not be limited to those with hormone deficiencies, why should they be available only to very short children? Why shouldn't all shorter-than-average children be able to seek treatment? And what about a child of average height who wants to be taller so that he can make the basketball team?

Some oppose height enhancement on the grounds that it is collectively self-defeating; as some become taller, others become shorter relative to the norm. Except in Lake Wobegon, not every child can be above average. As the unenhanced began to feel shorter, they, too, might seek treatment, leading to a hormonal arms race that left everyone worse off, especially those who couldn't afford to buy their way up from shortness.

But the arms-race objection is not decisive on its own. Like the fairness objection to bioengineered muscles and memory, it leaves unexamined the attitudes and dispositions that prompt the drive for enhancement. If we were bothered only by the injustice of adding shortness to the problems of the poor, we could remedy that unfairness by publicly subsidizing height enhancements. As for the relative height deprivation suffered by innocent bystanders, we could compensate them by taxing those who buy their way to greater height. The real question is whether we want to live in a society where parents feel compelled to spend a fortune to make perfectly healthy kids a few inches taller.

Sex selection

Perhaps the most inevitable nonmedical use of bioengineering is sex selection. For centuries parents have been trying to choose the sex of their children. Today biotech succeeds where folk remedies failed. One technique for sex selection arose with prenatal tests using amniocentesis and ultrasound. These medical technologies were developed to detect genetic abnormalities such as spina bifida and Down syndrome. But they can also reveal the sex of the fetus—allowing for the abortion of a fetus of an undesired sex. Even among those who favor abortion rights, few advocate abortion simply because the parents do not want a girl. Nevertheless, in traditional societies with a powerful cultural preference for boys, this practice has become widespread.

Sex selection need not involve abortion, however. For couples under-going *in vitro* fertilization (IVF), it is possible to choose the sex of the child before the fertilized egg is implanted in the womb. One method makes use of pre-implantation genetic diagnosis (PGD), a procedure developed to screen for genetic diseases. Several eggs are fertilized in a Petri dish and grown to the eight-cell stage (about three days). At that point the embryos are tested to determine their sex. Those of the desired sex are implanted; the others are typically discarded. Although few couples are likely to undergo the difficulty and expense of IVF simply to choose the sex of their child, embryo screening is a highly reliable means of sex selection. And as our genetic knowledge increases, it may be possible to use PGD to cull embryos carrying undesired genes, such as those associated with obesity, height, and skin color. The science-fiction movie *Gattaca* depicts a future in which parents routinely screen embryos for sex, height, immunity to disease, and even IQ. There is something troubling about the *Gattaca* scenario, but it is not easy to identify what exactly is wrong with screening embryos to choose the sex of our children.

One line of objection draws on arguments familiar from the abortion debate. Those who believe that an embryo is a person reject embryo screening for the same reasons they reject abortion. If an eight-cell embryo growing in a Petri dish is morally equivalent to a fully developed human being, then discarding it is no better than aborting a fetus, and both practices are equivalent to infanticide. Whatever its merits, however, this "pro-life" objection is not an argument against sex selection as such.

The latest technology poses the question of sex selection unclouded by the matter of an embryo's moral status. The Genetics & IVF Institute, a for-profit infertility clinic in Fairfax, Virginia, now offers a sperm-sorting technique that makes it possible to choose the sex of one's child before it is conceived. X-bearing sperm, which produce girls, carry more DNA than Y-bearing sperm, which produce boys; a device called a flow cytometer can separate them. The process, called MicroSort, has a high rate of success.

If sex selection by sperm sorting is objectionable, it must be for reasons that go beyond the debate about the moral status of the embryo. One such reason is that sex selection is an instrument of sex discrimination—typically against girls, as illustrated by the chilling sex ratios in India and China. Some speculate that societies with substantially more men than women will be less stable, more violent, and more prone to crime or war. These are legitimate worries—but the sperm-sorting company has a clever way of addressing them. It offers MicroSort only to couples who want to choose the sex of a child for purposes of "family balancing." Those with more sons than daughters may choose a girl, and vice versa. But customers may not use the technology to stock up on children of the same sex, or even to choose the sex of their firstborn child. (So far the majority of MicroSort clients have chosen girls.) Under restrictions of this kind, do any ethical issues remain that should give us pause?

The case of MicroSort helps us isolate the moral objections that would persist if muscle-enhancement, memory-enhancement, and height-enhancement technologies were safe and available to all.

It is commonly said that genetic enhancements undermine our humanity by threatening our capacity to act freely, to succeed by our own efforts, and to consider ourselves responsible—worthy of praise or blame—for the things we do and for the way we are. It is one thing to hit seventy home runs as the result of disciplined training and effort, and something else, something less, to hit them with the help of steroids or genetically enhanced muscles. Of course, the roles of effort and enhancement will be a matter of degree. But as the role of enhancement increases, our admiration for the achievement fades—or, rather, our admiration for the achievement shifts from the player to his pharmacist. This suggests that our moral response to enhancement is a response to the diminished agency of the person whose achievement is enhanced.

Though there is much to be said for this argument, I do not think the main problem with enhancement and genetic engineering is that they undermine effort and erode human agency. The deeper danger is that they represent a kind of hyperagency—a Promethean aspiration to remake nature, including human nature, to serve our purposes and satisfy our desires. The problem is not the drift to mechanism but the drive to mastery. And what the drive to mastery misses and may even destroy is an appreciation of the gifted character of human powers and achievements.

To acknowledge the giftedness of life is to recognize that our talents and powers are not wholly our own doing, despite the effort we expend to develop and to exercise them. It is also to recognize that not everything in the world is open to whatever use we may desire or devise. Appreciating the gifted quality of life constrains the Promethean project and conduces to a certain humility. It is in part a religious sensibility. But its resonance reaches beyond religion.

It is difficult to account for what we admire about human activity and achievement without drawing upon some version of this idea. Consider two types of athletic achievement. We appreciate players like Pete Rose, who are not blessed with great natural gifts but who manage, through striving, grit, and determination, to excel in their sport. But we also admire players like Joe DiMaggio, who display natural gifts with grace and effortlessness. Now, suppose we learned that both players took performance-enhancing drugs. Whose turn to drugs would we find more deeply disillusioning? Which aspect of the athletic ideal—effort or gift—would be more deeply offended?

Some might say effort: the problem with drugs is that they provide a shortcut, a way to win without striving. But striving is not the point of sports; excellence is. And excellence consists at least partly in the display of natural talents and gifts that are no doing of the athlete who possesses them. This is an uncomfortable fact for democratic societies. We want to believe that success, in sports and in life, is something we earn, not something we inherit. Natural gifts, and the admiration they inspire, embarrass the meritocratic faith; they cast doubt on the conviction that praise and rewards flow from effort alone. In the face of this embarrassment we inflate the moral significance of striving, and depreciate giftedness. This distortion can be seen, for example, in network-television coverage of the Olympics, which focuses less on the feats the athletes perform than on heartrending stories of the hardships they have overcome and the struggles they have waged to triumph over an injury or a difficult upbringing or political turmoil in their native land.

But effort isn't everything. No one believes that a mediocre basketball player who works and trains even harder than Michael Jordan deserves greater acclaim or a bigger contract. The real problem with genetically altered athletes is that they corrupt athletic competition as a human activity that honors the cultivation and display of natural talents. From this standpoint, enhancement can be seen as the ultimate expression of the ethic of effort and willfulness—a kind of high-tech striving. The ethic of willfulness and the biotechnological powers it now enlists are arrayed against the claims of giftedness.

The ethic of giftedness, under siege in sports, persists in the practice of parenting. But here, too, bioengineering and genetic enhancement threaten to dislodge it. To appreciate children as gifts is to accept them as they come, not as objects of our design or products of our will or instruments of our ambition. Parental love is not contingent on the talents and attributes a child happens to have. We choose our friends and spouses at least partly on the basis of qualities we find attractive. But we do not choose our children. Their qualities are unpredictable, and even the most conscientious parents cannot be held wholly responsible for the kind of children they have. That is why parenthood, more than other human relationships, teaches what the theologian William F. May calls an "openness to the unbidden."

May's resonant phrase helps us see that the deepest moral objection to enhancement lies less in the perfection it seeks than in the human disposition it expresses and promotes. The problem is not that parents usurp the autonomy of a child they design. The problem lies in the hubris of the designing parents, in their drive to master the mystery of birth. Even if this disposition did not make parents tyrants to their children, it would disfigure the relation between parent and child, and deprive the parent of the humility and enlarged human sympathies that an openness to the unbidden can cultivate.

To appreciate children as gifts or blessings is not, of course, to be passive in the face of illness or disease. Medical intervention to cure or prevent illness or restore the injured to health does not desecrate nature but honors it. Healing sickness or injury does not override a child's natural capacities but permits them to flourish.

Nor does the sense of life as a gift mean that parents must shrink from shaping and directing the development of their child. Just as athletes and artists have an obligation to cultivate their talents, so parents have an obligation to cultivate their children, to help them discover and develop their talents and gifts. As May points out, parents give their children two kinds of love: accepting love and transforming love. Accepting love affirms the being of the child, whereas transforming love seeks the well-being of the child. Each aspect corrects the excesses of the other, he writes: "Attachment becomes too quietistic if it slackens into mere acceptance of the child as he is." Parents have a duty to promote their children's excellence.

These days, however, overly ambitious parents are prone to get carried away with transforming love—promoting and demanding all manner of accomplishments from their children, seeking perfection. "Parents find it difficult to maintain an equilibrium between the two sides of love," May observes. "Accepting love, without transforming love, slides into indulgence and finally neglect. Transforming love, without accepting love, badgers and finally rejects." May finds in these competing impulses a parallel with modern science: it, too, engages us in beholding the given world, studying and savoring it, and also in molding the world, transforming and perfecting it.

The mandate to mold our children, to cultivate and improve them, complicates the case against enhancement. We usually admire parents who seek the best for their children, who spare no effort to help them achieve happiness and success. Some parents confer advantages on their children by enrolling them in expensive schools, hiring private tutors, sending them to tennis camp, providing them with piano lessons, ballet lessons, swimming lessons, SAT-prep courses, and so on. If it is permissible and even admirable for parents to help their children in these ways, why isn't it equally admirable for parents to use whatever genetic technologies may emerge (provided they are safe) to enhance their children's intelligence, musical ability, or athletic prowess?

The defenders of enhancement are right to this extent: improving children through genetic engineering is similar in spirit to the heavily managed, high-pressure child-rearing that is now common. But this similarity does not vindicate genetic enhancement. On the contrary, it highlights a problem with the trend toward hyperparenting. One conspicuous example of this trend is sports-crazed parents bent on making champions of their children. Another is the frenzied drive of overbearing parents to mold and manage their children's academic careers.

As the pressure for performance increases, so does the need to help distractible children concentrate on the task at hand. This may be why diagnoses of attention deficit and hyperactivity disorder have increased so sharply. Lawrence Diller, a pediatrician and the author of *Running on Ritalin*, estimates that five to six percent of American children under eighteen (a total of four to five million kids) are currently prescribed Ritalin, Adderall, and other stimulants, the treatment of choice for ADHD. (Stimulants counteract hyperactivity by making it easier to focus and sustain attention.) The number of Ritalin prescriptions for children and adolescents has tripled over the past decade, but not all users suffer from attention disorders or hyperactivity. High school and college students have learned that prescription stimulants improve concentration for those with normal attention spans, and some buy or borrow their classmates' drugs to enhance their performance on the SAT or other exams. Since stimulants work for both medical and nonmedical purposes, they raise the same moral questions posed by other technologies of enhancement.

However those questions are resolved, the debate reveals the cultural distance we have traveled since the debate over marijuana, LSD, and other drugs a generation ago. Unlike the drugs of the 1960s and 1970s, Ritalin and Adderall are not for checking out but for buckling down, not for beholding the world and taking it in but for molding the world and fitting in. We used to speak of nonmedical drug use as "recreational." That term no longer applies. The steroids and stimulants that figure in the enhancement debate are not a source of recreation but a bid for compliance—a way of answering a competitive society's demand to improve our performance and perfect our nature. This demand for performance and perfection animates the impulse to rail against the given. It is the deepest source of the moral trouble with enhancement.

Some see a clear line between genetic enhancement and other ways that people seek improvement in their children and themselves. Genetic manipulation seems somehow worse—more intrusive, more sinister—than other ways of enhancing performance and seeking success. But morally speaking, the difference is less significant than it seems. Bioengineering gives us reason to question the low-tech, high-pressure child-rearing practices we commonly accept. The hyperparenting familiar in our time represents an anxious excess of mastery and dominion that misses the sense of life as a gift. This draws it disturbingly close to eugenics.

The shadow of eugenics hangs over today's debates about genetic engineering and enhancement. Critics of genetic engineering argue that human cloning, enhancement, and the quest for designer children are nothing more than "privatized" or "free-market" eugenics. Defenders of enhancement reply that genetic choices freely made are not really eugenic—at least not in the pejorative sense. To remove the coercion, they argue, is to remove the very thing that makes eugenic policies repugnant.

Sorting out the lesson of eugenics is another way of wrestling with the ethics of enhancement. The Nazis gave eugenics a bad name. But what, precisely, was wrong with it? Was the old eugenics objectionable only insofar as it was coercive? Or is there something inherently wrong with the resolve to deliberately design our progeny's traits?

James Watson, the biologist who, with Francis Crick, discovered the structure of DNA, sees nothing wrong with genetic engineering and enhancement, provided they are freely chosen rather than state-imposed. And yet Watson's language contains more than a whiff of the old eugenic sensibility. "If you really are stupid, I would call that a disease," he recently told *The Times* of London. "The lower 10 percent who really have difficulty, even in elementary school, what's the cause of it? A lot of people would like to say, 'Well, poverty, things like that.' It probably isn't. So I'd like to get rid of that, to help the lower 10 percent." A few years ago Watson stirred controversy by saying that if a gene for homosexuality were discovered, a woman should be free to abort a fetus that carried it. When his remark provoked an uproar, he replied that he was not singling out gays but asserting a principle: women should be free to abort fetuses for any reason of genetic preference—for example, if the child would be dyslexic, or lacking musical talent, or too short to play basketball.

Watson's scenarios are clearly objectionable to those for whom all abortion is an unspeakable crime. But for those who do not subscribe to the pro-life position, these scenarios raise a hard question: If it is morally troubling to contemplate abortion to avoid a gay child or a dyslexic one, doesn't this suggest that something is wrong with acting on any eugenic preference, even when no state coercion is involved?

Consider the market in eggs and sperm. The advent of artificial insemination allows prospective parents to shop for gametes with the genetic traits they desire in their offspring. It is a less predictable way to design children than cloning or pre-implantation genetic screening, but it offers a good example of a procreative practice in which the old eugenics meets the new consumerism. A few years ago some Ivy League newspapers ran an ad seeking an egg from a woman who was at least five feet ten inches tall and athletic, had no major family medical problems, and had a combined SAT score of 1400 or above. The ad offered $50,000 for an egg from a donor with these traits. More recently a Web site was launched claiming to auction eggs from fashion models whose photos appeared on the site, at starting bids of $15,000 to $150,000.

On what grounds, if any, is the egg market morally objectionable? Since no one is forced to buy or sell, it cannot be wrong for reasons of coercion. Some might worry that hefty prices would exploit poor women by presenting them with an offer they couldn't refuse. But the designer eggs that fetch the highest prices are likely to be sought from the privileged, not the poor. If the market for premium eggs gives us moral qualms, this, too, shows that concerns about eugenics are not put to rest by freedom of choice.

A tale of two sperm banks helps explain why. The Repository for Germinal Choice, one of America's first sperm banks, was not a commercial enterprise. It was opened in 1980 by Robert Graham, a philanthropist dedicated to improving the world's "germ plasm" and counteracting the rise of "retrograde humans." His plan was to collect the sperm of Nobel Prize-winning scientists and make it available to women of high intelligence, in hopes of breeding supersmart babies. But Graham had trouble persuading Nobel laureates to donate their sperm for his bizarre scheme, and so settled for sperm from young scientists of high promise. His sperm bank closed in 1999.

In contrast, California Cryobank, one of the world's leading sperm banks, is a for-profit company with no overt eugenic mission. Cappy Rothman, M.D., a co-founder of the firm, has nothing but disdain for Graham's eugenics, although the standards Cryobank imposes on the sperm it recruits are exacting. Cryobank has offices in Cambridge, Massachusetts, between Harvard and MIT, and in Palo Alto, California, near Stanford. It advertises for donors in campus newspapers (compensation up to $900 a month), and accepts less than five percent of the men who apply. Cryobank's marketing materials play up the prestigious source of its sperm. Its catalogue provides detailed information about the physical characteristics of each donor, along with his ethnic origin and college major. For an extra fee prospective customers can buy the results of a test that assesses the donor's temperament and character type. Rothman reports that Cryobank's ideal sperm donor is six feet tall, with brown eyes, blond hair, and dimples, and has a college degree—not because the company wants to propagate those traits, but because those are the traits his customers want: "If our customers wanted high school dropouts, we would give them high school dropouts."

Not everyone objects to marketing sperm. But anyone who is troubled by the eugenic aspect of the Nobel Prize sperm bank should be equally troubled by Cryobank, consumer-driven though it be. What, after all, is the moral difference between designing children according to an explicit eugenic purpose and designing children according to the dictates of the market? Whether the aim is to improve humanity's "germ plasm" or to cater to consumer preferences, both practices are eugenic insofar as both make children into products of deliberate design.

A number of political philosophers call for a new "liberal eugenics." They argue that a moral distinction can be drawn between the old eugenic policies and genetic enhancements that do not restrict the autonomy of the child. "While old-fashioned authoritarian eugenicists sought to produce citizens out of a single centrally designed mould," writes Nicholas Agar, "the distinguishing mark of the new liberal eugenics is state neutrality." Government may not tell parents what sort of children to design, and parents may engineer in their children only those traits that improve their capacities without biasing their choice of life plans. A recent text on genetics and justice, written by the bioethicists Allen Buchanan, Dan W. Brock, Norman Daniels, and Daniel Wikler, offers a similar view. The "bad reputation of eugenics," they write, is due to practices that "might be avoidable in a future eugenic program." The problem with the old eugenics was that its burdens fell disproportionately on the weak and the poor, who were unjustly sterilized and segregated. But provided that the benefits and burdens of genetic improvement are fairly distributed, these bioethicists argue, eugenic measures are unobjectionable and may even be morally required.

The libertarian philosopher Robert Nozick proposed a "genetic supermarket" that would enable parents to order children by design without imposing a single design on the society as a whole: "This supermarket system has the great virtue that it involves no centralized decision fixing the future human type(s)."

Even the leading philosopher of American liberalism, John Rawls, in his classic A Theory of Justice (1971), offered a brief endorsement of noncoercive eugenics. Even in a society that agrees to share the benefits and burdens of the genetic lottery, it is "in the interest of each to have greater natural assets," Rawls wrote. "This enables him to pursue a preferred plan of life." The parties to the social contract "want to insure for their descendants the best genetic endowment (assuming their own to be fixed)." Eugenic policies are therefore not only permissible but required as a matter of justice. "Thus over time a society is to take steps at least to preserve the general level of natural abilities and to prevent the diffusion of serious defects."

But removing the coercion does not vindicate eugenics. The problem with eugenics and genetic engineering is that they represent the one-sided triumph of willfulness over giftedness, of dominion over reverence, of molding over beholding. Why, we may wonder, should we worry about this triumph? Why not shake off our unease about genetic enhancement as so much superstition? What would be lost if biotechnology dissolved our sense of giftedness?

From a religious standpoint the answer is clear: To believe that our talents and powers are wholly our own doing is to misunderstand our place in creation, to confuse our role with God's. Religion is not the only source of reasons to care about giftedness, however. The moral stakes can also be described in secular terms. If bioengineering made the myth of the "self-made man" come true, it would be difficult to view our talents as gifts for which we are indebted, rather than as achievements for which we are responsible. This would transform three key features of our moral landscape: humility, responsibility, and solidarity.

In a social world that prizes mastery and control, parenthood is a school for humility. That we care deeply about our children and yet cannot choose the kind we want teaches parents to be open to the unbidden. Such openness is a disposition worth affirming, not only within families but in the wider world as well. It invites us to abide the unexpected, to live with dissonance, to rein in the impulse to control. A *Gattaca*-like world in which parents became accustomed to specifying the sex and genetic traits of their children would be a world inhospitable to the unbidden, a gated community writ large. The awareness that our talents and abilities are not wholly our own doing restrains our tendency toward hubris.

Though some maintain that genetic enhancement erodes human agency by overriding effort, the real problem is the explosion, not the erosion, of responsibility. As humility gives way, responsibility expands to daunting proportions. We attribute less to chance and more to choice. Parents become responsible for choosing, or failing to choose, the right traits for their children. Athletes become responsible for acquiring, or failing to acquire, the talents that will help their teams win.

One of the blessings of seeing ourselves as creatures of nature, God, or fortune is that we are not wholly responsible for the way we are. The more we become masters of our genetic endowments, the greater the burden we bear for the talents we have and the way we perform. Today when a basketball player misses a rebound, his coach can blame him for being out of position. Tomorrow the coach may blame him for being too short. Even now the use of performance-enhancing drugs in professional sports is subtly transforming the expectations players have for one another; on some teams, players who take the field free from amphetamines or other stimulants are criticized for "playing naked."

The more alive we are to the chanced nature of our lot, the more reason we have to share our fate with others. Consider insurance. Since people do not know whether or when various ills will befall them, they pool their risk by buying health insurance and life insurance. As life plays itself out, the healthy wind up subsidizing the unhealthy, and those who live to a ripe old age wind up subsidizing the families of those who die before their time. Even without a sense of mutual obligation, people pool their risks and resources and share one another's fate.

But insurance markets mimic solidarity only insofar as people do not know or control their own risk factors. Suppose genetic testing advanced to the point where it could reliably predict each person's medical future and life expectancy. Those confident of good health and long life would opt out of the pool, causing other people's premiums to skyrocket. The solidarity of insurance would disappear as those with good genes fled the actuarial company of those with bad ones.

The fear that insurance companies would use genetic data to assess risks and set premiums recently led the Senate to vote to prohibit genetic discrimination in health insurance. But the bigger danger, admittedly more speculative, is that genetic enhancement, if routinely practiced, would make it harder to foster the moral sentiments that social solidarity requires.

Why, after all, do the successful owe anything to the least-advantaged members of society? The best answer to this question leans heavily on the notion of giftedness. The natural talents that enable the successful to flourish are not their own doing but, rather, their good fortune—a result of the genetic lottery. If our genetic endowments are gifts, rather than achievements for which we can claim credit, it is a mistake and a conceit to assume that we are entitled to the full measure of the bounty they reap in a market economy. We therefore have an obligation to share this bounty with those who, through no fault of their own, lack comparable gifts.

A lively sense of the contingency of our gifts—a consciousness that none of us is wholly responsible for his or her success—saves a meritocratic society from sliding into the smug assumption that the rich are rich because they are more deserving than the poor. Without this, the successful would become even more likely than they are now to view themselves as self-made and self-sufficient, and hence wholly responsible for their success. Those at the bottom of society would be viewed not as disadvantaged, and thus worthy of a measure of compensation, but as simply unfit, and thus worthy of eugenic repair. The meritocracy, less chastened by chance, would become harder, less forgiving. As perfect genetic knowledge would end the simulacrum of solidarity in insurance markets, so perfect genetic control would erode the actual solidarity that arises when men and women reflect on the contingency of their talents and fortunes.

Thirty-five years ago Robert L. Sinsheimer, a molecular biologist at the California Institute of Technology, glimpsed the shape of things to come. In an article titled "The Prospect of Designed Genetic Change" he argued that freedom of choice would vindicate the new genetics, and set it apart from the discredited eugenics of old. To implement the older eugenics . . . would have required a massive social programme carried out over many generations. Such a programme could not have been initiated without the consent and co-operation of a major fraction of the population, and would have been continuously subject to social control. In contrast, the new eugenics could, at least in principle, be implemented on a quite individual basis, in one generation, and subject to no existing restrictions. According to Sinsheimer, the new eugenics would be voluntary rather than coerced, and also more humane. Rather than segregating and eliminating the unfit, it would improve them. "The old eugenics would have required a continual selection for breeding of the fit, and a culling of the unfit," he wrote. "The new eugenics would permit in principle the conversion of all the unfit to the highest genetic level."

Sinsheimer's paean to genetic engineering caught the heady, Promethean self-image of the age. He wrote hopefully of rescuing "the losers in that chromosomal lottery that so firmly channels our human destinies," including not only those born with genetic defects but also "the 50,000,000 'normal' Americans with an IQ of less than 90." But he also saw that something bigger than improving on nature's "mindless, age-old throw of dice" was at stake. Implicit in technologies of genetic intervention was a more exalted place for human beings in the cosmos. "As we enlarge man's freedom, we diminish his constraints and that which he must accept as given," he wrote. Copernicus and Darwin had "demoted man from his bright glory at the focal point of the universe," but the new biology would restore his central role. In the mirror of our genetic knowledge we would see ourselves as more than a link in the chain of evolution: "We can be the agent of transition to a whole new pitch of evolution. This is a cosmic event."

There is something appealing, even intoxicating, about a vision of human freedom unfettered by the given. It may even be the case that the allure of that vision played a part in summoning the genomic age into being. It is often assumed that the powers of enhancement we now possess arose as an inadvertent by-product of biomedical progress—the genetic revolution came, so to speak, to cure disease, and stayed to tempt us with the prospect of enhancing our performance, designing our children, and perfecting our nature. That may have the story backwards. It is more plausible to view genetic engineering as the ultimate expression of our resolve to see ourselves astride the world, the masters of our nature. But that promise of mastery is flawed. It threatens to banish our appreciation of life as a gift, and to leave us with nothing to affirm or behold outside our own will.

5

What Is and Is Not Wrong
with Enhancement?[1]

Frances Kamm

Abstract

This article examines the arguments concerning enhancement of human persons recently presented by Michael Sandel. In the first section, I briefly describe some of his arguments. In Section II, I consider whether, as Sandel claims, the desire for mastery motivates enhancement and whether such a desire could be grounds for its impermissibility. Section III considers how Sandel draws the distinction between treatment and enhancement, and the relation to nature that he thinks each expresses. The fourth section examines Sandel's views about parent/child relations and also how enhancement would affect distributive justice and the duty to aid. In conclusion, I briefly offer an alternative suggestion as to why enhancement may be troubling and consider what we could safely enhance.

Should we enhance human performance? There are at least two types of enhancement. In the first, we make it the case that more people are above the current norm in ways that many people are already quite naturally. For example, we might increase intelligence so that many more people who would otherwise be only moderately intelligent function as well as

[1] This article is a revised version of "Is There a Problem with Enhancement?" *American Journal of Bioethics* [AJOB], 5(3): 1–10. It incorporates some of my responses to the very useful commentaries on that article. The commentaries appear in the same issue of AJOB and my complete responses appear at the AJOB website. It also incorporates some of my responses to Sandel's helpful commentary on my presentation of parts of this article at the Inaugural Conference of the University-Wide Program on Ethics and Health, Harvard Medical School, Nov. 19, 2005. I am also grateful to audiences at that conference, at the UCLA Program in Genetics and Society, at Bowdoin College, and at Harvard Law School.

those few who are geniuses. In the second type of enhancement, we introduce improvements that no human being has yet evidenced—for example, living to be two hundred years old and healthy. The question of whether we should engage in either type of enhancement has arisen recently within the context of human genetics. Here one generation would probably modify the next. However, enhancement can also occur by way of drugs or intensive training and be done by a person to himself or to another.

Michael Sandel has recently argued that there is a moral problem with both types of enhancement regardless of the way in which they would be brought about, even if there were agreement (which there often is not) that the changes would be improvements, that they were safe, and they were fairly distributed among socioeconomic groups (Sandel 2004). Sandel's discussion is worth significant attention both because he was a member of the President's Council on Bioethics and because it expresses in compact form, readily available to the general public, some prominent concerns. In this essay, I shall present what seem to me to be the important components of Sandel's argument and then evaluate it.

I. Sandel's views

Sandel thinks that the deepest objection to enhancement is the desire for mastery that it expresses. He focuses especially (but not exclusively) on the attempt of parents to enhance their children, whether by genetic manipulation, drugs, or extensive training. He says:

the deepest moral objection to enhancement lies less in the perfection it seeks than the human disposition it expresses and promotes. The problem is not that parents usurp the autonomy of a child they design. The problem is in the hubris of the designing parents, in their drive to master the mystery of birth . . . it would disfigure the relation between parent and child, and deprive the parent of the humility and enlarged human sympathies that an openness to the unbidden can cultivate. (Sandel 2004, 57)

And he thinks:

the promise of mastery is flawed. It threatens to banish our appreciation of life as a gift, and to leave us with nothing to affirm or behold outside our own will. (Sandel 2004, 62)

However, he believes this objection is consistent with the permissibility and even the obligation to treat illnesses by genetic modification, drugs, or training. He is, therefore, arguing for a moral distinction between treatment and enhancement. He says (Sandel 2004, 57): "Medical intervention to cure or prevent illness or restore the injured to health does not desecrate nature but honors it." He also thinks parents must "shape and direct the development of their children...," but he thinks there must be an equilibrium between "accepting love" and "transforming love."

Among the bad effects of mastery, he identifies the increasing responsibility that we must bear for the presence or absence of characteristics in ourselves and others and the effects this may have on human solidarity. The first point is concerned with the fact that we will no longer be able to say that lacking a perfection is a matter of luck, something outside our control. We might be blamed for not improving ourselves or others. The second point is (supposedly) related to this. Sandel believes that the more our characteristics are a matter of chance rather than choice, "the more reason we have to share our fate with others" (Sandel 2004, 60). He goes on:

Consider insurance. Since people do not know whether or when various ills will befall them, they pool their risk... insurance markets mimic solidarity only insofar as people do not know or control their own risk factors.... Why, after all, do the successful owe anything to the least-advantaged members of society? The best answer to this leans heavily on the idea of giftedness.... A lively sense... that none of us is wholly responsible for his or her success makes us willing to share the fruits of our talents with the less successful. (Sandel 2004, 60)

II. Desire for mastery

(A) Let us first clarify the nature of Sandel's objection to enhancement based on the desire for mastery over life processes. It implies that if (both types of) enhancements were occurring quite naturally, without our intervention, the desire for mastery objection to enhancement would not be pertinent. Indeed, interfering with the natural enhancing changes would itself require mastery over life processes, and so Sandel's objection might pertain to this. It is also important to keep in mind several distinctions.

Actual mastery is different from the desire for it. We could achieve and exercise mastery over nature as a side-effect of doing other things, without desiring it. This might be more acceptable to Sandel, but it might still raise the issue about responsibility and solidarity. For if we become able to control our natures despite never having wanted mastery and power, the question of how to deal with those who do not exercise the power well will arise.

Suppose we did desire mastery, however. We could desire it as a means to some other end (e.g., achieving such good aims as health, intelligence, or virtue) or we could desire it as an end in itself. So long as we desire it as a means to other things considered good, it is clearly wrong for Sandel to conclude that desire for mastery will "leave us with nothing to affirm or behold outside our own will" (Sandel 2004, 62). Even if mastery were desired as an end in itself, this need not mean that it is our only end, and so we could still continue to affirm other good aims (such as virtue, health, etc.) as ends outside our own will. I shall henceforth assume that if we desire mastery, it is as a means to good ends, as this seems most reasonable.

Such a desire for mastery is not inconsistent with an openness to the unbidden that Sandel emphasizes (Sandel 2004, 56), if the unbidden means just "those things that come without our deliberately calling for or causing them."[2] For if many good things were to come without our deliberately intervening to bring them about, presumably we would be happy to have them and not regret that they came about without our deliberately bringing them about. Such a form of openness to the unbidden does not, however, necessarily imply a willingness to accept whatever comes even if it is bad when one could change it.[3] Sometimes people are also unwilling to accept things that merely differ from their preferences or that are not as good as they might be, though the things are not necessarily bad. One or all

---

[2] Notice that not deliberately causing something is not the same as not causing it. For example, a parent may cause his child's IQ to move down from 160 to 140 by inadvertently eating improperly during pregnancy. This reduction is unbidden, though caused by the parent. It is in part because we might be causally responsible for making things worse than they could naturally be, that some may think that we have a duty to achieve at least the knowledge of life processes that prevents our interfering with naturally occurring goods.

[3] When one cannot change bad things that come, one could be open to them in the sense of being accepting of one's fate. This is consistent with desiring mastery so that one could change one's fate. I owe this point to an anonymous reader.

of these forms of being closed to the unbidden may be what Sandel is concerned with, as he speaks of enlarged human sympathies resulting from an openness to the unbidden.

So far, I have been distinguishing various attitudes and states of mind that might be involved in a desire for mastery. Suppose some form of the desire for mastery and nonopenness to the unbidden were bad. The further question is whether there is any relation between having even a bad desire and the impermissibility of enhancing. As noted above, even Sandel supports the efforts to find certain treatments for illnesses. But seeking treatments for illnesses by manipulating the genome typically involves desiring mastery as a means, not being open to all things unbidden, and attempting to master the mystery of birth. Hence, Sandel may think that while there is something bad per se about desiring mastery even as a means, not being open to the unbidden, and attempting to master the mystery of birth, these bads can be outweighed by the good of curing diseases (if not by the pursuit of enhancements). Alternatively, he may believe that when the unbidden is very horrible—not a gift, even in disguise—not being open to the unbidden is not bad at all. If he believes these things, the question then is why enhancements cannot outweigh or transform the negative value of seeking mastery and not being open to the unbidden in the same way that he thinks that treatments outweigh or transform them.[4]

There is a further, deeper problem about the relation between having bad desires and dispositions and the impermissibility of conduct. For suppose that desiring mastery as one's sole end in life is a bad desire to have. Suppose a scientist who works on finding a cure for congenital blindness is motivated only by such a bad desire for mastery. He seeks a cure but only as a means to achieving the goal of being a master over nature. Does this make his conduct impermissible? Presumably not. The good of treating diseases still justifies the work of the scientist even when his ultimate aim is not that disease be treated but rather to achieve mastery. This is a case where there may be a duty to do the work. However, even when the act one would do would produce a good that it is not one's duty to produce, I think the act can be permissible independent of one's desires or disposition in doing it. So suppose several people could be saved only if you do an act

---

[4] I shall return to this point below.

that has a high probability of killing you. It is not typically your duty to do such an act, though it could be worthwhile to do it. If the only reason you do it is to make those who care about you worry, this alone will not make saving the people impermissible. More generally, it has been argued, the intentions and attitudes of an agent most often reflect on the agent's character but do not determine the permissibility of his act (Scanlon 2000; Thomson 1990).[5] People often do permissible acts for bad reasons, not for the sake of factors that justify the act.

If desires and dispositions do not generally affect the permissibility of acts, and if Sandel were right that "the deepest moral problem with enhancement" is "the human disposition it expresses," then the deepest moral problem would provide no grounds at all for thinking that acts seeking enhancement are morally impermissible (Sandel 2004, 57). We would have to decide whether particular enhancements are permissible independently of the desires, attitudes, and dispositions of agents who act. Among the factors we might consider are the goods that would be brought about and the bad effects that might also occur. It is true that if these goods outweigh the bad effects, then it is possible for a rational agent to have as his ultimate aim the pursuit of the goods, rather than the (supposedly) bad aim of seeking mastery above all else. But still it is the evaluation of objective goods and bads, rather than the agent's actual aims, dispositions, or desires that play a role in accounting for the permissibility of producing the enhancement. If the only possible aim of a rational agent in seeking a

---

[5] Judith Thomson (1990, 1999) has argued that intention never matters to the permissibility of action. Thomas Scanlon (2000) makes a somewhat more limited claim.

Notice that sometimes, we think that an act is permissible only if it aims to satisfy a certain desire in an agent who does the act. For example, suppose we set aside scarce resources for a musical performance in order that those who desire pleasure from music shall have some. But if someone's only desire in going to a concert is to mingle with other people, this is an indication that he has no desire for music per se. Hence, it is an indication that an end (give pleasure from music) which justified the use of scarce resources for musical performances will not be achieved. Hence, if this agent should not go to the concert, it is not because of his having only a desire to mingle per se, but because the desire is an indication that some effect that justifies funding concerts (pleasure from music) will not come about.

Now, suppose someone has a bad motive or further aim (e.g., to show off) in doing something otherwise permissible, such as chewing gum. It might be appropriate for him to, in a sense, be punished for the bad motive with which he would chew the gum, by making it impermissible for him to chew the gum. This, of course, is not just any punishment. It specifically makes it the case that his bad motive is not efficacious. But if the achievement of an important good for others or the performance of a dutiful act (e.g., not harming someone) is at stake and this can justify the act, it would not be appropriate to require someone to forgo the act as a way of making his bad motive inefficacious. That would be to "punish" others for the agent's bad attitude.

particular change were to seek mastery as an end in itself, then presumably this would be an indication that no good effect achieved by the change would be able to justify the act and so the act would be impermissible for that reason.

Furthermore, we need not be restricted to a consequentialist weighing of goods and bads in accounting for the permissibility of an act of enhancement. Individual rights may be at stake and the causal role of bad effects (e.g., whether they are side-effects or necessary means to producing good effects) could be morally relevant to the permissibility of an act, even if agent's intention and disposition are not.

In connection with the effects of enhancing, there is a further point that Sandel makes, for he is concerned not only with the disposition that enhancement expresses but with "the human disposition it . . . promotes." Promoting the disposition to seek mastery could be an effect of seeking enhancements, and we have said that the effects of acts can be relevant to their permissibility even if the attitudes and aims of agents who perform the acts are usually not. Indeed, considering the disposition as an effect helps us understand that when Sandel says that "the deepest moral problem with enhancement is the human disposition it expresses," he may not so much be giving an explanation of the wrongness of acts of enhancement as simply focusing on the bad type of people we will be if we seek mastery.[6] But why would we be bad people if we have the disposition to seek mastery as a means, if this disposition always led to permissible acts, and, furthermore, the disposition always led us to act for the sake of the good effects that make the acts permissible because they make it permissible? (Such persons will be very different from the scientist described above who did not care about the good effect that justified his act [i.e., treating disease] per se but only about mastery.) Sandel's account implies that even people with such a disposition to mastery could be worse people in virtue of the disposition, and I do not believe this is true.

Perhaps even such a disposition, not in itself bad, could be bad to have, if it leads us to focus on certain types of acts to the exclusion of other worthwhile activities. Consider an analogy. An artist is always seeking to improve her paintings. She never rests content with just appreciating her own and other people's great works. Hence, other people may have a

---

[6] As emphasized by Paul Litton and Larry Temkin.

better appreciation of great masters that she lacks, and her worthwhile aim interferes with other worthwhile aims. However, often it is not possible to achieve all worthwhile aims, one has to choose. And it is not clear that her way of responding to value—by trying to create more of it—is inferior to an admittedly good alternative way of responding to value (i.e., appreciating valuable things that already exist). Furthermore, sometimes these two approaches to value may be combined to one degree or another. Similarly, the dispositions to enhance and to appreciate goods already present may be combined.

(B) I have considered the relation between the permissibility of acts and the desires and dispositions related to mastery that produce them and that are produced by them. It might be suggested that acts themselves can have meaning as well as being the result of intentions and followed by consequences.[7] Perhaps some reason for an act's being permissible or impermissible is given by what it means or expresses because we should not "say" certain things by our acts. Sometimes, meaning can be due to the intention of the agent, but it has been argued by some that it can also be due to context and to the properties of the act itself. If the meaning of an act can be affected by an agent's intention, and meaning is relevant to permissibility, this still does not show that intention per se is relevant to permissibility, but only that what the intention causes (i.e., the meaning) is relevant to permissibility. Consider a situation in which, it has been said, context, not intention, determines meaning. For example, suppose that in the United States, selecting a male rather than a female child to balance a female child one already has means no more than that one is balancing genders. That is, it has been said, with respect to the act's meaning, the context would "drown out" an agent's intention if the parent is actually choosing to have a male child in order to avoid having what he believes is another inferior female in his family. Is his intention, which we shall suppose no one will ever know of, a reason for his act being impermissible? Those who are concerned with an act's meaning would have no reason to think it is.

Now, suppose that, in a case where intention determines an act's meaning, no one will understand what an act means because no one knows the

---

[7] This was emphasized in A. Martin and J. Peerzada (2005). The discussion that follows is my response to their views and some of their cases.

intention. It is not clear that the act's actual meaning, as opposed to people's interpretation of its meaning, can be a reason for its impermissibility. Where a bad intention determines meaning and people will find out about the intention, this still does not imply that there is good enough reason not to do the act. For example, suppose parents want good educations for their children, but only as a means to their own social climbing. When the children understand this, they will get the message that their parents see them as mere tools. But, of course, despite their parents' beliefs, they are not mere tools, and whatever the parents' intentions, the parents do have a duty to give their children a good education. If it is clear that the children will understand their parents' view of them if and only if the parents give them the education and this understanding will be psychologically very harmful to them, then this must still be weighed against the good of their being educated.

The specific immoral meaning that some think enhancement has, and the immoral message some think it sends, is that the unenhanced have less intrinsic worth than others, where presumably this implies that they do not have equal moral status just in virtue of being persons. (Call this Message 1. Notice that concern about this message could also apply to nongenetic methods of enhancement, such as education and exercise.) Message 1 is to be distinguished from a message that says that some properties are not as good for people to have as other properties. (Call this Message 2.) Presumably, expressing Message 2 is not immoral if it is true. This is because we can show our concern for someone of equal intrinsic worth by trying to give him properties that it will be better for him to have.

I think that it is highly unlikely that enhancement could carry the immoral Message 1. This is because enhancement is to be done to individuals who are already within the normal range of properties typical of the species. Such people are far less likely to be thought to lack the equal moral status that persons have just in virtue of being persons.[8] By contrast, those people who would be improved by being given treatments are more likely to

---

[8] Julie Tannenbaum, however, pointed out (in discussion) that the equal moral status of nonenhanced persons may depend not only on their properties qua persons but possibly on the fact that the properties of the enhanced would make them different only in degree but not in kind. For suppose we were creating gods. It might then be an open question whether persons would have fewer negative and positive rights in relation to gods than in relation to other nongod persons.

be in danger of being mistakenly thought to lack such equal moral status, for they fall below the norm. Yet this is, presumably, not a strong reason against treating them. We should cure blindness by drugs or surgery or genetic means because sightedness is good for persons, and because blind persons as much as any persons are worthy of care.

(C) I have been focusing on the desires, intentions, and actions of *individuals* and whether their acts of enhancement could be made impermissible by their desires, intentions and the meanings of their acts. One reason why I have discussed the desires, intentions and dispositions of individuals is that Sandel seems to be concerned with why individual parents might seek enhancement in their offspring. Furthermore, one way to conceive of the dispositions and aims of a society is as the sum of the dispositions and aims of the majority of people in it or of its typical members.[9] It is possible, however, that one would not be concerned if some individuals did certain types of acts from certain dispositions unless there were collective action, in the sense that a good part of the society were acting in this way, perhaps in unison. Indeed, Sandel has said that he is really concerned with social practices, not individual acts, and that he thinks that these are constituted, in part, by dispositions as well as acts.[10] For example, we now have a valuable social practice of parenthood which is constituted, in part, by a disposition to love whatever child comes unbidden and not to predetermine its properties. We now have valuable competitive sports practices which are constituted, in part, by excellence in the skillful exercise of natural gifts. If we pursue enhancements, Sandel thinks, we will corrupt and even eliminate these valuable practices.

Consider how this might happen. If the current practice of parenthood is conceived of as constituted (in part) by an openness to the unbidden in a sense that is in conflict with predetermining a child's properties,[11] then the desire to seek mastery as a means to goods will indeed eliminate the current

---

[9] Of course, it is possible that in a society only its leaders have certain particular desires, intentions, or dispositions and they arrange rewards and punishments so that individuals in the society fulfill the leaders' aims without necessarily sharing their desires, intentions, or dispositions. However, I do not think Sandel deals with such a scenario.

[10] This was part of his response to me on Nov. 19, 2005. The following section C summarizes our discussion on that occasion.

[11] Recall that earlier I considered senses of "openness to the unbidden" that were not in such conflict.

practice. The question, however, is whether a new practice—which might include the disposition to seek mastery in order to improve children for the sake of the children themselves—would be an even more valuable social practice than the older one. One measure would be its effects on children's lives, parent-child relations, etc. (This is an issue I consider in Section IV (A) below). I have already argued that having the disposition to seek mastery as a means to good need not be a bad characteristic of persons in itself. Of course, if the means chosen to the good effect, even if prompted by a good disposition, were bad, there would still be a problem. For example, Sandel mentions the possibility that the new practice might involve selecting mates on the basis of their potential for producing children of certain types. But the problem with doing this lies in the inappropriate way it treats potential mates, for relations between adults who seek to be mates should, presumably, be based primarily on love between them, as a response to their noninstrumental personal characteristics. So impermissible behavior between adults could be involved if this particular means to achieve mastery were chosen and the new practice of parenthood should not use it. But that does not mean that other ways of giving children good properties could not be part of the new practice.

In the case of sports, one of Sandel's concerns is that when athletes enhance their physical strength as a way to win competitions, we have a practice that is no longer about exercising skill but about whose body mass can fell an opponent. If this were so, I would say that the problem is that a good aspect of our current practice is not replaced by anything else of equal value in the new practice. But no one is arguing for "body enhancing changes" that have overall bad effects. Sometimes, Sandel claims that athletes' eating large quantities of muscle-building substances as a component of the new practice, while not in itself an impermissible act, is problematic because the focus on body mass eliminates a practice that relies on the use of valuable skills. However, sometimes he claims that in making their bodies massive, athletes are degrading themselves. If this were so, then, I would argue, the new practice would not only be less valuable but also involve impermissible acts.

My conclusion is that whether we are concerned with individuals and individual acts or with social practices, we shall have to focus on whether outcomes are valuable and can help justify acts or practices, whether means are permissible, and whether disposition to mastery as a means to goods is inconsistent with being good people. Emphasizing social practices merely because the identity conditions of a social practice (as a matter of definition) include effects, means, and dispositions will not alter the basic terms of our evaluative analysis from what they are when we consider individual acts and individual character.

III. Treatment versus enhancement

As noted above, Sandel's view is that the desire for mastery, rather than letting nature "give" us whatever "gifts" it will[12] is bad. However, the goods of treatment do justify seeking mastery. We may resist unbidden disease and disability. Why does treatment justify what enhancement cannot justify?

I suggested above that it may not be true that people's mastering nature, uncovering the secrets of life, and trying to improve what comes in life are bad in themselves. If they are not bad, then we do not have to show that avoiding great harm but not achieving great goods can outweigh the bad, in order to permissibly engage in these activities. However, if mastering nature were bad, one would have to show not only that the goods of enhancement are not as important as the goods of treatment but that they are not good enough to outweigh or transform the bad aspects of mastery.

There are several possible routes to showing that the goods of enhancement are not as important as the goods of treatment. One is the idea of diminishing marginal utility, according to which the benefit someone gets out of a given improvement in his condition decreases the better off he is. Hence, we do more good if we help those who are worse off than if we help those who are already better off. A second route is the view that there

---

[12] Carson Strong emphasizes that the idea of a gift requires a giftgiver and that, therefore, from a secular perspective where we do not assume a God, it is not literally true that children or naturally occurring good properties are gifts, as Sandel speaks of them (Strong (2005)). However, Strong himself notes that Sandel might simply emphasize the role of chance and good luck—as in a Rawlsian natural lottery—and use a metaphorical sense of giftedness. Strong also suggests that literal giftedness would come into the world, in the secular point of view, if parents did deliberately give good traits to their offspring. But "gift" has another connotation that militates against this conclusion to some degree, I believe. For a gift suggests some good that one gives beyond the call of duty; the recipient is not entitled to receive it. Children, however, might be entitled to certain enhancements, let alone certain treatments, from their parents and then those would not be gifts in the strict sense.

is greater moral value in helping people the worse off they are in absolute terms, even if we produce a smaller benefit to them than we could to people better off. (This is the view behind the position known as giving priority to the worse off.) A possible third route is to distinguish qualitatively between what some call harmed states and merely not being as well off as one might be but not badly off in absolute terms (Shiffrin 1999). All these routes depend on its being true that those to be treated are worse off than those to be enhanced. However, this may not always be true. For example, some illnesses produce states that are less bad than, or equal to, being at the low end of a normal range for a property. Furthermore, none of these routes to comparing the ends of enhancement and treatment shows that enhancements are not in themselves great enough goods to justify mastery as a means, even if enhancements are not as important as treatment. They also do not rule out that providing enhancements might be endorsed as a means to achieving some treatments. That is, suppose it is only if we are much smarter than we currently are that we will find a cure for terrible illnesses quickly. Then the importance of finding treatments could be transmitted to the enhancement of intelligence. (Of course, not all means are permitted to even justified ends. So if mastering nature to produce enhancements were sufficiently intrinsically objectionable, it might not be permissible to use the only available means [i.e., enhancement] to acquire treatments.)

At one point, Sandel tries to draw the distinction between treatment and enhancement by claiming that "medical intervention to cure or prevent illness . . . does not desecrate nature but honors it. Healing sickness or injury does not override a child's natural capacities but permits them to flourish" (Sandel 2004, 57). The assumption behind the first sentence is that nature is sacred and should be honored. When Sandel claims that curing and preventing illness do not desecrate nature, he implies that enhancement is a problem because of the sort of relation we should have to nature, as if this could be a source of moral imperatives in addition to our relations to other persons. But should we believe this? Cancer cells, AIDS, and tornadoes are all parts of nature. Are they sacred and to be honored? The natural and the good are distinct conceptual categories and the two can diverge: the natural can fail to be good and the good can be unnatural (art, dams, etc.).[13]

---

[13] Similarly, the human and the good are distinct conceptual categories. Human traits (such as arrogance) could be bad, and inhuman altruism could be good.

However, it is an important claim made by some that when there are goods in nature, they can indeed be sources of moral imperatives in addition to our relations to persons. By this they mean that independent of their effects on people, certain natural goods give us reasons to protect or promote them. For example, a great oak or the Grand Canyon may give us reasons to protect it even if no persons were favorably affected by this. Furthermore, recognizing their worth means not supplanting them with some things of inferior worth that may be good for people, such as parking lots.

How does this claim—call it the Independent Worth of Nature Claim—bear on not enhancing people? I do not think it serves as any support for the idea that there is a duty to nature not to engage in enhancement. First, it does not imply that, insofar as a "gift" in a person is a good of nature, what is a "gift" should be determined independently of its effect on people (i.e., independently of what is good for, or what is the good of, the person). (So, if a person were turning into a magnificent oak, this would not be a gift because it is not good for the person, and we should act to prevent this transformation.) Second, the Independent Worth of Nature Claim need not imply that we may not enhance, supplement, or even transform the goods of nature with genuine additional or superior goods.

Now consider the idea embodied in the second sentence of the Sandel quote, that healing honors nature by permitting natural capacities to flourish rather than overriding them. If enhancement involves the opposite, then we would be overriding people's natural capacities if we enhanced their immune system (by genetic means or immunization) so that they were able to resist illnesses that they could not naturally resist. Is doing this impermissible because it does not honor nature? Surely not. Suppose nature were sacred and to be honored. We would clearly be overriding its dictates by making people able to resist (by immunization) illnesses that they could not naturally resist. Is doing this impermissible because it does not honor nature? Surely not.

And indeed, Sandel has said[14] that such enhancement of natural functioning in order to combat illnesses is to be understood as part of treatment and is not the sort of enhancement he opposes. This may be because overriding natural capacities leads to treatment (or prevention) that does not itself override other natural capacities but permits them to flourish.

---

[14] In discussion on November 19, 2005.

The position expressed by this view might be illuminated by the following diagram, where "E" stands for enhancement and "T" for treatment (including prevention).

Ends

		E	T
E		EE	ET
T		TE	TT

Means (left axis label)

Figure 1.

This figure brings to light a distinction that may be overlooked in most discussions of enhancement: enhancement can be used to refer to an end—enhancing end states—or to a means—enhancing in order to either treat or enhance as ends. In the immune enhancement, we would enhance people as a means to stopping illness that interferes with natural gifts (ET). But a way to treat Alzheimer's disease might also involve increasing general memory power enormously simply as a way to diminish the effects of eventual dementia. Here overriding natural capacities to treat or prevent an illness that interferes with natural capacities does not merely allow those natural capacities to flourish. It overrides by supplementing them. (This is because it does not enhance capacities other than the ones that we seek to protect from the disease.) So Sandel might see this not as a form of ET, but rather as EE. But it is a special form of EE: the alternative to it is not being treated for a disease rather than being in a normal state. Perhaps when EE is the only alternative to disease, Sandel would permit it. (He would presumably object to a more indirect route to stopping Alzheimer's disease, namely increasing intelligence of scientists so that a cure could more easily be found.) He would object to EE when the alternative is a normal state and also possibly to TE when one treats an illness one would otherwise ignore just because treating it also enhances an end state (in a way that is not intermediate to further treatment).

Treatment, even ET, is commended by Sandel because it permits some natural capacities to flourish by eliminating one impediment to them, namely illness. Why would it not honor nature to interfere with other impediments. That is, might Sandel's view be better expressed as the view that we may permissibly override and not honor nature when we get rid of the things in nature that interfere with the other parts of nature that are its gifts (i.e., good things)? If this is so, then Sandel's position would not rule out dramatically lengthening the human life span and preventing the ageing process. This involves getting rid of things that are normal and not illnesses, but do impede the exercise of natural gifts that we have had all our lives. Yet most people would consider this a radical enhancement. (And, indeed, life-lengthening seems in some respects like a form of EE [in Figure 1].) So, Sandel's original objection to enhancement, that it interferes with gifts that nature has given someone rather than allowing them to flourish, is not always true. It is not true, in some forms of ET and some forms of EE (such as life-lengthening). But sometimes his original objection is true of treatments, as in increasing memory power to stop Alzheimer's.

For another example, suppose that a child's natural gifts are those of a Down's Syndrome child and we seek to supplement these and provide greater gifts than nature provided by changing the child's genome. This would change or add to natural capacities, not merely permit them to flourish. Yet, presumably, Sandel would want to classify this with allowable treatment rather than enhancement because it compensates for a genetic defect that caused the Syndrome.[15] This form of treatment, which involves changing and supplementing nature's gifts with new ones, rather than curing or preventing conditions that interfere with gifts already present, raises the more general question of why appreciation of nature's gifts requires limiting ourselves to them. We can appreciate what is given and yet supplement it with something new, even when we are not compensating for a defect.

There are three primary conclusions to this section so far. First, Sandel's attempt to draw a distinction between treatment and enhancement, based on allowing natural capacities to flourish versus overriding natural capacities, does not seem successful. Second, on one interpretation of how he draws the treatment/enhancement distinction, Sandel's objection to enhancement

---

[15] An anonymous reader of this paper suggested the following: Suppose that we would permit the person's natural capacities to flourish, even if we compensate for a congenital disease by genetic intervention. On this view, the wrong genes would mask, but not alter, an individual's natural capacities. So what are natural capacities? Not those likely to exist given an individual's genetic endowment. If, instead, they are those capacities that can be achieved in an individual given practical genetic interventions, then we permit an individual's natural capacities to flourish however we intervene, whether through treatment or enhancement. (Perhaps, the natural capacities would be those given by the idea of the normal capacities for the species?)

does not rule out maintaining natural gifts (that would otherwise wither) throughout a greatly extended human life span. Third, we would need much more argument to show that there is some duty owed to nature which we offend against when we change natural capacities and that it is our relation to nature rather than to persons that should be a primary source of concern with enhancement.

Consider an alternative way to draw the treatment/enhancement distinction suggested by P. H. Schwartz.[16] We treat when we eliminate a dysfunction, not merely prevent anything that interferes with nature's gifts. Dysfunction is an interference with healthy human life, which involves the normal, proper functioning of the human being. The normal, proper functioning of a human being or its parts is the functioning that contributes to survival and reproduction to a degree that does not fall too far below the mean for individuals of the same age and gender. (Possibly, if we alter a genome to add to a Down's Syndrome child's gifts, we might be seen to compensate for the dysfunction that originally interfered with normal development.) Schwartz thinks that we should value healthy human life and that fixing dysfunction (i.e., treating the failure of a part to contribute to survival and reproduction to a degree that does not fall too far below the mean for individuals of the same age and gender) has "superior moral status" to modifying normal functioning (enhancing), because it alone has "a virtue of accepting the normal" and avoiding the implied rejection of normal human life (Schwartz 2005, 6).

Despite drawing the treatment/enhancement distinction in this way, and identifying treatment as morally superior in at least one way to enhancement, Schwartz thinks there is "no need to treat dysfunctions that are valued by their bearers (such as infertility in some)" and no rule against modifying people so as to produce valued dysfunctions (e.g., infertility by vasectomy). Hence, on his view, the way in which treatment is morally superior to enhancement—by accepting the normal—can be overridden by other ways in which not treating or even producing dysfunction can be morally superior to treatment (e.g., by providing people with things that they correctly value).[17]

---

[16] As described in P. H. Schwartz (2005).

[17] F. Miller and H. Brody (2005) suggest that induced infertility by contraception is an enhancement. Schwartz thinks of it as an induced dysfunction. This suggests that sometimes dysfunctions are enhancements. Miller and Brody at one point attempt to fit contraception into a narrow notion of

Let me raise the following concerns with Schwartz's analysis of treatment and enhancement.

(a) First, it draws the treatment/enhancement distinction by relativizing the normal to "the mean for one's age and gender." Hence, what would ordinarily be thought of as dysfunctions can be perfectly normal. For example, it is normal for brain cells to die as we age, heart muscle to atrophy, and joints to wear out. So, it turns out on Schwartz's account that common interventions to eliminate such conditions, for example, by providing drugs or doing surgery, is not treatment but rather enhancement. (Only dealing with abnormal dysfunctions would be treatment.) If these are enhancements, then undoing similar normal dysfunctions so that people have radically longer life spans with continuing capacities cannot be distinguished from what we already do by appeal to a treatment/enhancement distinction. (On Sandel's view, I argued, radically longer life spans might turn out to be treatments because they stop impediments to normal gifts. On Schwartz's view, they turn out to be enhancements because they do not deal with abnormal dysfunctions. But neither author's analysis distinguishes such life-lengthening from what they already consider permissible.)

(b) Now consider Schwartz's value analysis. He begins by saying that we should value a life without dysfunction and that it is morally superior not to reject the normal, but he then concludes by saying that it is not unreasonable to sometimes value a life with dysfunction (such as infertility) over a life without it. This, of course, implies that it can be right to reject the normal (either in end state or in mechanism leading to an end state). It seems that this could be true because it could be more important for a life to be good in nonnormal ways than for it to be normal. Hence, as Schwartz recognizes, it remains open that an enhanced life will be a greater good than a normal one, just as a life with a dysfunction can be a greater good than one without it. Furthermore, suppose a very small additional good gotten through abnormality (either dysfunction or enhancement) overrides any

medical care by suggesting that even though it is an enhancement, it prevents clear medical risks involved in pregnancy and mental health problems associated with unwanted births. But suppose (counterfactually) that pregnancy had no medical risks and hormonal changes in women made it possible for them to always adjust psychologically to each additional child. It could still be true that a woman could sometimes have a better life if she did something besides have another child, and she should use contraception to achieve that good. Here the provision within medical care of contraception, which itself has some medical risks, would be unrelated to avoiding health risks. Yet it could be appropriate for a doctor to prescribe it.

merit in normality. This would show that the merit in normality is very weak.[18]

(c) Indeed, it is not clear that there is anything morally preferable about normality at all, or anything morally superior about preserving the normal than rejecting it. First, as noted in (a), according to Schwartz's analysis, some dysfunctions (e.g., brain cells not working) will be normal, and if we should value life without dysfunction, this means that sometimes we should not value the normal per se.

Second, recall that on Schwartz's analysis, normal means "functions so as to survive and reproduce at not too far from the mean for one's age and gender." Presumably, survival and reproduction are worth valuing only if there is survival and reproduction of what is good; survival and reproduction of what is bad may be normal but not in any way morally good. Let us assume that what survives and reproduces is good, and this supports the view that survival and reproduction are morally good. Why cannot superior-to-normal performance of these functions be better than normal function? For example, if it were normal for a species to just barely survive and reproduce, could the normal not have less value per se than the supernormal?

In order to see a general problem with using the normal as a basis for deciding when to alter characteristics, it helps to imagine what it would be right to do if, counterfactually, the normal for us were what is, in fact, abnormal. (I shall call this the Shifted Baseline Argument.) So Down's Syndrome is abnormal for humans. But suppose it were normal for our species to have the intelligence of a Down's Syndrome person. Should we think that it would then be wrong for the abnormally intelligent members of our species to alter the rest of us so that everyone had the sort of intelligence that is now considered normal? Presumably not, unless there were bad side effects of doing this. Those currently opposed to enhanced intelligence or enhanced memory point to the possible problems that might accompany these, such as not being able to forget and noticing too many defects in life. But suppose it were normal for our species to have the same intelligence as a Down's Syndrome person or a weaker memory than we now have. Would we think it wrong for us to be altered so

<hr />

[18] There is also another sense in which enhancement is more important than normality-preserving treatments: We are all willing to risk some illness by spending money on life-enhancing activities (such as education) rather than on cures for disease. I owe this point to Julian Savulescu.

that we had levels of intelligence and memory now considered normal for us, despite some drawbacks relative to the lower states (as those lower states may involve blissful ignorance and a constant pleasant disposition)? Presumably not.

The appeal to the moral value of the normal may just be a hidden way of supposing that there is a delicate balance between all our properties (and between our species and the rest of the world), and things might go for the worse overall for people if they made a local improvement to the normal.

I conclude that we have so far not seen why treatment but not enhancement justifies mastery over nature.

IV. Parental and social relations

In this section, I shall examine Sandel's views on how enhancement may negatively affect our relations to persons, ourselves or others.

(A) One's Children

As noted above, Sandel paints with a broad brush in condemning enhancements due not only to genomic changes but to drugs and training. However, he also realizes that much of ordinary good parenting consists of what might ordinarily be called enhancement. Hence, he says the crucial point is to balance accepting love and transformative love. (Perhaps Sandel would want to apply this idea to changes adults seek to make to themselves as well.) But he also seems to think of transformative love as concerned with helping natural gifts to flourish, framing and molding them so that they shine forth. (Similarly, in sport, he thinks that good running shoes help bring out a natural gift by comparison to drugs that would change a gift into something else. Treatment was also said to help natural gifts but only by removing impediments to them.)

Let us first deal with the issue of balance. For all Sandel says, it remains possible that many more enhancements than he considers appropriate are ones that satisfy the balance between accepting and transformative love, even if we expand the latter idea to include adding to natural gifts, for it is not clear what falls under "balancing." For example, suppose my child already has an IQ of 160. Might balancing the two types of love in her case imply that I may (if this will be good for her) increase her IQ another 10 but not 20 points, and that a parent whose child has an IQ of 100 should not change her child as much as to give her a 120 IQ, for this would err on the side of too much transformation?

An alternative to this view of balancing might be called Sufficientarianism. It could imply that there is no need at all to increase the first child's IQ and that in the second child's case much more transformation (in the sense of adding to natural gifts) than acceptance is appropriate—that is the right balance—in order to reach a sufficient level. (Sufficientarians are not interested in perfection, though they want mastery as a means to getting sufficient goods.)

Let us now restrict ourselves to Sandel's sense of transformation— bringing out natural gifts—and consider the ways in which this may be done. To the extent to which Sandel allows training and appliances to be used to bring out and shape gifts, nothing in his argument rules out using drugs or genetic manipulation that do exactly the same thing. So suppose that a certain amount of voice training is permitted to strengthen vocal chords. Would a drug or genetic manipulation that could strengthen vocal chords to the same degree also be permissible? If the argument Sandel gives does not alone rule out training, it alone will not rule out transformation by drugs or genetic means because a gift is transformed to the same degree by each method. If appliances such as running shoes are allowed, why not genetically transformed feet that function in the same way? Ordinarily, such genetic changes would be considered enhancements, even if they are only traits in addition to one's natural capacities that allow the other natural capacities to flourish. An argument different from Sandel's, based on the possible moral difference in using different means to transform capacities, would be necessary to rule out drug or genetic means but permit training. As we have noted, Sandel treats training, drugs, and genetic manipulation on a par. This leaves his position open to endorsing many genetic enhancements (in addition to those that aim at treatment, as discussed in Section III).

While Sandel rightly condemns excessive pressure to transform oneself and one's children in a competitive society, especially if the societal values are shallow, he does not condemn moderate training for worthwhile transformation.[19] Unless he emphasizes a difference in means used, he

---

[19] Hilary Bok emphasized this point.

should then permit moderate, worthwhile genetic transformations that bring out natural gifts, even if not excessive ones driven by competitive pressures and/or governed by shallow values. (His argument against giving traits merely to give one's child a competitive advantage, on the ground that when everyone has the traits no one has gained a competitive advantage, will also fail against traits that are good to have even if everyone gets them.[20] For example, better eyesight or higher intelligence can raise the absolute quality of each person's life even if there is no change in relative advantage.)

Now consider one way in which Sandel may be wrong not to distinguish different ways of either bringing out natural gifts or bringing about more radical enhancement by introducing major new capacities. Perhaps we should separate how we treat changes that are made before a child exists (what I shall call ex-ante changes) from those that are made once a child exists (what I shall call ex-post changes). The former are primarily genetic, while the latter will include drugs and training.

Love, it has been said, is for a particular. Consider love for an adult. Before we love someone, we may be interested in meeting a person who has various properties, such as kindness and intelligence. When we meet such a person, we may be interested in him or her rather than someone else because he or she has these properties. However, though it is through these properties that we may be led to love this particular person, it is the particular person that we wind up loving, not his or her set of properties. For if another person appears with the same set of properties, that does not mean that we could as easily substitute him or her for the person we already love. Even if the person we love loses some of the properties through which we were originally led to love him or her (e.g., his beauty), we would not necessarily stop loving the particular person that we love (Nozick 1977).

It seems then that when we love a particular person, this involves much of what Sandel calls accepting love. If we do seek transformation in the properties of the person we love, this may be because of moral requirements he would fail to meet without the properties, or because we want what is good for the person and can see a way of achieving it that is consistent with what he wants for himself. By contrast, before a particular person whom we love exists (just as before we find someone to love), it is permissible to

---

[20] This point was emphasized by Marcia Angell in discussion.

think more boldly in terms of the characteristics we would like to have in a person and that we think it is excellent for a person to have, at least so long as these characteristics would not be bad for the person who will have them and are consistent with respect for persons.

The latter side-constraint—respect for persons—could even conflict with seeking properties that are good for someone. For example, suppose peace of mind and equanimity are goods for a person. Nevertheless, ensuring their presence by modifying someone so that she is self-deceived about awful truths or about her duties to others would be inconsistent with taking seriously that one is creating a person, an entity worthy of respect. Both the side-constraint of respect and the side-constraint of concern for the person's best interests could conflict with what has been called a "genetic supermarket," wherein parents choose traits for offspring according to their own preferences. I agree with Sandel that such a consumer model is out of place when creating persons. Sandel says, "Not everything in the world is open to whatever use we may desire or devise" (2004, 54). This is certainly true of persons.

Still, before the existence of a person, there is no one with certain characteristics that we have to accept, if we love him and do not want to impose undue burdens necessary for changes. Hence, not accepting whatever characteristics nature will bring but altering them ex-ante does not show lack of love. Nor can it insult or psychologically pressure a person at the time changes are made the way ex-post changes might. This is because no conscious being yet exists who has to work hard to achieve new traits or suffer fears of rejection at the idea that they should be changed. Importantly, it is rational and acceptable to seek good characteristics in a new person, even though we know that when the child comes to be and we love him or her, many of these characteristics may come and go and we will continue to love the particular person. This is an instance of what I call the distinction between "caring to have" and "caring about." That is, one can know that one will care about someone just as much whether or not she has certain traits and yet care to have someone, perhaps for their own sake, who has, rather than lacks, those traits (Kamm 2004).[21] Sandel says that "parental love is not contingent on talents and attributes

---

[21] I previously argued for this distinction in Kamm (2004) when discussing the compatibility of (a) a disabled person caring about his life as much as a nondisabled person cares about his life, and (b) a disabled person caring to have a nondisabled life rather than a disabled one.

a child happens to have" (Sandel 2004, 55). This is true because love is for a particular about whom one cares, but this is consistent with caring to have, and seeking better attributes in, a person-to-be, at least ex-ante. Hence, it would not be correct for a child to think that just because his parents tried and succeeded in giving him certain good traits, they would not have loved him as much if he had not had these traits.

Applying what I have said to the issue of enhancement suggests that even if transformative and enhancing projects should be based primarily on what is best for the child-to-be, determined independently of mere competitive advantage, this is consistent with trying to achieve ex-ante a child with traits that will be desirable per se, so long as these traits will not be bad for the child and are not inconsistent with respect for persons. By contrast, ex-post enhancement may have to be more constrained for it could involve psychological pressure on the child and lead to fear of rejection. However, even ex-ante enhancement, given that the child knows about it ex-post, can lead to some forms of psychological pressure. For example, if you know that you have been deliberately given a talent for music, you may feel under pressure to use it, though you would prefer not to.[22] It might be suggested that we could avoid this problem by modifying the person-to-be so that the person would always prefer the traits that we have given them. But doing this would be inconsistent with respect for persons, for the exercise of independent judgment should not be restricted; if anything, it should be enhanced. An alternative way to reduce pressure ex-post is to provide traits that either add value simply in being present (such as better eyesight) or by increasing options for someone (for example, to either play or not play music).

Drawing a distinction between the methods of ex-ante and ex-post "designing" people does not, however, put to rest different sorts of objections to even nonpressuring ex-ante enhancements. Let us consider some.

(1) First, Sandel thinks that people are not products to be designed. I agree that people are not products in the sense that they are not commodities, but rather beings worthy of concern and respect in their own right. But I do not think this implies that it is morally wrong to design them. Consider first if it would be acceptable to redesign oneself. We are accustomed to people having replacement parts, such as knees and transplants. Suppose

---

[22] I owe this point to Seana Shiffrin.

when our parts wore out, we were offered alternatives among the new ones—for example, teeth of various colors, joints that were more or less flexible, limbs that were longer or shorter—it might well make sense to make selections that involved redesigning ourselves. Similarly, if we could replace brain cells, it might make sense to choose ones that gave us new abilities. This would also be redesigning ourselves.

Now consider creating new people. We already have much greater control over the timing of pregnancy, over whether someone can conceive at all, and over which embryos are chosen (via pre-implantation diagnosis) for development. Rather than humility, we have justifiable pride in these accomplishments. Suppose that we each had been designed in detail by other persons. (We all know that the story about the stork bringing babies is a myth. Just suppose that sexual reproduction and the natural lottery in traits are also myths, and we have really all been designed.) Presumably, we would still be beings of worth and entitled to respect. But might it be that although a being retains its high status despite such an origin, it is inconsistent with respect for persons to choose such a designed origin for them? (Analogously, a person retains his status as a rights bearer even when his rights are violated, but it is not, therefore, appropriate to violate his rights.) To answer this question, imagine that the natural way of reproducing required that important properties be selected for offspring, otherwise they would be mere lumps of flesh. Surely, selecting properties would then be permissible. If this procedure were working well, would we nevertheless be obligated, out of respect for persons, to introduce a lottery based on chance as a way for definite properties to come about? I do not think so. If this is correct, then the designing of persons is not per se inconsistent with respect for persons.[23]

(2) Some associate designing people with engineering them rather than raising them and letting them grow, and criticize designing for this reason.[24] However, I do not think these necessarily are contrasts. One could put together the innate mechanisms that are now present in people at birth (thus engineering them) and then they could grow and be raised as they are now. Some may think that putting together a living being according to a design would threaten our ability to worship, revere, and love it; we

---

[23] Notice also that there is an alternative of designing the gene pool so that only enhanced options are available and this is compatible with chance determination of the properties of any given individual.

[24] R. E. Ashcroft and K. Gui (2005).

could not have what might be called the "ooh-response." Worse, the idea of putting something together might suggest that there is nothing wrong with taking it apart (thereby destroying it). But many things we revere and love are created by us, and not just as the result of acts of inspiration. Works of art and craft, literature, hybrid plants and animals are composed, revised, put together in parts that we can come to understand completely. And yet we can respond to these as more than the sum of their parts, revering and loving them. Of course, such entities are not persons and do not have the moral status of persons. But that is because they do not have the properties of persons. If we gave such properties (as rationality and emotion), the worth that supervenes on them, and the response to the worth, would be present, too.

Crucially, it is a mistake in criticizing enhancement to focus on its occurring by a mechanical, piecemeal construction process (engineering) for enhancement does not essentially involve it. Consider that parents typically wish and pray that their children be good people, have good judgment and worthwhile capacities. Suppose that wishing made it so and one could be assured that one's prayers would be answered. This would be a means of enhancement. Should parents then not engage in such efficacious wishing and praying, even if they wish and pray for the right things?[25]

(3) A third general objection to ex-ante designing asks, if someone wants to have a child, should she not focus only on the most basic goods, such as having a normal child to love? If so, then if she focuses on achieving many superior qualities, does that not show that she is interested in the wrong things in having a child? To answer this worry, consider an analogy. If the primary concern for a philosopher in getting a job should be that she be able to do philosophy, does that mean that it is wrong to choose between possible jobs that equally satisfy that characteristic on the basis of higher salary? If not, why is the search for properties other than the basic ones in a child wrong, when the basic ones are not thereby put in jeopardy? (Of course, in the case of the child-to-be, unlike the job, the enhanced properties are usually to be for its benefit, not only for those doing the selecting.)

---

[25] It is true that when we pray and wish now, we may hope there is a superior being who will grant our prayers only when they are appropriate. (This is the point of the "if it be Thy will" part of the prayer.) But this can signal our concern that we may not really be enhancing in getting what we want. I discuss this problem of limited wisdom and imagination in the last section of this article.

Furthermore, as noted above, searching for more than the basics does not by itself imply that if one could not achieve those enhancements, one would not still happily have a child who had only the basics, and love the particular person she is. In this way, too, seeking enhancement is consistent with being open to the unbidden. What about disappointment? It is true that the more one invests in getting enhancements, the more resources one will have wasted if the enhancements do not come about; the lost resources, rather than the child one has, could be a source of disappointment. There may be disappointment for the child when enhancements fail—that one could not bring about something good for it. But that is different from disappointment in the child. Further, while someone who would refuse to have a child without enhancements might thereby show that he did not care about the core reasons for having a child, even this does not show he is unfit to be a parent. For he could still come to love the child if he actually had it, through attachment to it as a particular (as described above).

(4) I have argued that often ex-ante changes would be preferable to ex-post changes because there would be less pressure on, and less opportunity for feelings of rejection by, the child. But a fourth concern about ex-ante enhancements is that a parent will simply have greater control over the child's nature, whether she seeks it or not. (As Sandel agrees, this does not mean that the child will have less control, for it is chance, not the child, that will determine genetic makeup, if other persons, such as parents, do not. Nor does it mean that the issues of "designing" children and of parental control are not separable in principle. For if someone other than the parent designed the child, relative to the parent the child would still be part of the unbidden.) Is it possible that if we could produce a certain desirable trait in someone equally well and as safely by genetic means or by ex-post drugs or training, we should prefer the latter means because they give the child greater freedom relative to its parent?

Consider the following argument for this position:[26] Suppose a parent is told that its fetus has a gene that will make it aggressive to a degree that is undesirable from the parent's point of view though not outside the normal range. The gene could be altered so that the person that will develop will be less aggressive. Alternatively, the person who will

---

[26] Presented by Anja Karnein and based on one by Jurgen Habermas.

develop could take a drug through her life that will successfully reduce the aggressiveness caused by the gene. The latter course is to be preferred, the argument maintains, because when the child reaches maturity she can decide to stop taking the drug, if she decides that she prefers being a more aggressive person. By contrast, if her parents had made the genetic change, the claim is, she would not have this freedom to choose to be more aggressive.

This argument does not succeed, I believe. For it rests on the assumption that a genetic trait for aggression can be altered perfectly well by taking a drug. But if that is so, then it is also possible that the alternative genetic trait for less aggression can be altered by taking a drug that increases aggressiveness. Hence, the child whose parents made the genetic change could have the same freedom to alter her temperament as the child whose parents did not make the genetic change. On the other hand, if drugs could not alter traits as well as genetic modification, this would leave each child with a genetic makeup either given by nature or by a parent; the child would still be unfree to modify itself by drugs ex-post.

Suppose parents would have greater control than they now have over their children's characteristics with either ex-ante or ex-post enhancement. In numerous areas of life, persons now justifiably stand in relations of control over other people where once chance ruled. The important thing is that this be done justly and well. Furthermore, if we choose certain characteristics in particular in offspring, the balance of control over the child's life may shift to the child rather than the parent, even if the child does not have the capacity to further alter the characteristic ex-post. What I have in mind is that if we could ensure that a child had such enhancing traits as self-control and good judgment, then the child would be less, not more, likely to be subject to parental control after birth. This is what is most important.

(5) A fifth concern is that if each parent individually tries to do what is best for its child, all parents will end up making the situation worse for all their children. This can come about if we give traits that could benefit a child only by giving her a competitive advantage. If all children are similarly altered, everyone may be overall worse off, in virtue of efforts made that do not alter any individual's benefit. To avoid this prisoner's dilemma situation: I have already suggested that we focus on characteristics that would benefit someone independently of competitive advantage. With

respects to other traits some rule that coordinates the choices of parents seems called for.[27]

[27] Larry Temkin emphasized this problem of prisoner's dilemmas. Another objection to some ex-ante enhancements was raised by Matthew Liao (in Liao (2005)). Liao argues that some ex-ante enhancements (which I contrast to ex-post enhancements) are impermissible, even though the person does not yet exist, and this is not because of any property the person eventually comes to have, but because of the morally dubious intention of the enhancer (2005, 2–3). For example, suppose someone sex-selects a female child for the purpose of selling her into prostitution, or (in my own illustration) creates a brain-enhanced child for the purpose of exhibiting her in a zoo. However, each creator then comes to love the child for her own sake and treats it properly. Liao notes that I suggest that characteristics sought ex-ante should not be bad for the person who will have them and should be consistent with respect for persons. But being female or brain-enhanced is not bad for a person or inconsistent with creating a person worthy of respect. Hence, he thinks, it is not because of the properties that would be given, but because of the further intentions of the agents that their acts are wrong (2005, 5).

He also thinks that I mean to imply that properties that are morally undesirable (such as being subject to self-deception) make persons no longer worthy of respect, but he counters that having a morally dubious property does not do this. Yet, he agrees, it is still wrong ex-ante to do what gives this property to someone. This cannot be, he thinks, because of what the property is in itself, or because the person could have existed without the property and been better. The latter claim, Liao thinks, cannot be true because an individual comes into existence at the same time as his ex-ante chosen properties and the person without that property would have been a different person. Hence, the person now in existence with the property cannot complain that he was harmed by being given the property, assuming his life is worth living. Liao concludes from all this that the wrongness of giving such a property lies in the morally dubious intentions of the agent (2005, 6).

I do not think Liao's arguments succeed. First, consider the person who creates a female child intending to make her a prostitute, or a brain-enhanced person intending to exhibit her. I would say that the first creator is attempting to create a prostitute and the second an exhibition animal, and each of these properties is not one that persons should have. But suppose that an agent attempting to create someone with these properties cannot succeed, perhaps because he is bound to love each of the people he creates. Then I would say that his actual act of creating the people is not impermissible, though what he attempts to do (make prostitutes or exhibition animals) is impermissible. I would say that a morally worse event or act has taken place in virtue of the bad intention prompting his act, but this does not mean his act is impermissible.

Second, contrary to Liao, I do not mean to imply that giving a person a morally dubious property makes the person not worthy of respect. The person just remains someone worthy of having properties more appropriate to his respect-worthy status. Similarly, violating someone's rights can be inconsistent with respect for a person without in any way altering his status as a creature worthy of respect. Most disturbing, from the fact that a naturally disabled person remains a person worthy of respect, Liao concludes that the wrongness of deliberately creating a disabled person cannot be due to his winding up with the property of being disabled; the act must rather be wrong because of the motivation or intention of the agent. But surely it can be wrong to do what gives people properties that do not diminish their worth but just make their lives much worse for them to live, regardless of one's motivation or intention (for example, as a mere side effect of some useful act). Now consider Liao's arguments based on identity considerations for the claim that an act creating a person with a certain property cannot be wrong because of the property. First, it is not always true that a person would not have existed at all if he had not existed with a certain property. For not all properties are essential properties (i.e., properties without which that person would not exist), and we could imagine having changed a given embryo for the better by affecting one of its nonessential properties. Then that person could have been better than he actually is. Now consider the cases in which a different person would have been created if a property had been different—perhaps because an essential property is at issue. Liao says that in such a case, the person created with the nonoptimal property cannot complain

(6) Of course, many would reject both ex-ante and ex-post genetic and drug modification, whether controlled by parents or by the offspring themselves, rather than modification by effort or exercise. Such opponents try to distinguish means of enhancement that Sandel does not distinguish, but in another way than I have. Sometimes it is said that the struggle involved in effort and exercise has moral value. Or, it is said, that if our performance is not the result of our consciously bringing it about by trying and effort, then there will be no connection that we understand as human agents between our performance and ourselves. There will be no intelligible connection between means and ends. The performance will come about as if by magic.[28] However, these points suggest that it would be better if most members of our species did not have, for example, the genetic tendency that they in fact have toward fellow feeling, but rather, like the few amongst us who are very aggressive, had to produce fellow feeling in themselves by great effort or through a process that intelligibly led to fellow feeling. But this would not be better. Similarly, imagine the following imaginary case. Your high intelligence and natural grace, which in someone else would be due to an enhancement, is your normal luck in life's lottery, and it is due to a large degree to your genetic makeup. Then normal changes in your physical makeup lead to your losing the automatic presence of high intelligence and grace. Would you now be thankful that you had the freedom to decide whether or not to work extra hard and, by a humanly intelligible process, bring these good things about, or even take many drugs each day to bring them about? Or would you prefer genetic surgery so that your system worked automatically the way it always had? Presumably the latter. Here I have again employed the Shifting Baseline Argument, by imagining that a characteristic that is normally genetically controlled, either in the species or just you, is absent. Then we consider whether there is anything offensive per se in introducing a genetic trait to restore or produce the desirable characteristic.

The basic point is that people do not now complain that many good capacities they have come about independently of their will and not through

---

that he is worse off than he might otherwise have been. But it does not follow from this that we cannot say it is impermissible to have created a person with the property rather than someone else without the property, in virtue of what the property is. Hence, we need not refer to the intentions of the creator in judging the permissibility of his act.

[28] This point is especially emphasized by Leon Kass. See Kass (2007).

an intelligible process. Indeed, one might analogize genetic changes (or taking drugs) in order to improve performance to maturation. Often, when someone cannot do or appreciate something, we tell them to wait until they mature. This means that no act of will or effort in an intelligible process can substitute for a physical change that will, as if by magic, make them capable of doing or appreciating something.[29]

One major conclusion of this subsection is that Sandel does not show that seeking to enhance children, especially ex ante, is inconsistent with a proper balance between accepting and transforming love.

(B) Social Justice

Finally, we come to Sandel's views on the connection between enhancement and the twin issues of burdens of responsibility and distributive justice. Consider responsibility first. If people are able to enhance themselves or others, can they not be held responsible in the sense of being blamed for not giving themselves or others desirable characteristics? Not necessarily, for one does not have a duty to do everything that could make oneself or someone else better, and if one has no duty, then one is not at fault in not enhancing and so not to be blamed. Even if one has certain duties, for example, to be the best doctor one can be, and taking certain drugs would help one to perform better, it is not necessarily one's duty to take the drugs. One could retain a right not to alter one's body even in order to better fulfill one's duties as a physician. Hence, one need not be at fault even if one does not do what will help one perform one's duties better. But retaining the right not to alter one's body does not imply a right to make such alterations impermissible for anyone who wants them. Of course, if the characteristics one will have must be determined by others (for example, one's parents), then one could not be blamed for causing or not causing the characteristics, as one could not have directed one's parents' behavior.

What about cases in which one can be blamed for a choice not to enhance? Thomas Scanlon has emphasized that one can hold someone responsible for an outcome in the sense of blaming him for it without thereby thinking that it is also his responsibility to bear the costs of his

---

[29] Asian traditions involve many techniques that produce good results by exercise (such as repetition of a mantra) that do not involve trying or moving by intelligible steps toward a goal.

choice.[30] These are conceptually two separate issues. For example, suppose someone is at fault for acting carelessly in using his hairdryer. If he suffers severe harm and will die without medical treatment, his being at fault does not mean that he forfeits a claim on others he otherwise had to medical care.

By contrast, Sandel thinks that the issue of responsibility for choosing to have or to lack certain characteristics is intimately related to how much of a claim we have against others for aid. However, he is not always clear in distinguishing the role of choice from the role of mere knowledge of one's characteristics. For example, in discussing why we have insurance schemes, he seems to imply that even if we had no control over our traits but only knew what they were (for example, via genetic testing), we would lose a claim against others to financially share the costs of our fate. For, if people knew they were not at risk, people would not enter into insurance schemes that mimic solidarity. So Sandel's argument based on solidarity against enhancement seems to be an argument against knowledge of genetic traits as well as against control of them. But those who urge us to use a veil of ignorance in deciding whether and when we should share others' burdens (via allocation of resources) are, in effect, saying that even if we have knowledge of one another's traits, there are sometimes moral reasons for behaving as though we lack the knowledge.

Let us put aside the issue of blameworthiness for, and the effect of mere knowledge of, traits. How should the mere possibility of making responsible choices that determine one's traits affect responsibility for bearing costs for the outcome of choices? Sandel here seems to share with some philosophers (known as luck egalitarians) the view (roughly) that if we have not chosen to have traits but have them as a matter of luck (or other people's choices), the costs of having them should be shared among everyone. However, if we choose the traits (by action or by omitting to change them if we can), then even if we do not in any deep sense deserve to have made this choice, there is no reason for the costs of having the traits to be shared. (According to some luck egalitarians, however, we may choose to buy insurance that will protect us against bad choices.) Sandel says he cannot think of any better reason for the well-off to help those who are not well off except that each is not fully responsible for his situation. (It is important

---

[30] In Thomas Scanlon, *What We Owe to Each Other* (Cambridge, Mass.: Harvard University Press, 1999).

to remember that some do not find lack of responsibility a compelling reason for sharing with others. Robert Nozick, for example, argued that one could be entitled to what followed from traits that one was not at all responsible for having.[31])

Contrary to Sandel, it seems that often we want to give people new options without taking away from them help they would have gotten from others when they had no control over their fates. One example given above involved someone whose choice—even a faulty one—to use a hairdryer should not lead to his forfeiting aid to avert a major disaster. Similarly, if someone for reasons of conscience refuses to take advantage of the option to abort a difficult pregnancy, we do not think that she should forfeit medical care simply because she could have avoided the need for it. In many cases, arguments for the duty to aid others seem to have more to do with respect and concern for persons and a willingness to support their having an opportunity for autonomous choice without fear of costs[32] than with whether they have or have not gotten themselves into whatever situation they are in. Of course, in cases I have been considering, someone chooses in a way that leads to a bad outcome he does not per se choose. But recall that Kant thought we had a duty to help people pursue even the ends they themselves had deliberately chosen because people matter in

---

[31] See his *Anarchy, State, and Utopia.* Unlike luck egalitarians, Rawlsians may think that what is necessary to justify shared responsibility as a matter of justice is the fact that a particular social structure is, to a large degree, responsible for what sort of fate in life one's genetic properties will yield. By contrast, in the case of bad luck that is the result of socially unmediated natural effects, a Rawlsian might think that shared responsibility is not a matter of justice. Notice that the problem for shared responsibility of outcomes (solidarity) with which Sandel is concerned is different from another problem that concerns J. S. Robert in Robert (2005). Robert is concerned that giving people the choice of enhancement before we take care of the many who lack basic necessities is already to show a lack of solidarity with others (2005, 6). The fact that we have such priorities tends to weaken Sandel's view that we are more likely to help people when our traits are not chosen. For they are not chosen now, and yet, as Robert sees it, we are unwilling to share with the needy now. But does seeking enhancement indicate a lack of solidarity? Robert himself thinks that it is only psychologically realistic to demand moderate self-sacrifice from each of us. But such a degree of self-sacrifice may be consistent with seeking enhancement for oneself while others are in need of basic necessities. Further, if we were trying to provide the autonomous choice of enhancement to everyone, even though this is not what many need most, this itself would be an instance of solidarity, in the sense that we care for others as well as ourselves. And if it were unrealistic to expect—or not morally required of—us to sacrifice a great deal for others, helping them to enhance themselves at small additional cost (if this were possible) may leave them better off overall than if there were no opportunities for enhancements. However, none of this would solve the problem of solidarity with which Sandel is concerned, as that only arises after people have the option of autonomously enhancing themselves, and thus are thought (by Sandel) to both lose a claim to further assistance and to lose the motivation to assist.

[32] The latter point in particular is emphasized by Seana Shiffrin.

their own right, rather than because they could not be held responsible for outcomes or because it was only the unwilled consequences of their choices with which we were asked to help.

It may throw further light on (a) the effect of the option to enhance on shared responsibility to consider (b) the effect of the option to treat on shared responsibility. Sandel, of course, is not against giving individuals the option to treat or prevent their diseases. This is so despite the fact that one might construct an argument concerning the option to use treatments and preventions parallel to the one he constructs for the option to use enhancements. That is, someone might say that giving the option to use treatments and preventions will destroy the willingness of the healthy to aid the sick who had the option to avoid illness by earlier treatment or prevention but did not, especially when the healthy attribute their own health to their choice to use such earlier interventions. The fact that this is not a successful argument against spreading the option of treatments—presumably because we think many will make use of the treatments and then not need the help of others—should lead us to question its success against enhancements.

Might it be that Sandel also believes that people should be able to call on the assistance of others when they need it, regardless of many individual choices they make? Such a belief might account for the subterfuge of eliminating the possibility of individual choice for enhancement, as a device to sustain a duty to aid. This would be somewhat like the strategy of pretending that one cannot figure out what share of an outcome each person is responsible for producing as a way of ensuring equal shares of a social product. The fact that one seeks such a subterfuge suggests that one simply believes that equal shares are right, regardless of differential input. But it also suggests that one cannot really see how this could be so. One deals with this intellectual conflict by eliminating the factor one is having trouble seeing as not inconsistent with an outcome that one wants.

I think that a good account of the worry that lies behind Sandel's view focuses on a conflict between the right and the good. Here is an analogy that helps make this clearer. From the point of view of considering the good of a person, we may want to be sure that he gets help when he needs it. Suppose someone has the option of declaring himself emancipated. We can see the attraction in this status for him, but if we are concerned about his welfare, we may recommend against it. This is because we take seriously the idea of emancipation as implying that he will have to be self-reliant and can no longer be shielded by his parents from complaints against him. It is not open to us to say, "We care about your good, yet we see the attractions of being emancipated. So, we will combine emancipation with the continued care and protection by a parent when you need it." This would not be taking emancipation as a component of the right seriously; if we take it seriously, we can be constrained from dealing with that to which it leads, even when this is contrary to the good of the person. Hence, one's concern for his good could lead us to urge against emancipation, even though concern for the good is not the only basis for deciding what to do, for we agree that the good may not override a consideration of the right (e.g., emancipation) when the latter is present. Hence, eliminating choice or the ability to determine differential productive input might indicate that one thinks one should take these factors very seriously if they are present, and they would militate against good outcomes. A solution to this quandary is to show that appropriate respect for considerations of the right is often consistent with a duty to help, even when someone has made a choice. (I have focused on this in my previous discussion.) Another solution, to which I now turn, is to show that the good would be overall promoted, even were the duty to help less strong due to choice.

Let us suppose it were true that to some degree, as we increase the range of individual choice, we limit the claim of a person to the assistance of others. (For example, choosing to be or remain paralyzed, given the option of a cure, because one preferred that sort of life might be considered an "expensive taste," and public assistance to make such a life go as well as an unparalyzed life might justifiably be denied.) Does this mean that we will have lost valuable solidarity? If it is appropriate that people who have equal opportunity to choose enhancements but decline to do so bear more responsibility for their condition, then the moral status of solidarity will have changed; it will no longer be the only correct, valuable, and virtuous response that it is in other circumstances.[33] If so, its absence will not necessarily be bad. Furthermore, it is still true that if having the option to enhance leads many people to improve themselves or others, there will be fewer instances of people who are badly off, hence fewer who require

[33] This point was emphasized by Alexander Schwab.

the assistance of others. For example, rather than redistributing wealth that only the talented can produce in a certain environment, each might have a relevant talent and so have the opportunity to be more productive in that environment. Most importantly, each person would not only have the material benefits that can be redistributed from some to others. Each person could have the intrinsic rewards of exercising abilities and talents, something that cannot be *redistributed*.

Let me conclude this section by noting that if Sandel were concerned with the increased burden of responsibility for one's traits and one's children's traits, not at the individual level but at the social level, there would be no way to completely avoid the burden of increased responsibility. For suppose a society or species knows that it could change traits of its members by using or developing genetic or chemical means. Those who decide that the society will not use these means will be to some degree responsible for the absence of enhanced traits. (This is so even if some other individuals will not be responsible because others in the society made it impossible for them to have a choice about use of the means at the individual level.) However, society will be to blame for failures to improve people only if there were no good reasons not to engage in enhancement. Some seem to think that preventing individuals from becoming responsible for individual outcomes could be offered as such a good reason. But can preventing more *social* responsibility for outcomes be offered as a reason, if society already has increased responsibility when it is responsible for denying use or development of enhancement techniques? Possibly this reason would still be available, if a distinction could be drawn between degrees of responsibility, so that there is less social responsibility for genetic traits, if society chose to let chance determine them than if society actually selects the traits.

The primary conclusions of this subsection are that Sandel does not successfully show that we should limit options to enhance ourselves or others as a way of ensuring a right to social assistance.

V. Conclusion

Sandel focuses on the desire for mastery and the unwillingness to live with what we are "given" as objections to enhancement. (He also focuses on the more contingent issue of the misuse of the ability to enhance ourselves and others that is likely to occur in a competitive environment, especially one governed by shallow values.) I have argued that what is most troubling about enhancement is neither that there will be people who desire to have control over nature, offspring, and themselves, nor unwillingness to accept what comes unbidden. However, I do think that there are major problems with enhancement. Some are the ones Sandel puts to one side. Given our scarce resources, where should enhancement be on the list of things to do? Will there be a fair distribution of benefits of enhancement? Could we really safely alter a system as complex as a person (by genetic enhancement or treatment) without making disastrous mistakes? Consider the last point further.

It has been pointed out that in a complex system such as a human being, whose parts are densely interdependent, even small alterations can have unexpected bad effects. Extreme caution, at least, seems called for.[34] Genetic manipulation has been contrasted with surgery or taking drugs in this respect. (Sandel's complaint holds equally against all these means of enhancement, and he deliberately puts to one side issues of differential safety to focus on an objection that he thinks would be present even if there were no safety issues.)

In rebuttal, it might be suggested that genetic changes to individuals that would not affect their offspring could be made no less safe for the individual and the species than use of drugs. For in using drugs or even surgery, one usually thinks that one can, at least often, stop a change and revert to one's original condition if things go badly. If genetic changes could also be reversible, or at least counteractable in some way, then the risk of using them would also be diminished.

Further, it might be pointed out that the dense interdependence of the parts of our system also creates great risks even with therapeutic interventions, so it would be good to know specifically why enhancements present greater potential threats than treatments. And then there is the interdependence of human beings with the rest of the world. Is it possible that treating a defect in individuals that eliminates the normal presence of such defects in the human species would upset some delicate balance

---

[34] M. Coors and L. Hunter, 2005.

between our species and the rest of nature? Would we let this possibility interfere with our search for treatments?

Another issue in enhancing, I think, is that we will be doing it, and so our lack of imagination as designers may raise problems. That is, most people's conception of the varieties of goods is very limited, and if they designed people their improvements would likely conform to limited, predictable types. But we should know that we are constantly surprised at the great range of good traits in people, and the incredible range of combinations of traits that turn out to be good. For example, could we predict that a very particular degree of irony combined with a certain degree of diffidence would constitute an interesting type of personality? In Section IV (A), I mentioned the view that potential parents should focus on having children with basic good properties rather than seek improvements beyond this. Oddly, the "lack of imagination" objection to enhancement I am now voicing is based on a concern that in seeking enhancements people will focus on too simple and basic a set of goods.

How does the lack of imagination objection relate to Sandel's view that an openness to the unbidden (excluding illnesses) extends the range of our sympathies? One construal of his point is that if we have no control, we are forced to understand and care about people, as we should, even when they are difficult and nonideal. By contrast, the lack of imagination objection emphasizes that when creatures of limited imagination do *not* design themselves and others, they are likely to extend the range of their appreciation of great positive goods because the range of such goods is likely to be larger. Fifty years ago, a parent who would have liked to design his child to have the good trait of composing classical music, could not have conceived that it would be good to have a child who turned out to be one of the Beatles. (To have conceived it, would have involved creating the Beatles' style before the Beatles did.) The lack of imagination objection is concerned that too much control will limit the number and combination of goods from what is possible. Hence, at least in those cases where greater goods are more likely to come about if chance rather than unimaginative choice is in control, the desire for enhancement will militate *against* control.

Finally, if the controlled selection of enhanced properties is a morally acceptable means, at least sometimes, what are the good ends to which it could safely be used? Presumably, if it were at all possible, it would be a safe end to enhance our capacities to recognize and fulfill our moral duties, at least if the enhancement involved our appreciating the reasons for these duties and not a purely mechanical response. Recognizing and fulfilling moral duties is a side constraint on the exercise of any other capacities and the pursuit of any ends. There is no point in worrying that having such moral capacities would interfere with unimagined goods. For if such moral capacities interfere with other goods, this just means that those other goods are not morally permissible options for us.

References

Ashcroft, R. E., and Gui, K. 2005. 'Ethics and world pictures in Sandel and Kamm', *The American Journal of Bioethics*, 5(3): 19–20.

Coors, M., and Hunter, L. 2005. 'Evaluation of genetic enhancement: Will human wisdom properly acknowledge the value of evolution?', *The American Journal of Bioethics*, 5(3): 21–2.

Kamm, F. M., 2004. 'Deciding whom to help, health-adjusted life years, and disabilities', in S. Anand, F. Peters, and A. Sen (eds.), *Public Health, Ethics, and Equity* (Oxford: Oxford University Press, 225–42).

Kass, Leon, March 19, 2007. 'Deeper Disquiets with Biotechnological Enhancement'. Presented at Harvard Law School, March 2007.

Liao, S. M., 2005. 'Are "Ex ante" enhancements always permissible?', *The American Journal of Bioethics*, 5(3): 23–5.

Martin, A., and Peerzada, J. 2005. 'Impermissible attitudes, impermissible enhancements', *American Journal of Bioethics*, 5(3): 25–7.

Miller, F., and Brody, H., 2005. 'Professional integrity and enhancement technologies', *American Journal of Bioethics*, 5(3): 15–17.

Nozick, R., 1977. *Anarchy, State and Utopia* (New York: Basic Books).

Robert, J. S., 2005. 'Human dispossession and human enhancement', *American Journal of Bioethics*, 5(3): 27–9.

Sandel, M., 2004. 'The case against perfection', *Atlantic Monthly*, 293(3): 51–62.

Scanlon, T., 2000. 'Intention and permissibility I', *Proceedings of the Aristotelian Society*, Suppl. 74: 301–17.

——— Unpublished article. 'Blame'.

Schwartz, P. H., 2005. 'Defending the distinction between treatment and enhancement', *American Journal of Bioethics*, 5(3): 17–19.

Shiffrin, S., 1999. 'Wrongful life, procreative responsibility, and the significance of harm', *Legal Theory*, 5(2): 117–48.

Strong, C., 2005. 'Lost in translation: Religious arguments made secular', *American Journal of Bioethics*, 5(3): 29–31.

Thomson, J. J., 1990. *The Realm of Rights* (Cambridge, Mass.: Harvard University Press).

—— 1999. 'Physician-assisted suicide: Two moral arguments', *Ethics,* 109(3): 497–518.

6

Enhancements Are a Moral Obligation*

John Harris

If it wasn't good for you it wouldn't be enhancement. In terms of human functioning an enhancement is by definition an improvement on what went before. Not necessarily, as we shall see, an improvement on normal species functioning or species typical functioning, nor are enhancements justified, as many seem to believe, primarily in terms of their contribution to equal opportunities.

There is a continuum between harms and benefits such that the reasons we have to avoid harming others or creating others who will be born in a harmed state are continuous with the reasons we have for conferring benefits on others if we can.[1] In short, to decide to withhold a benefit is in a sense to harm the individual we decline to benefit. We have reasons for declining to create or confer even trivial harms, and we have reasons to confer and not withhold even small benefits.[2]

The opportunity to create healthier, longer lived and altogether 'better' individuals is one that there are moral reasons to take. To say that, is to say that parents would act ethically if they attempt to achieve such an objective for their children for example, and those of us who are autonomous enough to consider such questions, have good reasons to confer such benefits on

* This chapter follows closely lines developed in John Harris, 2007, *Enhancing Evelolution* (Princeton and Oxford: Princeton University Press). I am grateful to Princeton University Press for their indulgence in my use of these ideas here.

[1] See John Harris, *Wonderwomnan and Superman: The Ethics and Human Biotechnology* (Oxford: Oxford University Press, 1992), and "Is there a coherent social conception of disability?", in *Journal Of Medical Ethics*, vol. 26: 2, April 2000, 95–101.

[2] An extended argument for these assertions was given in John Harris, *Violence and Responsibility* (London: Routledge & Kegan Paul, 1980).

ourselves.[3] As with all opportunities, we have also to consider the risks that they may entail and there is of course a relation between the magnitude and probability of the benefit and the degree and size of risk we are prepared to run to get it. So far so familiar.

Enhancements are so obviously good for us (if they weren't they wouldn't be enhancements) that it is odd that the idea of enhancement has caused and still occasions so much suspicion, fear, and outright hostility. In particular, two influential sets of arguments by philosophers who do not in principle oppose enhancements, have nonetheless placed constraints on the legitimacy of using enhancement techniques either in terms of the motivation or the objectives to be achieved on the one hand or on the tests that enhancements have to meet on the other, which constrain enhancements in ways that seem hard to justify.

In Part I of this chapter I will consider briefly some arguments often adduced against enhancements. The brevity is justified by the weakness of the arguments and the familiarity of the objections to them. In Part II, I will reconsider three essays on enhancement, two of which seem to place unsustainable constraints on the use of enhancement technology, and use these as a way of trying to state clearly what the justifications for enhancements are.

Part I

The Precautionary principle

Discussions of the ethics of genetic manipulation or of human reproductive cloning are bedevilled by appeals to the sanctity of the human gene pool or to the importance of preserving the genetic inheritance of human-kind. UNESCO's International Bioethics Committee (IBC), for example, reflecting on the ethics of scientific progress, has maintained that "the human genome must be preserved as common heritage of humanity."[4] This clearly involves an appeal to the widely accepted but none the less

---

[3] John Harris, "One principle and three fallacies of disability studies", in *Journal of Medical Ethics*, vol. 27: 6, December 2001, 383–8.
[4] UNESCO Press Release No. 97-29. See also UNESCO, *Universal Declaration on the Human Genome and Human Rights*, published by UNESCO December 3, 1997.

incoherent Precautionary Principle.[5] The idea is that human evolution, which is responsible for the "human genome . . . as the common heritage of humanity", has done well for us and is likely to continue to do well for us. Therefore in the absence of reliable data, any proposed changes are to be considered of uncertain consequence and presumed disastrous. A more moderate version of the precautionary principle simply stipulates that dangers are to be considered more probable and of greater magnitude than benefits. The Precautionary Principle therefore requires that we leave well alone.

A number of questionable assumptions are involved here. The first is that our present point in evolution is unambiguously good and not susceptible of improvement. Secondly, it is assumed that the course of evolution, if left alone, will continue to improve things for humankind or at least not make them worse. The incompatibility of these two assumptions is seldom noticed. However, the common heritage of humanity is a result of evolutionary change. Unless we can compare the future progress of evolution uncontaminated by manipulation of the human genome with its progress influenced by any proposed genetic manipulations, we cannot know which would be best and hence where precaution lies.[6] Put more prosaically, it is unclear why a precautionary approach should apply only to proposed changes rather than to the status quo. In the absence of reliable predictive knowledge as to how dangerous leaving things alone may prove, we have no rational basis for a precautionary approach which prioritizes the status quo.

Playing God

Another commonly held objection to deliberate interventions in the human genome or in evolution is the idea that the human genome and Darwinian evolution are "natural phenomena or processes", and that there is some sort of natural priority of the natural over the artificial. This is often coupled

[5] In this section I draw on: John Harris and Søren Holm, "Extended lifespan and the paradox of precaution", in *The Journal of Medicine and Philosophy*, vol. 27: 3, 2002, 355–69. In this paper we detail the incoherence to which I refer.

[6] While some maintain that human evolution of the Darwinian sort is at an end because most humans now survive long enough to reproduce, this view overlooks the role of parasites in evolution. It also of course ignores our deliberate interventions in the evolutionary process.

with an argument from superstition; that it is tempting fate or divine wrath to play God and intervene in the natural order.

These suggestions are superstitious, fallacious or, more usually, both. If it were wrong to interfere with nature we could not, among many other things, practice medicine. People naturally fall ill, are invaded by bacteria, parasites, viruses or cancers and naturally die prematurely. Medicine can be described as "the comprehensive attempt to frustrate the course of nature"[7]. There is undoubtedly a widespread, but equally undoubtedly an irrational, respect for what is natural or part of the course of nature. Famines, floods, droughts, storms are all natural and all disastrous. We only, and rightly, want the natural when it's good for us. What is natural is morally inert and progress-dependent. It was only natural for people to die of infected wounds before antibiotics were available or of smallpox and polio before effective vaccines.

Thomas Hobbes famously took a more realistic view of nature, describing life in a state of nature thus:

. . . and which is worst of all, continual fear, and danger of violent death; and the life of man, solitary, poor, nasty, brutish and short.[8]

Cloning and preserving the human genome as the common heritage of mankind

We have noted that some, including some who speak for UNESCO regard "the preservation of the human genome as common heritage of humanity" as an important moral duty. However, if the preservation of the human genome were really a rational goal we would have to abjure sexual reproduction which involves a random recombination of genes to form a new genetic constitution at each "throw of the dice".[9] Normal sexual reproduction does not preserve the human genome, rather it almost always varies it, the exception being monozygotic twinning which produces

---

[7] See John Harris, *The Value of Life* (London: Routledge, 1980).

[8] Thomas Hobbes, *Leviathan*, ed. Michael Oakeshot (Oxford: Basil Blackwell, 1960), p. 82. Julian Savulescu and I made similar points in our Julian Savulescu and John Harris, "The Creation Lottery: Final Lessons from Natural Reproduction: Why those who accept natural reproduction should accept cloning and other Frankenstein reproductive technologies", *Cambridge Quarterly of Healthcare Ethics*, vol 13: 1, January 2004, 90–6.

[9] The mixed metaphor is in the interests of propriety and therefore, I trust, excusable.

clones. If *preservation* were the issue however, cloning on a universal scale would be the best way to achieve that (clearly dubious) objective. Only if all future reproduction were by cloning (monozygotic or identical twinning) or somatic cell nuclear transfer would the human genome be "preserved" intact.[10] UNESCO, with characteristic clarity of thought and of purpose, therefore wants to characterize cloning simultaneously as the only or at least the clearest case of acting contrary to human dignity[11] and at the same time oppose cloning on the grounds that it is essential to preserve the human genome, failing to notice that in fact cloning is the only reproductive path that can preserve the human genome.

Part II

I want now to look at two important essays that discuss enhancement in some depth. In doing so I will look again at a now rather antique discussion of enhancement in my own book *Wonderwoman and Superman*, first published in 1992.

The essays, by two of the most interesting writers on these themes, are by Norman Daniels, in this volume, and Alan Buchanan, taken from part of the book *From Chance to Choice* by Alan Buchanan, Dan Brock, Norman Daniels, and Dan Wikler. Much of what I want to say is critical of the approach taken in these two essays but they constitute icebergs in the ocean of discussions of enhancement. They must be negotiated in one way or another if we are to proceed.

In *Wonderwoman and Superman*, I was concerned with the ethics of changing for the better both the genetic constitution of the individual and changing people on a scale that would affect both society and the world at large, and with the question of what "change for the better" means. Society-wide changes are now often framed in terms of changes to populations. I argued that if the gains were important enough (sufficiently beneficial) and the risks acceptable, we would want to make the relevant alterations and be justified in so doing; indeed that we would have an obligation to make such changes. The ethical question seems still to be the same as then

---

[10] See John Harris, *On Cloning* (London: Routledge, 2004), ch. 2.
[11] *The Universal Declaration on the Human Genome and Human Rights*, published by UNESCO as a pamphlet December 3, 1997.

envisaged, and whether any proposed changes amount to changes in human nature, or to involve further evolution, seem ethically uninteresting. In particular whether the enhancements might be judged to involve creating a new species, "a new breed", or amount to "self-evolution", or "post humanism" are semantic rather than moral issues. In recent literature a distinction has often been drawn between the supposed moral significance of changes to the germ line and changes to the somatic line—that is between changes that involve the gametes and so are transmissible via reproduction to future generations and those which, because they do not affect the gametes, remain one-off changes to the individual him or herself. Changes to the germ line once demonstrated to be safe enough are merely issues of efficiency. If the change is important enough to make in the individual then, if it can be made on the germ line and passed on indefinitely to future generations, that simply avoids the necessity of a separate alteration to each and every future generation.

Daniels has reminded us that the high safety standards routinely now applied to human subject research will often rule out enhancements, whereas Alan Buchanan has suggested that the motive for all enhancement therapy must be, or at least include, the pursuit of equal opportunities. If the ethics of changing human nature or changing the nature of individuals (creating freaks as Daniels calls this) is principally a matter of cost/benefit analysis, safety versus advantage, then the question as to what an appropriate safety standard might look like becomes crucial. This is one of Daniels' main themes so we will start with Daniels' stimulating and fruitful analysis of what might be meant by changing human nature.

Daniels and the fruit fly

*To summarize the lessons from my excursion into fruit fly nature: fruit fly nature is a **population** concept: to characterize the nature of fruit flies we must aggregate phenotypic variations across allelic variations among fruit flies. It is a **dispositional** concept, since the phenotypic traits we take to be the "nature" of fruit flies vary within some range under different conditions. Finally it is a **selective**, theory-laden concept: not every trait of fruit flies is likely to be considered part of their nature, but only those that we use to explain something of importance to us about them. Putting these points together, the concept of fruit fly nature applies to what we consider the central explanatory features of the **phenotype** fruit flies manifest under some range of conditions . . .*

So we can modify human nature, but it takes a very tall tale. We must affect the (or at least a) whole population of humans, and we must do so with a trait central to that nature.

Still, what the modification does at most is change the particular individual's nature into something beyond human.... By itself, this does not alter human nature. It creates freaks. If it operated on a population level, we might well, as we have seen, count it as a change in human nature. A world full of mind readers instead of liars would be one in which we would not encounter human nature as we know it. Not many traits fit this description, I suspect.[12]

Daniels then is rightly sceptical about the idea that most changes about which people worry can in a meaningful sense be thought of as changes to "human nature". He thinks, surely correctly, that for most likely changes this is the wrong question to ask or a misleading specification of the task. He concedes that we can change the nature of some humans (if not human nature) creating the equivalent of freaks. However while we may have justifiable motives for running the inherent risks in order to ameliorate dysfunction Daniels believes we do not have such justification for improving upon "an otherwise normal trait".

For example, if we are trying to ameliorate or eliminate a serious genetic disease, or disease for which there may be some genetic or other medical remedy, the probability of potential benefit from the experimental intervention, may plausibly outweigh the certainty of catastrophic illness. But if we are trying to improve on an otherwise normal trait, the risks of a bad outcome, even if small, outweigh the acceptable outcome of normality. So we cannot ethically get there from here. I believe this argument has great force.

Talking of a cognitive trait, improvement in short-term memory loss, Daniels says:

We would have to know that the increased short-term memory involved here actually plays a role in enhancing the more complex cognitive task rather than ..., interfering with it.... Without some clear sense of these complex issues, we could not have any confidence that improving the component capability has the intended or desired effect on the more complex one. And all of this information goes well beyond the standard worry that the intervention itself carries with it risks that non-interference lacks. In short, a careful human research protocol would most likely stop this experiment in its tracks.

---

[12] From Norman Daniels, "Can anyone really be talking about ethically modifying human nature?" Norman Daniels believes the concept of human nature is problematic in ways that can be elucidated by reference to the fruit fly.

Daniels notes that in some fields (he cites plastic surgery) surgeons routinely experiment by modifying techniques "on the hoof" but he seems to feel that:

our incomplete adherence to appropriate patient-protection concerns should not count as an argument in favor of ignoring them in the case of medical—genetic or not—interventions to improve on human cognitive or behavioral traits.

It is also difficult to know whether the caution that Daniels regards as mandatory is better founded than that of UNESCO already considered. It is also unclear whether Daniels' precautionary approach is intended to apply only to cognitive and behavioural traits or whether he would also include enhancements to achieve longevity, or resistance to disease. These may all involve the same degree of "incomplete adherence to patient protection concerns", and "the standard worry that the intervention itself carries with it risks that non-interference lacks". With the result that "a careful human research protocol would most likely stop" experiments like this in their tracks.

These arguments illuminate the ethics of enhancement in important ways. In my *Wonderwoman and Superman: The Ethics of Human Biotechnology*[13] I considered many of these issues in some detail. When these passages were written, the probable technologies were not exactly those envisaged today. In particular I imagined the following scenario:

It is time to take further the resolution of problems associated with the idea of improving human beings. We'll suppose the possibility of introducing genes coding for antibodies to major infections, or, coding for repair enzymes which would correct the most frequently occurring defects caused by radiation damage, or which might remove pre-dispositions to heart disease, or which would destroy carcinogens or maybe permit human beings to tolerate other environmental pollutants. These techniques will also eventually enable us to insert genes which could repair DNA and have the effect of retarding the ageing process.

In Chapter VII we examined the problems associated with doing this either via hybridization or in a way which changed human nature. Our concerns then were in a sense personal. We were worried about the effect this would have on the individuals themselves. We must now think more in terms of the effects on society and indeed on the world at large. . . .

In the case of genes coded for antibodies to major infections, the effect would be that a new gene or genes would be inserted into the human genome which would effectively "immunise"

---

[13] *Wonderwoman and Superman: The Ethics of Human Biotechnology* (Oxford: Oxford University Press, 1992). I quote from ch. 9.

the individual against the infection in question. We will imagine that the infections include AIDS, malaria, and hepatitis B. It is likely that the gene would have to be inserted in the early embryo before implantation . . . However, it is possible that the gene could be inserted surgically, or via a catheter inserted into the fallopian tube via the uterus, but this would presuppose very early detection of pregnancy. Another possibility might be to insert the gene at the gametes stage by operating either on the egg or on the sperm prior to fertilization . . .

Individuals whose genome had been genetically modified in this way would become what might reasonably be termed a "new breed". This term, while doubtless controversial, is I think fair because the modified individuals would indeed be both "new" and a "breed", first in the sense that they would have what is an entirely new and unprecedented genetic constitution and also in the sense that their genetic constitution would differ systematically from other human individuals. Their claim to be a breed, though of course they might not themselves wish to make any of these claims, rests clearly but decisively on the fact that they could pass on this new constitution by normal reproduction with other members of the same "breed".[14]

In 1990 the word "breed" had a resonance that is now partially lost. If I had penned these passages today, I would probably have "processed" them and might well have followed some others in talking of "human nature", "post humanism" and, I might even have referred to "populations" rather than to effects on "society and the world at large", but the points are essentially the same. However I would still conclude the argument as I then did, on an optimistic note about the prospects and the desirability of enhancements:

For my own part I welcome the possibility of a new breed of persons with life chances not available to us now. Of course engineering genetic protections of various kinds into the human genome will not automatically make the world a better place to live in, nor will it necessarily make people happier. We will still have to work as hard as ever to reduce disease, new diseases are after all always liable to arise. We will still have to work as hard as ever to reduce prejudice, including prejudice against the new breed, to combat injustice, to eliminate poverty, starvation, cruelty and the thousand unnatural shocks that flesh is heir to; as well as the natural ones.[15]

---

[14] I have deleted unnecessary footnotes from this quotation, but the following is perhaps worth bearing in mind: "Of course members of the New Breed could pass on their genetic constitution with its advantages even if they do not procreate with other breed members. In subsequent generations 50% of children of any 'outbreeding' carrier would always inherit. Therefore, even if the individual did not breed within the carrier group transmission and spread of the gene and its effects would be fairly wide (assuming of course as we do, that the gene is able to be expressed in the homozygous condition). However, and I owe this suggestion to Susan Kimber, it would not be satisfactory from the parents' point of view to know that only half their children (statistically) will be likely to benefit from the new technology. It would also open up interesting and perhaps serious inter-sibling problems."

[15] Ibid.

But the fact that we cannot cure everything has never been an argument for failing to cure something, particularly when it is something that causes pain, misery and premature death.

Let me bring these possibilities up to date; consider the following three scenarios:

1. Suppose there are some infectious diseases we can eliminate by operating on the environment. We can, we shall suppose, kill airborne infectious agents by introducing into the atmosphere a substance harmless to flora and fauna but lethal only to the target infectious agent, whether a bacterium or a virus. If we could be satisfied that the atmospheric additive was harmless to everything but the target virus, bacteria or whatever, we would surely welcome such a discovery. Everything speaks for it and nothing against. Such an intervention would not however be an enhancement technology; it would not change human beings in any way. Rather it would have the effect of rendering them safe from, if not immune to, these infections.

2. Now suppose we could eliminate the same infectious diseases by the use of effective vaccines in the way we have succeeded in doing with polio and smallpox. Presumably we would welcome this as a wonderful and effective public health measure, which saved lives, saved money, and minimized suffering and distress. Everything speaks for it and nothing against. Vaccination is of course an enhancement technology and one that has been long accepted (since smallpox vaccine was first used in the middle of the eighteenth century). Interestingly there has been very little resistance to this form of enhancement.

3. A number of the world's leading laboratories are currently working on radical therapies which would also constitute enhancements. For example David Baltimore's lab at Caltech is working on the possibility of engineering resistance or possibly immunity to HIV/AIDS and cancer into cells.[16] The benefits of this and related work around the world are incalculable. Whatever else they were they would also constitute radical enhancement since, alas, immunity to HIV/AIDS

---

[16] Baltimore, D., 2003. Using stem cells as targets for gene therapy approaches. *First International Congress of Stem Cell Research, Singapore*, conference presentation.

or cancer is not part of "normal species functioning" or "species typical functioning" for our species. Other groups[17] are working on life-extending therapies using a combination of stem cell research and other research in the ways that cells age to both regenerate ageing or diseased tissue and to switch off the ageing process in cells. Again to live several hundred years and perhaps eventually to become "immortal" is no part of normal species functioning for our species.

Curing dysfunction and enhancing function

It is traditional to draw a distinction between repairing or curing dysfunction on the one hand and enhancing function on the other. Those who, like Boorse, Daniels,[18] and others define disease in terms of a departure from normal species functioning or species-typical functioning are often drawn to this distinction because for them enhancement is also a departure from normal species functioning and species-typical functioning. Repairing dysfunction is on this view restoring species-typical functioning from below so to speak, whereas enhancement is departing from species-typical functioning in an upward trajectory. On this view treating disease is restoring species-typical functioning whereas enhancement is interrupting species-typical functioning. However, it is of course always true that restoring species-typical functioning is enhancing for the individual concerned unless they are functioning above par and the restoration is injurious or damaging to them. Most of what passes for therapy is an enhancement for the individual relative to her state prior to therapy.

[17] Bodnar, A. G., Ouellette, M., Frolkis, M., Holt, S. E., Chiu, C. P., Morin, G. B., Harley, C. B., Shay, J. W., Lichtsteiner, S., Wright, W. E., 1998, "Extension of life-span by introduction of telomerase into normal human cells", *Science* 279, 5349: 349–52. Weinrich, S. L., Pruzan, R., Ma., L. B., Ouellette, M., Tesmer, V. M., Holt, S. E., Bodnar, A. G., Lichtsteiner, S., Kim, N. W., Trager, J. B., Taylor, R. D., Carlos, R., Andrews, W. H., Wright, W. E., Shay, J. W., Harley, C. B., Morin, G. B., 1997, "Reconstitution of human telomerase with the template RNA component hTR and the catalytic protein subunit hTRT", *Nature Genetics* 17, 4: 498–502. McBrearty, B. A., Clark, L. D., Zhang, X. M., Blankenhorn, E. P., Heber-Katz, E., 1998, "Genetic analysis of a mammalian wound-healing trait", *Proceedings Of The National Academy Of Sciences Of The United States Of America*, vol. 95: 20, 11792–7. For a comprehensive round-up of related work see de Grey, A. D. N. J. (ed.), "Strategies for Engineered Negligible Senescence: Why Genuine Control of Aging May Be Foreseeable", *Annals NY Acad. Sci.*, vol. 1019, 2004.

[18] Boorse, C., 1981, "On the distinction between disease and illness", in Cohen, M., Nagel, T., and Scanlon, T., *Medicine and Moral Philosophy* (Princeton, N. J.: Princeton University Press). Daniels, N., 1985, *Just Health Care* (Cambridge: Cambridge University Press). Daniels, N., 1996, *Justice and Justification* (Cambridge: Cambridge University Press), 185.

One problem for this distinction arises because the very same therapies, which for some might help restore normal, or as I would prefer to characterize it, "better or more adequate" functioning, may for others be radically enhancing. Regenerative stem-cell treatments for people with brain damage would clearly be therapy. The same treatment in those with normal or undamaged brains might however enhance brain function, likewise treatment for memory loss in damaged brains might enhance memory in normal brains.

Elsewhere I have criticized the therapy/enhancement distinction:

Suppose due to further depletions to the ozone layer, all white skinned people were very vulnerable to skin cancers on even slight exposure to the sun, but brown and black-skinned people were immune. We might then regard whites as suffering substantial disabilities relative to their darker-skinned fellows. And if skin pigmentation could be easily altered, failure to make the alterations would be disabling. . . . in such circumstances whites might have disabilities relative to blacks even though their functioning was quite species-typical or normal.[19]

We do not die of old age but of the diseases of old age.[20] It is species-typical of us to die of these as we normally do, but it is not necessarily necessary that we do. If we could systematically treat these diseases in a way that enabled tissue to regenerate (using stem-cell therapy perhaps) and at the same time switch off the ageing process in cells, this too would be enhancing, but it would be another case when treating disease in particular ways that also constituted an enhancement therapy. Systematically treating the diseases of old age with the result that people lived substantially longer, to the extent perhaps that some would even become immortal, would appear to constitute both therapy and enhancement. This however is only because treating disease seems typical of therapy not because normal species functioning does or can play any role at all in the argument.

However, as Boorse and Daniels define disease, treating the diseases of old age would not be therapeutic (indeed the diseases of old age would not be diseases) in any sense because diseases of old age are species-typical (or

---

[19] See my "One principle and three fallacies of disability studies", *Journal of Medical Ethics*, vol. 27: 6, 2001.

[20] John Harris, "Intimations of Immortality", in *Science*, vol. 288: 5463: 59, April 7, 2000, and John Harris, "Immortal Ethics", in de Grey, A. D. N. J. (ed.), "Strategies for Engineered Negligible Senescence: Why Genuine Control of Aging May Be Foreseeable", *Annals NY Acad. Sci.*, vol. 1019, 2004.

of course constitute normal species functioning) and it is species-typical, and a part of normal functioning that we cease to function in old age and that we die.

Of course in view of these examples those who wished to cling to the therapy/enhancement distinction could simply say "yes, therapy and enhancement sometimes amount to the same thing but not always." But now consider that routine therapies, vaccination for example, are enhancement technologies and the moral significance of the distinction as well as its utility collapses. It does not draw either a morally significant or an explanatorily significant distinction and so fails utterly to be useful. We will shortly return to the question of what is a morally relevant distinction in this field.

This forces a reconsideration of the distinction between therapy and enhancement and a reconsideration of the question of our motives for and the justification of our interference in the natural lottery of life. Here it is fruitful to look at Alan Buchanan's attempts to grapple with this.

Our commitment to intervene in the natural lottery of life

In one of the most famous and influential philosophical books on this subject, Allen Buchanan has argued that the motive we have for intervening to treat or cure disability, and the same would presumably go for the treatment of disease, is "for the sake of equal opportunity". He says "... some of our most basic social institutions reflect a commitment to intervening in the natural lottery for the sake of equal opportunity".[21] To be sure, Buchanan's main concern is to show how the concept of equality of opportunity requires extension to embrace what Scanlon and others have termed a "brute bad luck" conception of equal opportunity—a conception which believes in intervening to mitigate disadvantaging factors which are beyond the control of the subject of those factors.[22] This is a constantly repeated, but not universal, gloss on the moral reasons Buchanan gives for therapeutic or even enhancing interventions. Again: "In other words, equal

---

[21] Buchanan, A., Brock, D., Daniels, N., and Wikler, D., 2000, *From Chance to Choice* (Cambridge: Cambridge University Press), ch. 3, 71.

[22] Scanlon, T., 1989, "A Good Start: Reply to Roemer", *Boston Review* 20, 2: 819.

opportunity has to do with ensuring fair competition for those who are able to compete *and* with preventing or curing disease that hinders people from developing the abilities that would allow them to compete".[23] Buchanan et al. are self-consciously following Daniels and Rawls here. "As Norman Daniels has argued, the case for a moral right to health care relies, at least in part, on the fact that health care promotes equal opportunity."[24] Here the move from simply extending a conception of equality of opportunity to confirming that conception as an important part of the moral right to health care becomes clearer. It is this idea, the idea that the moral reasons we have for pursuing health or for enhancing the functioning of human beings, in short, our "commitment to intervening in the natural lottery" of life has much to do with equal opportunity, or the "ability to compete" that is genuinely bizarre.

Of course equality of opportunity is something we should try to maximize in the delivery of improvements in health or in functioning, but it seems only tenuously and contingently connected with our moral reasons for so doing. Suppose there was a painful condition that affected some people but not others. It did not however affect people's ability to compete or affect the pursuit of opportunities. I believe we would have exactly the same compassionate motive and moral reasons for intervening in the natural lottery to remove this condition as we would have if it was also "competition affecting". This latter factor seems to add nothing to our moral reasons for alleviating the condition.

Of course the reverse is also true. Where a feature frustrates equal opportunity, that fact also provides a sufficient and complete moral justification for trying to remove it. What it does not do is provide a necessary justification. The commitment to intervene in the so called "natural lottery" would (or should) surely be compelling quite independently of any contribution it makes to equal opportunity, although, as I have indicated, in pursuing health and/or enhancement for the good reasons we have for so doing, we should attempt to ensure equal opportunity to access such goods. But the claim that "the case for a moral right to health care relies, at least in part, on the fact that health care promotes equal opportunity" seems false. Equal opportunity might in some circumstances be a further additional reason to support the moral right to health care, or of course a separate

---

[23] Buchanan et al., op. cit. 74.   [24] Ibid., 73.

one, but to regard equal opportunity as an essential part of the moral basis for such a right or indeed the moral motivation for establishing such a right is doubtful. I have argued elsewhere[25] that where the provision of health care will prevent harm to human beings, the moral argument for delivering that care is as complete as it needs to be. Equal opportunity can say something about selecting who to help in conditions of scarcity, but it seems an inappropriate candidate for a factor which might have any priority in explaining or justifying "a commitment to intervening in the natural lottery".

Suppose now all people were affected by a debilitating condition so that there was no *inequality* of opportunity, but, *inter alia*, the opportunities for all were reduced. The unnecessarily reduced opportunity would itself constitute sufficient moral reason for "intervening in the natural lottery", not for the sake of equal opportunity (nor surely for the sake of competition), but for the sake of enhanced opportunity or enhanced functioning. Equally if, as we discussed when considering enhancement, a new protective treatment were to be developed then, even though before implementing it all would be equally disadvantaged by not having the treatment, the moral imperative to introduce it would not refer to equal opportunity at all and that case would not be enhanced by any such appeal.

Buchanan et al.[26] note that: "It is possible, however, that some natural inequalities are not departures from normal species functioning,[27] but nonetheless so seriously limit an individual's opportunities that he or she is precluded from reaching the threshold of normal competition. In such cases, genetic intervention might be required if it were necessary to remove this barrier to opportunity." Anticipating the question as to the precise circumstances in which this might be true Buchanan et al. answer: "Whether it does will depend on what the normal distribution of various characteristics is and how that relates to the most fundamental requirements for successful participation in social cooperation in a given society."[28] It seems implausible to think that either normal species functioning or successful social cooperation are the key ideas that

---

[25] *The Value of Life* (London: Routledge, 1985) and *Violence and Responsibility* (London: Routledge & Kegan Paul, 1980).

[26] Op. cit., 74.

[27] This way of defining health and illness is derived from Boorse (1981) but is used also by Daniels (1996, 185) and many others.

[28] Op. cit., 75.

licence interference in the natural lottery of life, and it is not hard to see why.

Consider again the enhancement technologies we discussed earlier: those involving engineering resistance to HIV and cancer into cells, or enhancing the life expectancy of human beings. These two sets of possibilities would be radically enhancing to the extent that if we manage to find ways to make such changes permanent, to insert them into the germ line for example, "we" might no longer be human, we would perhaps have evolved into a new distinct species. Whatever one thinks of these prospects, it is parochial in the extreme to imagine that our ethical response to them would depend on whether or not the failure to introduce these possibilities would "so seriously limit an individual's opportunities that he or she is precluded from reaching the threshold of normal competition". We have to ask, what is the motive to introduce these and other new therapies in the first place? It cannot be to restore normal species functioning because immunity to cancer is not part of this. Nor would we plausibly want to make people immune to cancer in order to help people reach "the threshold of normal competition". Normal competition and normal species functioning do not constitute reasons for considering the introduction of these and many other new therapies or enhancements. Nor could the idea of equal opportunity help us here, opportunity perhaps, but not equal opportunity.

Consider twin sisters both of whom suffer from cancer. One is curable, the other not. We do not think that equal opportunity requires us to leave the curable twin untreated because we cannot treat both. And our moral motive and reason for treating the curable twin has nothing to do with equality. It has everything to do with saving a life that can be saved or alleviating pain, suffering, and distress when presented with an opportunity so to do.

The moral imperative for David Baltimore's work, for example, is that it is required for what Hobbes referred to as "the safety of the people"[29] and for what others have called "beneficence or non malificence", or welfare. These are imperatives quite independent of their impact on or compatibility with equal opportunities or equal justice. A moment's reflection shows why this must be so. There is a vast shortfall in the availability of donor

---

[29] "*The office of the sovereign, be it a monarch or an assembly, consisteth in the end for which he was trusted with the sovereign power, namely the procuration of the safety of the people; to which he is obliged by the law of nature...*" Hobbes, 1960, 30: 1.

organs for transplantation in the world, certainly in the United States and in the United Kingdom. While we cannot treat all who need life saving transplants, we treat as many as we can and we do so because to fail to do so would cost lives. We do not say we will perform no transplants at all unless and until we can secure equal access to transplants for all those who need them. Hopefully we allocate access to those organs that become available in ways that are consistent with equal opportunity; but the reason why we save lives in this way is not to secure equal opportunity or to secure access to "normal competition".

What is clear is that the moral motive for using technology to intervene in the natural lottery of life is for the sake of the goods that this will bring about. Equality of opportunity may sometimes be one of these goods. More usually it will be a constraint on the way the goods may be achieved legitimately. Saving lives or what is the same thing, postponing death, removing or preventing disability or disease or enhancing human functioning are the more obvious and usually the more pressing reasons. These are the primary reasons we have to prevent or mitigate disability and to treat or cure disease.

Daniels and the limits to enhancement

In view of the moral imperatives that underlie enhancement just identified, Daniels' precautionary approach fails in its prime protective function. Consider again Daniels' argument for precaution:

For example, if we are trying to ameliorate or eliminate a serious genetic disease, or disease for which there may be some genetic or other medical remedy, the probability of potential benefit from the experimental intervention, may plausibly outweigh the certainty of catastrophic illness. But if we are trying to improve on an otherwise normal trait, the risks of a bad outcome, even if small, outweigh the acceptable outcome of normality. So we cannot ethically get there from here. I believe this argument has great force.

Daniels' argument here has two essential elements. In the first he suggests that the benefits of intervening in the natural lottery may outweigh the risks where there is a "certainty of catastrophic illness" as the alternative. It is important here to be clear as to whether the certainty of illness is statistical or personal. For example where we seek to engineer immunity to HIV/AIDS into the genes of future people there is no certainty that any individual will be exposed to HIV, let alone contract it, but the risk to individuals and to populations is such that the lack of certainty in any particular case seems irrelevant to the justification of taking the requisite risk. Of course the degree and magnitude of risks that might be worth taking to protect ourselves from major diseases are importantly relevant, but the assessment of these seems not to depend upon the certainty of contracting the disease in question. The same was true of vaccination for smallpox, polio, and other diseases. This is a case where there may be no direct benefit to the subject of the research or therapeutic procedure but where the procedures are justified by their expected benefits to society or to populations and to the interests of the subject more broadly conceived.[30]

This of course challenges some of the standard elements of the international conventions that purport to govern research. For example, when Daniels notes above that "a careful human research protocol would most likely stop this experiment in its tracks", examples might be those which follow paragraph 5 of The Declaration of Helsinki which notes: "In medical research on human subjects, considerations related to the well-being of the human subject should take precedence over the interests of science and society."[31] However the coherence of this provision is challengeable and depends crucially on how narrowly the interests of the subject are conceived.[32]

The second element to Daniels' argument places great weight on the idea that if we are "trying to improve upon an otherwise normal trait the risks of a bad outcome, even if small, outweigh the acceptable outcome of normality". It is not clear here what Daniels thinks the link is between the normality of a trait and the acceptability of the outcome. He seems to imply that normal traits are of themselves acceptable, perhaps because he thinks that disease is always a departure from the normal and hence that normality is a disease-free state. But as we have seen disease and unnecessary death are hideously normal, and although they impair normal functioning at some stages of life they do not do so in old age when it is normal to succumb to them.

[30] See John Harris, "Ethical genetic research", in *Jurimetrics: The Journal of Law, Science, and Policy*, Fall 1999 issue (vol. 40: 1), 77–92, and John Harris, "Scientific Research is a Moral Duty", in *Journal of Medical Ethics*, vol. 32: 4, April 2005.

[31] The World Medical Association Declaration of Helsinki, adopted by the 52nd General Assembly, Edinburgh, Scotland, October 2000. With the note of clarification of paragraph 29 added by the WMA General Assembly, Washington 2002.

[32] See Harris, "Scientific Research is a Moral Duty".

Clearly if we are trying to improve upon an otherwise acceptable trait then small risks may not be worth running. The problem even with this formulation is that awareness of the possibility of improvement is likely to affect the acceptability of a trait. Short sightedness at a certain age is normal and was perhaps acceptable before spectacles; and the pains of childbirth were thought not only acceptable but mandatory even after the advent of effective analgesia, they were certainly perfectly normal species functioning.

Increases in life expectancy are an even clearer case. It is certainly not normal for humans to live beyond 100 years and so far as we know no one has yet lived beyond about 122 years (although many believe it probable that the first 150-year-old person is already alive and some serious scientists believe the first 1000-year-old person is already alive.[33] Dying of old age is acceptable[34] only because it is regarded as inevitable. Absent the inevitability, the acceptability is problematic. We can, perhaps somewhat artificially, try to separate dying of old age and dying of the diseases of old age. We have noted that dying of the diseases of old age is normal, but perhaps if we were able combine regenerative treatments of the diseases of old age with the ability to switch off the ageing process in cells, even longer and healthier life-expectancy might be achieved. This would even more clearly have little to do with normal functioning and yet this fact seems of little help in thinking about either the ethics or the desirability of such enhancements, let alone about the question of what risks it might be worth running to achieve them.[35] If we are trying to improve on an otherwise normal trait, like old age, it seems implausible simply to assume or to stipulate that "the risks of a bad outcome, even if small, outweigh the acceptable outcome of normality".

The normality of the trait in question is clearly doing no work at all in the assessment of its moral acceptability or of the risks it might be worth running to change things. If we subtract the acceptability from the normality, we are left with nothing of moral nor of argumentative force.

---

[33] This is the view of Aubrey de Grey in a personal communication March 21, 2005. See also de Grey A. D. N. J., "Escape velocity: why the prospect of extreme human life extension matters now", *PLoS Biol.* 2(6), 2004, 723–6, in which he speculated that "the first 1000-year-old is probably only 5 to 10 years younger than the first 150-year-old".

[34] To those to whom it is acceptable.

[35] I have discussed some of these questions in my "Intimations of Immortality" in *Science*, vol. 288: 5463, 59, April 7, 2000, and in my similarly titled but fuller treatment, "Intimations of Immortality—The ethics and justice of life extending therapies", in Michael Freeman (ed.), *Current Legal Problems* (Oxford: Oxford University Press, 2002), 65–95.

Traits in short are not acceptable (in the normative rather than of course the simply descriptive sense of "acceptable") because they are normal, they are acceptable because they are worth having. If they are not worth having, or if they are worth not having, their normality seems bereft of interest or force. This it seems to me obviously applies to saving life, that is to postponing death or to increases in longevity, resistance to the diseases of old age and to those which strike at any time like HIV, cancer, and heart disease. Whether it also applies to enhancements in cognitive function like memory or other processing skills, or to personality, is more problematic only in so far as the benefits are more problematic in many ways. There seems to be no difference in principle here and so no difference in the relevant ethical considerations.

When Daniels says, "we cannot ethically get there from here" this seems doubtful; and I am unclear as to why he believes "this argument has great force". The problem seems to be an unjustified assumption that normal traits are acceptable by reason of their normality and that the risks of new "treatments" are justifiable only when the alternative is an inevitable catastrophic disease. Weaken or qualify the argument so that the inevitability applies to a population but not on an individual basis, and so that normal traits are only acceptable when they are desired or beneficial and the argument revives, but only at the cost of abandoning the therapy/enhancement distinction altogether, and only if disease is defined relative, not to normal species functioning or species-typical functioning, but relative to *possible functioning*.[36] The only remaining question then is whether or not the possibilities are worth attempting given the benefits offered and the degree or magnitude of the risks involved. To answer this question neither reference to normality nor to disease is required.

What is required is, as we have noted, the recognition that the moral imperative and the most usual moral motive for using technology to intervene in the natural lottery of life is for the sake of the harms this will prevent and the goods that this will bring about. Saving lives, or what is the same thing—postponing death, removing or preventing disability or disease, or enhancing human functioning, are examples of these goods. The only remaining question is what risks are worth running to achieve these goods either for individuals or for populations. Where the risk is only to

---

[36] This is indeed how I would be tempted to characterize it.

the individual she surely should decide for herself. Where the risk is to future individuals or to future populations society must have a say, which is why it is societies rather than populations that should stay in our central focus. The principles upon which societies may decide these things are not a subject to be tackled in this paper.[37] What can now be said however is that societies have a responsibility to address these issues and that their responsibility is not clarified or simplified by reference to what is normal, natural, nor species-typical. Nor is it much use thinking about how disease or illness or disability have traditionally been defined, nor by reference to equal opportunity except in so far as this refers to equal opportunities to access to the relevant technologies.

The moral question is and remains: how beneficial will be the proposed enhancements and whether or not the risks of achieving them are worth running for individuals or societies? The moral imperative is the safety of the people and the duty to compare risks with benefits, not on the basis of the normality of the risks nor of the benefits, nor on the basis of their contribution to equality of opportunity, but on the basis of their magnitude and probability, on whether they will save life, or what is the same thing, postpone death[38] and on how much harm and suffering may be prevented or avoided by the enhancements in question.

Therapy and enhancement are not mutually exclusive

Daniels, with a somewhat magisterial waft, records that he sees "the issue as largely semantic and not central to the distinction between treatment and enhancement. Indeed, had we no vaccine for HIV/AIDS, and no genetic modification providing protection, but instead found a diet that included dandelion leaves gave protection, we would hardly say we had enhanced human nature."[39] I do not see the differences between Daniels' approach and my own as "largely semantic", since I reject as inconsistent

---

[37] Some indications as to how I would address these issues are to be found, *inter alia*, in my *Violence and Responsibility* (London: Routledge & Kegan Paul, 1980), John Harris and John Sulston, "Genetic Equity", in *Nature Reviews Genetics*, vol. 5. October 2004, 796–800, and my "Sex Selection and Regulated Hatred", in *The Journal of Medical Ethics*, Vol. 31: 5, May 2005: 291–5.

[38] This may seem problematic at first glance but I think this equivalence is ultimately unassailable.

[39] In footnote 1 to his essay in this volume.

and unhelpful the way Daniels draws the distinction between normal and enhanced functioning. Daniels' analogy with dandelion leaves seems to me to be unconvincing. At first sight it looks as though it would be like saying in the context of a debate about the ethics of radical surgery: "indeed had we no option of bi-lateral mastectomy for breast cancer but instead found that a diet that included dandelion leaves gave protection we would hardly say we had undertaken radical surgery." Of course I was not assuming that all methods of achieving an objective would be enhancing if any of them were, it is obviously more likely that only some methods of protection constitute enhancement but not all, but even here the distinction is difficult to draw and more difficult to sustain, ultimately it collapses altogether. Consider Daniels' dandelions: depending on an understanding of their mode of operation and the durability or permanence of the protection afforded, we might come to think of dandelion leaves as the ultimate enhancement technology! When Daniels says: "[i]n another sense, providing the vaccine stimulates a normal immune system to produce antibodies it is capable of producing so that individuals and a population are protected against serious diseases",[40] he begs the question. Superman presumably had a normal physiology before exposure to Kryptonite. Kryptonite would "stimulate a normal physiology to produce powers it is capable of producing"—if that physiology was not capable of producing those enhanced effects in the presence of Kryptonite then Kryptonite would have no effect. On a Daniels analysis, Superman is actually Normalman. Finally on the issue of mode of operation, Daniels says: "I have generally characterized vaccines as part of the array of 'treatments' for departures from normal functioning—although this is stretching the idea of treatment to include preventive measures, a stretch I have made explicit in my writings. In effect, anything to do with maintaining normal function falls under the scope of 'treatment' as opposed to enhancement." But this simply assumes the point at issue, which is whether making a normal immune system do something it normally doesn't do constitutes "normal functioning".

Daniels' assumption that vaccines are treatments and indeed are also preventive measures is of course unassailable. But my point is that treatments or preventive measures that protect humans from things to which they are normally vulnerable, or which prevent harm to that individual by

---

[40] In footnote 1 to his essay in this volume.

operating on the organism by affecting the way the organism functions, are necessarily also enhancements. That goes for drugs, foods, vaccines, implants, and whatever else; whether they are "natural" or "artificial" and regardless of whether they are part of a self-selected diet or treatment, or are recommended or prescribed as a result of scientific research. The boundaries between treatment and enhancement, between therapy and enhancement, are not precise nor are these categories mutually exclusive as Daniels seems to think they must be. If we wear a suit of armour and the slings and arrows of outrageous fortune simply bounce off, that may not constitute an "enhancement" of the human being (though it seems to me that even here the protection/enhancement distinction in the way that Daniels sees it at least, is on the borderline of fracture to the point at which I myself am unclear as to which side of the border we are on). We already use prostheses and implants (heart pacemakers for example) as technological and mechanical aids or enhancements. Although the more familiar prostheses replace say lost limbs or teeth or even breasts they often do things that the originals could not do! In the future silicone chips and other electrical and computer prosthetic devices or implants may assist and enhance memory, vision, and many other functions. Nanotechnology may enable us to make some of these so tiny and lightweight as to be unnoticeable. On the other hand if we change human physiology, or metabolism or genetics, or whatever, by dietary modification, vaccination, stem-cell therapy, dandelions, or other organic means so that the organism becomes immune or resistant to slings and arrows, or automatically repairs the damage they do from within, the changes may seem more natural and more intrinsic to the human organism as traditionally understood. Either way the distinction between therapy and enhancement, between protection and improvement cannot be coherently or consistently maintained. Whatever else this distinction does it fails to identify two mutually exclusive categories and those wonderful dandelions will have enhanced human functioning.

Another reason the issue is not largely semantic is because consequences flow from whether or not something is classified as or "semantically constitutes" normal functioning. As Daniels admits: "anything to do with maintaining normal function falls under the scope of 'treatment' as opposed to enhancement." For Daniels maybe, and this is what he is trading on because for many people, including most doctors and those who run health care systems, treatment constitutes an obligation in a way that enhancement (as yet) does not.

The overwhelming moral imperative for both therapy and enhancement is to prevent harm and confer benefit. Bathed in that moral light, it is unimportant whether the protection or benefit conferred is classified as enhancement or improvement, protection, or therapy. For Daniels it does matter because for him "anything to do with maintaining normal function falls under the scope of 'treatment' *as opposed to* enhancement"[41] and for many purposes (although for none of mine) therapy is given a higher priority than enhancement. For Buchanan the most important moral imperative seems to be equality of opportunity. I have shown that both these views fail to capture the moral purposes which both therapy and enhancement standardly serve. I have also shown that existing and accepted enhancements, such as vaccination, make more sense when seen as conferring benefits or protecting from harms, than when seen as serving either the interests of equal opportunity or those of restoring normal functioning.

[41] My emphasis.

7

Playing God

C. A. J. Coady

The accusation of "playing God" is one commonly levelled against proposals to use science and technology to make dramatic changes in the way
we live and cope with the many ills, boons, misadventures, and adventures
of living today. It is also used in many other contexts to reject a proposed
course of action, including, as we shall see later, in the world of sport. I
want to scrutinize this charge of playing God to see what it means and
what, if anything, it amounts to as a moral criticism. I will not therefore
be concerned so much with whether particular proposals fall prey to this
accusation, but with what sort of objection those who present it are making.
To get clearer about this, however, it will be necessary to look at some
proposals, or proposal schema, in the area of genetic modification that have
been subject to the criticism of playing God.

To begin with, we should be clear that the allegation of playing God
need not be the preserve only of religious critics, though it is common
enough for the words to be on the lips of those who believe that there
is a God whose part is being usurped by the innovators. It may seem
strange that the non-religious could object to proposals on the ground that
they violate the prerogatives of a non-existent being. Put thus, it is indeed
strange, but there are, as we shall see, other ways of putting the point that
are amenable to the non-theistic or anti-theistic outlook.

The religious perspective

But first, let us look at the problem from the religious or theistic perspective.
Here, I think, the idea is that there are certain things that it is presumptuous
for human beings to undertake because those matters are really in the care

of God. The theological concept of "providence" is clearly at work here, at least in the background, and theistic religions have characteristically held that there is some sense in which God is in control of creation. Not only did God make the world but God conserves, shapes, and cares for what goes on in that world. Certainly, this idea of providence is powerful in Christianity despite the difficulties it creates for explaining the presence and persistence of evil in the world. These difficulties are met in a variety of ways that we will not be concerned to assess here, but it is worth noting that a prominent part is played in those responses to the problem of evil by the idea that human beings have been given free will by God as part of the providential plan. Such are the benefits of human freedom that the accompanying capacity for evil-doing, and the realization of that evil, are worth suffering.

The "free-will defence", as it is often called, has some well-known problems, but, for our purposes, it is significant in reminding us that the idea of providence allows for human freedom to act and create. God may have made the forests, but it is no violation of God's proper sphere for human beings to make paintings of forests or other representations of them, or to plant more trees. God may heal disease in response to prayer, but the majority Christian view has been that this does not prohibit medical research to discover earthly cures or the resort to those cures by the devout. The slogan "God helps those who help themselves" is a crude reminder of the theological insight that God has given human beings parts to play or perhaps better still has allowed them to find parts to play themselves in the unfolding of the providential design. In this sense, "playing God" may be a description of what theology teaches us that God has called people to do. To the degree that we are co-workers with God, as much Christian tradition teaches, and I dare say other traditions as well, then playing God is no accusation.

This much seems to me to be right, and it provides a caution against what might be called too "pietistic" an interpretation of God's rule and role. I say "pietistic" because the admission of an important role for resignation to and acceptance of God's will in a variety of religious traditions need not require the passive submission in a spirit of (surely false) piety to all that happens or is likely to happen. Such passivity would after all disavow the spirited opposition to evil that has always been a mark of mainstream Christianity.

So what then remains of the accusation of playing God? One interpretation I want to rule out from the beginning is that sin or immorality is *ipso facto* playing God. I rule this out because it is implausible to think that deliberate evil-doing is some form of imitating God. Perhaps there is a sort of self-assertion involved in sin that amounts to a defiance of God but this seems to me too uninteresting a sense of "playing God", if a sense of it at all. If playing God is to be an interestingly specific allegation it had better not collapse into just any form of wrong-doing.

One way of approaching the interpretation of "playing God" begins with distinguishing three traditions of response to the relationship between human beings and the natural order. The governing images associated with these are: domination, stewardship, and co-creation. The first two have been prominent in debates about the role of Christianity in promoting what many have seen as bad attitudes to the natural environment. Writers such as John Passmore have charged Christianity with promoting the idea that human beings have been given untrammelled sovereignty over nature and they see this idea as at least a contributing cause of the environmental degradation that has been such a feature of modern times.[1] They cite such texts as Genesis 1: 28 where God addresses Adam and Eve telling them "to fill the earth and subdue it. Have dominion over the fish of the sea, the birds of the air, the cattle and all the animals that crawl on the earth." (Confraternity version). Again, in Psalm 8, the psalmist claims that God has made human beings "a little lower than the angels" and "to have dominion over the works of thy hands; thou hast put all things under his feet." (King James version). The dominational (or as Passmore calls it "despotic") attitude is supposed to involve a lack of respect for the rest of creation which is seen purely in terms of its instrumental value for human beings. In response to this, some Christians have emphasized the stewardship tradition in Christianity, associating this with such models as St Francis of Assisi. Instead of viewing God as handing the created world to humans for domination and exploitation, the picture is one of God giving humans the task of caring for the creation on God's behalf.

---

[1] John Passmore, *Man's Responsibility for Nature*, 2nd edn (London: Duckworth), 1980. Passmore distinguishes the domination and stewardship traditions, grudgingly allowing that the stewardship tradition is present in Christianity but insisting that it is very much a minority response. He also goes part of the way towards recognizing something like co-creation in ch. 2.

It seems plausible that there are elements of both these outlooks within Christian tradition though the idea of dominion contained in the Genesis quotation is not necessarily that of ruthless instrumentalist exploitation. Dominion is not necessarily tyranny, though being "underfoot", as the Psalmist would seem to require of the rest of creation, is certainly to be in a dominated position. The Genesis text gives humans a special place in the creation, a place that many animalists and environmentalists want to deny or downplay, but it does not licence despoliation. After all, a ruler may rule with respect for those ruled and Jews and Christians could stand as much in awe of the wonders of the natural world as anyone else, though, as Passmore points out, there is a certain amount of Christian theology that shows an indifference, if not contempt, for the value of the natural world.[2] But the matter is quite complex since Christian tradition is committed to the view that God created the world as good and this suggests that the natural order has a value independent of humanity. St Augustine, whom Passmore plausibly treats as within the dominator tradition, is nonetheless capable of recognizing the value in the natures of all created things and of rebuking the human tendency to see the natural order purely in terms of its utility to human purposes. So he objects to those who "find fault with the sun itself; for certain criminals or debtors are sentenced by the judges to be set in the sun. Therefore it is not with respect to our convenience or discomfort, but with respect to their own nature, that the creatures are glorifying to their Artificer."[3] St Augustine is here putting human beings in their place, and, in a way, accusing them of playing God by imagining themselves to be entirely the beneficiaries of creation. This involves a sort of hubris, and, as we shall see, hubris is the vice that seems most naturally associated with the allegation of playing God.

But, if the domination model is at fault in not showing sufficient respect to the rest of nature, then its fault may be of several different kinds. One is the fact that it may have failed to understand the bad consequences for human beings themselves of the human drive to dominate and transform the natural world. Much environmentalist criticism makes this point. Pursuing human purposes such as destroying insects for better crop production or genetically modifying food crops to make them disease resistant may

---

[2] Passmore, *Man's Responsibility for Nature*, ch. 1. Passmore's discussion shows how complex the different strands of Christian theology could be on this point.

[3] St Augustine, *The City of God*, Marcus Dods (trans.) (New York: Random House), 1950, xii, 4.

increase human sickness. But the second way human domination can bring bad consequences is the actual damage to the environment and to animals that it causes. Many believe that this is wrong irrespective of the good or bad outcomes for human beings. They hold that there are intrinsic values in nature that can be transgressed by human domination, even where no obvious harm to humans is involved. Even the quotation from St Augustine might be taken to imply as much. The destruction of a species of plant or wildlife, for example, strikes many people as wrong per se even if human beings don't suffer from it at all.

It is worth noting at this point, that it may indeed be possible to capture much of the content of this second form of objection without resorting to the moral ontology it commonly deploys. The idea that there is much in the natural order that is "intrinsically valuable" need not, I suspect, be required to invoke intrinsic values as entities inhering in forests, whales, and the like. A morality adequate to the best insights of the environmental movement, in other words, need not be so construed that it departs radically from "a human-centred ethic" in the way many of its supporters believe. I do not think that a morality based upon the deepest needs of human nature must involve the superficial aggrandizement of human interests. But the further pursuit of this issue in the foundations of morality will take us too far from our topic. We should note the different possibilities here and move on.

Stewardship and co-creation

The stewardship model tends to the opposite faults of the domination model. Where the latter seems to ignore or fail to acknowledge properly the respect that is due to the non-human world, the stewards seem to have too passive an attitude to what there is. Admittedly, the model generates an attitude of care and tendering, but this seems to lack the dynamism to which human beings are called and for which they have abundant, if ambiguous talents. In particular, the astonishing achievements of human creativity in medicine, transport, architecture, labour-saving, and communications seem to be inconsistent with the picture of human beings as mere stewards and caretakers of what is given by God. Perhaps this criticism takes the image of stewardship too simplistically but the interpretation is natural enough, and it corresponds to a certain mood of excessive reverence for how things have been and are that devalues the genuine successes of human ingenuity and intervention. Those who stress that human beings are part of the natural order and not separate lords of it commonly fail to draw the implication that the natural order includes our dynamic, creative, and disturbing propensities. True, there are those who profess that they would prefer to live without the benefits of the modern technological world, but there is I fear a fair degree of bad faith in this nostalgia. Life in pre-modern times was all too often an approximation to the philosopher Thomas Hobbes's description of the state of nature as "solitary, poor, nasty, brutish and short".[4] Can anyone seriously maintain that the discoveries of the efficacy of sanitation, antibiotics, anaesthetics, and blood transfusion were undue interventions in the divinely established order of nature?[5]

Partly in response to considerations of this sort, theologians have been moved to the metaphor of co-creation as a more adequate picture of the relation between God and man.[6] The idea is that God has called human beings into a creative partnership in the ongoing creation of the world. It has long been theologically orthodox to view God's creative act as an ongoing sustaining thing and it is no great stretch of this idea to see the process in creaturely time as an ongoing enterprise. The official spokespeople of the Catholic Church have often been in the forefront of the campaign against playing God, yet the German Catholic Jesuit, Karl Rahner in the late 1960s was very positive about the partnership of God and humans in the creative process, even to the point of seeing human beings as legitimately engaged in an ongoing self-creation. Yet the image of co-creation has its own difficulties. Co-creation calls attention to the human role in the enterprise, but it may, from the theocentric point of view, misleadingly suggest that humans have a sort of equality with God. If so, any trace of a problematic "playing

---

[4] Thomas Hobbes, *Leviathan*, ed. Edwin Curley (Indianapolis: Hacket), 1994, ch. xiii, para. 9.

[5] Of course, there are those, such as Seventh Day Adventists, who do object to blood transfusion, and the glorious diversity of human thought processes is such that there may be sects, unknown to me, who object to anaesthetics and sanitation. But so few people take such objections seriously, that I shall persist in treating them as marginal.

[6] The image is employed in T. Peters, *Playing God? Genetic Discrimination and Human Freedom* (New York: Routledge), 1997. A similar model, implying a partnership between God and human beings, can be found in some Jewish and Islamic thought. Rabbi Dorff holds that "we are God's 'partners in the ongoing act of Creation' when we improve the human lot in life"; R. E. N. Dorff, "Human Cloning: a Jewish Perspective", testimony before the National Bioethics Advisory Commission in the USA, March 14, 1997. And an Islamic scholar talks of human beings "as participants in the act of creating with God"; see A Sachedina, "Islamic Perspectives on Cloning", testimony before the National Bioethics Advisory Commission in the USA, March 14, 1997.

God" would disappear, but so too would the distance between God and creatures, a distance that (despite the Christian mystery of the Incarnation) has always been a central element in the Judeo-Christian tradition.

It seems to me that all three pictures have an element of truth in them and that the dialogue between them exhibits the tensions that need to be kept in view by believers in negotiating the mystery of humanity's place in the created order. I shall say more about this after considering the non-religious viewpoint on "playing God". Before leaving the theological perspective, however, it should be remarked that there is no tension in this matter for believers who think that they know precisely from Revelation in its various forms (scripture, tradition, Church authority) that God has reserved certain matters for divine determination and these must never be usurped by human beings. This certainty must, as we saw earlier, concern more than the knowledge that certain behaviours are immoral or against God's commandments. God-playing behaviour may indeed be sinful, but it must be sinful because it is known to be behaviour that somehow usurps the role of God and so transcends what humans may legitimately strive to do. Some religious people argue against euthanasia, for instance, that it is God's prerogative to determine when our lives are over. They accuse even those who seek to end a life of dreadful suffering (with the consent of the sufferer) of overstepping the limits and seeking to occupy the role of God. Even here, they do not entirely avoid the tensions mentioned above since the idea that only God has domain over the ending of our lives has to be consistent with the legitimate human role in curing disease, preventing death, and alleviating suffering. In the end, I suspect that the complaint in the case of euthanasia will collapse into the idea that it is morally wrong to kill the innocent intentionally, even where one's motive is compassion, and where, for understandable reasons, they want to die.

The non-religious perspective

The non-religious can make sense of the accusation by thinking of the attributes God would possess if there were a God. They can insist that human beings clearly lack these attributes and go wrong by acting as if they didn't. Naturally, they will have to avail themselves of some common understanding of God's nature in order to proceed in this way, and there are a variety of such understandings. Nonetheless, I think it clear enough that a certain picture of the Godhead that is deep in Christian tradition is the one most often invoked in objections to playing God in the medical and other spheres. To expand this point, let us begin with a homely example from the realm of sport. (I should apologize in advance to those readers for whom this particular sport, cricket, is sadly mysterious.)

The New Zealand cricket umpire Steve Dunne was the official standing at the other end when Australian umpire Darrell Hair created an international incident by no-balling Sri Lankan spin bowling genius Muttiah Muralidaran during a Test match in Australia. Muralidaran had never been publicly and officially "called" for throwing instead of bowling, though doubts had been privately held in many parts of the cricketing world. Although Dunne, like many other people, also believed that Muralidaran's bowling action was suspect, he did not call "no-ball" for any of the bowler's deliveries when he was officiating at the bowler's end. In his recent memoirs, Dunne says that he had been keeping to an international agreement that umpires should rather report suspicious bowling actions to the match referee. He added, however, that an additional reason for not "calling" Muralidaran for bowling illegally was that he didn't believe that detecting the illegality of the Sri Lankan's arm action was humanly possible, without the aid of technology. As he put it: "I don't believe it's possible to do so with the naked eye, and I wouldn't want to play God."

One thing Steve Dunne was getting at is clear enough. He didn't think that he (or any other mortal umpire) had the power or knowledge to determine the truth about the spin bowler's action at or near the point of delivery. He seems to have thought that resort to sophisticated technology in a cool hour could have done so, but recent analyses seem to suggest that even this may not be the case. The rule about illegal deliveries is itself imprecise, and close slow-motion photographic analyses seem to indicate that, on a natural interpretation of the rule, as it was then, most fast bowlers (which Murali is not) violate the rule too constantly for it to be a sensible rule for the game. In addition, photographic evidence from different angles yields conflicting pictures of Muralidaran's action.[7]

---

[7] These claims are to be found in a newspaper article by Jason Kemp and Damian Farrow in the sports section of the Melbourne newspaper, *The Age*, August 9, 2003, Sport p. 9. See also their book *Run Like You Stole Something* (London: Allen & Unwin), 2003. As a result of these difficulties of interpretation the no-ball law has subsequently been amended.

In any case, Dunne is concerned that he would have been exceeding his standing, his competence, and his position to have given the verdict in those circumstances. His perceived incapacity seems to have been partly that of inadequate powers and inadequate knowledge. Given that a verdict was beyond his powers of perception and the knowledge he could build on that, he thought it arrogant over-confidence to have produced the cry of "No ball". No doubt it was also relevant that the verdict would have had momentous consequences for Muralidaran's career and for the game of cricket. He was partly asking himself the question "Who am I to make this sort of decision?" and partly asking "Who is any umpire to think they can do so?"

The example seems to raise some of the key questions about interpreting the playing God complaint in more serious contexts. The God of Christian natural theology (and of many monotheisms) is omnipotent, omniscient, and supremely benevolent. By contrast human beings are eminently fallible, limited in power, and only partially benevolent. They are also tempted to the exercise of undue power over others. This is surely evident to natural reason even if it is also the lesson of much religion. As the philosopher Thomas Hobbes argued, the drive for pre-eminence over others, either from motives of competition or love of glory, is deep in human nature and potentially destructive.[8] Umpire Dunne seemed to have been conscious of the temptation and he viewed it as akin to mimicking some elements of Divine power and wisdom. Playing God can be interpreted as going beyond the limits we have in these three respects, acting in ways that ignore the in-built constraints on our knowledge, power, and benevolence.

This is a complaint that has been often levelled in philosophy against the outlook of Utilitarianism, at least in its simpler forms. The utilitarian philosopher produces a theory that licences people to form their policies and guide their actions by the impossible idea of acting to produce "the greatest happiness of the greatest number". Critics call this "impossible" because they think that mere humans cannot know enough to foresee what actions will have these happy outcomes and, in addition, cannot forge the institutions and policies that will have the power to effect this goal. It has been further objected in the same spirit that the simple utilitarian has too optimistic a view of human nature and assumes wrongly that

---

[8] Hobbes, op. cit., ch. xiii, especially paras. 3 to 8.

the injunction to promote the greatest happiness of the greatest number will unleash universal benevolence whereas it is all too likely to produce universal manipulation in favour of a certain kind of self-assertion. Unlike God, human beings have deep springs of malignance in their make-ups as well as motives of benevolence, and this too makes their "do-gooding" impulses liable to misfire. I mention this reaction to Utilitarianism, not to endorse or pursue it, but merely for its illustrative significance.

Away from philosophy and sport, many other examples could be cited from everyday life to illustrate the perils of well-intentioned motives that ignore or underestimate the limits of our capacities with respect to knowledge, power, and benevolence. For example, the introduction in 1935 of cane toads from Hawaii into Queensland, Australia, in order to control sugar cane pests, has proved an ecological disaster. Adult animals have few natural predators so their population has exploded throughout north and central Australia, and threatens regions further south. They have high toxicity and are fatally poisonous if eaten by most native animals (including crocodiles) and they are capable of eating small native toads and native frogs. Commenting on this well-intentioned importation on Australian radio recently, one scientist said: "It's pretty dangerous to play God, especially with complex eco-systems."

The reference to Utilitarianism suggests a scenario that can be extended well beyond philosophical disputations. The great achievements of science and the prospects they open up for us can lead us to an exaggerated sense of what we know, to misplaced confidence in our powers to change the world and blindness to our own moral deficiencies. The point about knowledge concerns the knowledge of the consequences of our present discoveries and inventions as much as, if not more than, the security of our grasp on the present realities. A degree of humility about how much we now know needs to go hand in hand with a frank regard for the uncertainty of future developments consequent upon the application of our present knowledge or theorizing. Scientists are among themselves very often suitably aware of the tentative and revisable nature of much of their thinking and experimenting. But the public image of science tends to be much more triumphal and dogmatic. Part of this is the result of the media's relish for scientific "breakthroughs" and the public's appetite for the wonderful, though scientists are themselves no less prone to the Hobbesian temptations of competition and glory than the rest of us. But part of it is the work of that pervasive contemporary phenomenon, public relations. Scientists of all kinds need funding, and a public image of ongoing triumphs can be a powerful recipe for success. In addition to this, applied science is marketed by companies that need to make profits; an emphasis on the fallibility, unpredictability, and potential dangers of science and technology is seldom good for sales.

We may conclude that when people worry about the application of the latest scientific and technological discoveries and put this worry in terms of "playing God", they are concerned that these applications may embody an unjustified confidence in knowledge, power, and virtue beyond what can reasonably be allowed to human beings. How should we then judge the pertinence of this worry? In the first place, it should be seen as a cautionary criticism.[9] If indeed there is insufficient knowledge of outcomes and consequences, or no social or institutional regulatory regime for prudent implementation of the innovations and for continuing scrutiny of their effects, or no room for overview of the commercial exploitation of the innovations, then the critics clearly have a point. I have no doubt that much of the hype and some of the reality associated with the rise of biotechnology are vulnerable to this style of criticism. On the other hand, in particular cases, these problems can equally clearly be addressed. Of course, they cannot be infallibly or impeccably addressed. Any technological innovation will have risks and our information about future effects of present interventions is always limited. Hence the demand that we have absolute certainty about outcomes is too strong. We do well to be on guard about exaggerated claims, public relations hype, and insufficient efforts to discover what can be known about effects and implications. We are also generally right to insist on safeguards and regulation, both scientific and ethical. The cautionary attitude is appropriate since we need to be aware of deeply-seated human limitations. This awareness may well lead to the rejection of various proposals and the cautious, safeguarded introduction of others. But the warnings can be heeded. In the first instance, so it seems, the critique of playing God is primarily a criticism of an *attitude* and only derivatively of a programme or proposal. It is the attitude of

---

[9] This is a point similar to that made by Ruth Chadwick when she describes the criticism of "playing God" as "a counsel". See Ruth Chadwick, "Playing God", in *Bioethics News*, vol. 9:4, 1990, 45. (The article was reprinted from *Cogito*, 1989.) In this connection, she also makes reference to the idea of aspiring to divine attributes, notably omniscience and omnipotence (though not omnibenevolence).

hubris or, in homely English, "being too big for your boots".[10] We may admit that the temptation is to be avoided and be glad of the warning, but can we go further and regard certain proposals and programmes as inherently committing their proponents to "playing God"? This question, in its sharpest form, asks whether certain limits should not be exceeded, even where we have the power to do so, act with a good will, and know that our benevolent aims can be achieved. As Ronald Dworkin has put it: "Playing God is thought wrong in itself, quite apart from any bad consequences it will or may have for any identifiable human being. Nevertheless, it is deeply unclear what the injunction really means . . . ."[11]

To keep the question interesting we should, as mentioned earlier, set aside cases that can already be easily condemned on straightforward moral grounds. If hubris leads people to use science to murder others, as was the case with Mengele and the other Nazi death doctors, the comment that they are playing God is at least discordant, since they are better described as playing Satan. If it were appropriate to talk of playing God, the criticism would be secondary, if not redundant, since the actions are deeply wrong on other grounds. The best cases to consider are those in which the intentions of the agent are benevolent, but are criticized for seeking to transcend the legitimate limits on what it is to be human.

Playing God with genes

The revolution in genetics has since its beginnings provided good grist to this mill. As early as 1970, the Princeton theologian Paul Ramsey railed against the genetic optimism about transforming human nature that was even then gaining ground. One of the objects of his criticism was the idea that science could and should change human nature itself. Since then, the advance of genetics has brought this spectre (or prospect, if you are that way inclined) somewhat nearer than Ramsey could have thought, though

---

[10] Several authors make reference to the idea of hubris in connection with the "playing God" objection. See, for example, Chadwick, p. 43; Cynthia S.W. Crysdale, "Playing God? Moral Agency in an Emergent World", *Journal of the Society of Christian Ethics*, vol. 23:2, Fall–Winter 2003, 243–59; and Gareth Jones, "Playing God: Scientific, Ethical and Technological Challenges", Lecture given at St Edmund's College, Cambridge, June 22, 2004.

[11] Ronald Dworkin, "Playing God: Genes, Clones and Luck", in his *Sovereign Virtue: The Theory and Practice of Equality* (Cambridge, Mass.: Harvard University Press), 443.

it is remarkable how prescient some of his concerns were. Even so, of course, much of the debate about genetic transformations of the human condition remains in the sphere of science fiction. Yet it is important to discuss the prospects, partly because yesterday's science fiction is sometimes today's science fact, and also because even remote possibilities can provide the stimulus for significant moral reflection.

Let us look at two areas of concern raised by genetic technology that may help clarify the worry about playing God. First the use of human genetic material for the "improvement" of food that human beings may eat. Many people find this disturbing. Some of the reasons for their anxiety concern the possibility of bad consequences and relate to the knowledge strand in the playing God accusation. But let us suppose that this can be satisfactorily addressed. One study reported by the former Vice Chancellor of East Anglia University, and Chairman of the Advisory Committee on Novel Foods and Processes (1989–1997), Professor Derek Burke, considered the introduction of a human gene for Factor IX, which is involved in blood-clotting, into sheep.[12] The project requires injecting fertilized sheep eggs with the gene. The experiment is successful in only one animal in 100 in that only one in a hundred develops the IX Factor to a significant degree. A survey found widespread unhappiness amongst the public even with eating sheep from the programme that contained no novel gene or inactive novel genes. Amongst the religious groups involved in the survey, only Jews were unconcerned—"If it looks like a sheep, then it's a sheep!" was what most of them said. The sheep with the gene would have only one human gene in 100,000 (at least by the method of counting genes then in fashion).[13] Leaving aside the possibility of bad health consequences, what could be the moral objection to eating such meat?

Perhaps the idea is that we should resist changing the nature of God's creation (or the natural world) in anything like this way. The intrusion of this one human gene into the sheep's make-up is seen as changing the sheep's nature (and perhaps human nature?). But this conclusion is hardly warranted. Improving the health of sheep (or of humans) by making them less prone to certain diseases can hardly be thought of as a radical alteration in what they are. Perhaps there is lurking in the background here the idea

---

[12] Derek Burke, "Genetic Engineering of Food", in *Christians and Bioethics* (London: Society for Promoting Christian Knowledge), 2000, 26.

[13] Ibid., 26–7.

that is often promoted by various versions of popular science to the effect that "we are our genes". But human beings (and, for that matter, sheep) are more than a bundle of genes. But what if there were a proposal to put so many human genes into the sheep that 50 per cent of their genetic make-up was human? Burke considers this and thinks that everyone would be concerned about it. But it is not altogether clear what Burke's imagined scenario means, since, as I understand it, we already share much more than 50 per cent of our genes with sheep. Maybe he means 50 per cent of the genes we otherwise don't share with sheep. But even here, abstracting from the proposal's practical feasibility, it presumably depends upon what difference this genetic importation makes to the sheep's dispositions and behaviour. Perhaps the reported Jewish response is a little narrow. If it looks, thinks, and acts like a sheep, that may be enough to forget about the genes. But, of course, it may be that such a lot of genes make too much of a difference.

The example raises some more interesting issues. Suppose it was suggested that we should eliminate some unwanted species by genetically transforming them into another more wanted species—turning them from pest to pet, let's say. There are no doubt huge scientific and practical problems with this, and it may be much more sensible simply to exterminate the pests (at least the really dangerous ones) and make do with the pets we have, but would there be anything wrong with it? Or with the analogous proposal to alter those features of certain plants that make us call them weeds, so that we could now have them as flowers? I confess that I cannot see anything intrinsically problematic about this sort of suggestion. After all, rabbits are pests in Australia and harmless, and often loved neighbours elsewhere. And even where they are pests, some of them are kept as pets. There are even people who keep rats as pets, and many a mouse is a pet-like hero of children's books. But, it may be objected, such changes involve no genetic transformations, merely those that are circumstantial or attitudinal. The response is reasonable, but there has been plenty of traditional genetic manipulation by breeders in the evolution of such pets as dogs. Categories like pest and pet are so geared to human interests and particular circumstances that it is hard to believe that the transfer from the troublesome to the enjoyable category by any means that do not harm the animal can be an interference with God's purposes or an exercise in hubris, unless there is some over-confident ignoring of potentially bad consequences. This, of course, there might often be, since a proposal, for example, to change some predating species into mild-mannered vegetarians is very likely to have disastrous effects on ecological balance.

Some might still insist that, even in the absence of such harmful consequences, genetic changing of animals is a disrespectful usurping of God's role, so we may get further by directly examining the human case. Those who resist the validity of genetic changes to animals will presumably resist even more strongly genetic changes to human beings, and they will be joined by others who do not share their concern about the animal proposal. There are many problems associated with proposals for genetic changes to human beings. Some people worry that effecting a genetic change in an embryo or fetus with the good intention of eliminating the existence of or tendency towards a disease will have various effects on future generations. They could put this point by invoking the injunction against playing God. For the religious, the idea is that we would be determining the future in a way that is basically up to God. For the non-religious, the problem is more difficult to frame, but it would be the concern that we are going beyond the proper limits of human endeavour. Just what this could mean, we will explore below.

But first, it is surely important to distinguish mere genetic change from harmful genetic change. The idea that one should avoid passing on any genetic change to future generations is hard to take seriously. Suppose there were some medical technique that acted on the current generation's genes in some sample population so that they developed resistance to a lethal disease and would pass the resistance on to successive generations. Someone who objected that this was wrong simply *because* of the change being transmitted would surely be irrational. It would not help to insist that we must leave it up to God or Nature to decide on what disease resistance people were going to have. This is far too close to saying that we must leave it up to God to determine what diseases people will have, a position that rejects all programmes of preventive medicine in the name of God. A further story about harms, potential or actual, needs to be told.

Elsewhere, Loane Skene and I have criticized the suggestion, implicit in some writing of C. S. Lewis's, that future people are somehow harmed by the present genetic intervention simply because they will have different "dominated" choices than the ones they would otherwise have had.[14] This line of criticism is difficult to sustain, though it is related to a more complex view of Jurgen Habermas that will be considered later. It is true that the absence of that disease will mean that some people will not have the opportunity to care for those diseased, to exercise compassion for them and so on. But there will be plenty of opportunities for the exercise of good dispositions on the victims of other diseases and disabilities. In any case, surely no one thinks that the diminishing of such opportunities for currently existing people by saving some others from disease constitutes any form of unjustified "domination" of their choices or those around them. Why should our attitude be different to future people?

It also needs to be recalled that we are altering the choices available to future people by all manner of non-genetic interventions in our social and physical environment that it would be absurd to consider illegitimate on that account. The development of widespread education, modern medicine and anaesthetics, and domestic labour-saving gadgets has had these sorts of choice re-arrangements as consequences, but this is no objection to them. Indeed, many of our perfectly legitimate choices affect what people will actually exist in the future. Statistics show that more extensive education for women leads to lower birth rates, but the resultant loss in future population is not by itself an argument against female education.

Changing human nature?

A deeper fear of genetic interventions comes from the idea that we cross the limits of human sovereignty when we decide to change human nature itself. Ramsey's book in protest against playing God by scientists was called "Fabricated Man" and he is explicitly anxious about the value of any project to bring about deep changes in what human beings are.[15] This is a widely shared apprehension, even when playing God is not invoked. There are several important issues here.

The first is that when we move beyond obviously beneficial or remedial changes to the make-up of individual human beings (and possibly their

---

[14] Loane Skene and Tony Coady, "Genetic Manipulation and our Duty to Posterity", *Monash Bioethics Review*, 21:2, 2002, 12–22.

[15] Paul Ramsey, *Fabricated Man: the Ethics of Genetic Control* (New Haven: Yale University Press), 1970.

successors) we raise critical questions about what constitutes a human defect. The elimination of a tendency to breast cancer seems perfectly legitimate if we can be reasonably assured that it has no negative side-effects, but what of dwarfism? What also of deafness? In both these cases, and in other disability areas, there are arguments from people affected that claim either that any disability they have is simply the result of bad social arrangements imposed by the wider community or that, although they have certain inbuilt dis-advantages, their lives are worth living and programmes to prevent people being born with those disadvantages show a disdain for this fact. I cannot deal with these claims fully here but some few comments seem appropriate. First, there can be no doubt that a great deal of improvement in the effect of disabilities on the disabled can be achieved by improving their social circumstances rather than any form of genetic engineering, and it may well be that an emphasis on the whiz-bang prospects of genetic intervention obscures this fact and impedes this progress. This can be conceded without conceding that disability is entirely a "social construct". Second there is a world of difference between disvaluing an existing human being who has some handicap, defect, or disadvantage and trying to ensure that others are not born or become handicapped in the same way. Those currently disabled are tempted to deny this "world of difference" because they fear that the negative attitude to the handicap entailed by the desire to eliminate it will carry over to a negative attitude to them as so handicapped. This would indeed be deplorable, but I see no reason to think it inevitable. So the second argument seems to me to fail, even though its emotional power is under-standable. In the case of deafness, the evident disadvantages of lacking a basic sensory orientation to the world that most others possess speak in favour of eliminating it if you can. Against this, the deaf community raise many issues about the beauty of deaf language, the need to maintain the bonds of the deaf community and so on. I don't doubt that there is something in all of this, but not enough, I think, to sway the scales. In the case of dwarfism, the issue is much more difficult. Certainly, exceptional height or lack of it is not a defect in the way that lack of a sensory modality is. The question turns therefore on what other health consequences, if any, there are to dwarfism.

Others argue that people with certain disabilities have developed qualities of character and achievement that might not have been possible had they not suffered from the handicap. Some valuable qualities may indeed inherently accompany the disability, such as the emotional warmth and lack of inhibition that seems to go with Down's Syndrome. I have no simple answer that will accommodate every putative case of defect or disability; we need to examine the cases and the arguments in their particularity. Nonetheless, I am sceptical of the general form that the arguments tend to take. This is to point to achievements, qualities, virtues that have come about, at least in part, because of the disability, and to suggest that eliminating the disability amounts to eliminating, or at least devaluing, these traits. The problem with this is that all sorts of bad things can be made good use of without thereby becoming good things. Consider the remarkable achievements of many people afflicted after accidents with quadriplegia or paraplegia. Not only do they display remarkable qualities, but they often evoke impressive responses in their carers. But none of this means that we should cease to try to reduce or eliminate car accidents. Or consider the parallel with the effects of injustice. Some victims of injustice find in their condition the source of new strength and capacity. It may even be that in the absence of the suffering unjustly inflicted, they would never have achieved the insights and strength they now have. But this does not mean that the injustice was a good thing and it would be preposterous to claim that, on these grounds, we should cease efforts to prevent injustice. Orthodox Christian teaching on suffering has usually held that suffering can be an occasion for spiritual growth, but mainstream theologians have never suggested that suffering was in itself good. Nor has it been orthodox teaching that suffering should be sought for its spiritual benefits, though the ascetic tradition perhaps come close to this in its advocacy of certain discomforts and self-denials in pursuit of detachment from the world.

Of course, beyond the moral case, there are further issues about respecting choice and autonomy in a liberal, pluralist society that would need to be addressed. Such respect needs to be extended to parents though there are clearly limits to the freedom that the community can allow parental choices, as the child abuse problem illustrates. This political issue becomes acute when there are reasonable grounds for suspecting that something widely regarded as a defect is not so at all.

Next, there is the issue of improving, rather than rectifying, by genetic intervention. This is sometimes characterized as the difference between positive and negative eugenics. Mention of "eugenics" needs of course to be treated with care. The word rightly has bad connotations because of those eugenic programmes, such as the Nazis', that proceeded to murder people judged defective. Nothing that I am interested in here involves anything of the sort. Another cause of the infamy of eugenics was its racism and the assumption of a superior knowledge about what were defective forms of human life. The failings of that earlier eugenics movement should rightly give us pause about genetic interventions to remedy or improve, but I am assuming that the cautionary model of playing God legitimately requires us to think twice or more about such matters. That said, can we reject any proposal to enhance human nature by biotechnology? Can any such proposal be rejected out of hand as playing God?

Suppose scientists discovered a gene for intelligence. I suspect that this idea, like that of a gene for criminality, is not altogether coherent, but let that pass. Would it be usurping God's role (or a role that could only be played by God, were there a God) to offer this enhancement to parents? Well, there are already various devices that parents use in the hope of enhancing the intellectual and artistic capacities of their children. It is unclear how well they work, but playing Bach to the pregnant mother, getting her to take various vitamins and so on, do not seem to most people to be any usurpation of God's prerogatives. Intelligence is perhaps universally prized, so what about characteristics that are valued by some parents but not others. What about genetic manipulation for red hair? Or for powerful muscles? Or for musical talent? There is indeed the problem of unknown side-effects. Perhaps the intelligence enhancement comes at some cost to other capacities. But two things need to be said about this. One is that we are asking whether the enhancement is wrong because of God-playing regardless of these other possible consequences, and the other is that there are surely acceptable and unacceptable costs. On the latter point, if we were reasonably assured that the costs would be low then going ahead need not constitute God-playing.

Damaging autonomy?

But if it is not God-playing because of excessive confidence in our powers of understanding, there might yet be another perspective on such "designer babies" projects that needs to be considered. This is the fact that parents are deciding in such cases issues about important endowments for their children that would otherwise be contingently bestowed by nature (or

God?). Might not children so endowed have a sort of grievance against those who deliberately chose these endowments and these pathways for their orientation to life? Jurgen Habermas puts it this way: " ... genetically programmed persons might no longer regard themselves as the sole authors of their own life history; and second, (that) they might no longer regard themselves as unconditionally equal-born persons in relation to previous generations."[16] This interesting objection concentrates upon the potential invasion of autonomy that genetic intervention can bring about.

Consider the child who is contingently naturally endowed with musical talents, but who would prefer to be an athlete. She has a gripe against nature but cannot blame her parents or other human agents. At least, she cannot blame them for her natural endowments. She may blame them for the intensive training in music they put her through as a child and various other incitements, disincentives, and so on that went with their desire for her musical future. But at least, she reserves some room for further free choices not to pursue the musical path. Habermas wants to contrast this with the case of genetic choice, but, as he acknowledges, the contrast is not sharp, though he thinks the genetic example is more reprehensible. In both cases, the degree to which the social training or the genetic modification is irreversible seems to him to be what is crucial for moral disapproval. What both (but especially the genetic interventions) threaten is what he calls "the irreducible ethical responsibility that one bears for one's own life, and the assumption (even if counterfactual) that each of us is able to appropriate our own life histories critically, rather than being doomed to the fatalistic acceptance of the consequences of socialization."[17]

This case against "alien co-authorship"[18] as he calls it raises important issues just because it puts the focus on morally significant issues of autonomy and freedom. Autonomy and freedom are, moreover, plausibly regarded by those religious people who value them (and some, of course, don't) as special gifts of God, and this gives particular point to the criticism of "playing God". Nonetheless, I do not think the objection from autonomy is as powerful as Habermas imagines. No one can regard themselves as the sole authors of their own life history, there is too much contingency and inevitable dependence on others for that claim to be plausible. There is

---

[16] Jurgen Habermas, *The Future of Human Nature* (Maldon, Mass.: Polity), 2003, 79.
[17] Ibid., 84–5.   [18] Ibid., 85.

also a problem about shifting issues to do with autonomy from the arena of interfering with the autonomy of palpably existing persons to that of setting the conditions under which such persons will come to be. Presumably a child has no legitimate moral complaint against her musically gifted parents who were attracted to each other partly because of their musical gifts and wanted to have a musically gifted child. But, if not, why would she have a legitimate complaint against parents who, with benevolent intent, genetically engineered musical talent for her? In either case, she may be unhappy with the outcome, but she doesn't have to use the talents, so she is left plenty of room for authoring her life in so far as this phrase makes sense. She need not be condemned to "fatalistic acceptance" nor to failure to "appropriate her own life history critically".

What of the claim that such a child may not regard itself as having unconditional equality with previous generations? It is not altogether clear what this means but if some sort of moral or political equality is at issue, then there seems no reason to deny such equality on the grounds of differential parental choices, whether genetic or otherwise.

It is interesting to consider the situation in which the techniques are available for such modifications, but parents decide not to avail themselves of the choice, preferring to leave the talent outcome to nature. Could not a child who later became interested in a musical career, but had only the modest talents of its parents, complain that they had opted for the natural outcome with much less prospect of high musical talent? They had the option and rejected it. In context, letting nature take its course is no longer a neutral response. Is it nonetheless somehow fairer, given that no one can know what a future person's response to the relevant talent will be?

John Broome has considered an analogous case where the complaint of "playing God" is sometimes raised, namely, that of determining who shall receive scarce medical resources, in particular, kidney dialysis. Some people say that recipients for the scarce treatment should be decided randomly because to decide on the basis of, say, likely longevity on receipt of the treatment, is to play God. They say this because they think that it is not up to human beings to decide that some lives are worth more than others. If anyone can make such a decision, it must be God. In the absence of God, the decision is avoided by resort to random means. Allocating the treatment in any other way than by a random procedure is to deny the equal worth of human beings. Suppose we decide to treat patient A rather than B because A will live forty years with the treatment whereas B will live only twenty. Then we are deciding that A is more worthy of life than B and this denies their equal worth as human beings. Random selection involves no such denial. Broome claims that the argument is confused because deciding randomly *is* to make a decision about differential worth, namely, that "twenty years of one person's life is roughly equal in value to forty years of the other's. A year of one person's life is worth roughly twice as much as a year of the other's."[19] This is an interesting rejoinder, and serves to remind us that devices for avoiding reasoned choice can implicitly invoke the reasons supposedly avoided. Even so, in this case, it seems to me that Broome's response is not entirely successful, since the supporters of random selection do not seem to be principally concerned with the comparative worth of life spans, but with the equal worth of all human beings. It is not altogether clear what this respect for equal worth entails about the comparative value of life spans, and Broome's criticism at least raises a challenge for the equal worth school to meet. Presumably, a random procedure would be out of place for a choice between someone with the prospect of many years of life with dialysis and another who could only live a further two months with this support. Here, we touch upon the concept of futile treatment; this may be difficult to apply in some contexts, but cannot in general merit the criticism of playing God. Yet there is no purchase for the idea that treatment that extends life for twenty years is futile or pointless. On the other hand, respect for the equal dignity of all human beings does not seem to preclude judgements that some lives are more worthy or valuable than others—the life of a compassionate carer seems more worthy than that of a dissolute sadist.

Returning to the case of the choice between genetic intervention for talent and leaving it to nature, we can see that, once the technology is in use, the choice not to use it is something like choosing the random over the reasoned. And again, one might argue that this is better because deliberately choosing this or that talent for the child for reasons of one's own is somehow being unfair. But here it is hard to see in what the unfairness consists. It cannot be that the parents have done something that burdens the child with some talent they haven't chosen, because this will also be true of the choice of leaving it to nature.

[19] John Broome, "Selecting People Randomly", *Ethics*, 95:1, 1984, 52.

One source of our alarm at such proposals, and of our sense that we may be playing God, is related to the way they shift the boundary of the choice and chance factors in our lives. Ronald Dworkin has called this "the spine of our ethics and our morality", and he adds that "any serious shift in that boundary is seriously dislocating."[20] What we can be praised or blamed for takes place against a background that we have no responsibility for and the "givenness" of this background functions in a variety of important ways in our thinking. We take pride in our natural endowments of beauty, grace, or strength and we should probably have a different attitude to such attributes were they the product of human intervention (think of attitudes to the powerful bodies of steroid-dependent athletes). But although we can find such boundary-shifting disorientating, it is unclear that it must always be adjudged wrong. Shifting the boundary between what is given and what is made need not involve a damaging departure from what is truly valuable, though it may take some getting used to.

But none of these enhancements or talent interventions constitutes a change in human nature. They may constitute a change in that elusive entity, identity, but not exactly nature. What if that were in prospect? (Habermas's book about these issues is called, interestingly enough, *The Future of Human Nature*.) Well, there are various difficulties in knowing what is meant by human nature, and there is no doubt that appeals to human nature are sometimes used merely as a device for propping up various versions of the status quo. But it is equally certain that human beings have basic needs and orientations just as do plants and animals. Just as plants need nourishment so human beings need richer forms of nourishment, as well as food and drink. So let us consider the prospect of altering human nature by changing such basic things as the human capacity for love, the human capacity for autonomy and free-will, the human capacity for connection to the human past, the human capacity for involvement in community. Suppose there were a programme for changing some or all of these in the interests of forging a superior being. A particular problem now emerges about the morality appropriate to judging the changes. If you believe that our moral perspective is profoundly linked in some complex way to human nature, then that moral perspective is linked to human nature as it is. We do not have to be "natural law"

---

[20] Dworkin, op. cit., 444.

theorists to accept some such linkage, though an Aristotelian or natural law ethic will presumably accept a stronger link than other theories. Martha Nussbaum has argued, following Aristotle, that our perspective on morality is conditioned profoundly by our understanding of what it is for beings like us to flourish. Our quest for the good life takes place against a background of our natural limitations. We can shift and alter those limits in the process of seeking greater human achievements, just as the athlete surpasses what was thought possible by straining against the existing limitation of the human body. But we need the broad idea of such a limitation to make sense of the surpassing performance. Nussbaum considers the tale of Odysseus's rejection of the goddess Calypso's offer of immortality and divine status. In choosing to reject the superior status of a god, Odysseus sees clearly the fears and uncertainties that would be removed by the change in status and sees the delights that are on offer, but rejects them for the perils and pleasures of the human life that has already shaped his moral outlook.[21]

To make the issue more concrete, we have a powerful moral investment in obligations that are based on our deepest positive affections such as love and deep negative ones such as resentment. Our conceptions of well-being are broad and to a degree capable of divergence but they centre around various satisfactions and fears that are deeply anchored in the sort of beings we are. Proposals to change human beings at this level must themselves be based upon moral understandings that are prior to such changes. Of course, as we suggested in discussing Dworkin, some of the things we presently treat as the fixed background to our normative assessments could be changed without our moral outlooks being drastically disrupted. The fact that we live so much longer than our ancestors represents a change that has many reverberations in the way we confront our lives and deaths. Proposals to extend the normal life span even further should cause us to reflect carefully on what it would mean to lead a human life for 150 years in company with others doing the same, but it doesn't damage the moral fundamentals in the way that a proposal to make us immune to the hazards of love would do. Proposals like the latter have provided material for many of the striking dystopian fables of the twentieth century, such as Huxley's

---

[21] Martha C. Nussbaum, "Transcending Humanity", in her *Love's Knowledge: Essays on Philosophy and Literature* (New York: Oxford University Press), 1990, 365–91.

Brave New World, wherein simplified pictures of human happiness have been imposed without regard for the complex moral possibilities inherent in human nature. Here the charge of playing God may move beyond the caution against hubris (though it includes it) to an intrinsic moral objection to the very idea of changing human nature.

Concluding—A mildly anti-clerical postscript!

Since the accusation of playing God is invariably made against secular agents, such as scientists, and very often made by clergy and theologians, it is worth reflecting on the possibility that the charge could be turned in the opposite direction. After all, it is often religious authority that claims to be representing God and God's purposes. Have the Churches been playing God in the crisis created by the new technologies?

If we return to the attitudinal understanding of "playing God" fleshed out earlier then there is some plausibility to this reversing of the accusation. The temptation to act in ways that ignore or make light of the in-built constraints on human knowledge, power, and benevolence is certainly one to which all humans are prone, including bishops, theologians, and priests. Indeed, those who believe that they are privy to God's purposes through revelation, inspiration, or tradition or all combined are perhaps especially open to the temptation. We should recall in this connection the sad history of religious wars, crusades, inquisitions, the preaching of erroneous doctrines, and the failure to preach important truths. I am a Catholic, and my own Church has its blemishes in all these regards. Rather than proclaim a litany of such offenses, it is enough simply to stress the difficulty of knowing God's will and truth in so many complex settings and the deep tendency of the righteous to simplify both in the interests of the perceived good, but also, often enough, in the interests of power. Of course, for any given issue, the clergy are not playing God if they are actually in receipt of genuine information about what God has decreed. But the evident temptations for religious people to play God should at least give pause to those who believe themselves in that fortunate representative position. Moreover, the current reluctance of clerical authorities to identify with much that was so confidently proclaimed in their institutional past suggests that these temptations do not merely inhabit the realm of possibility.

A similar point can be made about conservatism in the face of technological or social change, whether that conservatism comes from a religious source or elsewhere. A conservative stance on innovation is often seen as necessarily less prone to the assumptions of omniscience, omnipotence, and omnibenevolence. But this does not ring entirely true. The attitudes involved in playing God can easily enough find a home in the defence of the status quo. Those who resisted the modernizing trends that promoted the equality of women were surely playing God with people's lives. They were assuming knowledge about a women's role in the world that was presumptuous and ill based. The gleam of hubris is as likely to be found in the eye of the ardent traditionalist as in that of the fervent revolutionary.

8

Toward a More Fruitful Debate About Enhancement*

Erik Parens

Bioethical debates often seem to feature smart and decent people talking past each other. The debate about the enhancement of human traits and capacities is no exception. Too often we interlocutors seem keener on winning a point than on advancing our shared understanding of the question at hand. This chapter proceeds from the sanguine premise that if we get better at noticing the structure of the debate about enhancement, we might engage in a more fruitful debate.

In my effort to illuminate the structure of the debate, I want to do three things. First, I want to suggest that both proponents and critics of so-called "enhancement technologies" proceed from a "moral ideal of authenticity," although they differ in how they understand it. Here I'm trying to emphasize that critics and proponents share more than they usually remember in the heat of academic battle. Second, I want to suggest that these different understandings of authenticity grow out of two different but equally worthy ethical frameworks, which stand in a fertile tension with each other. I will emphasize that reasons alone cannot account for why most of us feel more comfortable in one framework than in the other and that none of us feels comfortable only in one of them—we all move back and forth between them, to some extent. Finally, I will discuss two examples to show that, on reflection, none of us should want to speak only out of the framework in which we feel most comfortable. If understanding is what we are after, we should embrace rather than

* This chapter is adapted from my "Authenticity and Ambivalence: Toward Understanding the Enhancement Debate," *Hastings Center Report* 35, no. 3 (2005): 34–41.

suppress the ambivalence we often experience when we think about specific interventions.

The moral ideal of authenticity

In *The Ethics of Authenticity*, Charles Taylor reflects on the debate between "the knockers and boosters of modernity." According to Taylor, much of that debate, which simmered in the twentieth century and continues today, is rooted in each side's different mistake about the same moral ideal. The moral ideal of authenticity, which he says emerged fully at the end of the eighteenth century in Europe, is that each of us finds our own way of being in the world. It is my job as a human being to find my way of flourishing, of being true to myself. "If I am not [true to myself], I miss the point of my life, I miss what being human is for me."[1]

Taylor says that this debate about the moral ideal of authenticity is "inarticulate." He writes, "Its opponents slight it, and its friends can't speak of it."[2] What he means by that somewhat oracular formulation is, I think, important.

When Taylor wrote *The Ethics of Authenticity*, Allan Bloom's *The Closing of the American Mind* was still being widely discussed, and Bloom becomes Taylor's paradigmatic knocker of modernity. Much of *Closing of the American Mind* lambastes American college students (and their teachers) for their self-indulgence and shallowness, which Bloom says they cloak in "a certain rhetoric of self-fulfillment."[3] What Bloom doesn't get, according to Taylor, is that, even if some students and their teachers are guilty of self-indulgence and shallowness, many in fact are striving to live up to the moral ideal of authenticity. Whether or not they achieve it, they aspire to find self-fulfillment, to become who they really are. Bloom doesn't get that beneath what he takes to be rampant immorality is the expression of a thoroughly moral ideal.

I am not a serious student of political philosophy and do not mean here to play one. But I need to point out why Taylor thinks it's not just the knockers of modernity who make a mistake about that ideal. According to Taylor, the boosters' view of what's going on is obscured by what he calls

---

[1] C. Taylor, *The Ethics of Authenticity* (Cambridge, Mass.: Harvard University Press, 1991), 29.
[2] Ibid., 18.   [3] Ibid., 16.

"the liberalism of neutrality."[4] He suggests that this sort of liberalism (John Rawls is his first cite) has as one of its basic tenets "that a liberal society must be neutral on questions of what constitutes a good life."[5] To put Taylor's now familiar point even more bluntly than he does in *The Ethics of Authenticity* (or in *Sources of the Self*), there is an important respect in which no theory about living well together can be neutral about what constitutes a good life. A theory about living well together requires a conception of what is good the way seeing requires a horizon. Theories about living well together can pick out different horizons, but they cannot go without one, no matter how fervently we might wish it were otherwise.

In a nutshell, Taylor's complaint about the "the liberalism of neutrality" is that it forgets its tacit commitment to what he calls "the moral ideal of authenticity." It forgets that, insofar as it is committed to affirming persons in their own projects of self-fulfillment, it is not neutral.[6] In their commitment to refraining from specifying the particular forms that self-fulfillment should take, liberals of this sort forget their commitment to the goodness of finding self-fulfillment by implementing one's own life project. Moreover, Taylor suggests, to value self-fulfillment requires a view about the difference between a person who is fulfilled and one who is not. To believe that one understands that difference, one has to have some idea of what being a fulfilled person consists in.

Of course, Taylor is not talking about the debate over so-called enhancement technologies. ("Relativism" is his subject.) I offer his account of the different mistakes made by knockers and boosters of modernity because I want to offer a variation on his claim. Namely, the knockers and boosters—or critics and proponents—of "enhancement technologies" share the moral ideal of authenticity, but they understand authenticity differently: they have different views about what it consists in, and thus about how to achieve it.[7] (Hereafter I will distinguish between critics and proponents;

---

[4] Ibid., 17. [5] Ibid., 17–18.

[6] Here I will do no more than say I'm keenly aware (a) that Rawls has responded to this sort of charge, switching his focus over the years from justice to legitimacy, from metaphysical to political conceptions, and so on (Jim Nelson, personal communication) and (b) that Taylor is but one of many who level this sort of charge. Another is Michael Sandel in *Liberalism and the Limits of Justice* (Cambridge: Cambridge University Press, 1982).

[7] I believe one finds this sort of argument in Ronald Dworkin's *Life's Dominion* (New York: Alfred A. Knopf, 1993); I'm referring to his claim that we disagree so profoundly about abortion because "we interpret the idea that human life is intrinsically valuable in different ways" (70).

the labels "knockers" and "boosters" seem to connote simplemindedness, and I think it's a bad mistake to attribute simplemindedness to either side.)

While the idea of authenticity has a complex history, the core of it is that we are authentic when we exhibit or are in possession of what is most our own: our own way of flourishing or being fulfilled. To be separated from what is most our own is to be in a state of alienation.

Critics of enhancement technologies—and they are a distinguished and heterogeneous lot—worry that these technologies threaten our efforts at achieving authenticity. They worry that enhancement technologies will separate us from what is most our own. This is surely not their only worry, but I am suggesting it is central. Later I will emphasize that the difference between critics and proponents is not the same as the difference between political "conservatives" and "liberals"; indeed, some of the most astute and eloquent critics of enhancement technologies are political liberals like Susan Bordo, Alice Dreger, Carl Elliott, Thomas Murray, and myriad others. But I will begin with one version of the critics' concern, as articulated in *Beyond Therapy*, a report written by George W. Bush's President's Council on Bioethics.

In *Beyond Therapy*, Leon Kass and the members of the council (not all of whom are political conservatives) speak at length about, to take but one central example, mood-altering drugs like Prozac. In a word, they are concerned that mood-altering drugs will separate us from the actions and experiences that normally accompany those moods.[8] They worry that in separating us from those un-drug-mediated experiences, we will be separated from who we really are[9] and from how the world really is.[10] They write: "As the power to transform our native powers increases, both in magnitude and refinement, so does the possibility for 'self-alienation'—for losing, confounding, or abandoning our identity."[11]

Again, it is not only political conservatives who worry that such drugs will separate us from who we really are. Much of Carl Elliott's book *Better Than Well* is a trenchant analysis of what he takes to be the dominant contemporary American conception of authenticity, which holds that to achieve authenticity, we need to buy more stuff from the medical-industrial complex.

[8] President's Council on Bioethics, *Beyond Therapy: Biotechnology and the Pursuit of Happiness* (New York: Regan Books, 2003), 238–9.
[9] Ibid., 253.   [10] Ibid., 255.   [11] Ibid., 294.

Like many of us, Elliott isn't eager to get too explicit about the alternative conception of authenticity he favors. After all, the concept of the authentic self can seem awfully close to outré notions like "the essential self" or "the real self." As Elliott quotes someone else saying: "The real self as a belief went out in the 70s."[12] But he isn't prepared to jettison altogether the idea of the authentic self. "You can buy into the idea of an authentic self without buying into the idea of an essentialist self," he remarks.[13]

Though Elliott does not try in *Better Than Well* to get clear about his particular take on authenticity, he does in an earlier essay, "The Tyranny of Happiness."[14] Or at least he gets clear about a fundamental worry that helps us infer what he thinks authenticity is: the worry that a drug like Prozac might separate us from the way the world really is. In the "Tyranny of Happiness," Elliott invents a character of his own, an accountant living in Downers Grove, Illinois, who comes to himself one day and says, "Jesus Christ, is this it? A Snapper lawn mower and a house in the suburbs?" Elliott invites us to imagine that we're this man's psychiatrist. Should we prescribe Prozac? Or should we think that, "even though he's in a predicament, at least he's aware of it, which is a lot better than being in a predicament and thinking you're not"?[15] Elliott traces this idea about the value of knowing you're in a predicament to the novelist Walker Percy, who traces the same idea to Søren Kierkegaard, one of the progenitors of at least one understanding of authenticity. Indeed, the epigraph for Percy's *The Moviegoer* is taken from Kierkegaard's *Sickness Unto Death*: "the specific character of despair is precisely this: it is unaware of being despair."

I should hasten to add that neither Kierkegaard nor Percy nor Elliott says it is good to be depressed. They say, rather, that to live authentically is to perceive the world and oneself as they really are, in the face of the ever-present temptation to look away. In our new age of "exuberance,"[16] I hesitate to acknowledge that, on this sort of view, it is better to suffer because

---

[12] C. Elliott, *Better Than Well: American Medicine Meets the American Dream* (New York: Norton, 2003), 48.

[13] Ibid., 49.

[14] C. Elliott, "The Tyranny of Happiness," in *Enhancing Human Traits: Ethical and Social Implications*, ed. E. Parens (Washington, D.C.: Georgetown University Press, 1998): 177–88.

[15] Ibid., 180.

[16] P. Kramer, "Goodbye, Darkness: The New Science of Exuberance," *Slate*, September 20, 2004, at http://slate.msn.com/id/2106883.

of one's awareness than it is to relieve one's suffering by looking away. The point is not that suffering is good but that compromising our awareness is bad. Elliott's worry about Prozac is that it threatens that awareness; it threatens to separate us from who we really are and how the world really is.

Proponents of enhancement, of course, view these same technologies very differently. They see them not as a threat to authenticity, but rather as tools that can facilitate our authentic efforts at self-discovery and self-creation. Indeed, much of Peter Kramer's *Listening to Prozac* aims directly at the sort of argument one finds in Kierkegaard, Percy, and Elliott. Kramer's basic argument is that drugs like Prozac do not separate us from what is most our own. On the contrary, they give us what is most our own; they free us up so that we can encounter the world as it really is and authentically create ourselves. "There is a sense in which antidepressants are feminist drugs, liberating and empowering."[17] Prozac does not rob life of the edifying potential for tragedy; "it catalyzes the precondition for tragedy, namely, participation."[18] According to Kramer, Prozac enables people to embark on their own quest to find out or create who they really are.[19]

Along with Peter Kramer, Jonathan Glover, Julian Savulescu, and others, David DeGrazia makes a complementary argument when he invites his readers to consider the case of a young woman who had a traumatic childhood, who currently isn't leading the life she imagines for herself, and who asks her doctor to prescribe Prozac so that she can transform herself. Of this young woman's request, DeGrazia writes:

[I]t is hard to see the basis of paternalistically judging that her values and self-conception are not authoritative for her own life—not only for what is good in her life (best interests) but also for what constitutes her life (authenticity). I therefore conclude that Prozac . . . can be an authentic part of a project of self-creation.[20]

To put the point in the terms I'm employing, DeGrazia makes explicit how the proponent's view of enhancement technologies is consistent with

---

[17] P. Kramer, *Listening to Prozac* (New York: Viking, 1993), 40.   [18] Ibid., 258.

[19] In another essay ("Kramer's Anxiety," in *Prozac As a Way of Life*, ed. C. Elliott and T. Chambers (Chapel Hill: University of North Carolina Press, 2004)) I have tried to show that Kramer sometimes suggests that Prozac can be used to "discover" the authentic self (that is, to free the self from genetic and environmental constraints) and at other times suggests that Prozac can be used by an individual to "create" her authentic self. Whether talking in terms of discovering or creating the self, Kramer seeks to show that Prozac can promote as opposed to thwart "authenticity."

[20] D. DeGrazia, "Prozac, Enhancement, and Self-Creation," in *Prozac As a Way of Life*, ed. C. Elliott and T. Chambers (Chapel Hill: University of North Carolina Press, 2004): 33–47, at 41.

the liberal commitment to defending the individual's right to choose for herself what the good life is for her and what her life project will be.

As someone who deeply sympathizes with that position, for now I would just remind us of Taylor's earlier point about liberal neutrality. In their defense of the individual's right and obligation to use enhancement technologies to craft her own life project, proponents sometimes forget that their defense grows out of a commitment to a particular view of what it means to be a person: they are committed to the moral ideal of authenticity, to the idea that people who are fully persons should find self-fulfillment. As liberals, proponents are loath to foist on others their own conceptions of the good, but, like it or not, they must have some idea of what self-fulfillment means. To have an idea of what self-fulfillment is presupposes an idea of what a self or a person is. Below I will offer an example to try to persuade the proponent that her concept of personhood and self-fulfillment is thicker than she is accustomed to acknowledging.[21] (Of course, if the proponent's mistake is to profess too little understanding of what being a fulfilled person is, the critic's mistake is to assume too much.)

Different frameworks

Although there are important disagreements among both critics and proponents, I want briefly to describe what I take to be an important difference between critics and proponents.

I have come to think that these different understandings of authenticity grow out of what I will call two different ethical frameworks. By "frameworks," I mean a constellation of commitments that support and shape our responses to questions about, among many other things, new enhancement technologies. When I refer to those different frameworks as "ethical," I use that term in its broadest possible sense, as designating habits of thought and being. Were it a more felicitous neologism, I would refer to "psycho-ethical frameworks," to emphasize that these frameworks have an important psychological (and perhaps aesthetic) dimension. Instead, I will

---

[21] M. Nussbaum, "Human Functioning and Social Justice: In Defense of Aristotelian Essentialism," *Political Theory* 20 (1992): 202–46; and M. Nussbaum, "Non-Relative Virtues: An Aristotelian Approach," in *The Quality of Life*, ed. M. Nussbaum and A. Sen (New York: Oxford University Press, 1993): 242–69.

say simply that I believe these different conceptions of authenticity grow, at least in part, out of different pre-rational experiences and understandings of our selves and of our proper relationships to the world.

These frameworks are built of answers to questions that do not have only one good answer. In another place I have described some of those questions at length,[22] but for now I will merely mention some: Can we meaningfully distinguish between "natural" and "artificial" human interventions into nature? Should we conceive of technology as morally neutral or morally loaded? What do we mean when we claim that we are free, and to what extent are we free? And so forth.

To emphasize that these two frameworks are intimately related even as they are importantly different, I will dare to remind you of a single figure in an oft-cited book. In the book of Genesis, Jacob's wife Rachel, who was unable to bear children, begs him: "Give me children, or I shall die." Jacob famously responded to Rachel's injunction with a question, "Am I in the place of God?" With this question, Jacob expresses one of the book's central and best-known ideas: that we human beings are not the creators of life; we are creatures, whose job is to remember that life is a gift. It is our responsibility to express our gratitude for the mysterious whole, which we have not made.

This sort of attitude does not require a commitment to any particular religious tradition, indeed to any religion at all. Many an environmentalist (like Bill McKibben, author of The End of Nature and Enough: Genetic Engineering and the End of Human Nature) adopts such an attitude. Many a left-leaning critic of corporatization (like Rich Hayes, who directs the Center for Genetics and Society) adopts it. Michael Sandel invokes the secular version of this idea when he writes, "If bioengineering made the myth of the 'self-made man' come true, it would be difficult to view our talents as gifts for which we are indebted, rather than as achievements for which we are responsible. This would transform three key features of our moral landscape: humility, responsibility, and solidarity."[23] We can discern in his words the sort of view symbolized by Jacob's question: if we forget that life is a gift—albeit from an unknown giver—we will make a mistake about the sort of creatures we really are and the way the world really is.

---

[22] E. Parens, "Creativity, Gratitude, and The Enhancement Debate," in *Neuroethics in the 21st Century*, ed. J. Illes (Oxford: Oxford University Press, 2005).

[23] M. Sandel, "The Case Against Perfection," *Atlantic Monthly* (April 2004): 51–62, at 60.

But this very same Jacob, who exhibits a kind of gratitude that many today associate with "religion," also exhibits a radically different stance, which Genesis also celebrates. After all, as has been noted more than once, Jacob, the very one whose name would become Israel, was "the first genetic engineer"; he was the one with the creativity to fashion a device ("rods of poplar and almond, into which he peeled white streaks" (Gen. 30:38)) with which he induced his uncle's goats to produce only the valuable "speckled and spotted" (Gen. 30:39) young. According to Genesis, and it seems to me much of Judaism, our responsibility is not merely to be grateful and remember that we are not the creators of the whole. It is also our responsibility to use our creativity to mend and transform ourselves and the world. As far as I can tell, Genesis and Judaism do not exhort us to choose between gratitude and creativity. Rather, or so it seems to this pagan, it is our job to figure out how to maintain that fertile tension, making sure that neither stance gets more than its share.

When we observe scholars and others debate about "enhancement technologies," I believe that we often see people who have at least for the moment adopted either the gratitude or creativity framework, as I am calling them. As one side emphasizes our obligation to remember that life is a gift and that we need to learn to let things be, the other emphasizes our obligation to transform that gift and to exhibit our creativity. As one framework emphasizes the danger of allowing ourselves to become, in Heidegger's famous formulation, "standing reserve," the other emphasizes the danger of failing to summon the courage to, as Nietzsche put it, "create" ourselves, to "become who we are."

Indeed, sometimes the same scholar moves between frameworks in the same talk. I believe I saw my friend Eric Juengst, a philosopher who has thought deeply about human enhancement, do just that during a lecture at Hiram College in the summer of 2004; he operated out of the creativity framework when he criticized those who would oppose all efforts at extending life, and he operated out of the gratitude framework when he criticized efforts that would bring normal ageing under the control of medical science. Again, most of us can be comfortable in both frameworks, even if most of us are considerably more comfortable in one framework than in the other. I should hurry to add: moving between frameworks, being ambivalent, seems to me to be a sign of openness and thoughtfulness, not confusion.

It's not only because I love that we find both attitudes in one figure that I invoke Jacob. Yes, it is essential to remember that none of us who is thoughtful inhabits only one of those frameworks. But it is also useful to remember that the figure of Jacob appears in a book that is "religious." In fact, one might tell a creation story about bioethics that has the field grow out of a battle between two titans, both of whom were theologians: Paul Ramsey, the Ur-critic of biotechnology,[24] and Joseph Fletcher, the Ur-proponent.[25] If one looked to the history of presidential commissions that broached the enhancement question, one would notice that each of them has brought out theologians from both the gratitude and creativity frameworks: one side reminds us of the importance of letting things be, eschewing arrogance, and so on, while the other reminds us with equal passion of our obligation to find the courage to become creative in our efforts to ameliorate human suffering.

Suggesting that we find religious soil at the roots of the critical and the enthusiastic stances toward enhancement helps me bring to the fore concerns I have about both sides of the enhancement debate. Beginning with the side I feel most comfortable on: the critics. Sometimes, when we critics speak, we sound as if we have forgotten or don't even fully appreciate that, in principle, the creativity framework is as worthy as the gratitude framework. When we try to make the case "against perfection" or when we raise problems with the "ethic of willfulness,"[26] we risk forgetting that at the core of that ethic is the noble impulse to be creative, to mend and transform ourselves and the world. Were we to speak, instead, of "the ethic of *creativity*," we might be more prone to give the other side its due.

By calling attention to the religious element of the commitments on both sides, I am trying to emphasize what I take to be an obvious but under-appreciated fact: the proponent is not as neutral as she sometimes seems to believe. She has no more than anyone else escaped the maw of extra-rational commitments.

Having named these two ethical frameworks, I need to emphasize several caveats. First, I've tried to make abundantly clear that I don't think

---

[24] P. Ramsey, *Fabricated Man: The Ethics of Genetic Control* (New Haven, Conn.: Yale University Press, 1970).

[25] J. Fletcher, *The Ethics of Genetic Control: Ending Reproductive Roulette* (New York: Prometheus Books, 1974).

[26] Sandel, "Case Against Perfection," 56.

the difference between critics and proponents is the same as the difference between people who are religious and those who are secular. You find both kinds in both camps. Second, the distinction between the gratitude and creativity frameworks is not the same as that between political conservatism and liberalism; conservatives and liberals operate out of each.

Finally, I do not for a moment forget that distinguishing between the gratitude framework of the critics and the creativity framework of the proponents is a *very crude heuristic*. The outlines of the gratitude and creativity frameworks are neat only in speech. Nonetheless, I think that when we engage in debates about enhancement technologies, it can help to recognize that people on both sides are speaking out of the framework in which they feel most comfortable. And I think it is crucial to recognize that none of us, if we are reflective, feels comfortable only in one of these frameworks. Even if we settle in one for the sake of debating each other, in our day-to-day lives we shuttle between them. One might say that in our day-to-day lives we are often more prone to allow ourselves such thoughtfulness—and ambivalence—than when we sit down to engage in scholarship.

The limits of the frameworks

I have suggested that the gratitude and creativity frameworks deserve equal respect and that we should aspire to balance the commitments and insights of both. I should point out, however, what I think is patently obvious: most readers of this volume of essays live in a time and in places where the gratitude and creativity frameworks do not receive equal weight or enjoy equal respect. The two constellations of commitments are not in balance. At least on my interpretation of the current scene, the creativity framework dominates.

There is after all no money to be made in exhibiting gratitude, at least to the extent that exhibiting gratitude means letting things be. The money, as John Berger, Thomas Frank, Susan Bordo, Carl Elliott, and myriad others have pointed out, is in persuading consumers that they should garner the courage to purchase a product that will help them shape their life projects according to their own discovery of what is good for them. As the advertisers for a breast enlargement company called Mentor put it in an ad they called "Amber's choice": "Check it out for yourself. Then do it for yourself." Amber isn't the sort of young woman who can be co-opted by anybody else's conception of the good. As the ad tells us, her "pet peeve" is "People who pressure me into doing things" and her "life's mission" is to "Always be open to new ideas." As if we need to be told that a company called Mentor could appeal to someone who wasn't open to new ideas!

For the rest of this chapter I want briefly to discuss two "cases" that I think should make honest inhabitants of both frameworks acknowledge insight on the "other side." First to a difficult case for proponents.

To get at the difficulty, I need to rehearse a couple of facts about heterosexual men and Viagra. The drug enables men who cannot otherwise achieve or sustain an erection to engage in sexual intercourse. For the sake of this discussion, let's assume that the erectile dysfunction we're talking about is rooted in a plumbing, not a relationship, problem. Insofar as many heterosexual couples consider sexual intercourse to be an essential part of a loving relationship, which in turn they take to be an essential part of being a fulfilled person, Viagra can help to facilitate relationships and fulfill persons, and thus surely is a good thing.

According to the experts, Viagra works because most men are, sexually speaking, simple. If a pill can get blood to a man's penis, then he will experience the desire for sexual intercourse. Or as the experts put it, there is no gap between arousal and desire for most men. Arousal essentially entails desire.[27]

That's not true for many women. To get from arousal to desire, many women need to experience what is often summed up as "intimacy." Alas, Viagra can't bridge that gap. It can get blood to a woman's vagina, but it won't necessarily make her experience the desire for sexual intercourse.

This is disheartening if you're Pfizer and you want to break into the women's market. So what's a drug company to do? One obvious strategy is to try to close the gap between arousal and desire. As one female Pfizer researcher told a *New York Times* reporter, "What we need to do is find a pill for engendering the *perception of intimacy*" (my emphasis).[28] If Pfizer could develop a pill that could make women feel like they were experiencing intimacy, then the gap could be closed, and the market opened.

[27] M. Loe, *The Rise of Viagra: How the Little Blue Pill Changed Sex in America* (New York: New York University Press, 2004).

[28] G. Harris, "Pfizer Gives Up Testing On Women," *New York Times*, February 28, 2004, C1–2.

Whether that Pfizer researcher was speaking ruefully or in earnest, she raises an interesting question: What should reasonable proponents think about a pill "for engendering the perception of intimacy"? The easiest response is, of course, "Look, that's not a way of shaping a life project that I admire, but who am I to say?" While I share many of the assumptions behind that rhetorical question and acknowledge its power, I think that response gets us too quickly off the hook of thinking.

The second but by now nearly automatic response is: "Look, there's nothing new here. We've always used 'medicine' to create the perception of intimacy. What do you think alcohol is?" I will not rehearse here the problems that beset arguments from precedent. For now I will merely point out that it doesn't follow from the fact that humans have long sought a way around the need for intimacy that we should now be happy to get the world's largest industry in on the action.

I think that honest proponents will acknowledge that the idea of a pill that would, in the absence of genuine human intimacy, create the perception of intimacy, is perplexing—even for the clearest thinking and toughest minded among us. I think the honest proponent will find this case troubling because she has a thicker conception of what a person is—and thus how one fulfills the moral ideal of authenticity—than she is accustomed to acknowledging (at least in debates about enhancement technologies). An essential part of being a fulfilled person is experiencing intimacy with another person. In words that Taylor might use but that a proponent might at first find foreign: to live up to the moral ideal of authenticity, to be a true or authentic or fulfilled person, one needs to discover and cultivate intimate relationships with other people. If a person's relationship depended on a pill to engender the perception of intimacy, we—proponents and skeptics alike—would think that person was not living truly or authentically or was missing out on an essential, if not always easy, part of life.

I'm not saying that a reasonable proponent would want to outlaw a pill for the perception of intimacy. But if some proponents are indeed perplexed by some cases, it would deepen the understanding of the rest of us if they would offer an account of their perplexity. In doing so, they would likely find themselves temporarily adopting language native to the gratitude framework. I think they would find themselves appealing to the idea that there are some human problems we should not use technology to eliminate. Or, as Jim Edwards has recently put this idea: "Usually we demand that the facts answer to us, to our needs that the world be ordered as we see fit; some facts, however, have the demand on their side: it is we who must answer to them."[29] On this sort of view, instead of using technology to erase the problem that is the need for intimacy, we should let it be.

Notice, however, that no one from either framework would say, "Let the problem be," full stop. Rather, she would say something along the lines of, "Instead of using a pill to make that problem disappear, we should use some other means—like words—to try to grapple with it, if never fully 'solve' it." Nor does adopting the critics' language of gratitude entail giving up altogether the impulse to creatively transform the self and world. How could any of us simply give up that impulse? The language of gratitude merely gives the speaker a way of expressing what she takes to be a threat to authentic personhood. To fully express that, the proponent would likely be thrown back on some variation of the claim that a pill for intimacy would threaten to separate us from the true, if impoverished, state of a relationship without intimacy. She would, I think, be thrown back on some version of the claim that it is better to be without genuine intimacy and aware of it than to be without genuine intimacy and unaware of it.

Having briefly discussed a problem for honest proponents, now I want to discuss still more briefly a problem for honest critics. As many know, increasing numbers of men and women are seeking surgery to transition to the sex opposite the one they were born into. So-called transgender surgeries enable people who were born with male anatomies to adopt female anatomies (and people who were born with female anatomies to transition to male anatomies).

Now if one is, as I am, most comfortable working out of the gratitude framework, then one's first response to transgender surgery is that it is a very bad idea. We should let bodies be, not "mutilate" them. People who want to transition should, rather than changing their bodies, help the rest of us to change how we think about sexual and gender variation. We should realize that this is one more opportunity for all of us to learn to affirm the wide and marvelous range of phenotypic variation.

---

[29] J. Edwards, "Concepts of Technology and Their Role in Moral Reflection," in *Surgically Shaping Children*, ed. E. Parens (Baltimore, Md.: Johns Hopkins University Press, 2006).

If, however, you listen to people who have had to decide between living with a body they experience as alien and transforming their bodies into the shape they feel to be true, I think you will have to acknowledge the problem with that initial reaction. In his careful and persuasive book, *Becoming a Visible Man*, Jamison Green, a female-to-male transgendered person, reflects on the very responses voiced by those who feel most comfortable in the gratitude framework. The bottom line for Green, however, is that he did not feel at home in the body of a woman. In that body, he did not feel fully "present" or "visible" and thus was not able to share in what he takes to be genuine intimacy. He writes, "The only proof [that one has achieved real presence] is in the strength of one's connectedness with others, the kind of connectedness that I could not truly feel until I became a visible man."[30]

When someone hears this sort of argument, she has two obvious, if crude, interpretive options. She can say that this thoughtful and eloquent man is deceiving himself (he operates with "false consciousness"), or she can accept his claim that surgical transformation is a necessary condition for him to experience connectedness, intimacy, and relationship.

I cannot adopt that first, "false consciousness" response. If Jamison is not reflective and clear thinking about himself, then none of us is. So I'm left with the option of accepting his claim that the surgical transformation makes genuine relationship possible for him. This realization can be troubling for someone working out of the gratitude framework, who, like me, is committed to learning to let healthy bodies be, and who worries that medical technologies can threaten our authentic encounters with ourselves and the world.

But it seems to me it would be a bad mistake to let that commitment or worry get in the way of appreciating that, however you understand authenticity or flourishing or personhood, the capacity to enter into intimate relationships must be central. Different from the "pill for intimacy," which undermines the purpose of achieving genuine intimacy and relationship, Jamison's surgeries seem to promote that purpose. So, as much as it disturbs my neat theoretical objections to using medical means to shape selves, or disturbs my commitment to letting healthy bodies be,[31] I cannot deny that in this context, the medical means seem to promote a purpose I should

---

[30] J. Green, *Becoming a Visible Man* (Nashville, Tenn.: Vanderbilt University Press, 2004), 169.

[31] E. Parens, "Is Better Always Good?" A Special Supplement to the *Hastings Center Report* 28, no. 1 (1998): S1–S16.

endorse. As one working out of the creativity framework can too quickly forget that means matter, one working out of the gratitude framework can too quickly forget that purposes matter.

Coda

At the New York City meeting out of which this volume of essays grew, Jonathan Glover observed that enhancement technologies force us to think anew about the oldest, most pressing, and most infuriatingly difficult of questions: What does human flourishing consist in? Indeed, it is a very good thing that we are engaged in a debate about how enhancement technologies will promote and thwart human flourishing.

As we engage in that debate, we should recall Socrates's famous distinction between *dialectic* and *elenchus*: between arguing for the sake of understanding a question and arguing for the sake of refuting one's opponent. I have suggested that when we argue about enhancement, too often we aim at refutation. The problem of course is that we then fail to recognize insight on the other side.

I have tried to suggest not only that we should recognize the value of the ethical framework in which we are less comfortable, but that most of us actually do recognize its value. Indeed, when we're not waging argumentative war, we sometimes find ourselves exploring our ambivalence, shuttling between the frameworks we're more and less comfortable in. As I've tried to say, it would be very difficult to live in this culture and not appreciate the virtues of the creativity and gratitude frameworks. Each of us is, as it were, Jacob.

It may be that on other topics, passionate refutations are warranted and productive. But I don't see how it helps when we're talking about the sorts of self-shaping technologies that I've just mentioned. Given that, by definition, we're talking about interventions that someone thinks aim at improvement, and given that pursuing them will usually entail different sorts of considerable costs to the individual, some large and potentially noble human ideal seems at work. Insofar as one is, critics should be slow to criticize. But if we are trying to talk together about the difference between interventions that stand a good chance of promoting "authenticity" and those that don't, then proponents should be slow to stand up and cheer. Or at least they should be quick to acknowledge their perplexity.

Anyone who has used the word "authenticity" or has tried to track how others use it knows how slippery it is. It is tempting to say that we use it in different ways at different times because we are confused, or because we are trying to dress up our preferences in fancy philosophical garb. I have tried to suggest, instead, that its slipperiness reflects the fact that we think about authenticity in different ways; we think out of different frameworks at different times. I do not have an account of why we adopt this framework and then that one. Nor do I have an account of how we should evaluate this or that use of the frameworks. My hope is merely that by calling attention to these two different frameworks and to the fertile tension between them, I have made a small contribution toward helping us to aim less at refutation and more at understanding—less at talking past and more at talking with.

9

Good, Better, or Best?

Arthur L. Caplan

The rise of anti-meliorism

Excellence has come in for a lot of bad press recently. A torrent of books and articles have appeared [see list of References, 1–10, 20] all raising serious ethical questions about the wisdom and morality of trying to use new biomedical knowledge to perfect ourselves or our offspring. Of course, beating up on the literal pursuit of perfection is silly. As the artist Salvador Dali famously pointed out, "Have no fear of perfection—you'll never reach it".

Critics of those who allegedly seek to perfect human beings by means of bioengineering know this. Nonetheless, they often invoke the rhetoric of 'perfection' in their critiques since the pursuit of perfection seems arrogant at best and silly at worst. Perfection, however, while an easy target, is not their real target. What they really are attacking is the far more frequently expressed, albeit far less lofty, and, notably, far less controversial goal—improvement. The critics are very concerned about the drive to improve or enhance particular human behaviors, traits or features by the application of emerging biomedical knowledge in genetics, neuroscience, pharmacology and physiology.

Those who I will lump together as 'anti-meliorists' wonder how we will ever resist the obvious temptation to put the explosion of biomedical knowledge to use for the aim of improving ourselves. They are quick to note that we are already edging down the melioristic road. Breasts are being augmented, wrinkles smoothed, fat suctioned, blood doped and moods calmed. Where, the anti-meliorists wonder, will this all end?

Why is the drive to improve ourselves so disturbing to anti-meliorists? Their arguments cluster around these key worries: that the pursuit of perfection by biomedical means is vain, selfish and unrewarding [1, 2, 3, 6, 7], that improving ourselves is unfair [1, 3, 4, 10], that the happiness achieved through engineering with an eye toward improvement will lead to a deformation of our character and spirit [1, 2, 4, 9], improvement in performance that is bioengineered is not authentic and therefore not morally proper [1, 2, 9, 10], accepting enhancement will undermine and deform the role of parent [9] and, that enhancement or improvement violate human nature [2, 4, 5, 7, 8, 9] or worse still, may actually destroy it [2, 5, 7, 9].

I am going to spend little time examining concerns about vanity. Vanity and self-regard are not the same things. Self-regard, in moderation, is not a moral evil. And when examined carefully the anti-meliorist invocation of vanity seems to me to be based on the assertion that the pursuit of improvement by means of bioengineering is of necessity vain rather than simply an instance of legitimate self-regard. Wanting to look better or function more efficiently cannot justifiably be dismissed as mere vanity. The anti-meliorist must first tell us how to recognize morally suspect vanity from morally legitimate self-regard.

I will also pass over anti-meliorist arguments about inequity since they miss the relevant mark. When it comes to worries about fair access to melioristic biotechnologies, those concerned about equity worry either about the creation of more 'haves' and 'have nots'—as the rich get better, the poor will languish—or, the inequity of private companies earning massive profits by seducing us all into frivolous efforts to improve ourselves (10).

Equity and fairness are major problems in this and every society. But, concerns about equity do not speak to why improvement is wrong. Rather, equity arguments tell us whether a pattern of inequality or a particular distribution of resources is right or wrong. It is important to decide what is fair in the distribution of access to enhancement technologies or what to do about greedy, manipulative pharmaceutical or cosmetics industries that fool us into wasting our money on silly things when real health needs go unmet—but these are matters that are quite distinct from and hardly unique to improvement via new biological knowledge. Equity arguments do not show what is inherently wrong with the desire to use biotechnology to improve ourselves and our children [11].

The remaining arguments of anti-meliorism do engage improvement on its own terms and thus do merit a response. It is the last of these arguments, which I believe is at the core of anti-meliorist concerns. So I will engage the view that it is wrong to tamper with human nature first and then return to the remaining concerns of anti-meliorists. I do not think that any of the arguments that have been brought forward provide a convincing case against improvement.

Human nature inviolate?

It cannot simply be the pursuit of improvement that is making anti-meliorists nervous. Many religious traditions, self-help, and spiritual movements seek improvement, even perfection [12, 13, 14] but these evoke no negative commentary from the anti-meliorists. Nor, interestingly enough, do recent and sustained efforts to improve animals and plants using biotechnology evoke much more than an ethical yawn (with the exception of McKibben [2]). Rather, it is the use of biomedical knowledge applied to you and me that is the crux of their concern. Those who worry about what will become of human nature fear that in applying new biomedical knowledge to improve human beings something essential about humanity will be lost. If biomedical tinkering is allowed we will destroy the very thing that makes us human—our nature.

Anti-meliorism rests, however, on a very shaky foundation. To support their position the anti-meliorists must state what human nature is. Despite a great deal of hand-waving about this they do not. They must also be very clear about why they see human nature as static. They are not. And they must advance an argument about why human nature, which has evolved in response to an enormous array of random forces, accidental environmental contingencies, and stochastic genetic events, tells us anything about what is good or desirable in terms of the traits humans should possess. They cannot.

The products of the 'random walk' of evolution, where a series of contingent events intersect to produce the patterns of life we call organisms, do not teach any lessons about what we should become any more than they can tell us what is right or wrong, good or bad. They merely are what they are.

Is there a 'nature' that is common to all humans, both those that exist now and those that have existed in the past? The fight over whether there is any such thing as human nature is a long-standing one [15, 16]. But one can concede that we have been shaped by a causally powerful set of genetic influences and selection forces and still remain skeptical as to whether these have produced a single 'nature' that all members of humanity possess. What exactly is the single trait or fixed, determinate set of traits that defines the nature of who humans are and have been throughout our entire existence as a species on this planet? Unless they can articulate this Platonic essence, anti-meliorists who invoke the sanctity of human nature as the basis for their moral concerns about improvement lack a foundation for their argument. If one surveys all humans, across cultures, those of all ages and varieties of congenital defects, and those from different times in the past it becomes hard to believe any single trait is defining of human nature.

Without a demonstration of a 'nature' there is no basis for the claim that change, improvement, and betterment always represent grave threats to our essential humanity. In fact, perhaps the only lesson that evolution teaches is that adaptation to change is the key requirement for life on this planet.

Worse still for anti-meliorists, even if there is an amalgam of traits that might be roughly described as constituting human nature, that does not show that it is wrong to tamper with those traits to try and improve upon them. We are creatures who have long tinkered with ourselves using all manner of technologies from clothing to medicines to agriculturally produced foods to telescopes to computers to airplanes.

Our view of our 'nature' is closely linked to the technologies that we have invented and to which we have adapted [17]. We don't think of ourselves as being engineered for improvement but we are. We have already engaged in systematic meliorism using science and technology. We are traveling, eating, flying, computing, and perceiving in ways that are distinct improvements upon what would be possible using only our natural endowments. Each of these 'improvements' comes at a price but it is not clear that it is a price not worth paying [18]. And more to the point, there is no reason to think that this creative manipulation of our environment, including our own bodies and minds, is any less worthy of inclusion as part of human 'nature' [19].

Nor is there any normative guidance offered by our evolutionary history that shows why we should not try to improve upon the biological design with which we are endowed. Augmenting breasts or prolonging erections may be vain, self indulgent, trivial, and a waste of scarce resources but seeking to use our knowledge to enhance our vision, memory, strength, learning skills, immunity, or metabolism are not obviously any of these things.

Ultimately, anti-meliorism posits a static vision of human nature to which the anti-meliorists mandate we reconcile ourselves. If anything is clear about human nature it is that this is not an accurate view of who we have been or what we are now, or a view which should determine what we become [16]. So, if human nature does not provide a foundation for anti-meliorism what other arguments are there? The inadvisability of settling for 'cheap' thrills and the importance of resisting the lure of the inauthentic are two prominent lines of argument in the anti-meliorist camp.

The 'loss' of authenticity

It is estimated that nearly one and a half million Americans have undergone laser surgery to improve their vision. The purveyors of this procedure often promise that those who have it will see better than they ever have before, even with the aid of glasses or contact lenses. Laser surgery sometimes can give eyes better than 20–20 vision. So, have those who have undergone this type of procedure and achieved enhanced vision done something immoral? If you were to read the report of the President's Council on Bioethics entitled *Beyond Therapy: Biotechnology and the Pursuit of Happiness* [1] you might think so.

Admittedly the eye is not the only part of the brain that people want to improve. Interest in brain enhancement is enormous. Already a number of pharmaceutical companies are interested in selling drugs such as Provigil, that allow individuals to go without sleep for longer periods of time than they otherwise could or Ambien that provides sleep with fewer side-effects than older sleeping aids. Herbal and nutritional companies are also peddling substances that allegedly can improve memory, mood, or sexual enjoyment. Many students are keenly interested in any drug, say Atavan or Ritalin or Prozac, that might improve their performance on tests or in musical, dramatic, or athletic performances by allowing for greater attention span, increased short-term memory, fewer muscle twitches or reduced anxiety. The military has an interest in seeing mental performance improved so as to increase the combat effectiveness of individuals or entire units. And not a few of us drink coffee, tea, colas, and other stimulants to try and enhance our cognitive performance. Many take various drugs, foods and herbs, or utilize technology such as virtual reality to try to enhance their mood, emotional state, or sexual enjoyment. While these activities can and sometimes are abused, it would hardly seem self evident that it is morally wrong to seek to try and improve one's mental abilities. Surely it is the critics of efforts to improve or enhance what the brain can do that bear the burden of showing why this is wrong.

So what is the basis for the moral concern of those who authored the Council's Report about efforts to improve, enhance or optimize our brains, vision, or any other human trait? To some extent they worry that since the brain is the seat of our nature then altering it is to alter our very nature. But as we have already seen this argument presumes both a clear, static, and inviolate nature that is not consistent with any evolutionary view of how our brains came to be what they are. So what other arguments do the anti-meliorists make? Among other concerns are these:

1. the happiness or satisfaction achieved through engineering is seductive and will lead to a deformation of our character and spirit;
2. improvement in performance that is engineered is not authentic and is, thus, not earned and is, therefore, not morally commendable.

Neither of these arguments provides a sufficient reason to oppose enhancement or optimization of our vision or our brains, our own or our children's. Each argument carries some emotive force, but is not a sound basis for rejecting choices that individuals or parents might make to improve or optimize their children. That is not to say that every choice for enhancement or optimization is beyond moral criticism or even morally valid. But it is to say that those who would have us turn away in principle from all forms of enhancement or optimization have not made a convincing case.

Consider these questions from the President's Council which suggest that all efforts at enhancement will distort or deform the nature of our experience:

Indeed, why would one need to discipline one's passions, refine one's sentiments, and cultivate one's virtues, in short, to organize one's soul for action in the world, when one's aspiration to happiness could be satisfied by drugs in a quick, consistent, and cost-effective manner? [1]

The concern expressed here is that, if we enhance ourselves and our pleasures, achievements and enjoyments come easily, then why would we strive to be good or virtuous people?

The problem with this argument is that many people now do not strive to be virtuous or good, and they are not biologically or biotechnologically enhanced or optimized in any way. Laying the blame for vice, sloth, or the willingness to settle for cheap thrills at the feet of enhancement ignores the inconvenient fact that the desire for quick returns, easy money, and instant gratification have nothing at all to do with whether some or all of us choose to use biotechnology to become enhanced beings with different experiences. Vice is a trait of many if not all human beings. The notion of what we must seek and what we must avoid to facilitate character development and what that character should be that is implicit in the President's Council report has deeper roots in fictionalized accounts of young men at boarding schools, then anything that accurately describes how human beings actually evolve the character traits that they manifest or what psychologists and social scientists tell us about the process [18].

Still, the Council broods in *Beyond Therapy*, easy pleasures and cheap thrills will likely make us weak and spineless. There is nothing like misery to make us stronger. Sorrow, courageously confronted, can make us stronger, wiser, and more compassionate.

To what extent might the new antidepressants, the serotonin reuptake inhibitors or SSRIs, when used to reduce our troubles and sorrows, endanger this aspect of affective life? Although they do not prevent psychic pain, SSRIs may generally dull our capacity to feel it, rendering us less capable of experiencing and learning from misfortune or tragedy. They may make it difficult to empathize with the miseries of others. If some virtues can only be taught through experiencing very trying circumstances, those virtues might be lost, or at least less developed in a world of biological enhancement.

Put aside the fact that sorrow can also drive some to suicide and bring others to dysfunction and despair. And ignore the fact that using drugs to dull or blunt experience is not clearly linked in any way to the goals of enhancement or improvement. After all one might use drugs to intensify experiences that lead to the formation of virtue or empathy rather than to avoid such experiences. Putting these points aside, is it really true that improvement and virtue cannot co-exist?

This argument is a bit like those who worried what the airplane would do to the virtues of the combat ground soldier. The improved technology would make obsolete the kind of courage needed for a frontal assault. Oh really? Tell that to the fighter pilot who needs to evade a ground to air missile or land on an aircraft carrier at night, or to the helicopter pilot evacuating a wounded soldier under a barrage of ground fire. Improving performance is not necessarily toxic to virtue. It simply shifts how virtue is manifest. It is highly unlikely that those with enhanced vision, muscles, or brains would lack for challenges in the real world.

So the case is not made that improving our brains will destroy our 'authentic' character. What then? The Council wring their collective hands at the prospect that enhancement of the brain or optimization of brain performance will cheapen the value of our experiences:

But seldom do those who win by cheating or who love by deceiving cease to long for the joy and fulfillment that come from winning fair and square or being loved for who one truly is. Many stoop to fraud to obtain happiness, but none want their feeling of flourishing itself to be fraudulent. Yet a fraudulent happiness is just what the pharmacological management of our mental lives threatens to confer upon us [1]

Translation: If you don't really earn your performance, if you do not sweat and toil at it, then it will not be authentic and it will ultimately prove unsatisfying. One is tempted to ask who is writing this stuff—is the Council somehow psychically channeling our Puritan ancestors?

Certainly it is exciting to achieve satisfaction by testing one's limits, by seeing what one can achieve by striving, struggling, and working to overcome innate limits. But it also very satisfying to have benefits that simply come from out of the blue or through good fortune. No one who has enhanced vision as a result of laser surgery whom I have ever encountered feels the least bit of guilt, shame, or doubt that the improved vision they enjoy is fraudulent because they did nothing to deserve or earn it except pay their money and let a laser do its thing. Life is full of many pleasures that are not earned by testing our limits but which are fully and thoroughly enjoyed. Think of the joy in winning the lottery, or in finding out that your friends like you even though you cheat at cards, cannot stop smoking, eat too much, or are sometimes boring, or the pleasure you can find in solving problems using computers and every form of technological assistance you can muster to aid your fallible brain.

We do not always have to "earn" our happiness to be really and truly happy. Nor do we always reject as fraudulent those things that make us happy that we do nothing to earn. In fact it could be argued that a mix of both types of experiences, the happiness that is earned and the happiness that we enjoy as a matter of good fortune, is a more accurate reflection of authentic human experience. An enhanced brain or improved cognitive functioning would not in principle undermine the ethos of authenticity that undergirds human satisfaction because that infrastructure is not as the Council depicts it. Nor is it clear that improvement through bioengineering must always be inimical to authenticity.

Neurotic parenting and improvement

Lastly, consider the concerns of Harvard's Michael Sandel writing in the *Atlantic* [9, 21] and in this volume. He is worried that if we seek to perfect our children, to enhance them and optimize them we will no longer see them as "gifts". They will instead become objects, things to manufacture.

In a social world that prizes mastery and control, parenthood is a school for humility. That we care deeply about our children and yet cannot choose the kind we want teaches parents to be open to the unbidden. Such openness is a disposition worth affirming . . . it invites us to abide the unexpected, to live with dissonance, to rein in the impulse to control. [9, p. 60]

Put aside the irony of a Professor at a school to which parents devote enormous resources to enhance their children's capacities and abilities so that they may enter there counseling acceptance of the impulse to control the fate of their children. Ignore the fact that the vision of parenting that is put forward seems unduly bound by an upper class, American vision of what makes for desirable parenthood—no collective parenting or parent–child estrangement cloud this vision. Is there value to be found in accepting the random draw of the genetic lottery with respect to one's children? Should a point mutation that produces a slight change in a trait or a recombination of genetic material really be seen as the source of value in creating the unexpected in our offspring? If the genetic endowment of our children is a gift then to whom ought we feel grateful—our microbial forebears, the dinosaurs, Neanderthals for not wiping our ancestors out? The metaphor of the gift makes no sense in the secular context such as Sandel proposes. Gifts require a giver but nature offers no likely suspects to occupy this role.

Much of what parents try to do is shape and control their children. They do not value much about their design but rather try to work with the tools and abilities that nature has given to parent a child that can be happy and productive. Would changing what the accidents of nature produce in terms of a child's endowment of traits and behaviors at birth really result in a child that is less the object of parental design or less on parental affection for a child [21]? Is it self evident that this must be so?

No doubt there are neurotic parents. And no doubt some parents can and do get caught up in trying to 'perfect' their children. We are all familiar with the stereotypes of the demanding soccer parent or the overbearing parent who forces their child to do piano, math, tennis, or gymnastics regardless of the child's own wishes and even at the cost of the child's emotional and physical health.

But, adding more bioengineering possibilities to what is already there in terms of environmental and social tools that parents can use does nothing except broaden the armamentarium available to parents. The parents who are neurotic, overly demanding, and compulsively driven to change and shape their children according to their own values will be trying to do this with or without biological tools. The fact that there are some neurotic parents around should not be enough to prohibit the use of biological engineering to improve eyesight, enhance memory, or allow a child to learn languages with greater facility. The problem is bad parenting, not bad technology.

The case against all enhancements, in adults or children, is not made. Which, again, is not to say that all enhancement is, of necessity, good or desirable. But it is to say that, in principle, objections to perfection and enhancement should not deter those who seek to improve or make better use of biotechnology for themselves or their children. What we must do is take each proposed enhancement technology under consideration and decide whether what it can do is worth whatever price it might exact.

References

1. President's Council on Bioethics. *Beyond Therapy: Biotechnology and the Pursuit of Happiness*, Harper Collins, 2003.

2. W. McKibben. *Enough: Staying Human in an Engineered Age*, Times Books, 2003.

3. D. Callahan. *What Price Better Health*, University of California Press, 2003.

4. C. Elliott. *Better Than Well: American Medicine Meets the American Dream*, W. W. Norton & Company, 2003.

5. F. Fukuyama. *Our Posthuman Future: Consequences of the Biotechnology Revolution*, Picador, 2003.

6. S. Rothman and D. Rothman. *The Pursuit of Perfection: The Promise and Perils of Medical Enhancement*, Pantheon, 2003.

7. L. R. Kass. 'Life, Liberty and the Defense of Dignity: The Challenge for Bioethics', *Encounter*, 2002.

8. W. Kristol and E. Cohen (eds.), *The Future Is Now*, Rowman & Littlefield, 2002.

9. M. Sandel. 'The Case Against Perfection', *The Atlantic Monthly*, April 2004, 51–62.

10. C. Elliott. 'Pharma's Gain May Be Our Loss', *PLOS Medicine* 1:3, 2004, 52–3.

11. A. L. Caplan. 'Nobody is perfect—but why not try to be better?', *PLOS Medicine*, 1:3, 2004, 52–4.

12. W. Isaacson. *Benjamin Franklin: An American Life*, Simon and Schuster, 2003.

13. J. Whorton. *Crusaders for Fitness: The History of American Health Reformers*, Princeton University Press, 1984.

14. 'Saint Teresa of Avila: The Way of Perfection'. Available at: www.ccel.org/t/teresa/way/main.html

15. S. Pinker. *The Blank Slate: the modern denial of human nature*, Viking, 2002.

16. H. W. Baillie and T. K. Casey (eds.), *Is Human Nature Obsolete?*, MIT Press, 2005.

17. E. Tenner. *Our Own Devices: The past and future of body technology*, Knopf, 2003.

18. A. L. Caplan. 'Is biomedical research too dangerous to pursue?' *Science* 303, 2004, 1142.

19. J. C. Gibbs. *Moral Development and Reality*, Sage, 2003.

20. J. C. L. Wells, S. Strickland, K. Laland (eds.), *Social Information Transmission and Human Biology*, Taylor and Frances, 2006.

21. M. Sandel. This volume, 2008 and *The Case Against Perfection*, Harvard University Press, 2007.

22. M. Sagoff. 'Nature and human nature', in H. W. Baillie and T. K. Casey (eds.), *Is Human Nature Obsolete?*, MIT Press, 2005.

10

The Human Prejudice and the Moral Status of Enhanced Beings: What Do We Owe the Gods?

Julian Savulescu

... "improved posthumans would inevitably come to view the naturals" as inferior, as a subspecies of humans suitable for exploitation, slavery, or even extermination. Ultimately, it is this prospect of what can be termed "genetic genocide" that makes cloning combined with genetic engineering a potential weapon of mass destruction, and the biologist who would attempt it a potential bioterrorist.

George Annas

The first victim of transhumanism might be equality. ... Underlying this idea of the equality of rights is the belief that we all possess a human essence that dwarfs manifest differences in skin color, beauty, and even intelligence. This essence, and the view that individuals therefore have inherent value, is at the heart of political liberalism. But modifying that essence is the core of the transhumanist project. If we start transforming ourselves into something superior, what rights will these enhanced creatures claim, and what rights will they possess when compared to those left behind? If some move ahead, can anyone afford not to follow?

Francis Fukuyama

1. Introduction: radical modification of humans

It has been possible since about the 1980s to transfer genes taken from one species into another. ANDi is a rhesus monkey who has had a jellyfish gene incorporated into his DNA. This results in a unique fluorescent green glow. Alba is a genetically engineered rabbit created by French scientists for artist Eduardo Kac. She also has a fluorescent glow. These transgenic animals show that a gene from one species can be successfully transferred and activated in a completely different genome in a different species. There is no reason why genes from other species could not be transferred to human beings, creating transgenic humans. (For elaboration of this Introduction, see Savulescu 2003b.)

Transgenesis could be used to radically enhance human beings. For example, it has been hypothesized that ageing in human beings is related to the degradation of telomeres, the regions on the end of our chromosomes (Rudolph et al. 1999; Blasco 2005). Suppose that this were true, or some other genetic program for ageing were discovered. It may well be that there is genetic variation across species responsible for different rates of ageing. It may well be that we find that animals that have a significantly longer lifespan than humans, such as turtles and rockfish (Guerin 2004), contain genetic sequences that reduce the rate of telomere degradation or some other genetic contributor to ageing. It could then be possible,via transfer of these sequences into the human genome, to delay the ageing of human beings.

There are other techniques in biological sciences besides transgenesis which might bring about radical modification of human beings. Stem cell science also has the potential to extend human lifespan radically further than this, by replacing ageing tissue with healthy tissue (Harris 2000, 2002, 2004). We could live longer than the current maximum of 120 years.

Genetic memory enhancement has been demonstrated in rats and mice. In normal animals during maturation expression of the NR2B subunit of the NMDA receptor is gradually replaced with expression of the NR2A subunit, something that may be linked to less brain plasticity in adult animals. Tang et al. 1999 modified mice to overexpress the NR2B. The NR2B "Doogie" mice demonstrated improved memory performance, both in terms of acquisition and retention. This included unlearning of fear conditioning, which is believed to be due to learning a secondary memory (Falls, Miserendino, and Davis, 1992). The modification also made them more sensitive to certain forms of pain, showing a potentially non-trivial trade-off (Wei et al. 2001).

Increased amount of brain growth factors (Routtenberg et al. 2000) and the signal transduction protein adenylyl cyclase (Wang et al. 2004) have also produced memory improvements. Neural stem cells have also been identified which could potentially be induced to proliferate and differentiate (Rietze et al. 2001), mediated through nerve growth factors and other factors (Palma et al. 2005). In principle, human beings could be biologically modified to have significantly greater cognitive powers.

Other psychological characteristics besides cognitive power may be improvable. Gene therapy has been used to turn lazy monkeys into workaholics by altering the reward centre in the brain (Liu et al. 2004). In another experiment, researchers used gene therapy to introduce a gene from the monogamous male prairie vole, a rodent which forms life-long bonds with one mate, into the brain of the closely related but polygamous meadow vole (Lim et al. 2004). Genetically modified meadow voles became monogamous, behaving like prairie voles. This gene, which controls a part of the brain's reward centre different to that altered in the monkeys, is known as the vasopressin receptor gene. It may also be involved in human drug addiction (Savulescu 2006).

Not only may the mental abilities of human beings be radically modified but so too may physical abilities. Anabolic steroids and growth hormone have been used for some time to increase muscle strength but newer designer drugs are constantly being developed. Growth hormone is very difficult to detect. Myostatin is a growth factor which controls muscle growth. One family has been identified with a genetic mutation resulting in no myostatin production (Schuelke et al. 2004). This resulted in extraordinarily strong and developed muscles in the child affected. Genetically modified mice which do not produce myostatin have enormous muscles and have been called Schwarzenegger mice (Lee 2004). Administration of myostatin blockers causes significant increase in muscle mass in mice (Lee and McPheron, 2001). Genetic manipulation to stop myostatin production or administration of blockers would be expected to significantly increase strength in athletes and are likely to offer real potential for doping in the future (Savulescu, Foddy, and Clayton 2004).

Insulin-like growth factor injected into the muscles of mice increases strength (Barton–Davis 1998). Vascular endothelial growth factor stimulates the development of new blood vessels and could also be of use to athletes in the future.

Transgenesis could be used to introduce genes coding for superior physical abilities from other animals. For example, humans could have the hearing of dogs, the visual acuity of hawks, the night vision of owls, or even be able to navigate by sonar employed from bats.

This is merely a sketch of some of the ways humans may be biologically modified and improved. Besides biological modification of human beings and non-human animals, other technologies could be used to enhance human functioning. Nanotechnology could be used to create artificial blood cells with greater life, durability, and oxygen carrying capacity. See [http://new.foresight.org/Nanomedicine/Respirocytes.html; http://www.transhumanist.com/volume11/vasculoid.html]. Indeed, nanotechnology could be used to reconstruct and enhance all parts of the human body.

Neurocience, together with computing technology, offers radical opportunities for enhancing cognitive performance. Already, chips have been introduced into human beings for the purposes of tracking and computer-assisted control of biological functions. Minds are connected through the internet and there may be no barrier in principle to direct mind-reading and thought-sharing across human minds. Uploading of human minds to artificially intelligent systems represents one of the most radical possibilities for human development.

Indeed, artificial intelligence offers an alternative form of existence with superior capacities to human capacities. The "spike" of exponentially increasing computing power will probably be reached this century resulting in computers with unimaginable abilities. It is possible that artificial intelligences vastly superior to human intelligence will exist this century.

We can, then, identify several different possible life forms:

- plants
- non-human animals
- humans
- enhanced humans
- transhumans—humans who have been so significantly modified and enhanced that there are significant non-human characteristics, e.g. chimeras, cyborgs
- post-humans—beings originally "evolved" or developed from humans but so significantly different that they are no longer human in any significant respect
- alien life forms

What are our obligations to other beings who are not human beings like us? This question has traditionally arisen in discussion of animal rights: what we owe other non-human animals. But as technology progresses in the twenty-first century, a new question emerges: what do we owe radically different and technologically altered human beings, or post-humans? And what would we owe to other intelligent non-human life forms, such as aliens or intelligent robots or non-carbon based life forms?

Humans have enjoyed dominion over other animals until this point in human history. According to the book of Genesis,

And God said, Let us make man in our image, after our likeness: and let them have dominion over the fish of the sea, and over the fowl of the air, and over the cattle, and over all the earth, and over every creeping thing that creepeth upon the earth.

So God created man in his own image, in the image of God created he him; male and female created he them.

And God blessed them, and God said unto them, Be fruitful, and multiply, and replenish the earth, and subdue it: and have dominion over the fish of the sea, and over the fowl of the air, and over every living thing that moveth upon the earth. (26–8)

The basis of this was that humans were created in the image of God. For those of us, non-religious or religious, who do not accept this, another justification has had to be given for why we can kill, farm, experiment on, and generally use non-human animals for our purposes. One dominant explanation has been given in terms of the nature of human beings as persons, in terms of their capacity for self-consciousness and rationality. This accounts for our *greater* moral status. But this invites a problem—if beings existed with greater capacity for self-consciousness, greater rationality, our moral status would be downgraded.

This concern is common. George Annas believes "improved" post-humans would inevitably come to view "the 'naturals' as inferior, as a subspecies of humans suitable for exploitation, slavery, or even extermination." Another bioconservative, Francis Fukuyama, also believes the idea of equality is under threat, and implies that enhanced beings will claim greater rights. Wikler, in his chapter in this volume, argues that we would all be relatively disabled and requiring the legal protections which disabled people enjoy. All these views share the feature, and concern, that the rights humans would have would be *downgraded* if enhancement occurred. This runs deeply counter to our ordinary view of human moral status.

These writers are concerned to *protect* human beings in a world of enhancement or greatly superior sentient beings. This is a new and hypothetical issue. In the past, discussions of the moral status of human beings have addressed questions not of protection but of *privilege*: whether we are entitled to treat human beings in a special way.

2. The Human Prejudice

As human beings, we believe that being human has special significance, at least to us. In bioethical debates, this often grounds the claim that we must protect our humanity, human nature or human dignity. The great, recently deceased moral philosopher Bernard Williams called this the *human prejudice*. I will discuss his posthumously published paper of that title since discussion of it reveals much about the basis of and the limitations of according special significance and moral status to human beings. Indeed, I believe there is a folk view that humans do have special significance and Williams's argument is the most sophisticated defence of that view.

The Oxford English Dictionary defines Prejudice: "Preconceived opinion; bias or leaning favourable or unfavourable; prepossession; when used *absolutely*, usually with unfavourable connotation."

It also defines it in another sense: "Injury, detriment, or damage, caused to a person by judgement or action in which his rights are disregarded."

Williams uses the term in the sense of a bias by human beings towards human beings.

A central idea involved in the supposed human prejudice is that there are certain respects in which creatures are treated in one way rather than another simply because they belong to a certain category, the human species. We do not, at this basic initial level, need to know any more about them. Told that there are human beings trapped in a burning building, on the strength of that fact alone we mobilise as many resources as we can to rescue them. (Williams 2006, 142)

By human beings, he means members of the species *homo sapiens*. This view is sometimes called anthropocentrism.

Some of the characteristics of the human prejudice are that:

- we privilege human beings in our ethical thought
- we think that what happens to human beings is more important than what happens to other creatures
- we think that human beings as such have a claim on our attention and care in all sorts of situations in which other animals have less or no claim on us

Williams argues that the human prejudice is justifiable and is different to other prejudices such as racist or sexist prejudices. I will argue that his arguments fail and that there are strong moral reasons to care equally about non-human beings. Our obligations to post-humans and intelligent non-human life forms are greater than Williams argues and indeed than many people would pre-reflectively think. However, I will close by arguing that we may have special obligations to other human beings which are greater than our obligations to other animals or post-humans. I will sketch briefly the extent of those obligations. We should not defend the human prejudice, at least in the form advanced by Williams.

2.1. Bernard Williams's Argument for the Human Prejudice

Williams gives a historical analysis of the importance humans have had in the scheme of things, in particular, the absolute importance that both Christian and humanistic traditions have accorded to human beings: "a definite measure of importance" (Williams 2006, 136), and "that humans were particularly important in relation to the scheme of things" (Williams 2006, 136). But he rejects both of these justifications for the human prejudice because they presuppose metaphysically queer properties. In particular, he denies the existence of a cosmic point of view or any way in which things can absolutely matter in the Universe.

If there is no such thing as the cosmic point of view, if the idea of absolute importance in the scheme of things is an illusion, a relic of a world not yet thoroughly disenchanted, then there is no other point of view except ours in which our activities can have or lack a significance. (Williams 2006, 137)

Indeed, Williams believes that the human prejudice can only be and indeed is justified by reference to human beings and what matters to them.

There is certainly one point of view from which they are important, namely ours: unsurprisingly so, since the "we" in question, the "we" who raise this question and discuss with others who we hope will listen and reply, are indeed human beings. It is just as unsurprising that this "we" often shows up within the *content* of our values. Whether a creature is a human being or not makes a large difference, a lot of the time, to the ways in which we treat that creature or at least think that we should treat it. (Williams 2006, 138)

Williams argues that we can accord special significance to human beings without reverting to a belief in the absolute importance of human beings (cosmic significance). He wants to make a more limited claim: that "human beings are more important *to us*" (Williams 2006, 139).

Williams argues that opponents claim we need a reason for these preferences. Without a reason, the objection goes, the preference will just be a prejudice. If the justification is just that " 'it's a human being' or 'they're human' or 'she's one of us' " (Williams 2006, 139), then this is no reason. It is a form of speciesism, unjustifiably privileging one's own species, like racism or sexism.

Williams argues that the human prejudice is different to racial or sexual prejudice. Racism or sexism are unjustified prejudices because there is no answer to the question: "*What's that got to do with it?*" (Williams 2006, 139).

Let's call those who hold the human prejudice, "humanists", recognizing that this is a broader usage of the term than usual. It is however, neater than "speciesist". Williams argues that humanists are different to racists or sexists. "[N]ot many racists or sexists have actually supposed that a bare appeal to race or gender—merely saying "he's black" or "she's a woman"—did constitute a reason" (Williams 2006, 139).

They were at an early stage—they did not articulate a reason. Or they were at a later stage:

Something which at least seemed relevant to the matter at hand—job opportunities, the franchise or whatever it might be—would then be brought out, about the supposed intellectual and moral weakness of blacks or women. (Williams 2006, 140)

However, Williams claims:

" 'It's a human being' does seem to operate as a reason, but it does not seem to be helped out by some further reach of supposedly more relevant reasons, of the kind which in the other cases of prejudice turned out to be rationalizations." (Williams 2006, 140)

But does "It's a human being" really operate as a reason? It may be that "It's a human being" appears different to us because it is readily acceptable to us all because all who can understand this justification are human beings. It is psychologically more appealing. We are all in *that* club. This is different to "He's a man" or "He's white", which would not be acceptable to those human beings outside of the privileged club. Club members are ready to endorse rules and practices that protect the members of the club. Privilege disappears when club members are willing to consider the rights, interests, and claims of non-club members. This of course is not going on when we appeal to the human club.

Moreover, it is a contingent feature of other prejudices that they appeal to rationalizations. They could be simple like the human prejudice: it's a white. Skin colour could be just as relevant as walks on two legs and has opposable thumb or has 46 chromosomes.

There are other reasons to doubt whether there is the structural dis-similarity between humanism and other more discredited prejudices that Williams asserts. Williams claims as significant in favour of the human prejudice:

Told that there are human beings trapped in a burning building, on the strength of that fact alone we mobilise as many resources as we can to rescue them (Williams 2006, 142).

But what this means is: "Told that there are human beings trapped in a burning building, on the strength of that fact alone we *human beings* mobilize as many resources as we can to rescue them." This is very similar to: "Told that there are whites trapped in a burning building, on the strength of that fact alone we *whites* mobilize as many resources as we can to rescue them."

Williams claims that the human prejudice can't be based on some absolute importance to human beings, or their culture or achievements.

Of course, we can say, rightly, that we are in favour of cultural development and so on, and think it very important; but that itself is just another expression of the human prejudice we are supposed to be wrestling with. (Williams 2006, 141)

So there is something obscure about the relations between the moral consideration "it's a human being", and the characteristics that distinguish human beings from other creatures. If there is a human prejudice, it is structurally different from those other prejudices, racism and sexism. This doesn't necessarily show that it isn't a prejudice. (Williams 2006, 141)

I do not believe there is any structural difference between humanism and racism or sexism. It is a club privilege, which gives greater weight to the interests of the club members and is endorsed by the club members. I have argued that racists and sexists can use race and sex in the same ways as humanists use human. The reverse is true. Humanists could endorse the human prejudice in the early basic way. They could go on treating other non-human animals badly, just as racists treated blacks badly, without thinking to justify it. Or they could offer bad rationalizations—like humans have souls. I will close in the final section by arguing there is a sense in which humanism is justified, but not in the brute sense that Williams articulates and that this sense also justifies racism and sexism. But now I will argue that there is no *normative reason* why being a human should matter, in the way being a person, or an intelligent, empathic and sociable alien, should matter.

2.2. Personism

Part of Williams's strategy is to claim: what other view could there be? And then of course to discredit that. He considers a main competitor to humanism: personism.[1] Those who typically reject the human prejudice claim that what matters is not human beings per se but persons.

For the purposes of this argument, we need not settle the difficult question of the metaphysical relationship of persons to human beings, and questions of personal identity. There are at least two major positions. Those who claim that persons are separate entities to human beings and those who claim that persons are *phase sortals*. That is, we are human beings, but during a part of a human being's life, there is typically a phase where a person also exists. For the purposes of moral argument, this distinction does not matter. Personism is a moral view, not a metaphysical view. Personists claim that it is wrong to kill human beings who are persons, but not wrong to kill human beings who are not persons, or other non-persons.

---

[1] Another competitor is Classical Utilitarianism. On this view, it is wrong to kill animals because of the loss of valuable experience from the world. The death of human is worse than the death of a non-human because of richer psychological connectedness.

Michael Tooley and Peter Singer are the most famous or infamous proponents of personism. They argue that what matters morally is not being a member of the species *homo sapiens*, but some property of human beings—rationality and self-consciousness—which characterize us as persons (Singer 1993, 1995; Tooley 1983). It is wrong to kill persons because they can conceive of themselves as existing across time and have preferences for their continued existence into the future. Non-persons do not have such preferences. It is the frustration of these preferences that is wrong. Being human is merely having the property of being able to interbreed or having a certain chromosomal structure. These facts are not in themselves of normative significance.

It is these normative facts that differentiate personism from humanism, racism, and sexism. The latter do not appeal to relevant moral facts. Personism is not an arbitrary club. The relation of "has crosstemporal desires to live" and "should not be killed" is like "is suffering" and "should receive medical treatment." Having the feature of "suffering" is morally relevant to being a potential recipient of medical treatment. However, "being white" is not relevant to "should be considered for a job" in the same way.

Williams does not address this consideration directly but issues a related challenge: why are the properties which constitute persons morally relevant? He gives two possibilities:

- we "favour and esteem" (William 2006, 144) them—but he claims that also applies to human beings. I will return to this claim, which he does not develop
- it is better that such properties are instantiated—but this is again an appeal to absolute importance, which he rejects

Williams is correct that we favour and esteem these properties. But what he neglects is that we have a *reason* to favour and esteem them. The concept of a normative reason is a primitive one. We have a reason to relieve someone's pain. This reason is provided by or related to the badness of pain. It is not provided by the fact that we disapprove of that person being in pain. Similarly, we have a reason to satisfy the preferences of rational self-conscious beings for continued survival. That reason is provided by or related to the goodness of satisfying those preferences, according to personists.

Williams argues that utilitarians like Singer invoke the Ideal Observer (IO) to correct our irrationally restricted sentiments and beliefs which result in prejudice:

They deploy the model [of the IO] against what they see as prejudice, in particular the human prejudice, and the idea behind this is that there is a sentiment or disposition or conviction which we do have, namely compassion or sympathy or the belief that suffering is a bad thing, but we express these sentiments in an irrationally restricted way: in ways governed by the notorious inverse square law, where the distances involved can be of all kinds, spatial, familial, national, racial, or governed by species-membership. The model of the IO is supposed to be a corrective; if we could take on all suffering as he does, we would not be liable to these parochial biases and would feel and act in better ways. (Williams 2006, 145)

Williams identifies two problems with this line of argument.

Even if we thought that the IO's outlook were a reliable guide to what would be a *better state of affairs*, how is that connected to what we—each of us—should be trying to do? (Williams 2006, 146)

The second problem which Williams raises is: what would it be like to be the simple IO concerned to reduce suffering?

I will address each of these problems in turn.

2.2.1. Reasons and Caring   The first problem—of how a better state of affairs is meant to connect with what we should do—is a familiar problem in metaethics which Williams has addressed at length, which he calls internal/external reasons problem. It is the problem of how moral judgements or considerations are meant to connect to motivation and what we care about.

Williams divides reasons for acting into internal and external reasons. Consider the sentence—"A has a reason to $\tilde{\varphi}$". If A has some motive which will be furthered by $\tilde{\varphi}$-ing, if only in an indirect way, then A has an internal reason to $\tilde{\varphi}$. If there is a reason for A to $\tilde{\varphi}$, and yet A has no motive whatsoever which is furthered by or related in any way to $\tilde{\varphi}$-ing, then the reason is external. Thus a reason for acting can be either internal or external to the agent's "subjective motivational set" (Williams 1981, 102–13), S, as Williams put it. Note that S is the agent's *present* desire set.

Williams argues that there are no external reasons. He considers the example of Owen Wingrave, a character from one of Henry James's stories. Owen's father urges him to join the army because all his male ancestors were soldiers. Family pride demands that he join the army. Owen, however, hates everything about military life. The reason for Owen to join the army is an external reason (Williams 1981, 107).

Williams argues that external reasons must have some connection with motivation:

If something can be a reason for action, then it could be someone's reason for acting on a particular occasion, and it would then figure in an explanation of that action. Now no external reason statement could *by itself* offer an explanation of anyone's action. Even if it were true . . . that there was a reason for Owen to join the army, that fact by itself would never explain anything that Owen did, not even his joining the army. The whole point of external reason statements is that they can be true independently of the agent's motivations. But nothing can explain an agent's (intentional) actions except something that motivates him to so act. (Williams 1981, 106–7)

If there are external reasons for *intentional* action, then these reasons must give rise to a desire to act. But how can they, if they are unrelated to present desires in any way? Not only must external reasons give rise to motivation, but having deliberated over them, they must in virtue of this deliberation give rise to motivation. There must be a causal connection between deliberation and motivation.

Michael Smith has developed this kind of account. He argues that rational deliberation (1994, 156–8) entails that A (i) has no false beliefs, (ii) has all the relevant true beliefs and (iii) is deliberating correctly. Deliberating correctly is reasoning according to the means–end principle, considering how one's desires can be satisfied (by time-ordering, weighting what one plans to do to satisfy them) and exercising one's imagination.

The external reasons theorist will:

have to make the condition under which the agent appropriately comes to have the motivation something like this, that he should deliberate correctly; and the external reasons statement itself will have to be taken as roughly equivalent to, or at least entailing, the claim that if the agent rationally deliberated, then, whatever motivations he originally had, he would come to be motivated to $\tilde{\varphi}$. (Williams 1981, 109)

Williams concludes from this that there are no external reasons.

But if this is correct, there does indeed seem great force in Hume's basic point, and it is very plausible that all external reason statements are false. For, *ex hypothesi*, there is no motivation for the agent to deliberate *from*, to reach this new motivation. . . .
(Williams 1981, 109)

Williams's target is claims of duty and other moral claims. According to this line of argument, there could be no *external* reason to care about non-humans, including superhumans and the gods. There is no basis in terms of God or some Impartial Observer or, indeed, any impartial morality. The human prejudice is justified, on this line of argument, because we happen to care more about human beings.

2.2.1.1. Striking Implications of Desire-Based Accounts of Normative Reasons for Action and the Human Prejudice Williams's account of internal reasons can be called a Desire-Based (DB) conception of *normative* reasons. Many moral philosophers since Hume have held a DB conception of normative reasons. Michael Smith's book, *The Moral Problem* (Smith 1994), is probably the most sophisticated defence of a DB account of reasons, but the view dates from Hume.

On this view, we should care or have a reason to care more about human beings because that is what we desire, or, as Williams puts it, because "we favour and esteem them."

Desire-Based views of reasons have striking implications. It implies we have no reason to care about God, if one believes in God. For those of us who do not, it has equally striking implications. Hume famously believed that we can act irrationally in only two ways. Firstly, when we act on false beliefs. This is not really irrational action (practical irrationality) but possibly the result of irrationality in thinking (theoretical irrationality). Secondly, we can act irrationally when we choose means which are inappropriate to our ends (Hume 1978, 416, 459) (instrumental irrationality).[2]

Hume was one of the few to face up to this kind of implication. He admitted: " 'tis not contrary to reason to prefer the destruction of the whole world to the scratching of my little finger" (Hume 1978, 416).

---

[2] Hume, D., *A Treatise of Human Nature*, Second Edition (Oxford: Clarendon Press, 1978), 416, 459. For Hume, this instrumental irrationality really represented a special case of false belief: "we . . . deceive ourselves in our judgement of causes and effects" (p. 416). Thus for Hume, there was no true form of practical irrationality.

Thus, if we happened not to care about human beings, or persons, we would have no reasons, on the Williams-style account, to care about them. If parents did not care about their children, then they would have no reasons to care about them. And if we did care about persons, we would have a good reason to care about them. If we accept this kind of defence of the human prejudice, anything goes, or at least, anything could go depending on what we happened to care about. There is no reason to care about anything! God, your mother, your love, your children, or yourself.

2.2.1.2. A Value-Based Account of Normative Reasons Williams's external reasons can be called Value-Based (VB) Reasons. The question of whether reasons are DB or VB goes back to Plato. Socrates, in the *Euthyphro*, asks,

... is the holy approved of by the gods because it is holy, or is it holy because it is approved? (Plato 1993)

Socrates argues that what is holy is approved of by the gods because it is holy. According to a VB account, it is the badness or goodness of suffering, indignity, achievement, warm and sincere human relations, knowledge, development of skills, and talents, that provide reasons for action, independent of what a person's desires happen to be.

On a VB account of reasons, we should care about human beings because they instantiate certain valuable properties, such as personhood. It is this fact that gives us a reason to care about them, not that we happen to favour and esteem them. And to the degree that other animals and life forms instantiate these valuable properties, we have VB reasons to care about them.

2.2.2. The Impartial Observer   The second problem that Williams identifies is: what would it be like to be the simple IO concerned to reduce suffering?

But what would it conceivably be like for this to be so, even for a few seconds? What would it be like to take on every piece of suffering that at a given moment any creature is undergoing? It would be an ultimate horror, an unendurable nightmare. (Williams 2006, 146)

We would annihilate the planet, he claims.

This seems to be an attack on negative utilitarianism—the view that we should minimize suffering. However, it does not seem to apply to positive utilitarianism, that we should maximize the balance of pleasure over suffering. After all, if we consider happiness as well as suffering, there is much to be encouraged by. We would only annihilate the planet if the suffering outweighed the happiness and life for all or the majority was not worth living.

Williams's rejection of personism is in part based on scepticism about the IO. "It is not an accident or a limitation or a prejudice that we cannot care equally about all the suffering in the world: it is a condition of our existence and our sanity" (Williams 2006, 147). Perhaps the claim here is, that without giving greater concern to human suffering, we could not exist. This again is not true—some animal rights activists seem to be able to exist caring equally about all suffering. Peter Singer exists, even though he attempts in perhaps an imperfect human way to care about all suffering.

Williams continues:

But it is a total illusion to think that this enterprise (of caring for all animals) can be licensed in some respects and condemned in others by credentials that come from another source, a source that is not already involved in the peculiarities of the human enterprise. It is an irony that this illusion, even when it takes the form of rejecting so-called speciesism and the human prejudice, actually shares a structure with older illusions about there being a cosmic scale of importance in terms of which human beings should understand themselves. (Williams 2006, 147)

Personism, however, need not have any commitment to any supernatural entity or cosmic order. Personists appeal to properties human beings value and to normative properties, like the badness of suffering. They claim that this is what really matters to us not being a member of the species *homo sapiens*. We need to distinguish between two senses of human being:

- Human being qua member of species homo sapiens
- Human being qua rational being

The personhood approach, as I will now argue, considers a subset of human qualities as of moral significance. This does not posit some cosmic, unnatural significance to things. It simply says that not all human qualities are morally relevant and some non-humans share these relevant qualities so should be treated equally in virtue of possessing those properties. Williams foists on to personists metaphysical baggage they need not carry—their metaphysical commitments can be the same as the humanists. Talk of cosmic points of view and ideal observers is a distraction at best and a mischievous diversion at worst.

2.3. Is Species Membership Valuable?

Williams claims "It is hard to see any argument in that direction which will not turn out to say something like this, that it is *simply better* that culture, intelligence, technology should flourish" (Williams 2006, 141). On a Value-Based account of reasons, we could argue that it is simply better that culture and intelligence flourish. This is the view I will ultimately defend. But it is a mistake again to think that a Desire-Based account of reasons, like the one Williams advances, rules out personism. We can simply value, because we desire them, culture, intelligence, and technology with no commitment to the cosmic order of things. Thus, when Williams claims that we value being a member of the species *homo sapiens*, personists can respond that is not what we *really* value. They are not committed to ascribing some fancy value to these properties of persons. They can merely point out that we do actually value them and we are confused when we ascribe intrinsic value to the place holder, "members of the species *homo sapiens*". Indeed, it is hard to imagine how we could value merely being a member of a species. Species distinctions are arbitrary and turn on capacity to interbreed or some genetic structure. These are not what people have in mind when they say human beings have value. "The fact that we implicitly use this concept all the time explains why there is not some other set of criteria which we apply to individuals one by one" (Williams 2006, 150).

However, we may use this concept "all the time" as a rough and ready placeholder for the qualities of personhood. Rough equivalence is enough for everyday talk. The moral question is what is really of moral significance. Indeed, personists argue that there is confusion, or at least lack of rational development, in our beliefs about what we value. Consider a person who claims to value Equality. Through argument, such a person may be convinced that she does not value Equality but rather Priority to the worst-off people. She did not really value Equality, but she thought that she did because her thinking was insufficiently developed and her concepts too loose and vague. Personists claim that most humanists are guilty of such vague and undeveloped thinking, often influenced by religious dogma.

There may be people who truly and after great critical reflection subjectively value mere membership of the species. On a Desire-Based account of reasons we could have reason to go wherever our desires happen to lead us. Some people wish to carry anencephalic pregnancies. If that is what they want, knowing all the facts and thinking clearly about this, then that is what they have good reason to do. But most people would not choose to have an anencephalic child, who is a human being but not a person, or to continue such a pregnancy on its diagnosis. Most people are not really humanists in the thoroughgoing sense, though they might think that they are. Told that there are *permanently unconscious* "human beings trapped in a burning building, on the strength of that fact alone we mobilize as many resources as we can to rescue them."

I doubt many people would be prepared to risk their lives for human beings who are permanently unconscious. What we value is not human beings but something else that is generally but not always true of them: the characteristics that make them persons, and, as I will argue in the final section, our special relations with them. This is revealed by our practices of letting brain damaged human beings die and even killing them: those in a persistent vegetative state, sufferers from severe brain injury or advanced dementia. These are human beings but we do not value their lives when we disconnect their feeding tubes.

It is true that people believe that merely being a human being matters, but they are mistaken. It is other properties of being a human being that really matter, the personists argue. This is brought out by a hypothetical example of Covert Alien Coexistence.

2.3.1. Covert Alien Coexistence   Aliens have been living among us since time began. Half of all the human population are not carbon based but silicon based, even though they look, behave, and experience the same.

For humanists, this would be a tragedy. However, this would be a curiosity, if an astounding curiosity.

Imagine you discovered you were silicon-based. How would you react? Shocked and disappointed that you were not what you thought you were. How should you try to be—the same? The fact that you are made of silicon rather than carbon is of no rational significance.

For my part, I do not believe that fully informed rational agents deliberating properly would care about mere species membership, rather the characteristics which define persons. Prejudice in favour of the human is typical among the uneducated and the religiously dogmatic who do cling to a cosmic order. Moreover, even if we do care more about human beings intrinsically, it is clear we can come to care equally about lower animals, as some animal rights activists and pet owners do, and that we could come to care about post-humans and intelligent aliens. People can care about just about anything. So even in Williams's terms, our obligations to intelligent non-humans could be great, if we came to care about them enough. There is nothing special about our current pattern of concern in Williams's own terms: it is just now what we happen to have. We could come to be more concerned about post-humans—the human prejudice would then be reversed. Some people love their pets more than their children. Williams's argument, if it justifies humanism at all, seems to justify humanism only as long as we happen to care about the species *homo sapiens*. Since serious and considered argument about the moral status is a very recent event, there seems little reason to believe that the humanism will persist much longer than racism or sexism. People may well, in the light of argument and realization of technical possibility, simply cease to care.

Jeff McMahan has argued that humanism, or anthropocentrism as he calls it, must fail because we are not identical with our physical organism. He argues we are embodied minds. Since any definition of *homo sapiens* must be based on biological criteria, it must fail because we are not identical with some aspect of our biology. On any this kind of account of personal identity, humanism is based on a logical mistake. If we care about us, we should not care about our species (McMahan 2002, 226). He argues that if we are embodied minds, one's relation to a chimpanzee is closer and more significant than one's relation to an anencephalic infant.

But the confusion may be simpler than McMahan proposes. I have argued that humanity or the member of the species *homo sapiens* is a rough placeholder that typically includes a range of properties which we value. It is properties which are the operative differentiator. Williams argues, in effect, that DB account of reasons supports the human prejudice. It does not. It can equally well support personism. Appeal to the nature of reasons will not alone settle whether we should be personists or humanists. And those who value beings other than human beings need not be committed to any supernatural entity, cosmic order of things, or impartial observer.

2.3.2. DB Reasons, Values, and Rationally Changing the Objects of Concern
Since many people, including many economists, believe reasons depend on our desires or preferences, it is worth showing that even on this account, we can be required to modify our patterns of concern.

2.3.2.1. The Drowning Wife   George and Marion go on a hiking holiday with their three children. It has been raining heavily for the past three days. They pass by a river in flood. The three children sit on a hill watching their parents. Marion stands on a rock close by the river, while George photographs her against the spectacular backdrop of a deep ravine. A sudden torrent sweeps her away. Now she is one hundred feet downstream. George dives in after her. There is very little chance he will save her, or himself. A day later, their bodies are recovered several miles downstream.

George chooses to attempt to save his wife rather than attend to his responsibility as father to his three children. From an impartial morality, his act may be immoral if the chance of rescuing his wife is sufficiently small. Nonetheless, he may have most reason to attempt to save his wife. We can rationally submaximize value, that is, fail to realize as much value as we can in the world. But what matters is that, insofar as George is concerned for his wife's welfare, he should be concerned to promote it to the maximum extent possible, *ceteris paribus* (Savulescu 1998).

Thus, generally, whether we have reason to act so as to promote a certain value is tied to whether that act maximizes *that* value. George's act is rational because:

- George is devoted to a good end: his wife's welfare
- he is concerned not only that his wife be better off, but that she be as well off as possible
- in promoting that end, George is doing everything he can

As Hume put it, we are irrational when we adopt means which fail to maximally promote our ends. Rationality may require that we extend our present concerns in a more radical way. Consider:

2.3.2.2. The Drowning Children In this case, it is not George's wife who is swept away by the flood, but his three children who were playing on the banks of the river. He dives in. He sees that ahead the river diverges. One child is swept down the left fork, and two children are swept down the right. He swims down the right fork in an attempt to save the two.

If all other considerations of value are equal (such as the chances of effecting a successful rescue, the extent of George's love for each of the children, their physical and mental capacities, etc.), we should claim that:

(1) George has most reason to attempt to save the two children rather than the one. (Taurek and others deny this (Taurek 1977).)

This shows that we are rationally committed to maximizing what we value, unless there is some other value at stake. Personists argue that this applies to valuing relief of suffering, satisfying the desires for continued existence of the self-conscious.

If (1) is true, it might be objected that we should also accept:

(2) George has most reason to promote his three children's welfare rather than his wife's welfare.

We can accept (1) but reject (2). Consider a variant of the Drowning Children. In this case, the child who is swept down the left fork is George's own child; the two children swept down the right fork are someone else's children. Many people would accept that:

(3) George has most reason to try to save his own child rather than two other people's children.

Why might it be rational for George to save his own child in preference to two strangers (3), yet it is rational to save his two children rather than one (1)?

Consistency is a requirement of rationality. Consistency can be expressed as a principle of equality: to treat like cases alike, unless there is a relevant difference. Thus, if I care about A but not about B, and B is similar to A, I should be able to justify my not caring about B. Consistency requires that, if I care about A, and there is no relevant difference between A and B, then I should also care about B. The father who loves one child should also love his other children unless there is a relevant difference. He should extend his present pattern of concern. Let's call this the consistency requirement.[3] Imagine that George rescued the one child rather than his other two. He would need a relevant difference to justify his choice, one that truly related to what he cared about.

There would not typically be a relevant moral difference between George's three children. If George's three children all have an equal claim on him, and he can save one or two, he should satisfy the most claims which he can satisfy. Thus (1) may be true.

Why then can we reject (2)? While it is true that George has a special relationship with his children as well as with his wife, the relationship is of a very *different kind*. There is a relevant difference between the relationship one has with one's children and the relationship one has with one's spouse. Thus (2) does not violate the requirement for consistency.

Rationality, even on a DB account of reasons, thus requires that we extend concern even if it does not require that we adopt different concerns. It does not require that we should show equal concern to all worthwhile objects of concern.

Rationality, according to personists, requires that we extend our concern beyond humans. Other humans are like our children and non-human persons are like strangers. Even if we care more about humans, we should still care about non-human persons. Why? Because we do value the properties which non-human beings instantiate. If what we value is something like self-consciousness, it is irrational in terms of this value to restrict our concern to only humans. Unless we value species membership for its own sake, it is irrelevant that self-consciousness, or what-ever other property defines persons, resides in another species. And do we really value, for their own sake, the number of chromosomes we have, or the capacity to interbreed? Some humans have 45 chromosomes, some have 47—they matter no less because they are biologically different.

---

[3] Note that this does not require that I care about all worthwhile objects of concern. If C is relevantly different to A, I can consistently fail to care as much about C as I now care about A.

So a human could be rational if she saved one drowning child rather than three drowning dogs. This does not show that our values do not ground concern for dogs just as saving one's wife rather than two children does not imply we do not value our children. But if there are three drowning dogs and we can, at little cost to ourselves, save them, we should save them. The importance people have to us, partiality, and special relations, can justify our acting in ways which favour those we care about. This implies nothing about how other beings should be treated by third parties and what their moral claims are in other contexts.

2.4. How Much Human Prejudice Is Justified? Partiality and Special Relations

As I have argued, even on a DB account of reasons, we have some reason to care about non-human animals, though we might give greater weight to the interests of humans. This would ground some degree of human prejudice, though partiality is a better term. There are some reasons to believe that there are special ties, albeit much weaker than humanists want to assert, between members of the family of man. Human beings share a biological, genetic connection, just like family members. Indeed, the genetic differences between humans is small. There is a common history. Our physical and psychological attributes, despite conspicuous dissimilarities, are much more similar at the deepest level. We can understand the actions and behaviour of people from radically different cultures. This, however, only justifies weak partiality in favour of human interests.

McMahan notes that an alternative defence of anthropocentrism is in terms of not intrinsic differences between humans and non-humans, but based extrinsic or relational differences. We have reason to care more for humans because we are related to them in special ways (McMahan 2002, 217)—"the tie of birth" as Scanlon puts it. Thus we owe the severely retarded special duties because we are related through the tie of birth.

This conception of morality distinguishes two sorts of moral reasons. Firstly, the moral reasons which derive from the intrinsic properties of the beings affected by our actions. Thus if a being is sentient we have a reason not to inflict pain. Secondly, there are reasons deriving from our special relations to some beings. The existence of this second kind of reason means there is a *relevant difference* between George's own child and the children of strangers. We have more reason to save our own children than other people's.

McMahan distinguishes the view that reasons derive from special relations from the Personal Priority View, which, for the purposes of this paper, I will call Autonomy. The Autonomy View states that we must give some weight to what we value and care about, to what Williams has called our "ground projects". McMahan argues morality encompasses Autonomy but I will here contrast it with impartial moral reasons provided by Morality. George's own child has a special relationship to his life, and indeed is a part of his life and is valued in the way that the strangers are not. George's preference for his own children is rationally defensible and is consistent with the expression of his autonomy. Thus, as Nozick suggests, we may have more reason to care for severely retarded humans than animals with the same psychological capacities because we are related to them.

McMahan argues that Autonomy does not adequately account for the significance of special relations. A parent might care more about a child actor than his own child and on the Autonomy view would have more reason to care for that child. As McMahan notes, on the Autonomy view, we could care more for our pets than our children. McMahan argues that reasons derived from partiality are weak. While they may have benefits to those to whom we are partial, they have detrimental effects to others, numbing our sensitivity to them. Humanism is, he argues, like nationalism. He argues that those not specially related to severely retarded humans, say intelligent Martians, would be entitled on the partiality account to treat them like non-human animals: eating them, hunting them, and experimenting on them.

McMahan denies that species membership is a morally significant relation, or at least is only a minimally significant one.

Comembership of the human species is, like membership of the same race, a purely biological relation: it is a matter of genealogy, similarity of genome, or potential for interbreeding. It seems hardly credible that *these* commonalities could be morally significant, any more than membership in the same race could be. (McMahan 2002, 225)

However, the parent-child relation is biological and morally significant.

We could imagine a system where children are distributed at birth so that their biological parents do not rear them (Savulescu 2003). Such a system would correct for tracking of social with genetic advantage. But we do care about our biological ties, perhaps partly because they are responsible for our children's dependence on us and that pattern of concern seems justified. Our concern for our fellow human persons could be equally justified.

McMahan claims,

> The parallel with racial partiality is particularly instructive ... the moral effect of a special relation is to demand that one do more for those to whom one is specially related than one is required to do for others. ... The effect of a special relation is *not* to *lower* the moral barriers with respect to those to whom one is not specially related. ... Thus a rough guide to what we owe to animals is this: we owe to them whatever kind of treatement we believe the severely retarded would be owed in virtue of their instrinsic natures by morally sensitive Martians. We should, in short, treat animals no worse than we believe severely retarded human beings with comparable capacities should be treated by moral agents who are not specially related to them. (Mcmahan 2002, 227)

On McMahan's argument, partiality is icing on the cake. Our obligations are primarily determined by the being's intrinsic properties. Appeals to partiality can support only a very weak form of the human prejudice.

3. Post-humans and other intelligent life

Williams, in the closing part of the essay, considers beings superior to ourselves.

> Suppose that, in the well-known way of science fiction, creatures arrive with whom to some extent we can communicate, who are intelligent and technologically advanced (they got here, after all), have relations with each other that are mediated by understood rules, and so on and so forth. (Williams 2006, 148)

> The late Robert Nozick once gave it as an argument for vegetarianism that if we claimed the right to eat animals less smart than ourselves, we would have to concede the right to such visitors to eat us, if they were smarter than us to the degree that we are smarter than the animals we eat. In fact, I don't think that it is an argument for vegetarianism, but rather an objection to one argument for meat-eating, and I am not too sure how good it is even in that role (because the point of the meat-eater may not be the distance of the animals from our level of understanding, but the absolute level of the animals' understanding). (Williams 2006, 148)

Williams considers the aggressive alien who wants to annihilate us, as in the film *Independence Day*. He argues we can protect ourselves on grounds of self-preservation or self defence. This is surely correct. But then he considers benevolent aliens and asks whether the human prejudice is justified. Can we give greater consideration to us and our concerns?

The arrivals might be very disgusting indeed: their faces, for instance, if those are faces, are seething with what seem to be worms, but if we wait long enough to find out what they are at, we may gather that they are quite benevolent. They just want to live with us—rather closely with us. What should we make of that proposal? (Williams 2006, 149)

As I have argued, if any partiality towards humans is justified, then it is weak. Imagine an epidemic that leaves one of my children horribly ugly, say a smallpox epidemic. Even if I hate his ugliness, I am morally required to care for him the same as my other children, in virtue of the fact that he is one of my children. In so far as the aliens have the properties which we value in humans, we should care for them.

Williams's response would be: but they are humans. But again, why should chromosome number or capacity to interbreed matter? In Williams's language, how could we (if we really knew the facts and reflected on what was really of value), care about *that*? Most people, when they deliberate on the facts properly, would not care about that.

Or turn things round in a different direction. The aliens are, in terms of our preferences, moderately good-looking, and they are, again, extremely benevolent and reasonable; but they have had much more successful experience than we have in running peaceable societies, and they have found that they do need to *run* them, and that too much species-self-assertion or indeed cultural autonomy prove destabilizing and destructive. So, painlessly, they will rid us, certainly of our prejudices, and to the required extent, of some of our cultural and other peculiarities. What should we make of that? Would the opponents of speciesism want us to join them—join them, indeed, not on the ground that we could not beat them (which might be sensible if not very heroic), but on principle? (Williams 2006, 149)

Williams considers whether a non-aggression pact is possible and we could co-exist at a distance with the aliens:

There is no reason to suppose that the universal principles we share with the aliens will justify our prejudices. We cannot even be sure that they will justify our being allowed to have our prejudices, as a matter of toleration; as I said in setting up the fantasy, the long experience and benevolent understanding of the aliens may enable them to see that tolerating our kinds of prejudice leads to instabilty and injustice, and they will want to usher our prejudices out, and on these assumptions we should agree. (Williams 2006, 151)

Ushering out racist and sexist premises from local communities is a good thing: why not the human prejudice too? To remove our human prejudice is not to lose our cultural and other pecularities. It is to lose attachment to some biological fact. It is obvious that different cultures can coexist without harming each other and still retain sufficient cultural identity, even if some are radically different or even superior to others. Removing our human prejudice has no necessary implications for our lives or for our valued human activities. Removing our speciesist preference might mean we have to more peaceably co-exist with animals, not unnecessarily hurt them and perhaps stop eating them. But it does not mean that we cannot listen to music, do scientific research, admire our achievements, or play with our children.

But if this is so, doesn't something stronger follow? I said, in setting up these fantasies, that the *Independence Day* scenario, in which the aliens are manifestly hostile and want to destroy us is, for us, an ethically easy case: we try to defend ourselves. But should we? Perhaps this is just another irrational, visceral, human reaction. The benevolent and fair-minded and far-sighted aliens may know a great deal about us and our history, and understand that our prejudices are unreformable: that things will never be better in this part of the universe until we are removed.[4] I am not saying that this is necessarily what the informed and benevolent aliens would think. Even if they did think it, I am not saying that the universal moralists, the potential collaborators, would have to agree with them. But they might agree with them, and if they were reluctant to do so, I do not see how they could be sure that they were not the victims of what in their terms would be just another self-serving prejudice. This, it seems to me, is a place at which the project of trying to transcend altogether the ways in which human beings understand themselves and make sense of their practices could end up. And at this point there seems to be only one question left to ask: Which side are you on? (Williams 2006, 152)

As Williams alludes in response to Nozick, moral status may be a threshold concept. Above a certain level of intelligence, or rationality, or whatever defines person, all persons are equal and have an equal right to life. This

---

[4] This is the scenario in the new version of "Battlestar Galactica". They kick off the series with this question, do we deserve to be allowed to live?

is the common-sense view of moral status. Once humans have achieved a certain level of self-consciousness, they are treated equally, even if some have a greater self-consciousness in terms of having greater insight into self, being better able to project into the future, have richer life plans, and a more coherent sense of self. Smarter people do not have more of a right to live. On the threshold view, we have nothing to fear from the aliens if we are above the threshold of moral consideration.

But even on a scalar view, where our value varies according to the amount of property X, the property of persons, it does not imply that we should turn ourselves over to the aliens for the better. As Williams himself points out, self-defence is justified.

Williams seems to be tempting the would-be collaborators or personists to give themselves up to the superior aliens. But why should they? We do not have an obligation to die so that better beings might exist. Moreover, it is not reasonable to justify the human prejudice in terms of whom we are entitled to kill in self-defence. Self preservation is different: I should not be expected to allow myself to die to promote any equality. *Killing a black aggressor who attacks me is not racism.* It is mere self-defense. Even if we are morally entitled to kill superior aliens who threaten us, this does not give us any reason to believe that the human prejudice is justified.

Following Fukuyama's concerns about the inferiority of humans in a post-human world, consider the following objection. (Bennett Foddy, personal communication.) Suppose the post-humans are actually better: smarter, more compassionate, wiser, more creative. Suppose that they are so smart and so wise and so compassionate that they dwarf us in the same way as we dwarf houseflies. They are persons to a much greater extent than us. Why shouldn't they devalue us, just as we devalue flies? We consume resources and meet less of the post-humans' goals and values, and we fulfil fewer objective values. On every available theory except biological humanism, shouldn't we let them devalue us? This may present a problem for personism. If we are persons to the extent that we have minds, then aliens with bigger, more effective minds may be more like persons, just as we are more like persons than cows. On value-based personism, smarter people DO have more of a right to live.

Such concerns only highlight the need for good value-based normative frameworks. If being a person grounds a right to life, then our lives are not in jeopardy if there are people smarter than us. If intelligent culture is worth protecting, then we should not fear if there are more intelligent cultures. As humans, we now believe that all human cultures, regardless of their sophistication, age, intelligence, creative complexity, deserve protection. Human culture would be like this in a *moral* post-human world. What we must ensure is that the post-human world is sufficiently moral. We do have much to fear from immoral post-humans. But then again, we have much to fear today from immoral humans with great technological powers.

4. Value-based reasons: saving, killing, and creation

I have argued that on a DB view of reasons, we would have reason to care about non-human persons including aliens to the extent that they instantiate the properties we value, such as happiness, rationality, etc. Some preferential prejudice in favour of human beings could be justified if the relations between human beings are relevantly similar to relations between family members or close personal relations. There is another bleak view which would justify the kind of human prejudice that Williams and many people have in mind. If reasons were DB, and all we cared most about was humans, then our prejudice would be justified. But equally, if we cared more about our pets than our children, we should care more about our pets than our children. Most people do not have the pattern of values which would justify the human prejudice—most people do not care most about the number of chromosomes or our ability to interbreed. They care about the human properties of value: empathy, love, wisdom, etc. Indeed, it is hard to see how this is an adequate account of what we have reason to care about at all.

On a value-based account of reasons which I favour, how much we should care about non-human animals depends on their properties. If moral status is a threshold concept, we have nothing to fear from benevolent superior aliens or post-humans, provided we fall on the right side of the threshold. It is plausible we would, according to personists. We have enough self-consciousness and rationality to justify a right to life.

If moral status is a scalar concept, there are interesting problems thrown up by superior post-human or alien life which Williams only obliquely addresses. Let us return to the case of the benevolent superior aliens who wish to peaceably coexist with us. Imagine that an alien is dying and a human is dying. We cannot save both. Whom should we save? Or imagine some trolley case requires we kill an alien or a human, whom should we choose? Imagine a couple could have a normal human child or an enhanced being. Whom should they create?

It is useful here to compare normal human beings with disabled human beings. I will choose mild disability because my claims are hardest to justify in relation to deafness and deaf people have given structurally similar arguments to Williams's humanists to defend bias in favour of the deaf.

The relevant ethical concept is something like: loyalty to, or identity with, one's ethnic or cultural grouping, and in the fantasy case, the ethical concept is: loyalty to, or identity with, one's species. (Williams 2006, 150)

Such loyalty has been affirmed by Deaf people to the Deaf community.

Three Categories of Cases

Case A Threat.   A tries to kill a deaf person because A believes the world will be a better place without deaf people.

Case B Saving.   A doctor B saves a hearing person rather than a deaf person.

Case C Creation.   C decides to select an embryo which will be able to hear rather than one which will be deaf.

Case D Creation.   A deaf couple, D, select an embryo which will be deaf rather than one which will hear because they believe deafness is not a disability.

Case A* A post-human, A*, tries to kill me because he believes the world would be a better place without humans.

Case B* A doctor, B*, saves a post-human rather than a human.

Case C* A post-human, C*, decides to select an embryo which will be post-human rather than one which will be human. (He considers humans disabled.)

Case D* D* selects an embryo which will be human rather than enhance one to create a post-human.

The Threat cases, A and A*, which Williams primarily addresses are straightforward. The deaf person is entitled to resist A's attempts to kill him and I should resist the attempts of the post-human to kill me.

Why is this? Sidgwick described the dualism of practical reason, the conflict between duty and self-interest. Even on a VB view of reasons, self-interest and morality can be independent sources of reasons for action. Self-interest, like Autonomy, can give weight to what we do care about and value and the fact that we want our lives to go a certain way.

4.1. The Drowning Wife and Children

George's wife goes down one fork. His children go down the other. He saves his wife.

Utilitarians believe George is morally required to rescue his two children. He might care for his wife more. He might autonomously desire to rescue his wife—he might have most reason to do this, even though he has more moral reason to save his children.

People can be morally required to give up their life—for example for their country. But they might have most reason to desert their moral duty, depending on the values. Self-interest might rationally justify their desertion. How much weight we give to our own Self-interest or Autonomy and how much to Morality is not clear but both provide reasons for action.

The interesting cases are those of Saving and Creating (or killing in non-self-defence cases). Here I will briefly sketch my own position based on personism and moral status being a scalar not threshold concept.

I have elsewhere argued that we have a moral obligation to have the best child, that is the child with the best opportunity of the best life (Savulescu 2001). Morality requires that people have healthy rather than disabled children.

However, this does not settle whether people have most reason to have hearing rather than deaf children. If they strongly value having a deaf child, and have great loyalty to the Deaf culture, it is a "ground project" to have a deaf child, then they may have most reason to have a deaf child just as the husband might have most reason to save his wife rather than two children on the basis of his present pattern of concern. This of course is subject to the availability of resources, the impact on others, and the strength of other normative considerations.

And, even if the deaf couple do not have most reason to have a deaf child, it is plausible that they should be at liberty to have such a child, if there are no serious resource constraints, no one is harmed, etc.

In Cases B and C, saving a hearing person and conceiving a hearing child are grounded in the fact that their lives will go better, or at least have a greater chance of going better. Other things being equal, we should save and create beings with longer and better lives. When organs such as hearts are distributed, they go to children with better prognoses: that is, a better chance of a longer better life. (Savulescu 2001a)

In Case D, the deaf couple might have most reason to conceive a deaf child or at least they should be at liberty to do so as I have argued elsewhere (Savulescu 2002).

Compare these to the structurally similar cases. Post-humans and impartial third parties should give priority to post-humans rather than humans if they will have better, longer lives.

However, in Case D*, humans would be at liberty to continue to procreate their line, even if the value of such lives is inferior to what they could have created. However, it is plausible to claim that they should have silicon children, rather than carbon-based children, if these children are better and are expected to have better lives just as couples should have hearing rather than deaf children.

5. Concluding Remarks

There are many (over 20) definitions of species *homo sapiens*. It is remarkably difficult to say what is biologically different about *homo sapiens*. Chimps share 98.4 per cent of their DNA with humans. Sometimes the definition is genetic (for example, *homo sapiens* is a species with 46 chromosomes or some other defining genetic quality), or in terms of the capacity to reproduce with one another.

These definitions would exclude those human beings with chromosomal disorders who are infertile, such as people with Turner's Syndrome (45XO). Moreover, these definitions may work to define a species, but do not capture what is special about the species *homo sapiens*, which is different to all other plants and animals. Why is the capacity to interbreed morally relevant? Why does having some special genetic structure entitle a being to special concern and respect?

Existing definitions will struggle as genetic modification of animals continues and eventually humans are modified. Jeff McMahan imagines superchimp—a genetically enhanced chimp with the IQ of a 10-year-old. This is not science fiction. We could create human–chimp chimeras by fusing chimp and human embryos. Or we could substitute genes through transgenesis. These will raise interface questions—when does an animal become a human being? Would genetically altered human beings, with animal genes inserted, be members of our species? What matters is whether they are persons. As Jeff McMahan writes,

...it would be absurd to suppose that the moral status of any individual in the spectrum [from full chimp through chimera to full human] would be determined by how many, or what proportion, of its genes were human or were taken from a human being. Rather, it seems that the moral status of each individual would be determined by its individual phenotypic characteristics, particularly its psychological capacities. Compare, for example, two chimeras. In one, more than 99 per cent of its genes are of human origin, though the genes responsible for the growth and development of the brain are from the original chimpanzee zygote . . . In a second chimera, more than 99 per cent of its genes are of chimpanzee origin, but the genes responsible for the development of its brain have a human source. If membership in the human species is sufficient for a certain high moral status, the chimera with the intelligence of a chimpanzee should have the moral status at least equal to that of the one with human intelligence. This, I believe, is implausible. (McMahan 2002, 213)

What is special about the species *homo sapiens* compared to all other animals?

There are several candidate properties which differentiate us from other animals:

- capacity to reason
- capacity to act from normative reasons, including moral reasons
- capacity to act autonomously
- capacity to engage in complex social relationships
- capacity to display empathy and sympathy
- capacity to have faith (believe in a god)

I believe one necessary (but perhaps not sufficient) condition of humanity is the capacity to act on the basis of normative reasons. Let's assume this quality is one of the essential elements of humanity. Let's call this the capacity to display practical rationality. Scanlon claims that what matters is the capacity to have "judgement sensitive attitudes". Animals have desires and wants about what to do. Humans alone have beliefs about what they should do. Humans sometimes act on the basis of these (Savulescu 2003b).

Humans may become extinct just as Neanderthal man gradually became extinct. It is characteristic of evolution for species to come and go, to be replaced by others. There is something special about *homo sapiens*. But that specialness will continue in post-humans or another life form, unless we are annihilated against our will.[5] We will not give up what we value. Our rationality, creativity and patterns of care and concern—the things which we value and which are of value—will live on provided power is not exercised over value, in which case self-defence would be appropriate.

We have reasons to care about our descendants and other intelligent life forms, even if they are not human. What matters is whether and to what degree they display the properties of persons. Is moral status scalar or threshold? In most cases, it is likely to be threshold. But if the non-human life forms are greatly superior in the characteristics which define human persons, like the difference between us and Neanderthal man, it may be that we should care more for them than we do for humans. We might have reason to save or create such vastly superior lives, rather than continue the human line.

I have tried to make some general points about the relationship between metaethics and normative ethics. I have also argued how we can be mistaken about our values and the importance of rational deliberation in arriving at what we truly value. I have argued humanism or the human prejudice is no different to racism or sexism. I have argued that even on Williams's earthy Humean subjectivism, where our reasons are desire-based, and there is no cosmic or objective order, the human prejudice is not justified and we may have significant moral obligations to post-humans and other intelligent life forms based on the value we accord to persons. On more objective, value-based accounts, our obligations to these non-human life forms may be even greater. Considerations of partiality to the family of man may justify some partiality towards human persons, but such considerations are limited. According to Value-Based reasons, we may have more reason to

---

[5] Nick Bostrom has elsewhere outlined two dystopian scenarios, in at least one of which our specialness does not continue even without us being "annihilated against our will". See Bostrom, N. 2004. "The Future of Human Evolution" in *Death and Anti-Death: Two Hundred Years After Kant, Fifty Years After Turing*, ed. Charles Tandy (Ria University Press: Palo Alto, California, 2004), 339–71, available online at http://www.nickbostrom.com/fut/evolution.pdf.

care about our children and to a lesser degree about humans. But we should also care about non-humans, including post-humans, to the degree that they instantiate the features which are valuable. What those features are is a topic for another paper.

References

Annas, G. (2002), 'Cell Division', *Boston Globe*. Available from http://genetics-and-society.org/resources/items/20020421_globe_annas.html, April 21, 2006.

Barton-Davis, E. R., Shoturma, D. I., Musaro, A., Rosenthal, N. and Sweeney, H. L. (1998), 'Viral mediated expression of insulin-like growth factor I blocks the aging-related loss of skeletal muscle function', *Proc Natl Acad Sci U S A*, Dec. 22; 95(26): 15603–7.

Blasco, M. A. (2005), 'Telomeres and human disease: ageing, cancer and beyond', *Nature Reviews Genetics*. 6: 611–22.

Falls, W. A., Miserendino, M. J. D. and Davis, M. (1992), 'Extinction of fear-potentiated startle: blockade by infusion of an NMDA antagonist into the amygdala', *J. Neurosci*. 12: 854–63.

Fukuyama, F. (2004), 'Transhumanism', *Foreign Policy* (September–October, 2004). Available at http://georgeovermeire.nl/transhumanisme.nl/fukuyama.html. Accessed 30 August, 2006.

Guerin, J. C. (2004), 'Emerging area of aging research long-lived animals with "negligible senescence"', *Annals of the New York Academy of Science*, 1019: 518–20.

Harris, J. (2000), 'Intimations of Immortality', *Science* 288 5463: 59.

—— (2002), 'Intimations of Immortality—The ethics and justice of life extending therapies'. In Michael Freeman (ed.), *Current Legal Problems* (Oxford: Oxford University Press), 65–95.

—— (2004), 'Immortal Ethics'. In de Grey, A. D. N. J. (ed.), 'Strategies for Engineered Negligible Senescence: Why Genuine Control of Aging May Be Foreseeable', *Annals NY Acad. Sci.*, 1019.

Hume, D. (1978), *A Treatise of Human Nature*, 2nd edn. (Oxford: Clarendon Press), 416, 459.

Lee, S. J., (2004), 'Regulation of muscle mass by myostatin', *Annu. Rev. Cell Dev. Biol*. 20: 61–86.

—— and McPherron, A. C. (2001), 'Regulation of myostatin activity and muscle growth'. *Proceedings of the National Academy of Sciences of the United States of America* 98: 9306–9311.

Lim, M. M., Wang Z., Olazábal, D. E., Ren, X., Terwilliger, E. F., and Young L. J. (2004), 'Enhanced partner preference in a promiscuous species by manipulating the expression of a single gene', *Nature* 429: 754–7 (17 June, 2004), *online* doi: 10.1038/nature02539.

Liu, Z., Barry, J., Richmond, B. J., Murray, E. A., Saunders R. C., Steenrod, S., Stubblefield, B. K., Montague, D. M., and Ginns, E. I. (2004), 'DNA targeting of rhinal cortex D2 receptor protein reversibly blocks learning of cues that predict reward', *PNAS* August 9, *online* doi:10.1073/pnas.0403639101.

McMahan, J. (2002), *The Ethics of Killing: Problems at the Margins of Life* (Oxford: Oxford University Press).

Palma, V., Lim, D., Dahmane, N., Sanchez, P., Brionne, T., Herzberg, C., Gitton, Y., Carleton, A., Alvarez-Buyll, A., Ruiz, I., and Altaba, A. (2005), 'Sonic hedgehog controls stem cell behaviour in the postnatal and adult brain', *Development* 132: 335–44.

Plato (1993), *Euthyphro*, 10a trans. H. Tredennick and H. Tarrant (London: Penguin), 1993.

Rietze, R., Valcanis, H., Brooker, G., Thomas, T., Voss, A., and Bartlett, P. (2001), 'Purification of a pluripotent neural stem cell from the adult mouse brain', *Nature* 412: 736–9.

Routtenberg, A., Cantallops, I., Zaffuto, S., Serrano, P., and Namgung, U. (2000), 'Enhanced learning after genetic overexpression of a brain growth protein', *Proc. Natl. Acad. Sci. U S A*, Jun. 20; 97 (13): 7657–62.

Rudolph, K. L., Chang, S., Lee, H. W., Blasco, M., Gottlieb, G. J., Greider, C., and DePinho, R. A. (1999), 'Longevity, Stress Response, and Cancer in Aging Telomerase-Deficient Mice', *Cell* vol. 96: 701–12.

Savulescu, J. (1998), 'The Present-aim Theory: A Submaximizing Theory of Rationality?' *Australasian Journal of Philosophy*, 76: 229–43, Parts of this section of this chapter relate to material in this paper.

—— (2001), 'Procreative Beneficence: Why We Should Select the Best Children', *Bioethics*, 15: 413–26.

—— (2001a), 'Resources, Down Syndrome and Cardiac Surgery', *British Medical Journal*, 2001, 322: 875–6.

—— (2002), 'Deaf lesbians, "designer disability," and the future of medicine', *BMJ*. Oct 5, 325(7367): 771–3.

—— (2003a), 'The Public Interest in Embryos', in Gunning J and Szoke, H. (eds)., *The Regulation of Assisted Reproductive Technology Legislation* (Aldershot: Ashgate), 2003, 191–202.

—— (2003b), 'Human-animal transgenesis and chimeras might be an expression of our humanity', *Am. J. Bioethics*, 2003 Summer, 3(3): 22–5.

—— (2006), 'Genetic Interventions and the Ethics of Enhancement of Human Beings'. In Steinbock, B., (ed.), *The Oxford Handbook on Bioethics*, 2006, 516–35.

—— Foddy, B., and Clayton, M. (2004), 'Why we should allow performance enhancing drugs in sport', *Brit. J. Sports Med.* 38(6): 666–70.

Schuelke, M., Wagner, K. R., Stolz, L. E., Hubner, C., Riebel, T., Komen, W., Braun, T., Tobin, J. F., and Lee, S. J. (2004), 'Myostatin mutation associated with gross muscle hypertrophy in a child', *New England Journal of Medicine* 350(26): 2682–8.

Singer, P. (1993), *Practical Ethics*, 2nd edn. (Cambridge: Cambridge University Press).

—— (1995), *Rethinking Life and Death: The Collapse of Our Traditional Ethics* (Oxford: Oxford University Press).

Smith, M. (1994), *The Moral Problem* (Oxford: Blackwell).

Tang, Y. P., Shimizu, E., Dube, G. R., Rampon, C., Kerchner, G. A., Zhuo, M., Liu, G., and Tsien, J. Z. (1999), 'Genetic enhancement of learning and memory in mice', *Nature* 401: 63–9.

Taurek, J. M. (1977), 'Should the Numbers Count?' *Philosophy and Public Affairs*, 6: 293–316.

Tooley, M. (1983), *Abortion and Infanticide* (Oxford: Clarendon Press).

Wang, H., Ferguson, G. D., Pineda, V. V., Cundiff, P. E., and Storm, D. R. (2004), 'Overexpression of type-1 adenylyl cyclase in mouse forebrain enhances recognition memory and LTP', *Nat. Neurosci.* June 7(6): 635–42.

Wei, F., Wang, G., Kerchner, G. A., Kim, S. J., Xu, H., Chen, Z., and Zhuo, M. (2001), 'Genetic enhancement of inflammatory pain by forebrain NR2B overexpression'. *Nat. Neurosci.* 4: 164–9.

Williams, B. A. O. (1981), 'Internal and external reasons', in his *Moral Luck* (Cambridge: Cambridge University Press).

—— (2006), 'The Human Prejudice' in his *Philosophy as a Humanistic Discipline*, ed. Moore, A. W. (Oxford: Princeton University Press).

PART II
Specific Enhancements

11

Is Selection of Children Wrong?

Dan W. Brock

The following case is derived from Derek Parfit: a woman is told that if she gets pregnant now her child is almost certain to be seriously mentally retarded. However, if she takes a relatively simple medication with no significant side effects for two months and then gets pregnant there is every reason to believe that she will have a non-disabled child.[1] Some time ago at a meeting of a research project on disability issues I presented this case with the expectation that all would agree that she ought to take the medication and wait to get pregnant, and that it would be morally wrong not to do so. To my surprise, one disability rights advocate argued not only that it would not be wrong to fail to take the medication and wait to get pregnant, but that it would be wrong *to* take the medication and wait to get pregnant.

The reason offered for this view was that taking the medication and waiting would be selection, and that selection was wrong.[2] I found this position extremely implausible then, as I still do now. However, I believe that ethical concerns about selection when used to prevent the creation of disabled individuals, which I will here call negative selection, are common, and not just among disability rights advocates. The concern about selection is often connected with charges that such practices represent eugenics and are therefore wrong. Selection has a perhaps even broader potential application, not to avoid undesirable traits in children, but to produce or enhance desirable traits, for example through in vitro fertilization with pre-implantation diagnosis or genetic enhancement. This is the concern

[1] Derek Parfit, *Reasons and Persons* (Oxford: Oxford University Press, 1984).
[2] Of course, once the option of taking the medication and waiting to get pregnant has become available, it could be argued that not taking that option also becomes selection. In this view, new reproductive options such as that in the Parfit case make selection unavoidable, and so taking a particular option could not be wrong simply because it is selection. I set this problem aside in the rest of the paper.

with positive eugenics and so-called "designer children," with the choices we might someday have to select the genetic makeup of our children, which I will call here positive selection. So the concern about selection cuts more broadly than just the prevention of the creation of individuals who would be seriously disabled, though I believe it has its origins in that context. My aim in this paper is to examine whether, or when, selection is in fact morally problematic or wrong.

What is selection?

In order to try to get at what might be wrong with selection in the reproductive context, we need to specify more carefully what is meant by selection, or what kind of selection is thought to be morally problematic. Even the selection of a person with whom to procreate can be intended, at least in part, to transfer some of the procreative partner's genetically influenced features or traits to one's offspring. The selection of a procreative partner can be intended to influence the nature of one's offspring in other ways as well; for example, selecting a partner with a high probability of financial success or with strong nurturing traits can also be intended to help shape the nature of the children that will be produced. It would be unusual for a concern with the children that a procreative partner would likely contribute to producing, to be the sole or even dominant reason for selection of a partner, but where such concerns are one among other reasons for selecting a procreative partner, then the selection of the procreative partner is in turn intended to select one's children, or at least to select some of their attributes. There is a sense in which any decision made by prospective parents, and in particular by a prospective mother, that is intended to affect the nature of the child that will be born can be considered selection. So, for example, a pregnant woman's avoiding alcohol or drugs that would endanger her fetus, eating a healthy diet, taking folic acid supplements or securing prenatal care are all intended to affect the nature of the child that she will have, and in these examples to help ensure that her child will be born healthy and without serious disability. Yet far from finding such actions in any way problematic, they are nearly universally viewed as desirable and responsible. Parents typically hope for a healthy child, and this hope is endorsed and sympathized with rather than criticized by others. Stated differently, parents hope that the child they have will not be seriously unhealthy or disabled. So parents' negative attitude towards the possibility of serious disability in their child, as well as actions to try to prevent that outcome, are common and widely viewed as acceptable, indeed desirable.

Now some will object that these actions do not involve explicit selection of children. In this view selection involves choosing among different existing children, as one might in adoption contexts or as in "Sophie's choice." But that kind of selection is not present in Parfit's case, or in typical cases of positive selection. In Parfit's case, the choice is among different possible children, neither of which is an actual child at the time of the choice; the choice is of some of the properties her actual child will have once it comes into existence. In post-conception negative selection the choice is typically between an existing fetus found by genetic testing to have a serious disease or disability and a different possible child in a future pregnancy not expected to have that condition. This is not, in my view, a choice between different persons, but rather a choice between an actual fetus not yet a person and a different possible fetus and possible person. It is the choice between one actual being and another possible being, neither of which are actual persons, not just the choice of some property or properties that a single actual or possible being will have.

In a possible future case of selection involving genetic manipulation of an already existing embryo, whether the genetic change constitutes a change in the properties of a single being, or instead a transformation of one being into a different being, depends on the identity conditions for individual embryos at the stage of development at which the genetic manipulation takes place. But whether or not this is a choice between two different individuals, or of the properties that one individual will have, I believe it is clear that at least one moral concern with selection extends to both kinds of cases. That concern is with our taking control over, with choosing, what kinds of children we will have. However, there is a potential additional moral concern when the selection involves the destruction of one being and the creation of another being in its stead. There one chooses between two complete beings, albeit one still a possible being, on the basis of one or more differences between them and where the choice is which one will be born and live to become a person, and which will not. For people who view human embryos as persons, the use of in vitro fertilization (IVF) to create multiple embryos and then pre-implantation diagnosis (PGD) to select the embryo to be implanted, whether it is negative or positive selection, involves the choice of which person will be allowed to live and develop. Since "spare" embryos left over from IVF are often frozen and stored indefinitely in the U.S. rather than being destroyed, it is not strictly a choice between which one lives or dies.[3]

Is genetic selection special?

Is whether the selection is genetic, that is the choice of one's child's genetic inheritance, a morally important feature of selection? Some examples given above of actions that affect the nature of one's children, such as its mother harming it by smoking or alcohol use during pregnancy, do not affect its genetic inheritance. For some opponents of selection, it seems to be genetic selection, in particular, that is morally problematic. However, it is unclear why selection being genetic selection has moral importance in itself. Of course, if the genes selected against, or for, have particularly profound phenotypic effects on the child, such as selection against the genes causing Lesch Nyan or Tay Sachs disease, then that selection has great moral import, but that is because of the profound effects of those genes on the child and its life, not because the selection is genetic; these two examples arguably create lives not worth living and are instances of wrongful life. In the case of so-called "junk genes," on the other hand, which apparently have no phenotypic effects, although there would generally be no reason to select against or for them, doing so would not be ethically problematic just because the selection is genetic. If a woman aborted an early fetus because it had genes that would result in a seriously disabling disease, that would seem no different morally than if she aborted a fetus who would have the very same disabling condition as a result of an injury to the fetus or an environmental hazard that caused no genetic mutations.

A special concern with genetic selection, as opposed to selection of other conditions likely to affect one's child, could be grounded in an unwarranted belief in genetic determinism. If it were the case that a very strong form of

---

[3] In some developed countries such as Great Britain there is a time limit on how long embryos can be stored before being destroyed. In Germany creating more embryos than will be implanted is prohibited.

genetic determinism were true, say according to which one's gene's fully determined all one's phenotypic traits and even one's entire life course or history, then there would be good reason for special concern with genetic selection. That selection would be decisive for and would control the nature and life of the person. However, there is no reason whatever to believe such a genetic determinism to be true. Instead, we know that an individual's environment and choices also have profound effects on the nature and life of the individual. With regard to some traits or properties of the person and events in the person's life genes may have the more important causal role, and for others environmental conditions and choices will have the more important causal role. There is no reason to believe that genetic changes will systematically have more profound impacts or control over the individual.

A different source of special concern with genetic selection can derive from a belief that one's identity is in some profound sense determined by one's genome, so that genetic selection affects the very identity of the child. In this view environmental conditions, on the other hand, even if they have a profound impact on the child nevertheless do not affect its very identity. And it might be thought that explicit identity shaping is not properly our, or specifically parents', business. This view too is mistaken in its assumption that a person's genome alone shapes or determines his or her identity. This issue about identity is not about the numerical or philosophical sense of identity, the conditions that determine whether an individual at one time and an individual at another time are one and the same individual, but rather the psychological or narrative sense of identity. That is the sense of identity that constitutes the properties that for any individual contribute most importantly to his or her sense of who he or she is, the unique set of properties most important to his or her self-definition.

For most people, if their genes were different such that they had, for example, green eyes instead of blue, this would not cause them to believe that their identity had been altered in any profound or even significant way. Identity determining properties are in the great majority of cases phenotypic properties, not genetic properties and those phenotypic properties can be determined more by environmental or genetic causes depending on the particular case and property in question. It is a mistake to believe that interventions that change a person's genome must change his or her identity in a deep way, whereas environmental interventions only bring out what is already genetically fixed. There is no fixed phenotype given a particular genotype. Instead, there is a range of phenotypes associated with a given genotype and determined by the environment with which the individual interacts. This means that it is also a mistake to believe that one's genome is more controlling of one's phenotype than one's environment; again, one or the other may be more controlling depending on the phenotypic property in question. The upshot is that there is no reason to believe that attempting to select children on the basis of their genomes is in principle ethically more problematic than attempting to select them through the environmental conditions to which they have been or will be subject.

Negative selection against disability

Adrienne Asch has made a helpful distinction between a pregnant woman who aborts a fetus because she does not wish to be pregnant and have any child now, from a woman who aborts a fetus because of the specific nature of that fetus, in particular the presence of a serious disability in the fetus.[4] In the former case, the woman's choice to abort is only selection among the alternatives of having a child now and not having one now; use of contraceptives usually also represents this kind of selection. It does not represent selection of what kind of child to have, or selection against a particular kind of child. It is not the kind of selection in question here. In the latter case, on the other hand, a woman's choice of abortion represents a decision specifically not to have a child with this particular condition. That might be because she believes she has the prospect of a new pregnancy in which her fetus and child would likely not have this condition and so she wishes to substitute a healthy fetus and child for this disabled fetus and child. Or alternatively it might be because she would rather have no child than to have a child with this disability. Whether she aborts because she wishes to substitute a child without this disability for the child with it, or whether she simply does not want to have any child with that disability, in either case her action does seem to express a negative attitude towards not

---

[4] Adrienne Asch, "Why I Haven't Changed My Mind About Prenatal Diagnosis: Reflections and Refinements." In E. Parens and A. Asch (eds.), *Prenatal Testing and Disability Rights* (Washington, DC: Georgetown University Press, 2000).

only the disability, but to having a child with that disability, and perhaps as well to people or a life with that disability. It is this kind of negative selection especially, which is thought to be objectionable by many people, not just members of the disability community.

The message expressed by negative selection

Why would selection against having a child with a serious disability be thought objectionable? I have pursued some of the arguments from the disability community and others against genetic testing and negative selection elsewhere and will not pursue those points again here.[5] Here, I want to note several kinds of arguments and their import for policy. One form of objection holds that such selection is directly harmful to already existing persons with disabilities or to society more broadly. For example, it will reduce the numbers of disabled persons and in turn erode support for persons who are disabled, it will reinforce prejudice and discrimination against persons with disabilities, or it will reduce diversity in society and tolerance of difference in its members. These objections grounded in harm to others must be weighed against the benefit of reducing suffering and diminished opportunity from not creating persons with serious disabilities and substituting non-disabled persons instead. I have also pursued these objections and the non-identity problem raised by the claim of benefit from substitution elsewhere.[6] A specific version of the objection based in harm to others from selection focuses on harm that comes from the attitude expressed by genetic testing and selection against persons with disabilities, and the hurtful and humiliating message thought to be sent to already existing persons with disabilities; like other versions of harm to others objections to selection, this too requires balancing the harms against the benefits of selection. A second form of objection is directly expressivist, and is to the message the practice conveys, independent of whether that message also causes significant material harm to others. For example, it is said that the message sent by such testing and selection is that the lives of persons

---

[5] "Preventing Genetically Transmitted Disabilities While Respecting Persons With Disabilities," in *Quality of Life and Human Difference*, ed. D. Wasserman, R. Wachbroit and J. Bickenbach (New York: Cambridge University Press, 2005).

[6] Ibid. See also Allen E. Buchanan, Dan W. Brock, Norman Daniels, and Daniel Wikler, *From Chance to Choice: Genes and Social Justice* (Cambridge: Cambridge University Press, 2000).

with serious disabilities are of lesser value than the lives of non-disabled persons, or that it would have been better if such persons had never been born. I will come back to whether this is in fact the message that genetic testing and selection sends, but assume for the moment that it is.

Is that negative message about persons with disabilities, independent of the harm the message might cause, a sufficient ground for restricting the practice of genetic testing and selection, for example by legally prohibiting it? I believe that it clearly is not because doing so would unjustifiably violate two important moral and legal rights of persons who want to use genetic testing and selection. Deciding whether to continue a pregnancy or to terminate it is clearly within a woman's legal right in the United States to reproductive freedom, and, as I have argued again elsewhere, her moral right as well.[7] The law does not permit scrutiny of a woman's reasons for ending a pregnancy in order to determine whether her doing so is permissible, and typical understanding of a moral right to reproductive freedom also entitles a woman to choose to end a pregnancy even for reasons that others might find inadequate or even contemptible. Those who believe abortion violates a serious right to life of the fetus object to abortion itself, not to abortion only when it expresses this objectionable message. They will oppose the use of abortion for selection because it is abortion, not because it is used for selection.

The other important right that stands in the way of prohibiting genetic testing and selection on expressivist grounds is the moral and legal right to free expression.[8] The right to free expression is not unlimited, and can be restricted in specific circumstances, for example when expression imminently incites others to violence or endangers national security. However, it cannot justifiably be restricted merely on the grounds that the message expressed is found to be objectionable, offensive, or hurtful by others. When Nazi sympathizing anti-Semites or Ku Klux Klan members demonstrate or hold rallies in support of their views, their right to free expression protects their doing so no matter how despicable and offensive the messages they deliberately convey. If the objection to genetic testing

---

[7] "Reproductive Freedom: Its Nature, Bases, and Limits," in *Healthcare Ethics: Critical Issues for Health Professionals*, ed. David Thomasma and John Monagle (Gaithersburg MD: Aspen Publishers, 1994) and Buchanan, Brock, Daniels, and Wikler, op. cit. See also John Robertson, *Children of Choice* (Princeton: Princeton University Press, 1994).

[8] Thomas Scanlon, "Freedom of Expression and Categories of Expression," *University of Pittsburgh Law Review* 40 (1979): 519–50.

and selection is to the message it conveys about the lesser value of disabled lives, or that it would have been better if disabled persons had never been born, then however objectionable and offensive others may find that message the right to free expression should bar legal restriction or prohibition of the activity on the grounds that it expresses such a message.

Even if an objectionable message and the practice that conveys it should not be legally restricted because doing so would violate a woman's rights to reproductive freedom and to freedom of expression, selection conveying that message might nevertheless be morally bad or wrong; it is widely recognized that rights protect actions from interference by others that may be morally criticizable or even morally wrong.[9] If selection is morally objectionable because it is intended to convey a message, for example, that it would be better if individuals with serious disabilities had never been born, then it must be the case that this is in fact the intended message. Others have written about the ambiguity in what message is intended by genetic screening and testing in the reproductive context that has the goal of avoiding the birth of a seriously disabled child.[10] Indeed, a woman may intend no message at all in taking steps to avoid having a disabled child and to have a non-disabled child instead; she may intend only that she have a non-disabled child, which is probably the usual case. Thus, rather than asking only what message is intended, we need to ask as well what message may in fact be implied by and reasonably inferred from her actions. That may still be different from what message some other persons believe, mistakenly or unreasonably, is implied by her actions.

Here, it is useful to distinguish between three cases: first, where a woman (or a man) employs preconception testing to ensure against the conception of a disabled child; second, where she employs post-conception testing of her fetus that if found to be seriously disabled will be aborted, whereupon she will try again for a pregnancy with a non-disabled fetus; third, where she employs post-conception testing of a fetus that if found to be disabled will be aborted because she would rather have no child than a disabled child. What message is sent by her action in each of these three cases? In the first case all that need be implied by the woman's action is that she hopes to

---

    [9] Jeremy Waldron, "A Right to Do Wrong," *Ethics* 92 (1981): 21–39.

    [10] Buchanan, Brock, Daniels, and Wikler, op. cit. 272–81. James Nelson, "The Meaning of the Act: Reflections on the Expressive Meaning of Prenatal Screening," *The Kennedy Institute of Ethics Journal* 8: 2 (1998): 165–82.

give the child that she will have the best life possible and she believes that a serious disability, all else being equal, is likely to make the child's life more difficult or worse than a life without such a disability. Only more likely, of course, since she can know that such a disability does not in all cases make a person's life more difficult or worse, and in some cases may even make it better. Nothing need be implied about the value all things considered of a life with that disability, only that she believes the disability is a disadvantage that she would like the child that she bears not to have if possible. Nothing more seems to be implied than what is implied by a parent's attempt to prevent such a disability in his or her already born child. She takes steps to substitute before conception takes place a non-disabled child for a disabled child that she otherwise would conceive. In some cases, her action may imply nothing about the nature or value of a life with or without such a disability, but only that she believes a disabled child would create burdens for her family that she wishes to avoid; in this case, nothing is implied about what life would be like for the child, or what value its life would have for it. What is implied or what message is sent in a particular instance of this first kind of case depends on the reasons for the woman's action.

The second kind of case is more difficult. If she believes her fetus is a person with the same full moral status of any born person, then to abort it would imply that she believes it is justified to kill a disabled person if one could create a non-disabled "replacement" instead. That would be a morally grotesque message. But if she had that belief about the moral status of her, or any, fetus, then she should not, and no doubt would not, pursue genetic testing with the intention of possibly aborting her fetus. So the relevant version of the second case is where the woman believes that her fetus is not yet a person, and in particular that it lacks the moral status that would make it seriously wrong to destroy it whether or not it had a serious disability. If she believes that there would be no harm or wrong done to the fetus if it is destroyed, that it has no moral status with regard to protection against being destroyed, then this case for her would be like the first case. The judgments or message implied in the first case would be the judgments implied here as well. She would be substituting a child who would not have the disability for a child who would have it before any person has been created.

The more difficult version of this second kind of case is where she believes the fetus has some moral standing, or is deserving of some moral respect, but not that which a born child or full person would have or be deserving of. Here, the message implied would seem to be that she judges avoiding the disadvantage of the disability in her child (or the burdens that it would cause her or her family) to be of sufficient moral importance to outweigh whatever moral status or respect it deserves. How reasonable that judgment is depends on the precise moral standing she believes the fetus has, or what is required by the respect that she believes it deserves, together with how serious the disability is that she seeks to avoid for her child (or burdens for her or her family). But as in the first case, the only judgment implied by her action bearing on existing persons with disabilities is her judgment about how serious a disadvantage, other things being equal, the disability in question is likely to be, or how great a burden it might place on her family. Even if others, in particular others who have the disability in question, believe that she has overestimated the seriousness of the disadvantage or burdensomeness of the disability, her doing so need imply nothing about the moral value of their lives or that they are not the moral equals of non-disabled persons. To have a disadvantage in one's life is not to make one any less deserving of equal moral concern and respect, and to have overestimated the disadvantage or burdensomeness of a disability is not to have underestimated the moral status of persons with that disability.

The third case is the most problematic, but still does not necessarily imply any morally objectionable judgment or message about persons with disabilities, their moral status, or the value of their lives. In this case a pregnant woman aborts a fetus that will have a serious disability because she would rather have no child than a child with that disability when any child she has is highly likely to have that disability. It is because of her fetus's expected disability that she does not wish to continue her pregnancy. This may seem to imply that she believes it would be better if people with this disability were never born, but this implication is ambiguous about who it would be better for—the child, the mother or her family, or society generally. Except in the rare cases in which the child's disability would be so serious as to make its life not worth living, there is no reason to believe that it would be better for it never to be born. If a non-person like a fetus had a right to be born and become a person, then aborting a fetus might be thought to only be justified if the person the fetus would become would not have a life worth living. But non-persons like a fetus do not have a right to be born and become a person, although I shall not argue that here, and so a woman can abort her fetus without denying that the life that it would have if born would be valuable to it. Her action might be based on the belief that it would be better for her or her family that such a child not be born to her or them. This would also not imply that she believes that it would be better for other pregnant women or their families that a child with the same disability not be born to them. She may be unwilling to assume the burden that she assumes the child would be for her or her family, recognizing that others may be willing to assume that burden or even not finding such a child to be a burden. She need not believe that her child's life would not be a valuable life for it or for society generally, nor that it would be deserving of anything less than full moral status as a person if it were to be born. Women are neither morally nor legally obliged to bring an unwanted child into the world just because the child would be valuable to society. This means that her action need imply nothing about the value or moral status of others who have a similar disability to what her child would have. A pregnant woman who aborts an apparently normal fetus because she doesn't wish to have children now, or at all, also implies nothing about the nature or value of her child's life to it or others if it were not aborted, only that she doesn't wish to have children now, or at all. No one thinks that her action implies or sends a degrading message to children generally, a message that it would have been better if they had never been born or that their lives have diminished value or moral status.

Selecting against potential children who would be seriously disabled in any of these three cases then need not imply any message that it would be better if such children never were born, that their lives are not valuable to them or to others, or that they have a lesser moral status. Nevertheless, it cannot be denied that some persons, both persons with and without serious disabilities, will mistakenly infer some such judgment from a woman's decision to select against disabled children; they will mistakenly infer a morally offensive message even if it is not in fact there, a message they have misread. Especially to persons with disabilities who misread the message in this way it will be hurtful, and to others who misread it, it may reinforce attitudes and practices harmful to persons with disabilities. Avoiding that hurt and those harms constitutes a reason not to engage in selection against persons with disabilities. Of course, another alternative is to attempt to clarify the message in order to make clear that it contains nothing that should be hurtful or harmful to persons with disabilities, but such efforts would no doubt be only partially successful. So this constitutes a consequentialist reason not to engage in selection in reproductive contexts against persons with disabilities. How decisive that reason is depends on the degree of hurt or harm caused and the moral reasons that support selection in the instance at hand. There is clearly no consensus about the relative weight of these reasons, whether in general or in many specific cases. Some may discount the hurt or harm because it is based on a misunderstanding of the message implied, but consequentialists will correctly insist that it remains a real hurt or harm. I have already noted that the important moral rights to reproductive freedom and free expression support the moral permissibility of selection whatever its message. But there is an additional serious consequentialist reason for permitting selection of not forcing an unwanted pregnancy and its long-term consequences on a woman and her family. Except in very unusual cases, I believe the balance of moral reasons does not show negative selection to be immoral or bad.

Expressivist arguments against positive selection

Selection against persons who would have serious disabilities is often characterized as negative eugenics, whereas selection in favor of specific desired traits is characterized as positive eugenics; these parallel my use of negative and positive selection. Is selection itself morally different when it is positive rather than negative? Some such selection takes place now, as noted earlier, when individuals choose procreative partners in part in hopes of transmitting certain positive traits to their offspring. However, at the present time our capacity to use genetic selection for traits deemed to be positive is extremely limited. Genes have been identified, and tests for them in turn developed, for a number of diseases, in particular so-called single gene disorders. However, positive traits that individuals might wish to select for such as intelligence, memory, or physical strength or fitness, are almost certainly much more complex or multifactorial, determined by complex interactions between multiple genes and multiple environmental factors. One possible future form of positive genetic selection would involve genetic manipulation of genes so as to increase or improve a trait such as intelligence or memory. However, even without the ability to perform the necessary genetic manipulation, some positive genetic selection would be possible if genes having a positive effect on desired traits were identified.

Through PGD it is possible to test embryos created by IVF for genes associated with various genetic diseases. However, PGD can also be used now for sex selection, by selecting an embryo of the desired sex for implantation. This practice is highly controversial, in particular in social contexts in which strong gender bias, typically against women, is present. Sex selection is then seen as complicit in and reinforcing unjust discrimination towards women and the attitudes that underlie that discrimination. However, sex selection for other reasons, such as family balance, need not be implicated in these prejudicial and discriminatory attitudes and practices. In these cases, I believe that sex selection is not wrong. If genes associated with other desired traits are identified, PGD could in principle be used to select for them and in turn the traits with which they are associated. To avoid the complications of traits associated with unjust discrimination like sex, it is best to imagine that we could select for traits that were relatively uncontroversially agreed to be desirable, for example traits associated with certain forms of intelligence or memory.[11] That should help us to focus on the issue of whether positive selection of children is in itself ethically problematic.

It might be thought that there is again a hurtful or harmful message in such selection, despite the fact that the practice only identifies or singles out some traits as desirable, not as undesirable as in selection against serious disabilities. By singling out traits for positive selection, we imply that they are sufficiently desirable or important to justify trying to ensure that our children have them to a high degree; indeed, to justify choosing to create children with them instead of without them. The hurtful or harmful message then is presumably to those who have these traits in a lesser degree, for example those with lower intelligence or less good memories, the message that they lack valued traits that others have. But is it only the positive selection of these traits in children that sends this message? Instead, it would seem to be the presence of the prior and underlying

---

[11] Of course, some will deny that better intelligence or memory are always beneficial, and no doubt there are circumstances in which they are not. But the issue facing prospective parents considering whether to enhance these traits is the ex-ante question of whether enhanced intelligence or memory constitutes an *expected* benefit, and if the safety of the enhancement was well established, it seems reasonable to answer yes.

attitude or value judgment that these are desirable traits to have to a high degree that sends the message that those who lack the traits to a high degree lack something of important value. And of course these attitudes are widespread now, well before genetic enhancement is possible. Selection for the positive traits, were it possible, would merely be a prominent marker of the underlying attitude, though it could no doubt reinforce this message to others.

Although attitudes that males are superior to females, which underlie much sex selection, may be grounded in prejudice and stereotypes, the desirability of other traits, such as intelligence and memory, is much less controversial and not based on prejudice or stereotypes. Intelligence and memory are strong candidates for what John Rawls would call natural primary goods, capacities useful and desirable in carrying out nearly any plan of life.[12] The attitude that these are desirable traits and that it is good to have them to a high degree is justified. It is an unavoidable consequence of that justified evaluation that some will hear the message that it is unfortunate or bad if one has less of them, and this may be hurtful to those who in fact have less of them. But, of course, positive selection would only be one among myriad ways in which judgments about such traits being desirable or valuable are implied or expressed; in all the many contexts in which we find such traits valuable in ourselves or in others, that evaluation is implied or expressed as well. And the only way of avoiding the possibility of that possibly hurtful message being sent would be to abjure making any judgments about desirable human traits. Avoiding all such judgments, however, would be neither possible nor desirable; there are both desirable and undesirable human traits and it would be false and dishonest to pretend otherwise.

So with respect to the possibility of harmful or hurtful messages, it turns out not to be the practice of selection, but rather the prior and underlying value judgments that support and motivate the practice of selection, which are the culprits. It is worth underlining that this same point holds with regard to negative selection against disabilities. It is the judgment or attitude that serious disabilities are undesirable that is the source of any hurtful or harmful message, not the practice of selecting against such disabilities. And as with positive traits, it is neither possible nor desirable to abjure all such

---

[12] John Rawls, *A Theory of Justice* (Cambridge MA: Harvard University Press, 1971).

value judgments about disease and disability. To do so would, among other things, be to remove any reason we have to try to avoid diseases or injuries that would result in disabilities to ourselves or others. That is of course not to say that we do not have good reason to try to remove false beliefs, prejudices, and stereotypes about disabilities and the people who have them, which generally make those disabilities appear worse than they in fact may be, and in turn make the lives of those with disabilities worse than they need to be. But I believe that in the case of most serious disabilities that people typically try hard to avoid for themselves or others about whom they care, such as serious cognitive impairment or blindness, these conditions would remain undesirable and disadvantages even if all false beliefs, prejudices, and stereotypes about them and the people who have them were removed, though no doubt much less undesirable and disadvantageous than they in fact generally are now.

Other arguments against positive selection

If anything, positive selection of traits deemed desirable in our offspring is viewed by many as more problematic than negative selection against disabilities. But why would such selection be wrong? I will take up five answers to this question in turn: 1) that it is "playing God" and that is not a role for humans; 2) that it will undermine the attitude to children as gifts to be unconditionally accepted and loved as they are; 3) that there is no perfect child or best nature to aim at for our children; 4) that it is eugenics and therefore wrong; 5) that the risks of selection would always outweigh any benefits. It will be important to see that most of these objections can be made against negative selection as well, and so my responses to them will in turn generally apply to them as objections to both positive and negative selection.

Playing God

First, the playing God objection. In its most natural religious interpretation, this objection suggests that it is God who should determine the nature of our children, and that it is not a proper role for humans to intervene in that process. Note that this objection applies as much to negative selection against serious disabilities and diseases as to positive selection; even selection against devastating diseases like Tay Sachs and Lesch Nyan, which many consider incompatible with a life worth living, is playing God in this interpretation. If the objection is to interfering with natural processes presumed to be properly under God's dominion, then it is of course notoriously difficult to see to which human interventions this objection should apply. Building airplanes and cars enable humans to fly and travel long distances that they could not manage without these interventions, yet the playing God objection is rarely applied to them. God has presumably given humans the capacities to create these technological aids, and so it is not clear why it is incompatible with God's will for humans to use them. And so if God has also given humans the ability to develop the knowledge and means to make positive selection possible, for example through IVF and PGD now and perhaps through genetic modifications in the future, it is unclear why the use of that knowledge and those means is incompatible with God's will for humans. Intervening in natural processes for the betterment and benefit of humans is a fundamental human capacity and propensity, and there seems to be no principled line to demarcate when doing so would be usurping God's prerogatives.

Besides these and related difficulties in understanding and defending the playing God objection, it is also subject to the difficulty that basing public and legal policy on it would impose a particular religious view on all that many do not share, including those who do not believe that selection usurps God's prerogatives, as well as those who do not believe in the existence of a God at all. While I will not pursue this point here, I believe it suggests that the playing God objection in its religious interpretation is not a proper basis for public policy in a liberal democracy.

Preserving unconditional acceptance of children

Appearances perhaps to the contrary, however, I believe that what for many people underlies the playing God objection can be given a secular interpretation which avoids the liberal democrat's objection to imposing on all a particular religious view that many do not share as public and legal policy. Doing so will take us to the second objection to positive selection. Recently, the President's Council on Bioethics, as well as two of its members—Leon Kass and Michael Sandel—has argued that selecting our offspring undermines the attitude to human life as a gift to be unconditionally accepted as it is given.[13] In its religious interpretation, this gift is from God, whereas in its secular interpretation the gift is from nature and our capacity for reproduction. Selection mistakenly exaggerates the extent to which we can be in control of our own or others' lives; in reinforcing this desire for control over the nature of our offspring it undermines attitudes of unconditional love and acceptance toward them. But we know often from hard experience that our own and others' lives are full of uncontrolled and uncontrollable contingencies, and parents especially learn this quickly about their children's lives. The importance of parents' unconditional love and acceptance of their children for raising psychologically strong and healthy individuals is not in question. So if selection of children would lead to an undermining of these attitudes in parents that would be a strong reason against it. Sandel contrasts this sense of human life as a gift with the project of mastery. The project of mastery, when it is mastery of another, not self-mastery, can be tyrannical. And in highly competitive modern societies, like our own, many parents already carry the molding, shaping, scheduling, and general controlling of their children's lives to excess in a manner that can verge on tyrannical.

It is important that this objection too from the idea of human life as a gift to be accepted also clearly applies to negative as well as positive selection; indeed, I believe that it applies in one respect even more forcefully to negative than to positive selection. From this perspective, negative selection against prospective children expected to have disabilities could be likened to viewing children as consumer products that should meet certain quality standards, and if they do not are to be returned as "defective." In the context of negative genetic selection against potential children expected to have disabilities, the "returning" amounts either to their not being created at all because they would likely be defective, or their being destroyed after being created but before being born because they have been found through genetic testing to be defective.

Positive selection, either through IVF and PGD or through genetic enhancement, will lead to hopes and expectations that the child will have

---

[13] President's Council on Bioethics, *Beyond Therapy: Biotechnology and the Pursuit of Happiness* (Washington DC: President's Council on Bioethics, 2004); Leon Kass, "Beyond Therapy: Biotechnology and the Pursuit of Human Improvement," prepared for the President's Council on Bioethics, Washington, DC www.bioethics.gov, 16 January 2003; Michael Sandel, "The Case Against Perfection," *The Atlantic*, May 2004.

specific traits that are expected to be selected or enhanced. Since the kinds of traits people are likely to be interested in selecting or enhancing will generally be complex traits, for example intelligence or memory, whose causes will be multiple genes interacting with each other and with complex environmental factors, there will inevitably be cases in which the selected or enhanced traits fail to materialize as the child grows and develops. Although there will be no "returning" the child as defective, as in negative selection using prenatal genetic testing, there will be heightened expectations for the child's capabilities and performance in the relevant respects, and so in turn heightened disappointment when those expectations are not met. Since the child has been given the genetic endowment thought to be necessary for the enhanced capabilities and performance, some parents will no doubt blame the child for failing to successfully or optimally exploit or live up to that endowment. While parents now have hopes and expectations for their children which are often disappointed even in the absence of any genetic selection, negative or positive, these often amount more to hopes than to firm expectations and generally are less specific than they will be in the face of efforts to genetically select or enhance specific traits, which will in turn lead to more specific expectations that can be disappointed.

It is not controversial, as already noted, that parents' unconditional love and acceptance of their children is important for the children's development—the key issue for this objection to selection is whether a practice of negative or positive selection is likely to, or must inevitably, seriously undermine it. That is an empirical question that cannot be settled by ethical analysis or argument, but there are some reasons to be skeptical. First, unconditional love and acceptance of children by their parents is common across a wide range of social conditions and historical periods, suggesting that it may be at least to some extent genetically programmed in humans. To the extent that it is, it is likely to survive new capacities for selection. However much genetically programmed, there are also features of the environment, specifically typical child-rearing practices, such as the deep intimacy between parents and children that foster and reinforce it; these practices will continue after the advent of greater abilities for positive selection and enhancement. Second, both negative and positive selection take place before a child is born. Negative selection involves not conceiving, or aborting a fetus after conception, when the resulting child is likely to have a serious genetically transmitted disease or disability.

Once another child is conceived and born without the disability, the strong unconditional attachment that typically develops between parents and most children should develop then as well. Positive selection would be either through PGD or through genetic manipulation, presumably in each case at the embryo stage, to select or enhance certain positive traits. All the experiences of pregnancy, infancy, and early childhood that now develop strong unconditional bonds of love and attachment of parents to their children would still take place and so should still produce this unconditional love and attachment. Third, parents now typically exert great efforts to shape and mold their children's development during their childhood in myriad ways. While some parents overdo this and can even become tyrannical in the control sought over children, some attempt to shape their children's development is part of every parental experience; its presence is not incompatible with parents' unconditional love and acceptance of their children.

It would be extraordinary, as well as unfortunate, if parents did not care at all how their children developed. Parents now seek to prevent serious diseases in their children and employ a wide variety of interventions, sometimes at great sacrifice to themselves, to try to develop positive traits that will give their children a good life. These efforts are typically a reflection of, rather than incompatible with, their unconditional love and acceptance of their children. Nevertheless, some will argue that positively shaping an existing child is different than negative selection in which a potential child is either not conceived or aborted because it would or will have a serious genetic disease and another child expected to be healthy can be substituted instead. Does the unconditional love and acceptance objection apply to negative selection even if it is not persuasive against positive selection? Some critics of genetic testing have charged that it creates a tentative pregnancy in which the pregnancy and developing fetus is not fully acknowledged and accepted until genetic testing has shown it to be free of serious disease or disability.[14] But in the case of preconception testing and negative selection, no embryo ever exists that is destroyed because it will have a serious disease or disability. In the case of post-conception testing where a fetus is aborted because it will have a serious genetic disease, the choice to do so is often

---

[14] Barbara Katz Rothman, *The Tentative Pregnancy: Amniocentesis and the Sexual Politics of Motherhood* (New York: W. W. Norton, 1993).

extremely difficult and agonizing for those involved. The decision to abort will likely only be made by parents who believe that the fetus is not yet a full moral person and that aborting it would not be seriously morally wrong. Few if any parents would be prepared to kill an already born child because it developed a serious genetic disease or disability that had not been anticipated, or suffered a serious non-genetic disease or injury that was comparably disabling, and of course doing so would be in virtually all cases clearly morally wrong and legally prohibited. This suggests that the attitude of unconditional love and acceptance is indeed undermined toward the fetus when the pregnancy remains tentative because genetic testing and possible subsequent abortion is contemplated. But it does not follow that that attitude will likewise be undermined toward a fetus not aborted and the child that the fetus becomes. Once the decision is made to proceed to term with the pregnancy, all the experiences that typically foster parents' strong unconditional commitment to their children will still take place. So far as I know there is no evidence that having undergone genetic testing and decided to continue the pregnancy undermines parents' unconditional commitment to the child.

The perfect child

A different objection to positive selection is that it seeks to create the perfect child, and so assumes that we know what the perfect child would be.[15] However, there is no perfect child, not just in reality, but also even as an ideal. Just as adults' views of the good life are irreducibly different and conflicting, so their views of what a perfect child would be are irreducibly different and conflicting. So there is no defensible target at which positive selection could aim. There are two fundamental mistakes in this objection.

First, selection need not assume that we know what the perfect child would be, only that we know what would make a given child, or any child, better, what would likely give it a better life. And at least in some cases we do know this. It is uncontroversially good for people not to have serious genetic diseases or disabilities. Again, this does not mean that the life of every person with a serious genetic disease or disability is made all things considered worse by that disease. Examples of persons whose

[15] Glen McGee, *The Perfect Baby: A Pragmatic Approach to Genetics* (Lanham, MD: Rowman and Littlefield, 1997).

experiences with serious diseases and disabilities have enriched their lives by giving them insights, character strengths, or new possibilities that would not otherwise have been available to them show that to be false. But it does mean that serious diseases and disabilities are on balance bad for the entire class of persons that have them, that they make their lives as a class worse, even if they do not make each and every member of the class's life worse. At the time at which selection is undertaken, the information a prospective parent has is only about how a particular disability in general affects the lives of the persons who have it; this is what justifies the expectation in advance or ex-ante that the effect will be bad. So negative selection only presupposes that we can know that a serious genetic disease or disability can be expected to make the life of a person who has it on balance worse. I believe that we do know that in many actual cases. Indeed, if we did not believe that about many conditions, we would not characterize the condition as a genetic disease, but instead merely a genetic difference.

The same is true for positive selection, either through IVF and PGD or through genetic enhancement—all we need reasonably to believe is that the selection or enhancement can be expected to make a person's life better. And I believe that in some cases we can also know this, although perhaps less indisputably than in cases of avoidance of serious disease or disability. Of course, these judgments must be made relative to particular social, cultural, and economic conditions, but that does not belie the fact that well-grounded judgments can be made relative to such conditions. Increased intelligence, enhancement of some forms of memory, or increased powers of concentration, are all improvements in natural primary goods. Intelligence, memory, and powers of concentration are useful, which is not to say necessary, in nearly any plan of life. These judgments of better, but not best or perfect, are all that are needed to justify selection, and we are justified in making at least some such judgments.

The second difficulty with the perfect child objection is that even if parents may have reasonable beliefs about what a perfect or better child would be for them, this does not imply that they know, or claim to know, what would be a perfect or better child for anyone else. Acceptance of reasonable pluralism about the good life implies that there are different reasonable views of what a good person and a good life would be. The most that need be assumed in selection is that a particular choice of negative or positive selection would contribute to making the individual's life better, according to a particular reasonable view of the good life. It is perfectly compatible with this that the selection choice need not make a life better according to other reasonable conceptions of a good life. Reasonable pluralism about the good life implies reasonable pluralism about whether some lives are better than others, and in turn about whether selection that contributes to a particular way of life makes the life better from other perspectives about a good life. Even within a particular view of a good life there need not be only one conception of a perfect child for that way of life because there may be alternative pathways, and so kinds of individuals, that will achieve that life. But the main point is that neither negative nor positive selection need assume there is only one best life, nor in turn that there is only one best or perfect child.

Recognizing this pluralism about what is a good person and a good life raises the troubling issue of how far that pluralism should extend. To take a much-discussed case, recently a deaf couple sought to select for the trait of deafness in their offspring.[16] More commonly, both deaf and hearing parents sometimes reject cochlear implants for seriously hearing impaired children. The defense of these choices has generally been that deafness is a difference or even an advantage, not a disability or disadvantage, and that deaf culture and sign language represent reasonable alternatives to the language and culture of hearing persons. They want their child to fit into the deaf culture, especially when it is their own culture too, with its language, not only into the hearing world. Selecting for deafness would be positive selection in their view. Whether this case falls within the bounds of reasonable pluralism about the good life and a good person depends principally on whether we accept that deafness, with the deaf language and culture that support deaf persons, is a neutral or positive difference as claimed, or instead a serious disadvantage. I say "serious disadvantage" rather than simply "disadvantage" because despite the wide acceptance of the "best interest of the child standard" for decision making about children, parents are and should be entitled to make choices that are not the best choices for their children; for example they can properly give some weight to their own interests, the interests of other family members, or broader societal interests, that may conflict with an individual child's interests. But if deafness imposes serious enough disadvantages on a child then choosing it

---

[16] L. Mundy, "A World of Their Own," *The Washington Post*, March 31, 2002: W22.

for one's child will exceed the bounds of reasonable pluralism. Whether it in fact does so is controversial, and the controversy is exacerbated by dispute about the extent to which disadvantages from deafness are what might be termed natural disadvantages from the condition itself, as opposed to the result of unjustified discrimination and prejudice against deaf persons.[17]

Selection is eugenics

Is selection, whether positive or negative, wrong because it is eugenics? There is no doubt that many believe this, but we need to examine, even if only briefly, first, whether selection is eugenics, and, second, whether this makes it wrong. We cannot answer the second question without first fixing what eugenics is so that we can be clear whether selection is always eugenics, and if so what properties that means it has. Nevertheless, it is worth noting at the outset that primarily because of the Nazi use of eugenics, eugenics has come to have a near universal negative connotation. If a practice is considered to be eugenic, then it is simply accepted that it is wrong, and the charge that it is eugenics is often employed as a discussion stopper about its ethical character. In work done with others elsewhere, I have argued that the goal of eugenics of human betterment through selection is not obviously in itself or inherently immoral.[18] While eugenics does involve selection of who will reproduce and who will be born, as its goal suggests eugenics programmes were typically carried out with the intention of positively affecting the characteristics of a population. Both the negative and positive selection under discussion here, on the other hand, are carried out not from a population perspective but from the perspective of individual parents seeking to improve the life of the child that they will have; in this respect it is misleading to characterize them as eugenics.

Whether or not eugenics, we can at least consider how closely negative and positive selection resemble historical eugenics movements in other respects. There were other features of historical eugenics movements that are not inherent in selection itself that constituted the mistakes and in turn the evils of past eugenic movements and programmes. Among these features were a belief in the deterioration of the gene pool and a consequent encouragement of the "fit" and discouragement of the "unfit"

---

[17] K. W. Anstey, "Are Attempts to Have Impaired Children Justifiable?" *Journal of Medical Ethics* 28: 5 (2002): 286–8.

[18] Buchanan, Brock, Daniels, and Wikler, op. cit.

to reproduce. Who were typically considered fit and unfit was deeply influenced by racial, class, ethnic, and national stereotypes and prejudices. A second feature was an excessive belief in the heritability of behavioral traits, which supported the view, congenial to conservative political positions and groups, that the solution to social problems lay in biology rather than social reforms. A third feature was the failure to recognize and acknowledge the pluralism about what is a good person and a good society noted above; this led eugenicists to favor people like themselves and to be biased against others who were merely different, not worse. A fourth feature was the coercive role of the state in reproductive choices, which failed to recognize the important value of reproductive freedom. However, this is not to say that some bad features of eugenics cannot come about from uncoerced choices of individuals, what has been called "backdoor eugenics."[19] Finally, there was a failure of justice, a willingness to sacrifice the rights and interests of some individuals for a, often only putative, greater social good.

These are all mistakes and evils or injustices to be avoided, and they have perhaps permanently tainted any social practice or programme characterized as eugenic, but I believe none of these features is inherent in the practice of either negative or positive selection under consideration here. The charge of eugenics is too general and unclear to be helpful, much less dispositive, in evaluating the practice of selection. Instead, what is needed is an analysis of the specific features of a practice claimed to be eugenic and why those features make it wrong. At least the most prominent features that made historical eugenics movements wrong are not intrinsic to negative or positive selection of the sort of concern here.

Selection has excessive risks

The concern about the risks of selection applies much more forcefully to positive than to negative selection. If one assumes, as I do here, that the fetus at the time it is aborted in negative selection is not a person with a serious right not to be killed, then the principal risks of negative selection are to the mother from the genetic testing and abortion she undergoes, not to the fetus which will not live to become a person. At the typical time of abortion for negative selection, there is a consensus that the risks to a woman from abortion are not in general significantly greater than the risks

---

[19] Troy Duster, *Backdoor to Eugenics* (London: Routledge, 1990).

of childbirth, and even if they were a woman should have the right to assume them if she chooses. Positive selection where complex behavioral traits will be the typical target of genetic enhancement is more problematic. At present, we lack the ability to even identify the genes involved in likely target traits, much less to perform genetic manipulations of those genes and in turn traits. Some geneticists believe that the genetic complexity of such traits, together with the complex environmental variables that affect them, mean that we are never likely to be able to undertake positive selection or perform genetic manipulations to substantially enhance such traits, but this point is controversial among geneticists. Certainly, positive genetic enhancement should not take place until its safety for the embryo and subsequent person is well established. But just because selection is positive does not entail that its safety must necessarily always be inadequate, that is, that it could never be shown to meet appropriate safety standards. Moreover, the safety issue does not get to the heart of most concerns about positive selection. Therapeutic interventions, like non-therapeutic selection and enhancement, should also not be undertaken until their safely is adequately established.

Conclusion

Negative selection in the reproductive context to avoid creating or giving birth to persons who would be seriously disabled has come under widespread criticism, especially from members of the disability community. The limited current capacities, but even more the expanded future prospects, for positive selection of desired traits in our offspring have generated an even broader unease in the public at large. There are many possible sources of this criticism and unease. In this paper, I have examined one source—the idea that selection itself, whether negative or positive is morally problematic or wrong. To the extent that my conclusion can be summarized in one sentence: it is that selection of our children is not in itself morally problematic or wrong. If negative or positive selection should be rejected, it will have to be for other reasons, not simply because selection of our children is wrong.

12

Parental Choice and Human Improvement[1]

Peter Singer

Consider... the issue of genetic engineering. Many biologists tend to think the problem is one of *design*, of specifying the best types of persons so that biologists can proceed to produce them. Thus they worry over what sort(s) of person there is to be and who will control this process. They do not tend to think, perhaps because it diminishes the importance of their role, of a system in which they run a "genetic supermarket," meeting the individual specifications (within certain moral limits) of prospective parents.... This supermarket system has the great virtue that it involves no centralized decision fixing the future of human type(s).

> Robert Nozick, *Anarchy, State and Utopia* (New York: Basic
> Books) 1974, 315n.

Buying yourself a tall, brainy child

Advertisements in newspapers in some of America's most prestigious universities commonly offer substantial sums to egg donors who are tall, athletic, and have scored extremely well in scholastic aptitude tests. The fees offered range up to $50,000. Actual sums paid are said to be closer to $10,000, but that is still substantial, and indicates the willingness of some couples to pay for the chance—and by this method it is only a chance—of

[1] This is a substantially revised version of an essay that previously appeared in John Rasko, Gabrielle O'Sullivan, and Rachel Ankeny (eds), *The Ethics of Inheritable Genetic Modification* (Cambridge: Cambridge University Press), 2006.

having a child with above average scholastic aptitude, height, and athletic ability.[2]

Our rapidly increasing knowledge of human genetics already makes it possible for some couples to have children who are genetically superior to the children they would be likely to produce if they left it to the random process of normal reproduction. At present, this is done by prenatal, and sometimes pre-implantation, diagnosis of embryos and fetuses. These techniques are becoming increasingly sophisticated and will in future be able to detect more and more genetically-influenced traits. Later, it will most likely be possible to insert new genetic material safely into the *in vitro* embryo. Both of these techniques will enable couples to have a child whose abilities are likely to be superior to those offered by the natural lottery but who will be "theirs" in the sense of having their genes, not the genes of only one of them (as in cloning), or the genes of a third person (as when an egg is purchased).

Many people say that they accept selection against serious diseases and disabilities, but not for enhancement beyond what is normal. There is, however, no bright line between selection against disabilities and selection for positive characteristics. From selecting against Huntington's Disease it is no great step to selecting against genes that carry a significantly elevated risk of breast or colon cancer, and from there it is easy to move to giving one's child a better than average genetic health profile.

In any case, even if it is possible to distinguish between selection for disabilities and selection for enhancement, it would need further argument to show that this distinction is morally significant. If, as surveys in most developed countries show, at least 85 per cent of couples are willing to abort a fetus that has Down's syndrome, most of them will also be willing to abort one with genes that indicate other intellectual limitations, for example genes that correlate with IQ scores below 80. But why stop at 80? Why not select for at least average IQ? Or, since genetics is only one factor in the determination of IQ, select for genes that make an above average IQ likely, just in case the environmental factors don't work out so well? The existing market in human eggs suggests that some people will also select for height, which in turn correlates to some extent with income. Nor will

---

[2] Gina Kolata, "$50,000 Offered to Tall, Smart Egg Donor," *The New York Times*, March 3, 1999, A10; the suggestion that the amount paid is usually significantly less comes from Gregory Stock, personal communication.

we spurn the opportunity to ensure that our children are beautiful, to the extent that that is under genetic control.

How should we react to these likely developments? Do they point to a nightmarish future in which children are made to order, and wanted for their specifications, not loved for themselves, however they may turn out? Or should we welcome the prospect of healthier, more intelligent, happier, and perhaps even more ethical children? Do the likely benefits outweigh the costs?

First we need to ask what exactly the costs are going to be. This is itself highly controversial. Is it a problem if, as Michael Sandel has suggested may happen, genetic enhancement will "banish our appreciation of life as a gift, and to leave us with nothing to affirm or behold outside our own will."[3] I hope that human beings will continue to leave some natural ecosystems intact, so that we can always affirm and behold things that are outside our own will. Beyond that, I'm not sure that the idea of life as a "gift" makes much sense independently of belief in God. If there is no God, life can only be a gift from one's parents. And if that is the case, wouldn't we all prefer parents who try to make the gift as good as possible, rather than leaving everything to chance? Indeed, even Sandel does not think parents should leave everything to chance. He opposes "perfectionism", but not current practices of prenatal diagnosis that are aimed at eliminating serious genetic diseases and disabilities. The argument for taking life as a gift clearly has limits. If it is outweighed by the importance of avoiding children with serious diseases or disabilities, it may also be outweighed by the positive characteristics that genetic selection could bring.

Is this weighing of positive and negative aspects of genetic selection an issue for the legislature to resolve for all of us? Nozick's words cited at the head of this paper suggest a different approach: it is not up to government, he argued, to judge whether the outcome of this process will be better or worse. In a free society, all we can legitimately do is make sure that the process consists of freely chosen individual transactions. Let the genetic supermarket rule—and not only the market, but also altruistic individuals, or voluntary organizations, anyone who wishes, for whatever reason, to offer genetic services to anyone who wants them and is willing to accept them on the terms on which they are offered. Similarly, those

---

[3] See Michael Sandel, "The Case Against Perfection," *Atlantic Monthly*, April 2004, 51–62.

who wish to preserve the idea that their child's life, with all his or her inherited characteristics, is a gift, may do so, and hence avoid genetic selection or enhancement. Others for whom that idea makes little sense, or is unimportant, may choose to make use of the technologies available to give their child a better chance of having the characteristics that they favor.

That the United States should allow a market in eggs and sperm which goes some way towards fulfilling Nozick's prophecy is no accident. In other countries a practice that threatens to turn the child of a marriage into an item of commerce would meet powerful opposition from both conservative "family values" politics and from left of center groups horrified at the idea of leaving to the market something as socially momentous as the way in which future generations are conceived. In the United States, however, that leftist attitude is restricted to groups on the margins of political life, and the conservatives who dominate Congress show their support for family values merely by preventing the use of federal funds for ends that they dislike; in other respects, they allow their belief that the market always knows best to override their support for traditional family values.

There are strong arguments against state interference in reproductive decisions, at least when those decisions are made by competent adults. If we follow Mill's principle that the state is justified in interfering with its citizens only to prevent harm to others, we could see such decisions as private ones, harming no one, and therefore properly left to the private realm.[4] For who is harmed by the genetic supermarket? The parents are not harmed by having the healthier, handsomer and more intelligent children that they want. Are the children harmed? In an article on the practice of buying eggs from women with specific desired characteristics like height and intelligence, George Annas has commented:

What's troubling is this commodification, this treating kids like products. Ordering children to specification can't be good for the children. It may be good for adults in the short run, but it's not good for kids to be thought of that way.[5]

But to say that this is "not good" for these children forces us to ask the question: not good compared with *what*? The children for whom this is supposed not to be good could not have existed by any other means. If the

---

[4] J. S. Mill, *On Liberty*, first published 1859, available at www.utilitarianism.com/ol/one.html

[5] Lisa Gerson, "Human Harvest," *Boston Magazine*, May 1999, www.bostonmagazine.com/highlights/humanharvest.shtml

egg had not been purchased, to be fertilized with the husband's sperm, that child would not have been alive. Is life going to be so bad for this child that he or she will wish never to have been born? That hardly seems likely. So on one reading of what the standard of comparison should be, it is clearly false that the purchase of these eggs is not good for the kids.[6]

Suppose that we read "not good for kids" as meaning "not the best thing for the next child of this couple". Then whether the purchase of the egg is or is not good for the kid will depend on a comparison with other ways in which the couple could have had a child. Suppose, to make the comparison easier, they are not infertile—they bought an egg only in order to increase their chances of having a tall, athletic child who would get into a very good university. If they had not done so, they would have had a child in the normal way, who would have been their genetic child. Was it bad for their child to buy the egg? Their child may have a more difficult life because he or she was "made to order", and perhaps will disappoint his or her parents. But perhaps their own child would have disappointed them even more, by being less likely to be any of the things that they wanted their child to be. I don't see how we can know which of these outcomes is more likely. So I do not think we have grounds for concluding that a genetic supermarket would harm either those who choose to shop there, or those who are created from the materials they purchase.

If we switch from an individualist perspective to a broader social one, however, the negative aspects of a genetic supermarket become more serious. Even if we make the optimistic assumption that parents will select only genes that are of benefit to their children, there are at least three separate grounds for thinking that this may have adverse social consequences. The first is that a genetic supermarket would mean less diversity among human beings. Not all forms of diversity are good. Diversity in longevity is greater when there are more people with genes that doom them to an early death. The loss of this diversity is welcome. But what about the loss of the merely unusual, or eccentric? Antony Rao, a specialist in behavioral therapy in children, finds that many middle and upper class parents come to him when their children behave in unusual ways, wanting them to be medicated, because "they fear that any deviation from the norm may

---

[6] On the difficult issue of whether we can benefit a child by bringing it into existence, see Derek Parfit, *Reasons and Persons* (Oxford: Clarendon Press), 1984, 367, and Peter Singer, *Practical Ethics* (Cambridge: University Press), 2nd edn., 1993, 123–5.

cripple their child's future.''[7] If this is true of behavioral abnormalities that for many children are merely a passing phase, it is likely to be even more true of genetic abnormalities. It is easy to imagine genetic screening reports that indicate that the child's genes are unusual, although the significance of the abnormality is not well understood (usually medical shorthand for "We don't have a clue"). Would many parents decide to terminate the pregnancy in those circumstances, and if so, would there be a loss of diversity that would leave human society a less rich place?

I am more concerned about a second problem: many of the advantages people will seek to ensure for their children will be advantageous for them only in comparative, not absolute terms. Consider the difference between being tall, and living longer. Living longer than today's average lifespan today is something most of us would want, and the extent to which we want it is not, by and large, affected by whether everyone achieves this good, and so the average lifespan increases. For the purposes of this chapter, I'll call this kind of good an intrinsic good (ignoring the fact that most of us don't really think living longer is intrinsically good, since we would not want to live longer if we were in a coma for all of the additional years). Being taller than a specified height, however, is not something most of us would want for its own sake. True, being above average height correlates significantly with having above average income, and with being able to see over the heads of the crowd, but to gain these advantages we must be taller than the average in our society. To increase one's childrens' height, therefore, is beneficial only if it also moves them up relative to the height of others in their society. There would be no advantage in being 6'3" if the average height is 6'6". I will call this a positional good.

If everyone gains a positional good, no one is better off. They may all be worse off. In the case of height, arguably, it would be better if everyone were shorter, because we would require less food to sustain us, could live in smaller houses, drive smaller, less powerful cars, and reduce our impact on the environment. Thus being able to select for height—something couples are already doing, on a small scale, by offering more for the eggs of tall women—could start the human equivalent of the peacock's tail—an escalating "height race" in which the height that distinguishes "tall" people from those who are "normal" increases year by year, to no one's benefit,

---

[7] Jerome Groopman, "The Doubting Disease," *New Yorker*, April 10, 2000, 55.

at considerable environmental cost, and perhaps eventually even at some
health cost to the children themselves.[8] Genetic enhancement could lead
to a collective action problem, in which the rational pursuit of individual
self-interest makes us all worse off.

A third significant ground for objecting to a genetic supermarket is its
threat to the ideal of equality of opportunity. It is, of course, something of
a myth to believe that equality of opportunity prevails in the United States
or anywhere else, because everywhere wealthy parents already give their
children enormous advantages in the race for success. Nevertheless, a future
in which the rich have beautiful, brainy, healthy children, while the poor,
stuck with the old genetic lottery, fall further and further behind, is not a
pleasing prospect. Inequalities of wealth will be turned into genetic inequalities, and the clock will be turned back on centuries of struggle to overcome
the privileges of aristocracy. Instead the present generation of wealthy
people will have the opportunity to embed their advantages in the genes
of their offspring. These offspring will then have not only the abundant
advantages that the rich already give their children, but also whatever additional advantages the latest development in genetics can bestow on them.
They will most probably therefore continue to be wealthier, longer-lived
and more successful than the children of the poor, and will in turn pass these
advantages on to their children, who will take advantage of the ever more
sophisticated genetic techniques available to them. Will this lead to a *Gattaca*
society in which "Invalids" clean toilets while "Valids" run the show and
get all the interesting jobs?[9] Lee Silver has pictured a USA a millenium hence
in which the separation between "Gene-enriched" humans and "Naturals"
has solidified into separate species.[10] That is too far in the future to speculate
about, but Maxwell Mehlman and Jeffrey Botkin may well be right when
they predict that a free market in genetic enhancement will widen the
gap between the top and bottom strata of our society, undermine belief in
equality of opportunity, and close the "safety valve" of upward mobility.[11]

How might we respond to these three problems? I think the solution to
the first problem is easy. We would face a serious loss of genetic diversity

---

[8] Helena Cronin, *The Ant and the Peacock* (Cambridge: Cambridge University Press), 1991, ch. 5.
[9] *Gattaca*, written and directed by Andrew Niccol, 1997.
[10] Lee Silver, *Remaking Eden* (New York: Avon), 1998, 282.
[11] Maxwell Mehlman and Jeffrey Botkin, *Access to the Genome: The Challenge to Equality* (Washington,
DC: Georgetown University Press), 1998, ch. 6.

only if the genetic supermarket was very widely used for a long time in a way that tended to focus on a small number of genotypes. Before this had had any real impact, we could observe what is happening, and stop the social experiment. I therefore do not see this as a decisive objection to opening the genetic supermarket.

The other two problems, of the pursuit of positional goods, and of making genetic inequality more rigidly structured than it is now, are more serious. What choices do we have? We might try to ban all uses of genetic selection and genetic engineering that go beyond the elimination of what are clearly defects. There are some obvious difficulties with this course of action:

1. Who will decide what is clearly a defect? Presumably, a government panel will be assigned the task of keeping abreast with relevant genetic techniques, and deciding which are lawful and which are not. This allows the government a role in reproductive decisions, which some may see as even more dangerous than the alternative of leaving them to the market.

2. There are serious questions about whether a ban on genetic selection and engineering for enhancement purposes could be made to work across the United States, given that matters regulating conception and birth are in the hands of the states, rather than the federal government. In the case of infertile couples seeking to pay a woman to bear a child for them, attempts by various U.S. states to make the practice illegal, or to declare surrogacy contracts void, have had little effect because a few states are more friendly to surrogacy. Couples seeking a surrogate to bear a child for them are prepared to travel to achieve what they want. As Lee Silver remarks: "What the brief history of surrogacy tells us is that Americans will not be hindered by ethical uncertainty, state-specific injunctions, or high costs in their drive to gain access to any technology that they feel will help them achieve their reproductive goals."[12]

3. Assume that one nation, for example the United States, decides that genetic selection is not a good thing, and Congress bans genetic selection and engineering when used for enhancement. Suppose also that this ban can be enforced effectively within the nation's boundaries. We would

---

[12] *Remaking Eden*, 177.

still have to deal with the fact that we now live in a global economy. An effective global ban seems very unlikely. A small nation might be tempted to allow enhancement genetics, thus setting up a niche industry serving wealthy couples from those nations that have banned enhancement. Moreover, in view of the competitive nature of the global economy, it may pay industrialized nations to encourage enhancement genetics, thus giving them an edge on those that do not. Singapore's former Prime Minister, Lee Kuan Yew, used to speak about the heritability of intelligence, and its importance for Singapore's future. His government introduced measures explicitly designed to encourage university graduates to have more children.[13] Had genetic enhancement been available to Lee Kuan Yew at the time, he might well have preferred it to the government-sponsored computer dating services and financial incentives on which he was then forced to rely. It might appeal to Singapore's present Prime Minister, who is, not coincidentally, Lee Kuan Yew's son.

If a ban in one country turns out to be unattainable, ineffective, or contrary to the vital interests of that country in a competitive global economy, and a global ban is not feasible, a bolder strategy could be tried. Assuming that the objective is to avoid a society divided in two along genetic lines, genetic enhancement services could be subsidized, so that everyone can afford them. But could society afford to provide everyone with the services that otherwise only the rich could afford? Mehlman and Botkin propose an ingenious solution: the state should run a lottery in which the prize is the same package of genetic services that the rich commonly buy for themselves. Tickets in the lottery would not be sold; instead every adult citizen would be given one. The number of prizes would relate to how many of these packages society could afford to pay for, and thus would vary with the costs of the genetic services, as well as with the resources available to provide them. To avoid placing a financial burden on the state, Mehlman and Botkin suggest, the use of genetic technologies could be taxed, with the revenue going to fund the lottery.[14] Clearly universal coverage would be preferable, but the use of a lottery

---

[13] Chan Chee Khoon and Chee Heng Leng, "Singapore 1984: Breeding for Big Brother," in Chan Chee Khoon and Chee Heng Leng, *Designer Genes: I.Q., Ideology and Biology*, Institute for Social Analysis (Insan), Selangor, Malaysia, 1984, 4–13.

[14] Mehlman and Botkin, op. cit., 126–8.

would at least ensure that everyone has some hope that their children will join ranks of the elite, and taxing those who are, by their use of genetic enhancement for their own children, changing the meaning of human reproduction seems a fair way to provide funds for it.

If we are serious about equality of opportunity then, instead of providing genetic enhancement for everyone, we could use our new techniques to provide genetic enhancement for those at the bottom, and restrict enhancement for those at the top.[15] That's a possible strategy, for those who consider equality of opportunity so important a value that it should override the benefits achieved by providing enhancement for those at the top. If, however, equality of opportunity is embraced for consequentialist reasons, rather than its intrinsic value, that is a dubious judgment. Unless we take a gloomy view of human nature, there seems a fair chance that enhancement for all, including those at the top, will eventually improve the situation of everyone, including the worst-off.

There is still a further problem that state provision of genetic enhancement to all citizens does not solve. If the rich nations were to act on this, it would still leave those living in poor countries without enhancement. So the divide that we feared would open up within a society would instead open up between societies. Unless we argue for an obligation for the rich nations to provide genetic enhancement for people living in countries unable to provide similar services, it is difficult to see any way of overcoming this problem.[16]

There is therefore a strong argument that the state should be directly involved in promoting genetic enhancement. But this takes us back to the question of which enhancement services the state should fund, and so we come back to the issue of positional goods. One proposal would be that the state should fund genetic enhancement that provides intrinsic goods, but not genetic enhancement that provides positional goods. For what would be the point of funding everyone to improve their positional goods? It would be as if the authorities dealt with drugs in sport by handing out equal doses of performance enhancing drugs to all athletes. If the drugs pose even small risks to athletes, no one could sensibly favor such a proposal. But now we need a government committee to decide which forms of genetic

---

[15] Dan Brock made this point in discussion, although without endorsing the view that we should give this much weight to equality of opportunity.

[16] I owe this point to Art Caplan.

enhancement confer intrinsic goods, and which confer positional goods. Suppose, for example, that we can find genes that correlate with doing well on IQ tests and scholastic aptitude tests used as part of the admission process by elite universities. Doing well on university admission tests is obviously a positional good. If everyone does better, the scores needed to get in will rise. If the tests are well designed, however, a good score presumably indicates an ability to learn, or to solve problems, or to write clearly and well. That sounds more like an intrinsic good, and an important one.

Bizarre as it may seem, there are some who might deny that the ability to learn or solve problems is an intrinsic good. Suppose that it is shown that scores on scholastic aptitude tests correlate inversely with the belief that God has an important role to play in one's life—not a far-fetched hypothesis, since we know that educational level does correlate inversely with this belief.[17] Those who think that belief in God is necessary for personal salvation, and that nothing can be more important than salvation, might then deny that scholastic aptitude is good at all.

Recent research on voles—small mouse-like rodents—has suggested that a characteristic more likely to appeal to Christians may be influenced by genetic modification. There are different kinds of voles, and they show different forms of mating behavior. Prairie voles tend to be monogamous, whereas meadow voles are more promiscuous. Researchers noticed that variations in a single gene—the arginine vasopressin receptor gene, which determines the way the brain responds to the hormone vasopressin—correlate with this difference in mating behavior. By manipulating the gene, the behavior of the normally promiscuous meadow voles was altered, so that they became as monogamous as prairie voles. If something similar can be shown for human behavior, would parents who place a high value on sexual fidelity wish to select or modify their children so that they would be more likely to be faithful to their sexual partners? Instead of exchanging promises and rings will people want their potential partners to make a different kind of commitment. Will they ever say: "If you really loved me, you'd get your vasopressin receptors enhanced, so you wouldn't be tempted to stray!" Or is there, as Immanuel Kant might have held, greater moral worth in being faithful *despite* have a genetic tendency to

[17] Gallup International Millennium Survey, 1999. Available at http://www.gallup-international.com/ContentFiles/millennium15.asp

stray?[18] Does making it easier for humans to be faithful somehow reduce the value of faithfulness? Is the only moral virtue worth having that which is achieved through an act of will, rather than with the assistance of genetic modification? But what if having strength of will is itself something that is subject to genetic influence?

Conclusion

As these examples show, judgments about what goods we ought to promote will raise fundamental value questions that will not be easy to resolve.

In addition to distinguishing intrinsic and positional goods, each nation will have to consider whether to promote forms of genetic enhancement that have social benefits. Just as societies now spend money on education, especially in science and technology, in the hope of gaining an economic edge by having better-educated people than other nations, so too some nations will seize on genetic enhancement as a way of achieving the same goal. We may therefore have no choice but to allow it, and indeed encourage it, if we want our economy to remain strong.

In the case of promoting scholastic aptitude, the interests of the nation, of the person who is selected for the enhanced characteristics, and of the parents, may all coincide. But that will not always be the case. Some advocates of genetic enhancement hold out the prospect of improving human nature by selecting for children who are less aggressive, or more altruistic. In this way, they suggest, we can hope one day to live in peace, free of war and violence. The regulated and subsidized form of parental choice that I am suggesting might not lead to that happy outcome. There is a collective action problem here, the reverse of that we found with positional goods. We would all be better off if we each selected children who will be less aggressive and more altruistic, but unless the culture changes significantly, our own children may be better off—at least by conventional measures of what counts as "better off"—if we do not select them in this way. The only way we could get the desired outcome would be to use coercion. Moreover if the desired end is world peace, and not merely a better, more compassionate society in

---

[18] Immanuel Kant, *Groundwork of the Metaphysics of Morals*, trans. Mary Gregor (Cambridge: University Press), 1997.

our own country, this coercion would have to be carried out globally, perhaps by each government agreeing to enforce it on its own citizens. Politically, for the foreseeable future, this is fantasy. Genetic enhancement may have benefits, but it doesn't look as if world peace will be one of them.

13

Reasons Against the Selection of Life: From Japan's Experience of Prenatal Genetic Diagnosis

Susumu Shimazono

In this chapter, I describe the Japanese resistance to genetic selection in the form of prenatal diagnosis and selective abortion. I explain the reasons for this and the implications for the debate about enhancement and whether human nature should be improved. I contrast the Japanese resistance to enhancement and genetic selection with Western arguments against these practices. Japan provides a new perspective, I will argue, on why we should resist genetic selection and enhancement. Japanese resistance is based not on the sanctity of human life or feminist concerns, but rather on skepticism about scientific intervention in nature and the human body, on values which place primacy on interpersonal relationships and bonds rather than autonomy and dominance, and the inclusion of all people regardless of disability.

1. Prenatal genetic diagnosis and enhancement

This chapter will consider the use of prenatal genetic diagnosis in a broad sense for the selection of embryos as a form of genetic enhancement. This means dealing with the ethics of embryonic and prenatal genetic diagnosis for the purpose of determining whether to give birth to a fetus or not, as well as the problems raised by new eugenic concepts and selective abortion. The process of detecting an undesirable fetus and excluding it is sometimes called "screening." There are three reasons to consider the ethics of screening in the context of how human nature can be improved.

Firstly, prenatal genetic diagnosis is a field of enhancement where the biotechnology is already in use and where there has already been some debate. This allows us, with reference to published theses and books, to examine the ethical issues without falling into an abstract speculative discussion.

In fact, whilst pre-implantation genetic diagnosis is a relatively new technique, the prenatal diagnosis of fetuses (in a narrow sense) has been practiced since the 1960s, and has become quite widespread in developed countries. The bioethical question of screening is closely related to broader ethical questions about the eugenic policies taken by many countries in the twentieth century and to questions about the distribution of medical care. Medical treatments have been used since the 1920s to prevent the birth of children with particular characteristics, with or without the consent of the parents, in accordance with eugenic ideas. Although there is a great difference between the selection of embryos based on contemporary prenatal diagnosis and that based on past eugenic theories, there is a continuum from the past to the present. Marriage restrictions and forced sterilization based on eugenic considerations can be seen as spearheading a form of genetic enhancement.

A second reason to look more closely at the ethics of pre-implantion genetic diagnosis is the close relationship between prenatal diagnosis and induced abortion. Induced abortion and euthanasia do not directly satisfy the basic objectives of treatment of illness, but the ethics of these have long been discussed as matters in which medical personnel are necessarily involved. The term "enhancement" may not apply to induced abortion, but the term "beyond therapy" does. The question "How can human nature be ethically improved?" is a question about "enhancement" as well as one about eugenic concepts and selective abortion. By examining the problem of prenatal genetic diagnosis we can shed new light on the debate on induced abortion, one of the most contentious issues in bioethics today.

Finally, Japan has a special position on screening. In Japan today, the pre-implantation genetic diagnosis of test-tube fertilized eggs is not publicly permitted. In 2004, there was widespread public criticism when it was reported that the technique had been used to select the sex of an embryo. The Japanese Society of Obstetrics and Gynecology has a policy that does not allow pre-implantation genetic diagnosis for this purpose, and the doctor who conducted the procedure was dismissed from the Society.

However, in the same year, the Society allowed the pre-implantation genetic diagnosis of the fertilized egg from a parent who had the gene for severe Duchenne-type muscular dystrophy. This was the first case of the use of this diagnostic procedure in Japan to avoid the birth of a child with a disability. However, at around the same time, an application for such a diagnosis submitted by a parent with a less severe type of muscular dystrophy was turned down.

Prenatal genetic diagnosis past ten weeks of pregnancy began in 1968, but has not become widespread. Mass screening of mothers' blood serum markers is not performed in Japan. This is related to the abolition of a law allowing the prevention of birth on eugenic grounds in 1996 when the Eugenic Protection Law (enacted in 1947) was revised to become the Mothers' Body Protection Law. In other words, the right to receive an induced abortion for the purposes of enhancement was rescinded in Japan in the 1990s.

Following the revision of this law, and upon the advice of a special commission on prenatal diagnosis, the Ministry of Health and Welfare issued a notification in 1999 regarding its "view on the test of blood serum markers of mothers' bodies." The Ministry said in this document, "Doctors need not to actively inform pregnant women about this test. Doctors should not encourage them to take this test, and it is not desirable that corporations prepare and distribute documents in which they encourage women to receive this test." In short, the Ministry did not consider that mass screening was desirable.

Partly as a result of this decision, prenatal genetic diagnosis has not progressed in Japan. Dr. Takamichi Sato, an obstetrician specializing in diagnosing fetuses with Down's syndrome, stated in 1996 that, while nearly 50 percent of fetuses with Down's syndrome were selectively aborted in France and Britain, it was estimated that fewer than 10 percent of affected Japanese fetuses were aborted. In 1999, the number of mothers who took blood serum marker tests in the United States stood at 167 times greater than the number in Japan, and the number in Britain, France and Germany was 10 times that of Japan (Sato 1999, 53). In 2004, Sato estimated that this situation had not changed much. The rate of selective induced abortions in Japan has remained at 1999 levels with no sign of an increase.

The infrequency of the practice of selective induced abortion seems to be closely related to the lack of positive encouragement for pre-implantation genetic diagnosis in Japan. The often cited justification of pre-implantation genetic diagnosis is that mothers will suffer physical as well as psychological burdens if they undergo selective induced abortion based on prenatal genetic diagnosis, but that these burdens can be avoided by pre-implantation diagnosis of embryos. However, this argument loses its power to convince in Japan, at least in principle, as the number of mothers receiving prenatal genetic diagnosis itself is not large, and not many selective induced abortions are practiced.

From the above it is clear that the consensus on screening in Japan is very different from that in France, the United States, and the United Kingdom. Why is this? By considering the reasons for the difference, clues about the ethics of medical care that seeks to go "beyond therapy," and the rights and wrongs of "enhancement" may be found. As a scholar of comparative religion I have a strong interest in differences among the various religious cultures of the world. I have found it useful to consider bioethics not merely on an abstract theoretical level, but also through examining the sources of various bioethical concepts in relation to the religious cultures of different nations. From my academic background the differences between Japan and Western countries on prenatal genetic diagnosis are significant.

2. Criticism of prenatal genetic diagnosis

In the 1990s, prenatal genetic diagnosis was a common topic of public debate in Japan. Many supported the right for women to choose to terminate a pregnancy, but were against screening for reasons of prudence and parental self-interest. This view was supported by a wide range of people. In the following sections, I will introduce some of the major publications supporting this view (see References).

The practical intention of this body of scholarship is to argue against the move to expand prenatal genetic diagnosis, and particularly against the introduction of mass screening, especially in the light of the revision of the Eugenic Protection Law into the Mothers' Body Protection Law. The landmark text in this movement is Takamichi Sato's *Shusseizen Shindan—Inochi no Hinshitsu Kanri e no Keisho (Prenatal Genetic Diagnosis—Warning to (about) the Quality Control of Life)*, which has the keenest argument. Sato's book explores the ethics of fetal genetic diagnosis and though he is by profession an obstetrician and gynecologist, he develops philosophical ideas on self-determination in bioethics. The book provides a summary of recent Japanese arguments against fetal genetic diagnosis, and at the same time, puts forward his own influential ideas. His position on prenatal diagnosis is summarized in the following paragraph:

The author does not oppose either prenatal genetic diagnosis or selective induced abortion that individual women (couples) receive upon contemplation. The decisions on these matters belong to their reproductive self-determination. Prenatal genetic diagnosis by individuals has nothing to do with eugenics. This is because eugenics is a social "movement." Even if prenatal genetic diagnosis and selective abortion are chosen by individuals, if a third party entity such as society or a corporation has propagated or promoted it, or latently enforces it, the case will be eugenic. This is true for cases where the majority makes the same choice. (p. 48)

By using such terms as "movement" and "propagate or promote," he suggests his negative attitude towards the mass screening of serum markers of mothers' bodies, which is comparatively less expensive but not as accurate. In Britain, France, and the United States, serum marker mass screening has become widespread. This is, as Sato says, a new type of eugenic practice as well as a way to exclude the disabled.

Mass screening is intended to deprive the life of fetuses that are presumed to have a high risk of having disorders, and as a consequence, aims to exclude the disabled from society. Sato believes such a "movement" constitutes "eugenic selection."

The decision to continue with a pregnancy or to receive an induced abortion rests with women and couples. It should be a woman's choice to abort an unwanted fetus as a final resort after considering all options. However, if society, a corporation, or a doctor were to compel a pregnant woman to undergo screening to diagnose future potential disease, this would seek to intentionally manipulate couples' or women's self-determination and could as a result turn a wanted pregnancy into an unwanted pregnancy. An eugenic desire to exclude the disabled would have intervened. It is for this reason, according to Sato, that government and doctors should not cooperate in the promotion of mass screening.

The differences between those who support the promotion of prenatal genetic diagnosis and those who are against it, such as Sato, can be summarized in two points: 1) the interpretation of "self-determination" and "right to self-determination," and 2) the consideration of the life of the disabled. Two deeper questions underlie these. They are 3) the value of human life, and 4) the philosophy on which to base bioethics.

3. Concept and limits of self-determination

Reasons for being prudent about prenatal genetic diagnosis

Sato develops a well-prepared theory of "self-determination," in relation to induced abortion, and in particular selective abortion. He defines the concept of self-determination as the act of making decisions on matters relating to oneself. To realize self-determination, certain conditions must obtain, which are quite difficult to achieve. Furthermore, even with these conditions in place, there are problems with selective abortion that cannot be solved by self-determination. Self-determination has its limits, and hardly serves as the major criterion in Japanese bioethics.

Sato focuses first on prenatal diagnosis. It is not easy for mothers to obtain accurate information on this problem. It is difficult to provide suitable conditions for a mother to make an informed choice about whether to continue with a pregnancy. Although the information from an examination can be provided and mothers advised that they exercise the "right to knowledge", it is difficult to provide precise information on the purpose and the type of examination. Chromosomal disorders and genetic disorders vary in the symptoms they produce, and in the degree of gravity of the resulting conditions. In Japan, the main justification given for prenatal genetic diagnosis is to detect Down's syndrome (spina bifida is relatively rare in Japan). However, although a diagnosis can be given, mothers are not informed of the reality of the life of a child with Down's syndrome.

A pregnant woman can undergo tests if she is worried about her fetus, but often, this worry is something created by others. The act of going through an examination may in itself prove to be an obstacle to developing a good mother-and-child relationship, as when receiving an examination, women supposedly become prepared to cut the mother-and-child relation (by having to abort the fetus). At this stage, preparedness for a possible induced abortion emerges, and with this preparedness, the process of self-determination is manipulated. The medical, academic, and business communities who consider prenatal examination to be good, and the society that accepts eugenic concepts serve only to increase the concerns a mother might have for her fetus. Doctors in particular can fear legal action if a baby is born with a disorder. Encouraging women to take an examination by suggesting the chance of the fetus having a disorder intentionally can paradoxically prevent mothers from rationally pursuing self-determination.

There is a further ethical problem beyond the range of parental self-determination, or the limit of the right to self-determination, and applies to induced abortion in general: the right of the fetus to survival. As such, the parent's self-determination is limited. Sato asks if pregnant women have an unconditional right to accurate information on their fetuses (p. 76). In Japan and Germany, it is illegal to inform the parents of the sex of a fetus until a certain stage of pregnancy. The right to knowledge is conditional, which means that the parents' right to self-determination is limited.

Sato is in favor of entrusting mothers with the decision to abort their fetuses up to a certain stage of pregnancy. This is to allow women to terminate unwanted pregnancies under certain conditions. Despite this, he does not consider "induced abortion and selective abortion to be ethical" (p. 46). Support for self-determination has been useful in the past to protect people's rights. But the concept of self-determination can be used as a justification for immoral behavior. For example, it may be used as an excuse to impose a responsibility on the person who has allegedly made a decision. Self-determination cannot be used as the absolute criterion, and the concept of self-determination should be seen in the context of the goal to which it is linked.

Prenatal genetic diagnosis and selective induced abortion must be practiced according to the "self-determination" of the concerned parties as "part of efforts to realize a society in which diversity is recognized and every person can pursue their wellbeing to the maximum level." On the premise that prenatal diagnosis and selective induced abortion should be tolerated as emergency means, doesn't reproductive self-determination mean that women have children with a sense of security? (p. 114)

Prenatal genetic diagnosis practiced in an environment where mass screening and selective abortion are taken for granted may appear to be based on women's self-determination, but the conditions for self-determination in its true sense are not satisfied. Moreover, it ignores problems that are beyond the scope of the concept of self-determination.

4. New eugenics

Reasons for being prudent about prenatal genetic diagnosis

The problem beyond the parent's self-determination concerns the right of a fetus to life. This is linked to Sato's emphasis on parental attitudes towards child rearing. What, then, is the ground for denying the right to life of a fetus? Induced abortion cannot be ethically justified, and cannot be generalized as a "self-determination" right. Termination is only permissible for a woman to choose when no other choice is feasible to protect her right to survival. Is it justified to stipulate in law that a fetus can be aborted on the ground that it has a chance of having a disorder? No. If this were allowed, it would mean that the value of the life of disabled people is inferior to a non-disabled child, thus enshrining a discriminatory judgment in law as a universal fact.

In fact, many disabled people lead happy lives. Few of them deplore their own birth. Why is it considered natural to prevent disabled people from being born? It is because society has created the idea that disabled people should be excluded. This idea is based on a eugenic thought. Eugenics is designed "to avoid bad hereditary elements, and to improve the quality of descendants by maintaining good hereditary elements" (*Kokugo Jiten, Japanese dictionary*, Sanseido, Ver. 4, 1992). Eugenic selection is based on the concept that "it is appropriate to exclude the weak artificially" from the standpoint of social loss and gain calculation.

Eugenic thoughts and practices began at the end of the nineteenth century and were most frequently applied from the 1920s to the mid-twentieth century by restricting marriages and applying sterilization mainly to mentally disabled people. The new eugenic practices represented by fetal diagnosis that spread so widely towards the end of the twentieth century are called the "new eugenics" or "second eugenics." The latter eugenic practice does not seem to violate human rights directly as it does not deprive any living persons of their reproductive rights. Even so, both forms of eugenics are the same in nature in that their intention is to exclude the disabled from society. Fetuses aborted through fetal genetic diagnosis are deprived of their lives. There is a risk that children born without prenatal genetic diagnosis, or without being aborted after prenatal genetic diagnosis, may be treated as "children who are not supposed to be born" by their parents. Children who are born with disabilities, as a minority group, will have a weaker say in society, and as such will be disadvantaged.

The exclusion of the disabled according to this second eugenics is said by some to be a result of parental self-determination. In fact, there is an aspect of societal manipulation. The use of blood serum marker tests, for example, is intended to lead pregnant women to choose selective induced abortion. The use of tests can be used to manipulate a woman's self-determination as follows:

(1) Cause a woman to entertain the sense of uneasiness that she may deliver a disabled child.
(2) Tell a woman that prenatal genetic diagnosis is a standard medical care.
(3) Tell a woman that prenatal genetic diagnosis and selective induced abortion are "wise choices" to make.
(4) Tell a woman that prenatal genetic diagnosis and selective induced abortion are not immoral.
(5) Lead parents of a child with Down's syndrome to sue the obstetrician in charge, of a failure of not having applied prenatal genetic diagnosis. Encourages obstetricians to give information on prenatal genetic diagnosis in a positive light.

However, little explanation is given as to what will be examined to detect any disorder, and what will be the nature of the disorder. Often, the doctors themselves do not have sufficient knowledge. In particular, obstetricians have limited knowledge about how children with Down's syndrome will grow. A survey among the members of the parents' association of children with Down's syndrome in the Kyoto area revealed that obstetricians and gynecologists have a stronger negative image of Down's syndrome than pediatricians do. Obstetricians often observe parents in deep depression upon learning that their babies were born with Down's syndrome, but rarely see that these babies grow well and live happily. Obstetricians see the disappointed parents right after delivery but do not see the growing process of the child. They may make an arbitrary judgment about the wellbeing of a child with a disability without knowing about the actual life of such a child, and so may give (unnecessary) uneasiness to parents.

A greater problem is the theory of the social cost spent on the disabled. Those who support blood serum marker screening suggest that the cost of detecting disabled fetuses is much less than the future cost of caring for disabled persons. This cost-effect calculation is not always correct. It is only in 10 percent of the entire disabled population that disabilities appear by age three. Further, about 1 percent of neonates are born having severe mental retardation, but it is only around 0.13 percent of live births that are born with Down's syndrome. The expenses for the disabled are nominal in the entire national budget and medical expenses (p. 108). Therefore, the social cost theory can be regarded as giving a false impression that the congenitally disabled are causing extra burden on society and could wrongly increase parents' concern over having children with disabilities.

The exponents of new eugenic practices attempt to manipulate information, and to create, under the disguise of parents' self-determination, an environment in which it is difficult for individual parents to choose to give birth to a child with a disability. Doctors, biotechnologists, and corporations all attempt to profit: doctors and biotechnologists by boasting their genetic knowledge, and corporations through doing business in mass screening. Politicians who seek to build national profit by supporting interested scholars and corporations could also benefit. However new eugenic practices will bring far greater losses to society as a whole by expanding discrimination against disabled people.

5. Ethics of living with others

Reasons for being cautious about fetal genetic diagnosis

In the new eugenic practices, parents go through a process of determining whether or not to terminate a disabled fetus. So, how do they make this decision? It is necessary to understand how they justify their act of exclusion by looking deeply into parents' thinking. It is also important to consider attitudes to living without excluding the disabled, and to retain a respect for human dignity. Sato steps into this problem to discuss bioethics itself in general.

Parents who have learned that their child has a disorder often react by saying things like: "I feel pity for my child," "it will be difficult for my child to live," "my child will be unhappy to live," "it will be worthless for my child to live" and the like. In short, they find no value for the child to live. But is it really so?

What is "the purpose of living"? What is happiness and unhappiness for a person? These are difficult questions and I can hardly give answers. One thing I can say is that we should not interfere with another's purpose for living. [. . .] You are free to see others' way of living and to question whether they are happy or unhappy, but it is a sort of violence to tell others to live in a certain way. Isn't it the greatest form of violence to deprive a life through selective induced abortion? Is there any parent who desires to be told by others, "it is unhappy to have a disability," or "the baby will have an unhappy life if it is born"? It is a matter that the individuals concerned should decide. [. . .] Children with Down's syndrome, a type of mental disability, are in general cheerful, gentle and thoughtful towards their family. They live happy lives just as ordinary children do. Children don't consider the purpose of life in their daily life. They are interested in daily happenings. Whether they are disabled or not, children spend their days in the same way. Every living person has a purpose for living, unconscious though it may be, and the minimum condition for purposeful living is that one is living. (pp. 175–6)

As individuals, we each have our own purposes in life, and there is no unified criterion to evaluate the quality of another's life. Sato argues that it is through the perception of differences among people that one learns to accept others as they are and respect their individual purposes in life. Sato repeatedly emphasizes the importance of considering prenatal genetic diagnosis from the viewpoint of how parents will relate to their fetuses. Whilst admitting the paucity of research about the psychological reactions of parents after the prenatal diagnosis of a fetal disorder and what support should be provided, he quotes research on parents' reactions at the time of having learned that their child was born with a congenital disorder (pp. 85–6).

He introduces a model of the process "shock → denial → depression and anger → adaptation → recovery" through which parents come to make up their mind that they will live with the disabled child. The term "acceptance" is understood as the act of parents facing up to the unwanted reality, admitting the child with disability as a whole and developing a positive attitude to enable them to enjoy raising the child with love. This acceptance is understood as one important element in the consideration of bioethics involved in prenatal genetic diagnosis.

Whilst Sato is against prenatal genetic diagnosis where the subsequent termination of the foetus may be considered, he foresees that the practice will continue. The underlying psychology of the eugenic concept, is the desire for a "healthy child." Sato accepts that this is a common and natural desire, but it becomes problematic when this desire is transformed into the norm "a child must be born healthy."

When informed of the probability of their fetus having a disorder, the parents' desire for a healthy child is directed in one of two ways. One is "the child must be healthy," and the other is "we want the child even if it is not healthy" (or more accurately, "whatever condition the child may be in, it is our child"). Those who have the former idea will choose induced abortion. (pp. 188–9)

The former is the consciousness of exclusion and the latter is consciousness of acceptance of life with the disabled child. It is obvious that the latter contains the potential to develop into rich parent-and-child relationships, and living with others with mutual respect. The former, on the other hand, may nip this potentiality in the bud. As a result, parents' respect for themselves may weaken as well as their ability to socialize and live with others.

I mentioned that parents' desire to have a "healthy child" is natural. But what about the idea "I don't want the baby if it is not healthy"? This idea may suggest that "the surrounding society does not allow any parent to have a child who has a disorder or disability." The surrounding society could include relatives, corporations, or neighboring communities. The environment the parents grew up in may affect their decision. However, in most cases, the surrounding society does not consider a couple's interests first, and it is needless to say that it never considers a fetus's interests. True "self-determination" would consist of considering one's own and a child's happiness even in the context of a surrounding society that seeks to exclude those with disabilities. (p. 189)

The process of the development of parents' nurturing love and responsibility towards their children is linked to the attitudes needed to live in society where various people live together. In other words, maturity in ethical consciousness is required of parents in contemporary pluralistic society to live in harmony with others, respecting mutual differences, on the premises of diversity and heterogeneity. Sato considers this is viable bioethics in the "society of living together."

If we are truly going to respect "self-determination," it should start with wiping out the consciousness that "I don't want the baby unless it is born healthy."

   Although it is said that the future society is that of diversity, genetic supremacy is going to prevail. The society of diversity means a society of various people living together. Regardless of being disabled or not, and as a matter of course, regardless of the colors of skin and family status, or genes, every individual should be able to enjoy living to the full. (pp. 189–90)

This provides a summary of Takamichi Sato's views on prenatal genetic diagnosis and bioethics. According to Sato, induced abortion cannot be justified ethically, but must be permitted as a means to solve individual cases. Although induced abortion is legal and the decision to have an abortion should be entrusted to the woman concerned, Sato does not believe selective induced abortion is justified by a woman's right to self-determination. He rejects selective induced abortion because it is a means to exclude the disabled. He bases his arguments, not only on the fetus's right to life, but also on the grounds of forging parent-and-child relations and on the ethical viewpoint of the benefits of the coexistence of diverse people.

In his book, Sato's unique views are revealed in many ways. But although permitting induced abortion where a mother's life is in danger, he is part of the consensus in favor of rejecting genetic factors of a fetus as a justifiable reason for induced abortion. Sato's view is representative of the majority of the Japanese people who are predominantly critical of screening and other new eugenic practices.

6. Eugenics and induced abortion in Japan

Japan and Germany stand out among developed countries with advanced technologies in their prudent stance to prenatal genetic diagnosis in a wider sense, and new (second) eugenic practices. By contrast, policies in Britain, France, the United States and many other Western countries have promoted prenatal genetic diagnosis. What factors have caused such a difference?

In Germany, the memory of the massacres during World War II based on eugenic thought and involving medical scholars has strongly influenced policy on prenatal genetic diagnoses. In Japanese history, medical scholars from Unit 731 of Kwantung Army camped in Northeast China killed many Chinese and Russians in an organized manner in preparation for biological warfare. In this instance however, although racial discrimination was at work (Tsuneishi 1981), eugenic thought was not such a strong factor.

The reason for strong opposition to selective induced abortion in Japan society should first be found in its history of induced abortion and birth control. Even before modern times the Japanese widely accepted induced abortion (Chiba, 1983, Namihira 1996). Toward the end of the nineteenth century, when the birth control movement was imported in response to the rise of the concepts of New Malthusianism and feminism in the country, the need to control population increase was the major justification (Fujime 1999). The government of Japan was greatly shocked when the US Congress enacted a law to control immigration from Japan in 1924. It shows how great the concern over population increase was.

Eugenic thought was also widely accepted. A social evolutionary concept of strengthening the nation by excluding people with poor abilities that was imported from the West exerted a certain level of influence on the nation (Fujino 1998). The Eugenic Law was enacted in 1940 based enitrely on eugenic interest. The Eugenic Protection Law in 1947 put its main emphasis on the acceptance of induced abortion, but the eugenic interest remained and after World War II enforced sterilization of people who suffered from Hansen's disease and mental diseases was begun. It was not until the 1970s that the government and other parties concerned reflected on the practice (Morioka 2001).

Although eugenic thought did exert some influence in Japanese society, more serious were concerns over population increase, and it was these concerns which led to the legalization of induced abortion. Acceptance of induced abortion was already prevalent in the 1910s and 1920s. In the mind of the nation in those days, the birth control movement to check population growth was understood to a certain level, but supporters of eugenic thought hardly increased. After World War II, the nation shared the sense of self-reflection toward the colonial expansionist policy that the government had taken as a means of solving difficulties caused by the narrow land area of Japan. The need for population control became widely understood among people. Therefore, the population problem was better accepted as the justification for induced abortion than eugenic thought.

Induced abortion was strictly prohibited after the Meiji Restoration, and in 1880 a provision for feticide was included in the Criminal Law. The prohibition of induced abortion at that time was motivated by population policies as well as modernization policies, and was not based on religious considerations. Therefore, as population problems changed, people's views on the prohibition of induced abortion tended to change (Fujino 1998). Because of this background, induced abortion was legally permitted in Japan earlier than other Western countries. When feminism rose in the 1970s, and women demanded their right to choose whether to have children, their goal of gaining acceptance for induced abortion had been achieved.

After the 1970s, a movement to restrict abortion arose, and women had to insist on their reproductive rights. Along with women's movements, disabled rights movements came to the fore arguing that legalized abortion was based on eugenic thought. Some feminist activists sympathized with the movement for disabled rights and protested against "freedom of choice." A movement to review the Eugenic Protection Law was developed by the disabled rights movement and some feminists (Tamai 1999b).

The process above was reflected in the influential criticism of prenatal genetic diagnosis which developed after the 1980s. The movement to allow women to put an end to the life of a fetus by arguing for their right to choose was not strong. The strongest voices against selective induced abortion were from those advocating protection of the rights of women and the disabled rather than those opposed to all kinds of induced abortion according to religious principles. Unlike Western countries in which the belief in the sanctity of life and the belief in a woman's right to choose conflict with each other, the criticism of medical care that seeks to go "beyond therapy" in Japan arose from a standpoint of seeking to protect the rights and wellbeing both of pregnant women and fetuses with potential disabilities.

7. Bioethics concerning the appropriateness of prenatal genetic diagnosis

Prenatal genetic diagnosis that is based on the assumption of having an induced abortion if a disorder is found are likely to be more sophisticated than other prenatal diagnoses, with higher accuracy and lower risk. For example, if foetal elements in a mother's blood could be more accurately extracted, prenatal genetic diagnosis without fear of harming either the mother or the fetus would be enabled. With improved technologies we may be able to lower costs gradually. The problems of safety and costs will then be largely solved, and mass screening will be promoted. Then, only the question of ethics around the "selection of life" will be left.

Moreover, if knowledge and technology of pre-implantation genetic diagnosis and its safety were improved, this method of diagnosis would be promoted. To conduct the diagnosis, *in vitro* fertilization is required. And if *in vitro* fertilization were to become widely practiced, people would use the diagnosis procedure for more varied purposes beyond aborting fetuses with specific genetic factors leading to disabilities. Sex selection, the avoidance of various potential diseases, or the selection of genetic factors with favorable abilities and characteristics may occur. The tendency toward having a "designer baby" has already been practiced by those who are attempting *in vitro* fertilization using a strictly selected donor's sperm or an egg. If pre-implantation genetic diagnosis were to be practiced widely, human reproduction would become based on "selection," and enter a new historic stage.

Prenatal screening through mothers' blood serum marker tests and amniotic fluid tests conducted at present can then be considered as the first step towards selection on a larger scale. The spread of mass screening will be a great stride towards enhancement in reproductive medicine. Furthermore, once the practice of pre-implantation diagnosis on a large scale becomes the norm, medical care that goes "beyond therapy" will go beyond the current framework of screening intended to reduce potential patients. As human enhancement develops, screening will become directly related to many people's daily life, and the question of ethics in relation to the genetic selection will become more important. Already, discrimination in buying life insurance and in seeking employment is thought to be inevitable by disclosing individual genetic information. The range of bioethical problems would increase beyond current predictions if selection during a reproductive process were promoted.

Many people discussing the question of enhancement touch upon such problems as the above. For example, the President's Council on Bioethics chaired by Leon Kass discussed the use of biotechnology to bear and raise "better children" in chapter 2 of its report titled *Beyond Therapy*. Sex selection is taken up as an example for having better children, and the wide use of psychotropic drugs such as Ritalin supposed to be used for attention-deficit hyper activity disorder (ADHD) is dealt with as an example for raising better children. According to *Beyond Therapy*, sex selection may change the meaning of pregnancy and childbirth, and that of parenthood and parent-and-child relations. The report states that sex selection relates to gender discrimination but that it is not the central issue. The sex identity of the children born after sex selection has been determined by their parents' desire. The report argues that children should not be produced or chosen at our will, but that they are given to us as gifts. We become parents by accepting the gifts unconditionally. Reproduction is mainly a question of love, and not a question of parents' will. Sex selection will mean a change in parents' attitude from the unconditional acceptance of children, towards a situation where children's identities will be subordinated to parental will (pp. 68–71).

The report of the President's Council on Bioethics opposes sex selection on the grounds of respecting children's rights to live and to their own identities, and of preserving parents' "unconditional acceptance" of their children. This stance is similar to that of Takamichi Sato and other Japanese scholars who are opposed to the exclusion of the disabled from society, and hence, are opposed to the spread of mass screening. In this case, the President's Council's arguments against sex selection can be used to oppose prenatal genetic diagnosis that would lead to mass screening and the exclusion of the disabled. However, the movement to oppose screening lacks strength in the United States, compared with Japan.

This attitude is reflected in the report in that whilst the report uses sex selection as an example to show parents determining their children's identities, or "choosing in," "choosing out" the disabled or female fetuses is not emphasized. Likewise, whilst in Japan "acceptance," "exclusion," and "discrimination" are closely linked in discussion, similar discussions in the United States do not connect these opposite attitudes as closely as in Japan.

This difference may reflect differences in religion, culture, and history between the United States in which prenatal genetic diagnosis is often practiced, and in Japan in which it is not practiced so often. To conclude this chapter, I will summarize the differences in attitudes to screening between the East and West as I see them.

8. Differences in the ethics of prenatal genetic diagnosis

Culture and historical background

In terms of prenatal genetic diagnosis for the purposes of induced abortion or selection, the historical backgrounds and cultures of many Western cultures differ greatly from the history and culture of Japan. I will examine below the differences between Japan and the West (covering mainly Britain, France, and the United States) in their attitude towards the diagnosis of fetal genetic disorders prior to induced abortion.

(1) Difference in the strength of justification by women's right to choose   In the West, the sanctity of life is the principal argument against abortion by both the Catholic Church and conservative Protestant groups. Their views on the sanctity of the life of fetuses does not admit any exception, and hence opposes all induced abortions. In contrast, those in favor of allowing induced abortion rely on the woman's right to choose as the ground for induced abortion. Approval for fetal genetic diagnosis prior to induced abortion and fetal selection was incorporated in speeches insisting on a woman's right to choose as a topic that can draw people's sympathy relatively easily.

In contrast, in Japan, induced abortion has tended to be made legal as a measure to control population growth, rather than as an issue for women's rights. For this reason, prenatal genetic diagnosis for induced abortion was not strongly associated with women's rights. Moreover, when women in Japan advocated the right to choose, the concept of women's rights to choose was criticized severely by disabled people. It is possible that as disabled people in Japan had not publicly advocated their right to life before, the time of their delayed advocacy just happened to coincide with that of the rise of the feminist voice. We need to examine carefully the historical interrelation of these processes.

(2) Difference in the opposition to eugenic thought   Eugenic thought was accepted in the West along with modern theories of progress, and above all, social evolutionary theory. This theory led to the spread of Western culture across the world and those who acquired the culture of the West were accorded higher social status, as the West was in an economically superior position following the Industrial Revolution. Looking down on people who have not acquired intelligence and ethical personality in the model of modern Western people is still prevalent in many parts of the world long after decolonization has become the norm. The Western consciousness gives value to the control of the human body and nature by the conscious self, gives weight to the value of rationalistic performances

and accomplishments, respects the sovereign self that dominates nature and the human body, and fears any impediment to the free exercise of sovereignty. A sense of superiority that contains the residue of colonialism underlies such eugenic thought.

The Japanese had been deeply influenced by the Chinese sense of supremacy over the uncivilized world, and, during the process of the nation's modernization, began to develop a sense of superiority with some racist inclinations. Its influence still remains among present-day Japanese. However, the Japanese shared with the Chinese a feeling of being discriminated against by the West during process of modernization. Furthermore, their sense of superiority was smashed by their defeat in World War II. As a result, people came to reflect negatively on their past sense of superiority. Their historical experience may have made the Japanese move a little bit closer to an awareness of people of colonized regions with respect to the notions of cultural supremacy and inferiority.

(3) Difference in the sense of unavoidability of population adjustment   The Japanese have long been taught that the nation's land area is small. Its farm land is very limited and natural resources are scarce. Nevertheless a large population has to survive in spite of this.

Among the people of the Edo (Tokugawa) era (seventeenth to nine-teenth century) which started when the long military conflicts driven by expansionist warriors and religious groups ended, there may well have been a shared and acute awareness of the inevitability of the need for population control. During the Edo era frequent famines brought the shortage of farmland to the forefront of people's minds. During the country's seclusion in the seventeenth century, it was considered impossible to find new land to support the surplus population. The fact that infanticides and feticides were conducted widely until recent times can be connected to a fear of population increase. In the process of modernization, the government attempted to solve the population problem by promoting colonization and emigration, but World War II forced the government and people to realize the limits and evils of its expansionism.

During early periods of industrialization, European countries continued emigration and colonization into the New World and other areas. It is inferred that, in spite of Malthusian influence, the sense of unavoidability of population adjustment was not so strong in the West as in Japan.

Rather, fear for the relative population growth of farmers, working class people and people of the colonies was heightened, contributing to the rise of the popularity of eugenics. The fear of so-called "reverse selection" (the increase of the parts of the population considered to have inferior abilities) became prevalent. It was only towards the end of the twentieth century that Christian churches started reflecting on their expansionist past seriously.

(4) Difference in skepticism on scientific intervention in nature and the human body In the West, people take great pride in their culture for the emergence of modern science and the way it has improved standards of human welfare. This suggests that they have firm confidence in reasoning power that has become independent from, and dominates, nature and the body. Prenatal genetic diagnosis leading to induced abortion and hence selection can then be understood as a valuable tool, following other modern medical accomplishments, and has become a part of the process where human beings with sovereign selves build their dominance over the body and nature. Self-determination is stressed as indispensable for the value of freedom. This is related to the sense of value of the conscious self that dominates the environment.

In Japanese culture, people are more skeptical about the adequacy of the kind of reason and sovereignty of self that dominates nature and the body. People consider that the arrogance and destructive nature of reason are inseparable from modernization, and also from modern scientific technology. Thus the power of reason is estimated to have limited value. This criticism of modern rationalism is often connected with nationalism. But there are new ways of thinking that distance themselves both from expansionist universalism and nationalistic particularism. This may not be very different from the situation in the contemporary West where there is a growing willingness to accept multiple ways of life without diminishing their difference and to live together.

(5) Difference between individual autonomy-centered ethics and ethics which values interpersonal relationships and bonds In the West, the value accorded to self-determination and reason has been an important factor both in prenatal genetic diagnosis and more widely in bioethics. The concept of individual humans having dignity, and the way of thinking that connects the value of

life with self-consciousness and self-identity have functioned as the ultimate norm.

However, in Japan, far fewer people entertain these concepts. In Japan, the value of life can be found in living together with others and living in a continuous cycle of carrying over the life of past generations to coming generations. Rather than the life of individuals, the relationships between individuals and others, and linkages beyond individuals are emphasized. People place a high value on the nurturing parent-and-child bond. The arguments about respecting the accepting and caring attitude needed to live with the disabled may have been influenced by this value-orientation and by the weaker popularity of the concept of life selection by autonomous individuals in Japan.

This type of thinking tends to increase the value of group integration and to reduce the value of individual autonomy. But in Japan since the 1970s there has been a wider acceptance of the value of individual autonomy and a growing criticism of group integration and homogeneity. In this transformation, the rights of disabled people have become a cornerstone for the value of coexistence of different and multiple human beings. This may be parallel to the transformation of Western thought and Western ethics which are becoming more aware of the limits of individualism and rationalism, and are reconsidering the place of others and that of the human body which conditions the autonomous self.

Differences in the perceptions of prenatal genetic diagnosis among different nations suggest that the culture and historical background of each nation has an influence on bioethical decision-making. Needless to say it is not the intention of this chapter to discuss which cultures are superior. This way of thinking about the superiority and inferiority is itself the source of the hegemonic and competitive attitudes which lead to eugenic thought. Rather, it is essential to accept diverse ways of thinking, to identify the advantages and defects of respective ways of thinking, and to try to make proper judgments based on tolerance. At the same time, it is necessary to forge consensus through mutual understanding, and to compromise and coordinate various ways of thinking in matters that require a common judgment for all human beings. The unprecedented new challenges facing humanity as a whole may in fact be an opportunity to develop a new solidarity as we work together to achieve consensus.

References

1. Books published in and after the 1990s in Japan which contain criticisms against prenatal genetic diagnosis

Ebara, Yimiko, ed. *Seishoku gijutsu to gender* (*Reproductive Technologies and Gender*), Keiso Shobo, 1996.

Ishikawa, Jun and Nagase, Osamu (eds.), *Shogaigaku eno shotai* (*Invitation to Disability Studies*), Akashi Shoten, 1999.

Marumoto, Yuriko & Yamamoto, Katsumi, *Umu umanai o nayamu toki—Botai hogo-ho jidai no inochi to karada* (*When women contemplate whether to deliver a child or not—Life and the body in the age of the Mothers' Body Protection Act*), Iwanami Shoten, 1997.

Morioka, Masahiro, *Seimeigaku ni nani ga dekiruka-nohshi, feminism, yusei shiso* (*What can life studies do? Brain death, feminism and eugenic thought*), Keiso Shobo, 2001.

Ohno, Akiko (ed.), *Kodomo o erabanai koto o erabu—inochi no genba kara shussei-mae shindai o tou* (*Choosing not to choose a child: Questioning about prenatal genetic diagnosis from the workplace dealing with life*), Medica Press, 2003.

Saito, Yukiko, ed. *Botai hogo-ho to watashitachi—Chuzetsu, tatai- gensu, funin shujutsu wo meguru seido to shakai* (*Mothers' body protection act and us—Systems and society around abortion, reduction of multiple fetuses and infertility surgery*), Akashi Shoten, 2002.

Sakai, Ritsuko, *Reportage: shussei-mae shindan* (*Reportage: prenatal genetic diagnosis*), NHK Press, 1999.

Sato, Takamichi, *Shussei-zen shindan* (*Prenatal genetic diagnosis*), Yukikaku, 1999.

Tamai, Mariko, "Shussei-zen shindan to sentakuteki chuzetsu o meguru double standard to taiji joho eno access" (Double Standards on Prenatal Genetic Diagnosis and Selective Abortion and Access to Information on Fetuses), in Matsutomo, Ryo (ed.), *Chiteki shogaisha no jinken* (*Human rights of the mentally disabled*), Akashi Shoten, 1999.

——— "Shogai to shussei-zen shindan" (Disability and prenatal genetic diagnosis), in Ishikawa, Jun and Nagase, Osamu (eds.), *Shogaigaku eno shotai—Shakai, bunka, disability* (*Invitation to disability studies—Society, culture and disability*), Akashi Shoten, 1999b.

Tateiwa, Shinya, *Shiteki shoyuron* (*Private property theory*), Keiso Shobo, 1997.

——— *Yowaku-aru jiyu e—Jiko kettei, kaigo, seishi no gijutsu* (*Freedom to be weak: Self-determination, care, technology for life and death*), Seido-sha, 2000.

Yusei-shiso o Tou Network (Network Questioning Eugenic Thought) (ed.), *Shitteimasu-ka? shussei-zen shindan—mondo* (*Do you know about prenatal genetic diagnosis? Q & A*), Kaiho Shuppan-sha, 2003.

2. Others

Asad, Talal, *Formation of the Secular: Christianity, Islam and Modernity*, Stanford University Press, 2003.

Chiba, Tokuji and Otsu, Tadao, *Mabiki to mizuko—kosodate no folklore (Infanticides and aborted fetuses—childcare folklore)*, Nosangyoson Bunka Kyokai, 1983.

Fujime, Yuki, *Sei-no rekishigaku—kosho seido to dataizai taisei kara baishun boshiho to yuseihogo-ho taisei e (History of sexual practices—from the state-regulated prostitution system and abortion crime system to the system under the prostitution prohibition act and eugenic protection act)*, Fuji Shuppan, 1999.

Fujino, Yutaka, *Nippon fascism to yusei shiso (Japanese fascism and eugenic thought)*, Kamogawa Shuppan, 1998.

Ishii, Michiko, *Jinko seishoku no horitsugaku—Seishoku iryo no hattatsu to kazoku-ho (Legal science of artificial reproduction—Development of reproductive medicine and the family law)*, Yuhikaku, 1994.

Namihira, Emiko, *Inochi no bunka jinruigaku (Cultural anthropology of life)*, Shincho-sha, 1996.

Ogino, Miho, *Chuzetsu ronso to America shakai—Karada o meguru senso (Abortion debate and American society—War around the body)*, Iwanami Shoten, 2001.

President's Council on Bioethics, *Beyond Therapy: Biotechnology and the Pursuit of Haappiness, A Report by the President's Council on Bioethics*, Regan Books, 2003.

Shimazono, Susumu, "Ko toshiteno inochi to majiwari no nakano inochi (Life as an individual and life in interaction with others," in *Shiseigaku Kenkyu*, No. 2, 2003.

_____ "Why we must Be Prudent in Research Using Human Embryos: Differing Views of Human Dignity," in William R. La Fleur, Gerndt Böhme, and Susumu Shimazono (eds.), *Dark Medicine: Rationalizing Unethical Medical Research*, Indiana University Press, 2007.

Stock, Gregory, *Redesigning Humans: Choosing our Children's Genes*, Profile Books, 2002.

Trombley, Steven, *The Right to reproduce*, Weidenfeld & Nicolson, 1988, trans. Fujita Mariko, Akashi Shoten, 2000.

Tsuneishi, Keiichi, *Kieta saikin butai—kanto-gun 731 butai (Vanished biological war unit—Kwantung Army Unit 731)*, Kaimei-sha, 1981.

Yonemoto, Shohei, Matsubara, Yoko, Katsujima, Jiro and Ichinokawa, Yoko, *Yuseigaku to ningen shakai—seimei kagaku no seiki wa doko e mukaunoka? (Eugenics and human society—Where is the century of bioscience heading to?)* Kodansha, 2000.

14

Medical Enhancement and the Ethos of Elite Sport

Torbjörn Tännsjö[*]

Abstract

We should distinguish between negative medical interventions (intended to cure disease), positive interventions (intended to improve, within the normal range, functioning) and enhancement (where a person is pushed beyond species normal functioning). It seems that, within medicine in general, even if these distinctions can make a difference with respect to who shall pay for the service, they make no principled difference as to whether the services can be provided. However, in sports medicine, they do make a difference. In this chapter, I investigate what kind of difference. Negative interventions seem to be unproblematic, positive interventions problematic, and enhancement forbidden. Why? Is there a rationale behind this to be found within the ethos of sport as such?

1. Introduction

Medical intervention is viewed very differently in sports medicine than in medicine in general. The impression is superficially that there is more room for medical intervention in order to further the functioning of the organism in sport than in medicine in general. There is more tolerance with respect to medical risks in sports medicine than elsewhere. It is crucial that the athlete who suffers from an injury is quickly back in business again, and there is a liberal view of the risks that the physician and the athlete, individually and together, can accept in order to accomplish this.

[*] Claëson Professor of Practical Philosophy, university of Stockholm, and Director of the Stockholm Bioethics Centre.

In particular, this seems to be a fact in team sports. When it is crucial that a certain team is successful in a decisive match it might be of such importance to have the best player in action that his physician accepts some hazards concerning his long-time medical interests. The pressure on the player to undergo the medical procedure may be considerable, and it is yet generally considered acceptable. However, upon closer inspection, it transpires that sports medicine is in important respects also *less* liberal than standard medicine in allowing medical intervention. In this chapter I will focus on *this*—startling—difference between sports medicine and medicine in general.

2. Some crucial distinctions

In our assessments of medical interventions it is common to distinguish roughly between *negative* interventions, performed with the aim of curing a disease or eliminating a handicap or disability, *positive* interventions which aim at improving the functioning of a human organism within a natural variation, and *enhancement*, which aims at taking an individual beyond the normal functioning of a human organism. Here are some typical examples: to provide antibiotics to a person suffering from pneumonia in order to cure him or her from this disease would be a typically negative intervention; to give human growth hormone to an unusually small child, (merely) in order to increase the height of this child, would be a positive intervention; to provide a man with big (female) breasts would be a typical example of enhancement.[1]

These stipulated distinctions are problematic in many ways, but still useful for my purposes. Let me first indicate in what ways they are problematic and then indicate how, in the present context, they are helpful.

3. Problems with the distinctions

First of all, these distinctions are, in an obvious manner, vague. What does it mean to suffer from a disease (or handicap/disability)? In many cases,

---

[1] This is how I make these distinctions in Tännsjö, T., 1993, 'Should We Change the Human Genome?', *Theoretical Medicine*, vol. 14, 231–47. Of course, there are many other quite legitimate ways of using these terms. My use reflects a mere stipulation.

human characteristics are distributed according to a normal curve. This is true, for example, of intelligence (as measured through an IQ-score). But then it is hard to draw any sharp line between what is healthy and what is not. And this means that, if we could improve intelligence, it would in some cases be difficult to settle whether we had performed a negative intervention (and provided a cure) or whether we had performed a positive intervention (and improved the functioning of an individual).

A solution to the problem of the vague distinction between what is healthy and normal, on the one hand, and abnormal and a disability, on the other hand, is conventionally just to *draw* a line. With respect to intelligence, for example, it is sometimes assumed that an IQ-score below 70 should qualify as a handicap or disability. But why draw the line here?

The answer to this question is partly evaluative. It has to do with what could reasonably be required from autonomous citizens in the kind of society in which we, who are drawing the line, are living right now. Depending on what society requires of people, we draw a line between what is normal and healthy and what is abnormal and dysfunctional. An even more obvious example of this is how we tend to view dyslexia. In a literate society we are likely to classify dyslexia as abnormal and dysfunctional while, in an illiterate society, we would conceive of it as normal (we simply would not notice this phenomenon at all).

I do not deny that the distinctions between medical intervention that are negative, positive, and examples of enhancement, are vague, evaluative, and conventional, then. And yet, for all that, they play a role in our thinking about medicine. They do so since there are *some* clear cases of negative interventions, positive interventions, and examples of enhancement. Moreover, if we take for granted the conventions and values upon which these conventions are established in a society, such as ours, then we can apply these distinctions to many more cases. And, when we do, some interesting differences between sports medicine and medicine in general surface.

4. A difference between sports medicine and medicine in general

In medicine in general it is commonly held that negative interventions are of the utmost importance. In a system of collectively subsidized health care, if the resources are thought insufficient to cover all medical costs, these negative interventions are the ones that should be prioritized. Positive interventions, on the other hand, are of a more dubious nature when it comes to common public funding. One often hears that, to the extent that people want to go along with these kinds of interventions, they should pay for them themselves. People are different and our differences, as long as they fall within a normal range, are acceptable. For example, there is really no need to improve one's pitch, it is claimed, even if one is born with a poor pitch, since having poor pitch is a fate one shares with many people. In a similar vein, for an ordinary person, there is no real *need* to improve one's memory or capacity to distinguish different smells, let alone to undergo merely cosmetic surgery. And, when it comes to enhancement, there is certainly much scepticism that can be brought forward against such measures. Few would accept that society should pay the bill when a transvestite, for mere cosmetic reasons, wants to have his breasts enhanced to average female size. This is different from how we would view a transsexual person, who feels that being captured in the 'wrong' sex destroys his or her life. Here we are perhaps prepared to pay the bill. But the transvestite, who wants the female breasts in order not to become a woman, but merely to dress up like one, would have a hard time convincing the public at large that they should pay for his extraordinary breasts.

At least this kind of view of enhancement seems to be predominant right now, and with respect to many of the kinds of human enhancements that have just begun to be at focus of the debate. I think of enhancement of our cognitive skills, our moods, our life-span, and so forth. However, I submit that we may be just not used to thinking about them and eventually we may come to change our attitude to them and see them as candidates of services that should be subsidized through public funding. Note that there is one kind of enhancement, that we now take for granted, and that we take for granted that the publicly subsidized health care *should* take care of: vaccination. In vaccination we push the human resistance to diseases way beyond the normal variation (species range). This is certainly 'enhancement', as I have here defined the term. In the not too distant future we may come to view other kinds of enhancement as just as natural as vaccinations.

For the time being, however, irrespective of whether we find this reasonable or not, we must conclude that these distinctions between negative and positive interventions and enhancements, play *some* role when standard medical procedures are assessed from an economical point of view. In particular this is so in health care systems where medical services are supposed to be publicly subsidized. However, note that this does not mean that, once a measure is such that the public at large is not prepared to pay for it, the public wants to prohibit it. If a positive intervention, or an enhancement, would be medically safe, and the person who wanted to undergo it were prepared to pay the cost for it, only highly prejudiced people would object. In a liberal society, there would be no legal prohibition against positive measures, or medical interventions aiming at enhancement, at least not *in principle*.

This is not to say that there is no resistance whatever to enhancement, even in a liberal society. However, the resistance seems to relate mainly to two sources. There may be some *means* used for positive or enhancement purposes that would be rejected, such as germ-line genetic therapy for example, by the public at large, but the positive intervention, or the enhancement, would not *as such* be legally prohibited—if it could be achieved through less controversial means, such as a proper administration of food. And there may be *egalitarian* concerns, even in a liberal society, about enhancement, if the enhancement measures cannot be offered to everyone on equal terms. Once these concerns are met, however, and the methods used are not objectionable as such, and they are made available to everyone, then there would be no good liberal ground for a prohibition.

Consider for example a skilled piano player, who had found that, even though she was the most talented and technically skilled player in the world, she could not manage a certain piece. Suppose she had found out that, in order to play this piece, she would need 12 fingers. Now, suppose an equally skilled surgeon could somehow provide her with two additional fingers. She agrees to the operation, which successfully takes place. In the circumstances some may find this choice of the pianist and the surgeon strange, but few would *object* to it. And few would hesitate to listen to, and enjoy, the music played by this pianist, with her twelve fingers.

Now, let us turn to sport medicine. Here we notice that the situation is very different. Sports medicine is, as was pointed out above, not very risk averse. However, this doesn't mean that anything goes. Quite to the contrary. What has here been described as positive medical measures, and, even more so enhancement, would be ruled out of court. It would be prohibited.

If a skilled physician provided an athlete with three-metre long legs, allowing this athlete to walk over a height of three metres, sports authorities would be very concerned. And it would be of no avail if the athlete claimed correctly that he had himself paid for the operation. The sports authorities would not allow this individual to compete in high jump. Not even the use of beta blockers would be accepted in a sport like shooting, while it is no problem in piano playing.

This does not mean that, within sport, no sorts of methods are introduced, intended to bend the rules. Quite to the contrary. Medical advice relating to diet and training regimes is standard procedure, even if not a much publicized fact, in many sports. Cyclists are, for example, given infusions with carefully prepared nourishment at night during big races, in order to make them fit for the fight the next day. But there comes a definite point, which cannot be transcended within sport. While the very fact that a certain drug is efficacious outside sport, and the very fact that it does enhance you capacity is a good reason to take it, it renders the same drug, for this very reason, *prohibited* in the sport context.

Why this difference between sports medicine and medicine in general? It must have something to do with the ethos of elite sport.

5. The ethos of elite sport

So, what is the ethos of elite sport? Several components come to mind. Elite sport is, first and foremost, a cultural phenomenon. It is supposed to provide the *viewer* with a fascinating performance. This means that the performance should hold a certain *aesthetic* quality. Moreover, elite sport is *competitive*. It is a matter of winning or losing. The viewer is supposed to take an interest in who wins and who loses. This requires that the outcome is not too easily predictable. I here refer to what the philosopher of sport, Warren Fraleigh, has called 'the sweet tension of uncertainty of outcome'.[2]

---

[2] Fraleigh, W., *Right Actions in Sport. Ethics for Contestants* (Champaign, Ill.: Human Kinetic Publishers, 1984).

Finally, there is an element of fairness involved in elite sport. As far as possible, conditions that are irrelevant to the competition should be eliminated. In a sense, all who compete should have the same chance to excel.[3] However, the requirement of fairness is problematic, so let us for the moment set it to one side and focus on the rest of the requirements.

Why would we not allow a person who has been provided with three-metre long legs to compete in the high jump? It suffices here to note that this would spoil the high jump for simple aesthetic reasons. For now we would have changed the nature of the high jump. Unless people jump, it's not much fun watching them compete. If we could measure the length of their legs and then correctly predict the outcome of the competition (the one with the longest legs wins), then this would make for poor entertainment.

Suppose, however, that these very long-legged persons did jump and suppose that, even though the length of their legs had made them superior to the people who compete nowadays, their performance would not be a simple function of the length of their legs. Some would jump 3.50 metres, others 3.75, and it could well be the person with slightly shorter legs that jumped 3.75. Now it is hard to see that, with reference to the ethos of elite sport, there is anything to object to in this medical intervention, at least to the extent that the ethos is taken to be merely a matter of competition and aesthetics.

A comparison with pole vault is in order here. Originally the poles were made of steel and then bamboo. Today's pole vaulters benefit from poles produced by wrapping sheets of fibreglass around a pole template, to produce a pre-bent pole that bends more easily under the compression caused by an athlete's take-off; this has meant that the results have increased tremendously. Since the fibreglass poles are available to anyone, and since the use of them doesn't destroy the element of competition and entertainment, they were willingly accepted. It is even more interesting to see a person jump over 6 metres than over 5!

A different move was made in javelin throwing. In 1986, the centre of gravity of the men's javelin was moved forward 10 cm to make the javelin's

---

[3] For a good, nuanced, and illuminating discussion of this, see Loland, S., 'The Logic of Progress and the Art of Moderation in Competitive Sports', in Torbjörn Tännsjö and Claudio M. Tamburrini (eds.), *The Value of Sport* (London and New York: Routledge, 2000).

nose drop down faster. This accomplished two objectives: it eliminated flat landings, making the javelin both easier to spot and safer. It also made the distances shorter so that long throws can be accommodated in the infield. The change was undertaken for practical reasons, then. And since it did not destroy either the competitive or the entertainment aspect of javelin throw, quite to the contrary, there was little protest at the change. It is hard to claim that the ethos of javelin throwing requires any definite centre of gravity of the javelin in particular.

Now, if these changes were acceptable in the pole vault and in javelin throwing, does this mean that an increase of the legs would be acceptable in high jump? I think not, but why not? If there is a rationale behind a more restrictive view of the enlargement of legs than on poles, it must have to do with the ethos of (traditional?) athletics. And it must have something to do with an aspect of the ethos which is not reducible to a simple matter of competition and aesthetics. Where do we find this further aspect?

6. Elite sport and human nature—some questions

It might be helpful to consider some more (intermediary) examples, when we try to find out why it is acceptable to improve the quality of the pole in pole vault but not to enlarge the legs in high jump.

Here is another comparison. Suppose an extremely short-legged person gets the length of his legs increased through what I have classified as a positive intervention. His legs are now somewhat above average length. Would this disqualify him for high jump?

Or, consider the case with a person who is born with just one leg. Suppose through advanced medical techniques involving stem cell technology we can provide him with a prosthetic for his lacking leg. Is he then fit to enter the Olympic high jump competition?

Or, consider an athlete who has his Achilles tendon hurt. His physician offers him a new artificial elastic transplant, which he accepts. He is soon back in competition and excels as usual. I suppose we have nothing to object to. But then there is another athlete, who has always had trouble with his weak Achilles tendon and never been able to train as much as he has wanted. He too asks for the artificial transplant and receives it, even though, for the moment, his own Achilles tendon is healthy. He now becomes able to train much harder than before and, eventually, he takes over the world record. Would this be acceptable?

My intuitions are not quite settled here, but I tend to believe that none of this would be accepted, at least not if the person operated upon not only competes, but does so very successfully and excels. We would not be happy to celebrate any one of these persons as the winner of high jump in the Olympics. His world record would be looked upon with suspicion. An indication that this is so is a recently publicized case with a South African short distance runner, Oscar Pistorius, who had both his legs amputated below the knee when he was 11 months old and who runs with prosthetics. He claims, according to *New York Times*, that he is 'the fastest man on no legs'.[4] Pistorius wants, according to the same source, to be the first amputee runner to compete in the Olympics.

Pistorius has delivered startling record performances for disabled athletes, *New York Times* reports. His records are as follows: at 100 metres (10.91 seconds), 200 metres (21.58 seconds) and 400 metres (46.34 seconds). Those times do not meet Olympic qualifying standards for men, of course, but he is only 20 years old, and the Beijing Games are still, when this is being written, more than a year away. And there are other occasions following the Beijing Games. Pistorius is facing fierce resistance from the track and field's world governing body, however, which is seeking to bar him on the grounds that the technology of his prosthetics may give him an unfair advantage over sprinters using their 'natural' legs:

'With all due respect, we cannot accept something that provides advantages,' said Elio Locatelli of Italy, the director of development for the IAAF [track and field's world governing body], urging Pistorius to concentrate on the Paralympics that will follow the Olympics in Beijing. 'It affects the purity of sport. Next will be another device where people can fly with something on their back.'[5]

Is there a way of explaining this kind of reaction? He would, after all, both contribute to the aesthetic quality of the competition, if he were allowed to compete, and this would also render the outcome of the competition less certain. So we must query if there is some aspect of the ethos of elite sport, not yet commented upon by me in the present context, which can make sense of the reaction from the IAAF I think there is and I now turn to it.

[4] *New York Times*, 15 May 2007.   [5] Ibid.

7. Elite sport and human nature—some answers

Let us return to the person with three-metre long legs. I have a strong suspicion that many would protest against allowing him to compete, even if our allowing him to compete would mean that we could retain, and even improve upon, the aesthetic and competitive qualities in high jump. Why is that? Is there anything more to high jump than aesthetics and competition with an uncertain outcome? I think there is. And this is how we can get a grasp of it.

The first answer to the question of why this person should not be allowed to compete would be that this person had an unfair advantage over other persons. This is hinted at already in the comment from Elio Locatelli of Italy, the director of development for the IAAF However, this answer is much too simplistic. We could easily avoid it by ascertaining that everyone who wants to do so can have his (or her) legs increased in this manner. Indeed, if we are interested in levelling out differences, we could also have a rule about the maximum length of legs, actually levelling out existing differences. One could compare here with a limit to the permitted concentration of haemoglobin in the blood. So the problem with the enhancement of the legs doesn't seem to have anything to do with equal opportunities for anyone to excel.

So, why not accept three-metre long legs in high jump? Well, *I* tend to think that we should accept this. But I think I understand the rationale behind what seems to be the received wisdom, to wit, a denial that people should be allowed to compete in high jump with three-metre long legs. The rationale has to do with a notion of elite sport as a way of exploring the limits of human nature. We arrange the competition in order to find out where the limit is for what is possible for a human being to achieve. We want to explore, not only where the limit is, but also who is, in the relevant aspect, the most perfect human being. Once we find this out, we make this human being the subject of our admiration. At last we have found our *Übermensch*.

It might be thought that, while this reference to the ethos of sport explains why enhancement is not acceptable, it doesn't explain why *positive* measures are not acceptable. So long as we operate within the normal human range of capabilities, where Oscar Pistorius roughly seems to be, why should we not allow a person who is born weak to increase his strength, through all sorts of medical interventions? Why not accept that Pistorius uses his prosthetics when he is running? After all, he walks on prosthetics otherwise in life, even if the ones he uses outside competition and training are differently designed and look more like normal legs. And the ones he is using in competitions render it possible for him to compete on roughly equal terms with other elite runners.

I think the explanation *here* must refer to a further aspect of the ethos of elite sport, a very special notion of justice typical of it. This is a notion of justice insisting that we all must accept the ticket we have actually drawn in the genetic lottery. Genetic differences are *not* irrelevant to the outcome of the competition. Indeed, genetic differences are what *should* be decisive, once we have eliminated *other* differences.

This is a Nietzschean view of justice, according to which it is unfair if those who are less fit pool their resources and rob the genuinely strong *Übermensch* of his genetic advantage. I have elsewhere explained why I resent this element in the ethos of elite sport. It is there, all right, but we should try to get rid of it.[6] Nowhere else in a civilized society are we prepared to live with this notion of justice. And it is impossible to find a philosophical rationale behind it. It is a mere cultural atavism.

But if we do get rid of this very special notion of justice, what are we to replace it with?

Well, I am not sure that we need to find a replacement for it. It is enough if elite sport provides us with good entertainment: fierce, fair, and unpredictable competition—a sweet tension of uncertainty of outcome. However, if we do want to add something to this it could be the following. We have now reached a position where it is possible for us, human beings, to enhance our human nature (our genome, our physical bodies, our mental make-up, and so forth). In elite sport we can test out the results of such enhancements and see, not where the limits are of the (given) human nature, but how far we can push them. We can enjoy what we

---

[6] See my chapter 'Is Our Admiration for Sports Heroes Fascistoid?', in Torbjörn Tännsjö and Claudio M. Tamburrini, *Sports and Values: Elitism, nationalism, gender equality, and the scientific manufacture of winners* (London and New York: Routledge, 2000), reprinted in William J. Morgan, Klaus V. Meier, and Angela Schneider (eds.), *Ethics in Sport* (Kinetics, 2001).

see at the competition, and we can feel admiration for all the scientific achievements that have rendered possible the performances. And we can thank the athletes for taking the inconvenience to test them out before us.

8. Conclusion

There is a striking difference between sports medicine and medicine in general, as we have seen. In medicine in general we can accept both positive measures and enhancement. However, in sports medicine both positive measures and enhancement are viewed with suspicion. The rationale behind this suspicion has to do with a very special aspect of the ethos of elite sport, the idea that in elite sport we search for the limits of what a human being can do, together with a very special notion of justice according to which we are allowed to admire the individual who has drawn a winning ticket in the natural genetic lottery and excels.

If we give up this aspect of the ethos of elite sport we need no special medical ethics for sport medicine. Just as we can allow a piano player to acquire two extra fingers, in order to play better, we can allow an athlete to acquire three-metre long legs, in order to jump higher. What counts, in both music and sport, is the aesthetic quality, providing for good entertainment. And it is incumbent upon the medical personnel to see to it that the medical measures resorted to are safe.

As a matter of fact, I believe this is the direction in which we are heading. Once enhancement of all kinds become common outside the elite sport context, in particular within recreational sports, it will become increasingly more difficult to keep it out of elite sport itself.

15

Life Enhancement Technologies: The Significance of Social Category Membership

*Christine Overall**

Sceptical about the benefits of deliberately manufactured life enhancement, Michael Sandel advocates that we not "override a child's natural capacities [by means of artificial life-enhancement technologies] but permit them to flourish" (Sandel 2004, 8). Perhaps no one would disagree that natural capacities should be allowed to flourish.[1] But what is not clear is what constitutes a "natural" capacity. Since every human environment is a social environment, "natural" capacities do not and cannot reveal themselves as such. *What* is perceived as a capacity, *whether* it is recognized in a particular individual, and *how and to what extent* people believe it should be developed and permitted to flourish, are socially determined processes that make the existence of raw "natural" abilities an illusion.

Those who investigate the ethics of life enhancement must, therefore, not only be concerned with topics such as risks and benefits, costs, species-normal functioning, needs versus wants, and authenticity, important though all of those are. For, I shall argue, the ethics of life enhancement can be deeply affected by the socially-produced *identities* of the individuals who are (ostensibly) benefited or not benefited by life-enhancement technologies, and by the power over these technologies that is wielded by some at the expense of others. Life enhancement is a political issue, political in the sense that it is also about power, about differences in privileges, rights,

---

* Professor of Philosophy and Queen's University Research Chair, Ontario, Canada.

[1] In saying this I do not in any way deny the cogency of Frances Kamm's criticisms of Sandel's views of human capacities as "gifts" (Kamm, this volume, Ch. 5).

opportunities, and access, and about oppression and the ways in which oppression might be deepened or diminished by various forms of life enhancement and the policies that govern them.

In this chapter I explore the significance of membership in certain social identity categories for the ethical evaluation of human enhancement technologies. Plans and prospects for human enhancement are not always politically and ethically neutral with respect to group identities. Instead, they may, deliberately or not, affect various groups in different ways that are politically and ethically significant.

The point of this chapter is not to criticize or defend any or all forms of technologically engineered (ostensible) human enhancement. The latter is, after all, a large and expanding category of potential physical, intellectual, psychological, and moral improvements (Baylis and Robert 2004, 449). It includes such diverse and wide-ranging processes as fertility enhancements and pregnancy substitutes, pre-conception and prenatal sex selection, cloning, sex/gender changes, breast augmentation, cosmetic surgery, height augmentation, sexual performance enhancers, anti-depressants used as "mood brighteners," memory improvement, and intelligence enrichment. As the list indicates, enhancement technologies may be employed to change the individual during childhood or adulthood, or affect the individual during fetal development or even earlier, via the manipulation of gametes or embryos. Moreover, enhancement technologies may be used to improve individuals only, or to generate inheritable characteristics via germ-line genetic engineering. Given this enormous variation, moral generalizations about all enhancement processes and technologies are unwise, and they should instead be evaluated individually.

In a recent book, *Aging, Death, and Human Longevity: A Philosophical Inquiry* (Overall 2003), I argued that the extension of the human life span is a worthy objective, which ought to be supported by social policy initiatives, although not necessarily sought through every possible means. Obviously I can't rehearse all of the book's arguments here. But let us imagine, for the sake of the topic of this chapter, that there is a reliable and safe process available—perhaps via genetic engineering—that will increase individuals' life span. I shall use this hypothetical prospect of life extension as an example of a potentially important life enhancement process. I seek to demonstrate two main ideas. First, I shall show *that* questions about life enhancement can be deeply affected by social identity categories (that is, such questions are gendered, racialized, and affected by class). Second, I shall show *how* this latter fact affects, or should affect, some aspects of our ethics and social policy formation with respect to life enhancement.

Social category membership

Human individuals are, obviously, diverse with respect to their talents, gifts, abilities, and disabilities. We regard many of these variations as being the result of the "natural lottery"—the genetic happenstance that lays the foundation for making one person an athlete, another a violin player, and a third a mathematician. We also recognize that the outcomes of the "natural lottery" can be affected by social processes. A child born to a mother who contracts rubella during her pregnancy may be born with disabilities. A child born into a social group that does not value sports may not—whatever his "natural" talents—become a hockey or football player. So the results of the "natural lottery" can be individually shaped both after birth and before birth.

But there is another highly significant way in which the outcomes of the "natural lottery" are modified. All human beings are differently placed as a result of their membership in various groups that are treated by their society as being morally and politically significant. Many of these groups—sex/gender groups, racial groups, age groups—are not chosen.[2] Others, such as religion, appear to be subject to choice, but the beliefs, values, and ways of being that are associated with membership in the group are often inculcated so early in life as to become virtually unavoidable. And for still others, such as socio-economic class, mobility from one group to another is possible but often difficult, and dependent on factors that are outside an individual's control. Moreover, membership in some social identity groups is advantageous: in most cases, for example, being male or being a member of the middle class confers certain unearned privileges. Other group memberships can be liabilities; for example, being a person of colour or an aboriginal within a predominantly white society inflicts certain equally unearned burdens resulting from prejudice and discrimination.

---

[2] However, I would argue that these group memberships are not merely biologically given, since the significance of one's sex, colour, or age is socially, not naturally, constructed by virtue of how the culture collectively picks out the category, assigns value to it, defines membership in it, and then treats individual members of the category. See Overall 2006.

The fact that people belong to social groupings that create either benefits or liabilities also means that when new technologies are introduced, their potential harms or benefits are not only the product of harms or benefits accruing to particular individuals, but also the result of changing attitudes towards and beliefs about the entire social category. Peter Singer, in this volume, defends unrestricted access to certain technological enhancements on the basis of reproductive freedom and the potential value to individual children of life enhancements (Ch. 12, pp. 276–7). He attacks those such as George Annas who worry about the general effects of technological enhancements on children in society. However, I suggest that Annas's type of concern—the effects of enhancement processes on entire social categories—is justified, and is not merely reducible to the effects on individuals who receive the enhancement. In a society in which beautiful, highly intelligent, talented children are, in effect, available for purchase by the wealthy, we are justified in being worried about the objectifying and commodifying effects of such a market on attitudes toward and beliefs about all children. More broadly, in a society where the sex, the race, and the health of children can also be chosen and determined before birth and even before conception, we are justified in being concerned about the ways in which sexism, racism, and ableism may be reinforced against females, against persons who are not white, and against persons with disabilities. Similarly, whenever (ostensible) enhancements to women's procreative capacities are introduced, it is essential to consider not only their potential risks and benefits to the individual women who use them, but also the effects of reproductive enhancements on general attitudes toward women's procreative capacities and the treatment of women as a group.

The identities human beings have by virtue of their membership in broad social categories have two different though related implications, I would argue, for the ethics of human enhancement. Moreover, these two implications also affect social policy formation.

The effects of social category membership on access to and availability of life enhancement

One's group membership largely determines whether or not one has access to the benefits of life enhancement and whether or not one can pay the costs of these processes. There is nothing new about this. Long before so-called human nature could be broadly engineered, human beings' right of entry to and capacity to pay for low-tech and no-tech sources of personal preservation and development such as health care, medicines, adequate shelter, and education, were (and in some places still are) determined by one's sex, race, and class. To this century's catalogue of engineered life enhancements the wealthy and the white will most likely have much more ready access than the poor and the non-white. As a result, Nick Bostrom suggests,

The genetically privileged might become ageless, healthy, super-geniuses of flawless physical beauty, who are graced with a sparkling wit and a disarmingly self-deprecating sense of humor, radiating warmth, empathetic charm, and relaxed confidence.[3] The non-privileged would remain as people are today but perhaps deprived of some of their self-respect and suffering occasional bouts of envy. The mobility between the lower and the upper classes might disappear, and a child born to poor parents, lacking genetic enhancements, might find it impossible to successfully compete against the super-children of the rich (Bostrom 2004, 502).

Because of concerns such as these, access to and the capacity to pay for life enhancement processes raise questions of justice, and those questions cannot be taken into account without due recognition of the ways in which group memberships may have increased or compromised access and capacity to pay.

Arthur Caplan (this volume, Ch. 9) argues that critics of human enhancement technologies "miss the mark" when they worry about fair access p. 200. Equity arguments, he says, "tell us whether a pattern of inequality or a particular distribution of resources is right or wrong," but they do not show that the improvement itself is wrong. I'm not sure the two issues can so easily be separated in practice. What if an enormously valuable improvement is such that only a relatively small number of people can have it? It may be very scarce or extremely expensive. In such cases, which are likely to be common, equity concerns are not easily dismissed and impinge upon the value of the technology not so much to the individuals who receive it as to the *society* as a whole. For while a few may be benefited, socio-economic inequities may be exacerbated. Individuals who

---

[3] Bostrom's description of the privileged may be overly optimistic, since he assumes that enhancements will include positive and non-threatening characteristics. It seems just as (or more) likely to me that the "genetically privileged" would be more aggressive, not self-deprecating, determined to compete, not just relaxed, and very self-oriented rather than empathic.

have benefited from an enhancement technology may well be able to make better use of their education, or obtain more rewarding jobs, or live healthier lives, than those individuals who have not had access to the technologies. It therefore behoves those who argue in favour of the use of enhancement technologies to show, first, that they are aware of all the ways in which inequity might be reinforced or increased by the use of such technologies, and second, that distribution and access can be set up so that traditionally disadvantaged groups are not further marginalized by the technologies.

To take my example of human longevity, people who are poor and disadvantaged—and these are disproportionately people of color and aboriginal people—have a shorter life expectancy than those who are well-off and not disadvantaged by racism. Males also have shorter life expectancies. For instance, a male infant born in the USA in 2002 could be expected to live to the age of 75.1 if he was white, but only 68.8 if he was black. Comparable figures for female infants are 80.3 and 75.6, respectively (Arias 2004, 3). And because members of racialized groups are, on average, poorer than members of white groups, black males and females are less likely to have access to any technologies that would overcome these life-span liabilities. If life enhancement technologies are available only to the wealthy and privileged, then it is likely that the life expectancy differences between members of different racial categories and different socio-economic groups will be increased, and whites will live even longer than blacks. This observation suggests that if (as I assume) increases in life span are worthwhile, and a safe and effective technology is available to produce them, then the technology should not be available only to the wealthy people who can pay for it. As Bostrom suggests, one of the ways of counteracting inequality-increasing tendencies of enhancement technologies is to subsidize it or provide it free to children of poor parents (Bostrom 2004, 503).

But what if, instead, we deny the technology equally, to everyone? Wouldn't that at least be fair? Some bioethicists have argued at length that no special efforts, including the provision of life-extension technologies, should be made to extend the life spans of existing human beings. Thus, for example, Daniel Callahan claims, "All organisms have a life cycle.... While medicine has succeeded in changing some aspects of the human life cycle, that cycle remains a fundamental of human life as of all other life. With further thought and refinement in the context of present knowledge, the life cycle can serve as the *natural* foundation of a sustainable medicine" (Callahan 1998, 130, my emphasis). Unfortunately, this "naturalistic" approach entrenches inequalities based on class, race, and sex, because it fails to sufficiently recognize the significant life-span differences that result from membership in different social categories.

Biomedical ethicists who oppose increasing the human life span argue that with current life expectancies, individuals already are able to live complete lives, so that their ending at the current life expectancy is not an evil (Callahan 1998, 130–5; see also Hardwig 2000). Callahan claims that the average life expectancy that is now achieved in developed nations is sufficient to constitute a full life (Callahan 1998, 253). The existing life-span framework that is now provided by "nature," he says, is "perfectly adequate for human life, both collectively and individually" (Callahan 1998, 134). What is a full life? Callahan claims that it is an existence in which "one's life possibilities have on the whole been accomplished" (Callahan 1987, 66).

But is it the case that current life expectancies enable everyone to realize their "life possibilities"? This question brings us to the second way in which the identities human beings have by virtue of their membership in broad social categories have implications for the ethics of human enhancement.

The effects of social category membership on the meaning and value of life enhancements

Peter Singer points out that there is an important question as to what constitutes an enhancement: "Judgments about what goods we ought to promote will raise fundamental value questions that will not be easy to resolve" (this volume, p. 288). As examples, he suggests that some people might oppose the enhancement of intelligence on the grounds that it is not compatible with belief in God. And others might support an enhancement that made sexual fidelity more likely.

Notice that the individual and social meaning of such proposed enhancements would depend not only on individual and social values (whether, for example, you value belief in God more than the capacity for higher education), but also on the identity of the individuals to whom the enhancements are offered. Social oppression affects who one is, and whether and to what extent one can be benefited or harmed by enhancement or by withholding enhancement. What an (ostensible) enhancement *means* and whether and to what extent one benefits depend in part on one's identity. If, for example, the sexual fidelity enhancement is offered only to women (or perhaps works only for women), then it could work to (heterosexual) women's disadvantage, since they would be genetically programmed for loyalty to one man, whereas many men would be seeking multiple sexual relationships.

Various life stages and events, including youth, maturation, reproduction, illness, and death, also have different meanings depending on to which social category one belongs. The evil of death, for example, is not a simple function of the length of the life that is lived, and the strength of the entitlement to life is not inversely related to years lived. For, *contra* the opponents of life-span enhancement, we cannot assume that an old person, despite his or her age, has already enjoyed his or her fair share of life's goods.

In an article entitled "Death's Gender" (1999), James Lindemann Nelson contests the work of philosophers such as Daniel Callahan and Norman Daniels, who, he says, assume that "death's significance is, in the general case, a function of age alone" (Nelson 1999, 116). This purported "super-fact"—"a fact that characterizes a set of people in a manner so relevant to distribution of goods or assignment of duties that none of their other traits, nor any of the traits of potential claimants not in that group can, singly or in combination, defeat its dispositive relevance" (Nelson 1999, 116)—erases the significance for death of ethnicity, class, and gender. Rejecting this supposed superfact, Nelson states, "Different facts about death affect different people at different times in different ways" (Nelson 1999, 119). He argues convincingly that death itself is gendered, that "widely spread social understandings can contribute to the ways in which death is taken to be a harm," and that "one's place in a social structure can also affect the ways in which death is taken to be harmful". Death, he says, "is altered according to one's position in the system of class differences, and . . . it alters with one's position in the system of gender differences" (Nelson 1999, 117, 118, 124, emphasis in original removed).[4]

Nora Kizer Bell makes a comparable suggestion. She says, "There might be differences in the definition of 'natural life span' or one's perception of a 'tolerable death' that are gender-relative" (Bell 1992, 85; cf. 87). "The argument in favor of believing that there is an appropriate time in a person's

---

[4] I should acknowledge that while I find Nelson's idea of the gendering of death enormously useful, I draw different conclusions from it than Nelson does.

biography for claiming that her life could be considered full strikes me as advancing recognized forms of male bias: both a gender *devaluation of women's concerns* and *an indifference to a woman's 'life possibilities' apart from her abasement into more servile positions*" (Bell 1992, 85, her emphasis). The existence of gendered expectations about women's biological and cultural roles makes it less likely that women will have had a full human life than men may have had, and more likely that the quality of their lives may be lower than those of men (Bell 1992, 86).

It is therefore a mistake to think that it can only be young people who have not yet had the opportunity to enjoy the goods of human life. While the shorter one's life, the less one is likely to have experienced, it does not follow that a long life inevitably means a fuller life. As Anita Silvers points out, such a belief falsely assumes the existence of "a fair social system with a level playing field" (Silvers 1999, 217). But not all older people have received or experienced the things for which we automatically believe young people should have the opportunity. Older women, older people of color, and older persons with disabilities, despite their age, may very well not have benefited from their sheer quantity of life, and therefore are in no way necessarily advantaged as compared to young people. As a result of poverty, racial discrimination, or sexism, many elderly people have been deprived of material comforts, good health care, education, travel, fulfilling work, access to the arts and sciences, and so on.

So if the absence of opportunity to experience these things makes a longer life particularly of value to the young, it should equally make a longer life of value to many who are old—perhaps even the majority of elderly people worldwide. We cannot assume that two people of equally advanced age have both necessarily experienced all of life's goods and should be ready to die. There may be big differences between, for example, a poor seventy-five-year-old aboriginal woman and a wealthy seventy-five-year-old white woman in terms of the experiences they have had, the education and work to which they have had access, the nutrition and health care they have received, the sexual health and reproductive services they have been offered, and the respect and support they have been accorded.

It follows, then, that technologies for life-span extension will mean different things to people in different groups. The meaning of death is gendered. It is also inflected by race, by socio-economic status, and by health status. For those who have been disadvantaged and not able to live a full life, technologies of life extension could have a far greater effect than for those who have been privileged and whose life was full.

Policy implications

I have argued that those who favour the use of enhancement technologies must show, first, that they are aware of all the ways in which inequity might be reinforced or increased by the use of such technologies, and second, that distribution and access can be arranged so that traditionally disadvantaged groups are not further marginalized by the technologies. I turn now to the social policy implications of this claim with respect to the particular case I have chosen, the extension of the human life span.

We know that average life expectancy varies considerably among different social groupings. So *prima facie*, if there is an effective, low-risk process for extending the human life span, it should be used, at least in the short run, to increase the average life expectancy of members of groups that historically have been disadvantaged and that currently have low life expectancy. At the very least, equity would seem to require that, as far as possible, the life-span liabilities encountered by members of disadvantaged groups such as those who are poor and targeted by racial discrimination should be eliminated or at least reduced. Doing so means focusing upon the ways in which social policy might help not just individuals but entire groups.

This policy prescription for special attention to disadvantaged groups raises the interesting question as to whether the lower life expectancy of men should also be targeted. Richard Posner writes that a possible argument against directing resources to efforts to increase men's longevity is that governments should not attempt to "offset natural differences between the sexes" (Posner 1995, 274).[5] But if men do indeed suffer an "inherent" disadvantage, it is morally objectionable to disadvantage them further by refusing to reduce it when a remedy is possible.

I have also argued in this chapter that what an (ostensible) enhancement *means* and whether and to what extent one benefits depend in part on one's

---

[5] Of course, differences are never merely "natural," and men's relatively low life expectancy is substantially shaped by social practices including risk-taking, smoking, alcoholism, unprotected sex, and drug abuse (Perls and Silver 1999, 90). Elsewhere I have argued that it is urgent to take public health steps to diminish the impact of these factors (Overall 2003).

identity. Even if some members of disadvantaged social groups (women, for example) manage to live a long life, the nature of that life might be more impoverished than that of privileged people, and therefore both death, and a longer life, would have different meanings to them. Therefore, having already lived a long life does not necessarily make one less entitled to life extension technology. If by virtue of his or her membership in an oppressed group a person has been disadvantaged, then s/he must not be further deprived through the society's failure to recognize his or her special need for a longer life in which some of the deficits might be made up.

Nor, in addition, must elderly people "earn" an entitlement to an extended life through care of and service to others (as women are often expected to do), the provision of "wisdom" and support to others, or the willingness to enact any other social stereotype of the "good" old person. As Caplan points out, no one feels that people must "earn" laser surgery to enhance their vision. "Life is full of many pleasures that are not earned by testing our limits but which are fully and thoroughly enjoyed" (Caplan, this volume, p. 206). An increased life span should not have to be earned.

But while there is no case to be made here for meritocratic justice with respect to members of disadvantaged groups, there may be an issue of compensatory justice. That is, when it comes to life enhancement technologies, we may have some obligations to *compensate* for the social lottery that makes some group memberships a liability. We must consider the possibility that social policy with respect to life enhancement should not only be a matter of creating more equal opportunities, but possibly also a matter of redressing harms by providing appropriate compensations.[6] We might well have more of an obligation to provide life span enhancement to members of some groups than to members of others.

Silvers remarks,

On the 'fair life's share' argument, older persons who have been wronged as a result of their membership in groups misperceived as weak and incompetent now should be offered *more* opportunity than members of present and past dominant classes. For example, as women belong to a class disadvantaged by being considered, until very

---

[6] Callahan points out that the reform of health care to ensure that members of disadvantaged groups receive health care at an earlier time in life is preferable to providing after-the-fact compensation (Callahan 1999, 194). I agree entirely. Here, however, I am discussing people who have *not* in fact received earlier advantages. The question is, what is owed to them? And I am suggesting it would be just to provide compensation in the form of longer life.

recently, to be incapable and dependent, and thereby to be unsuitable recipients of the full range of competitive opportunities, the 'fair life's share' argument suggests that aged women be compensated by receiving *greater* support for actualizing their opportunities to flourish than is afforded to both young and old men (Silvers 1999, 217, emphasis added).[7]

Silvers may intend these comments to be ironic. Still, I think we should take seriously the ethical possibility that, if an effective low-risk technology for the extension of human life were discovered, society would have a particular obligation to ensure that it is available, if wanted, to those who, even if they otherwise have had a "normal" life span, nonetheless have been deprived or disadvantaged during their lifetime. The reason is that life is the precondition for any other good.[8] If society has collective obligations to individuals who have suffered because of oppression—and I think it does—then the only way to meet those obligations, for those who are already nearing the end of their life, is by offering them the opportunity to extend their life.

Speaking of providing health care for elderly women, Callahan objects, "to benefit one sex unilaterally while ignoring another unilaterally would surely result in unjust results in many cases" (Callahan 1999, 198). Indeed. My point is that under current circumstances, the reality is that the elderly members of some groups (particularly those who are poor, people of color, and women) have to at least some degree been ignored "unilaterally" when social goods were distributed. Therefore, society owes persons in these groups more than it owes to members of groups not similarly ignored or disadvantaged.

Conclusion

In this chapter I have defended several claims. First, the ethics of life enhancement (and the social policies that govern life enhancement technologies) must take into account the effects of social category identities.

---

[7] Similarly, feminists Hilde Lindemann Nelson and James Lindemann Nelson explicitly call for gender-based distinctions in health care interventions near the end of life, partly in order to correct for "the sexism that has trammeled their [women's] opportunities for self-development" (Nelson and Nelson 1996, 362).

[8] I set aside the possibility that there may also be some things that are good for an individual (for example, a long-lasting reputation or fame) that exist even after the person's death. (Individuals who have had a life of deprivation are unlikely to acquire them anyway.)

Second, one's membership in social categories of sex, race, and socio-economic class largely determines whether or not one has access to the benefits of life enhancement and whether or not one can pay the costs of these technologies. Third, what an (ostensible) enhancement *means* and whether and to what extent one benefits from it depend in part on one's social category membership. Therefore, those who favour the use of enhancement technologies must show two things: first, that they are aware of all the ways in which inequity might be reinforced or increased by the use of such technologies and second, that distribution and access can be set up so that traditionally disadvantaged groups are not further marginalized by the technologies. Equity may well require that life enhancement technologies be used, as far as possible, to eliminate or at least reduce the liabilities encountered by members of disadvantaged groups such as those who are poor and targeted by racial discrimination. And there may in some cases be a further responsibility to use life enhancement technologies to compensate for harms resulting from oppression based on social category membership.

References

Arias, Elizabeth. 2004. "United States Life Tables 2002". National Vital Statistics Reports, http://www.cdc.gov/nchs/data/nvsr/nvsr53/nvsr53_06.pdf (accessed January 17, 2006).

Baylis, Françoise, and Robert, Jason Scott. 2004. "The Inevitability of Genetic Enhancement Technologies". In *Health Care Ethics in Canada*, 2nd edn., ed. Françoise Baylis, Jocelyn Downie, Barry Hoffmaster, and Susan Sherwin (Toronto: Thomson Nelson), 448–60.

Bell, Nora Kizer. 1992. "If Age Becomes a Standard for Rationing Health Care...". In *Feminist Perspectives in Medical Ethics*, ed. Helen Bequaert Holmes and Laura M. Purdy (Bloomington, Indiana: Indiana University Press), 82–90.

Bostrom, Nick. 2004. "Human Genetic Enhancements: A Transhumanist Perspective", *The Journal of Value Inquiry* 37: 493–506.

Callahan, Daniel. 1987. *Setting Limits: Medical Goals in an Aging Society* (New York: Simon & Schuster).

—— 1998. *False Hopes: Why America's Quest for Perfect Health is a Recipe for Failure* (New York: Simon & Schuster).

—— 1999. "Age, Sex, and Resource Allocation". In *Mother Time: Women, Aging, and Ethics*, ed. Margaret Urban Walker (Lanham, Maryland: Rowman & Littlefield), 189–99.

Caplan, Arthur. "Good, Better or Best?" Chapter 9, this volume.

Hardwig, John. 2000. *Is There a Duty to Die? And Other Essays in Medical Ethics*. With Nat Hentoff, Dan Callahan, Larry Churchill, Felicia Cohn and Joanne Routledge).

Kamm, Frances. 'What Is and Is Not Wrong With Enhancement?' Chapter 5, this volume.

Nelson, Hilde Lindemann, and Nelson, James Lindemann. 1996. "Justice in the Allocation of Health Care Resources: A Feminist Account". In *Feminism and Bioethics: Beyond Reproduction*, ed. Susan M. Wolfe (New York: Oxford University Press), 351–70.

Nelson, James Lindemann. 1999. "Death's Gender". In *Mother Time: Women, Aging, and Ethics*, ed. Margaret Urban Walker (Lanham, Maryland: Rowman & Littlefield), 113–29.

Overall, Christine. 2003. *Aging, Death, and Human Longevity: A Philosophical Inquiry* (Berkely, California: University of California Press).

———2006. "Old Age and Ageism, Impairment and Ableism: Exploring the Conceptual and Material Connections". In *National Women's Studies Association Journal*—Special Issue on Aging, Ageism, and Old Age, 18:126–37.

Perls, Thomas T., and Silver, Margery Hutter. 1999. *Living to 100: Lessons in Living to Your Maximum Potential at Any Age* (New York: Basic Books).

Posner, Richard A. 1995. *Aging and Old Age* (Chicago: University of Chicago Press).

Sandel, Michael. 2004. "The Case Against Perfection". *The Atlantic Monthly*. April.

Silvers, Anita. 1999. "Aging Fairly: Feminist and Disability Perspectives on Intergenerational Justice". In *Mother Time: Women, Aging, and Ethics*, ed. Margaret Urban Walker (Lanham, Maryland: Rowman & Littlefield), 203–26.

Singer, Peter. "Parental Choice and Human Improvement". Chapter 12, this volume.

16

Paternalism in the Age of Cognitive Enhancement: Do Civil Liberties Presuppose Roughly Equal Mental Ability?

*Daniel Wikler**

1. Introduction

Advances in genetics and biotechnology may enable scientists to augment our cognitive powers. If this does become feasible, it is virtually certain that many people will want this kind of intervention for their children, or indeed if it proves feasible, for themselves.

Perhaps the maximum enhancement will be minor, say a 5 to 10 per cent increase in memory capacity, ability to concentrate, or speed of calculation. Some of us can achieve performance enhancements of this magnitude now, with training, coffee, or a good night's sleep. If many people achieved these gains, they might be more productive, and perhaps fewer accidents would occur. The aggregate benefit might be impressive. But their effect on our social institutions and relationships would be minor or non-existent.

But what if science will enable human beings, or at least some human beings, to be vastly smarter, passing by Einstein toward presently un-imaginable heights. We would certainly notice these changes.

It would make a difference if everyone in that future society were much more intelligent than we are, or if only some were. I would like to focus on a society in which only some people achieve this enhancement. Perhaps the

* Mary B. Saltonstall Professor of Ethics and Population Health, Harvard School of Public Health.

enhancement is expensive, and not all can afford it; or perhaps the technique for enhancing intelligence doesn't work with every candidate. Whatever the reason for making substantial cognitive enhancement less than universal, we should be prepared to face a difficult social problem; a potential threat to civil liberties. What once was "normal" intelligence might not be sufficient to navigate the society that the cognitively-enhanced create for themselves. The implications of this development for self-determination on the part of the un-enhanced may be dire.

2. A brief look backward: the eugenicists' concerns about intelligence

A neo-Nazi writer named Roger Pearson followed the Human Genome Program with great interest.[1] Pearson understood the Human Genome project to vindicate his racist and eugenic vision of society and social problems. The Genome Project would finally demonstrate, he thought, that people are *not* created equal, that some are much more gifted than others, and that the substrate for these differences are inherited (he also believed that they clustered along racial lines). And he took this to be an unanswerable refutation of egalitarianism.

Pearson's argument has a glaring flaw: egalitarians need not, and do not, assume or argue that everyone has the same intellectual capacity. The point of egalitarianism is to ensure that people do equally well, or have the same opportunities to do well, given the talents they are born with and those that they can acquire.

So of what interest is Pearson, or rather the kind of view he espouses, after all?

One reason is that if it becomes possible to increase the intelligence of appreciable numbers of our fellow-citizens, this development will inevitably

---

[1] Pearson is somewhat more interesting than other Neo-Nazis, *inter alia* because of his financial backing from the Pioneer Fund, a small but very controversial foundation whose research program was originally directed by the head of the Carnegie Institute's Eugenics Record Office, and because he later was included on the editorial board of *Policy Review*, the journal of the Republican-affiliated Heritage Foundation. See his *Heredity and Humanity: Race, Eugenics and Modern Science* (Washington: Scott-Townsend Publishers, 1996); "The concept of heredity in Western thought: Part two, the myth of biological egalitarianism," *Mankind Quarterly*, 35, 343−71 (1995) and Part three, "The revival of interest in genetics", *Mankind Quarterly*, 36, 73−98 (1995).

bring to mind the old eugenics movement and the calamities it brought about, and we will need to think whether this precedent has anything to teach us in our new venture. Indeed the Human Genome Project has already proven to be a stimulus for this kind of reflection.

Eugenics was not one movement, but many, and eugenicists varied considerably in both their methods and their goals.[2] In the UK, where Galton gave birth to eugenics, its advocates urged voluntary changes in mating patterns. In the US and Germany, involuntary sterilization ensued. In the Anglo-Saxon and Germanic countries, the focus was on who gets born, the "quality" of the population; while in France and Brazil, the movement was as concerned with healthy deliveries and child-rearing. It was a fractious, unorganized movement of cranks and scientists, Nazis, racists, feminists, democrats, and communists. Galton was concerned with breeding genius, and the British version generally was preoccupied with the caste of social class; while in Kansas and Arkansas, prizes were handed out at state fairs for "Fittest Family", alongside the prizes for best cow and best pig, to very ordinary farming people.

For all the disagreements over both means and ends within the eugenics movement, the historical record reveals a continuing preoccupation with one theme, and that is low intelligence (or "feeblemindedness", to use their stock phrase). The inherited stupidity of the genetic underclass[3] led these people, by one pathway or another, to their multiple antisocial transgressions. These people were "shiftless", lazy, immoral, menacing, and lecherous (and, partly as a result, unusually fertile). Not all eugenicists blamed every social problem and individual failing on cognitive deficits, but this hardy theme has survived even into recent times. The authors of the neo-eugenic tome, *The Bell Curve*,[4] intimated that the reason that the genetic underclass in America did not adopt proper middle-class morals was that morality is not easy to grasp and they simply did not have the mental capacity for it.

---

[2] Diane Paul's historical research has emphasized the heterogeneity of views within the eugenics movement, especially with regard to themes such as state coercion that are often associated with the eugenics movement as a whole. See her *Controlling Human Heredity* (Atlantic Highlands, NJ: Humanities Press, 1995) and *The Politics of Heredity: Essays on Eugenics, Biomedicine, and the Nature–Nurture Debate* (State University of New York Press, 1998).

[3] Diane Paul, "Chapter 4: The Menace of the Moron," in her *Controlling Human Heredity: 1865 to the Present* (Atlantic Highlands, N.J.: Humanities Press, 1995), 50–71.

[4] Richard Herrnstein and Charles Murray, *The Bell Curve: Intelligence and Class Structure in American Life* (Glencoe: Free Press, 1994).

What follows from this understanding of the problem—whatever "problem" it was that for which eugenics was supposed to be the answer—was that this country badly needed a smarter population. The eugenicists, of course, could not dream of intervening at the level of molecular biology. Their interventions were crude and barely effective, as the best-educated and candid eugenicists acknowledged. All they could do was to ask the fit to mate more often, preferably with each other, and try to prevent the unfit from mating at all. Worse, they had no way of identifying who might be carrying recessive genes that would poison the next generation, and who were presumably much more numerous than the people who failed the newly-devised IQ test and who, thus identified as genetically compromised, could be handed over to authorities for sterilization. The prospect of direct intervention on genes to increase intelligence would, we can speculate, have put them into orbit—unless all the talk of eugenics was just a cover story for committing violence on a class of people they did not like.

We take comfort in being far more enlightened than these pseudo-scientific zealots. We know that social problems stem largely from social failings and that the link between genes and behavior is in most cases indirect, complex, mediated, and nonspecific. But in fact some of the old controversy animates us. In debates over race, nothing is as germane and as incendiary as the belief, spoken or unspoken, that blacks are not as smart as whites. Though we all should know that (*pace* Pearson) egalitarianism does not rest on the assumption that everyone has the same cognitive capacity, the notion of inherited differences in capacity is widely assumed to be anathema to egalitarians and the left. Anti-racists and other egalitarians have been motivated to argue strenuously about IQ and its alleged heritability. Granted, Gould, in writing *The Mismeasure of Man*,[5] had no shortage of good targets. But in the debates over genes and intelligence, whether in connection with *The Bell Curve* or more broadly with sociobiology and twin studies, it is apparent that many scholars are moved to defend one side or the other by their political outlook. As we consider the prospects for intervening on the biochemical substrate of intelligence, especially if the resulting enhancement of that will be heritable, we might restimulate some of these controversies. This is especially the case if the enhancements will be extended, even if only at first, on a less than universal basis.

---

[5] Stephen Jay Gould, *The Mismeasure of Man* (New York: Norton Publishers, 1995).

3. Intelligence and civil liberties in the pre-genomic and post-enhancement eras

While distancing ourselves from Pearson's insistence that egalitarianism will crumble once we learn that people are not born equal, it should not escape our notice that there is at least one important respect in which unequal social status—a social fact—does seem to track unequal biological capacity for intelligence. We routinely restrict the freedom of people who are judged to be insufficiently intelligent to handle their own affairs. These are people who are classified as moderately retarded and who are found to be incompetent in respect to essential skills. In a humane society, their needs are met by caring family members or guardians, supported by government. Enlighted competency laws selectively permit the restriction of rights and liberties to be keyed to the abilities and challenges each faces as an individual rather than across the board. A person might, for example, have the right to buy her own clothes, but not to make long-term financial decisions.

We are used to this practice and it is uncontroversial, but I believe we can learn something by asking for its justification. In a paper I published some time ago,[6] I asked the reader to choose between two quite different accounts. These corresponded to two different notions of competence. A "relativist" account of competence points to the relative difference in intellectual ability between average people and the moderately retarded and to the corresponding (probable) difference in favorable outcomes of key decisions when made by the two categories of people. A rule of thumb is that people perceive others as mentally inferior—that is, they come to explain observed differences in function and behavior as stemming from differences in intellectual capacity—when their IQs differ by two standard deviations or more (about 28 IQ points). This perception occurs in the encounter between a person of average intelligence and someone who is very smart, just as it occurs between an average person and someone who has been (correctly) classified as mild or moderately retarded. For the relativist, the distinction between "smart" and "dull" applies equally well to either pairing, and so too for the boundary between those deemed competent and those judged incompetent.

---

[6] Daniel Wikler, "Paternalism and the Mildly Retarded," *Philosophy and Public Affairs*, 8(4): 377–92, 1979.

A second view, I argued, saw competence as what Rawls called a "range property", i.e, a property that is possessed in equal measure by all who possessed it. According to this view, what determines that one person is incompetent and the other competent is not the relative difference between them in respect to intelligence, but rather on which side of an absolute threshold their intellectual capacities fall. In this perspective, what matters is that one has the kinds of abilities typical of a person with, say, approximately 90 IQ points and who is otherwise sane and well balanced. I re-emphasize that the threshold should be expected to vary with the task, and a person judged competent for one task might be judged to require guardianship for another. Still, in respect to each of these competencies, there would, in this view, have to be a threshold. Above the thresholds, all are equally competent.

Each of these views has both problems and advantages. To summarize a fairly complex matter, the relativist view needs fewer suppositions and assumptions about the somewhat mysterious threshold of competence; it points to relative differences, each measurable in an objective, standard (if disputed) way. But it is vulnerable to a follow-up question: if the relative difference between average people and the mildly or moderately retarded person justifies steps by the former to curtail the liberties of the latter—for his or her own good, of course—would the same consideration not justify similar action by a much smarter-than-average person vis-à-vis the average person? This would not necessarily be a pure hypothetical, if the gap in question is merely the least perceivable difference, i.e. two standard deviations in IQ. But even if the gap would have to be much greater, the hypothetical is troubling. Is this all that it take to justify lifting our rights to control our lives—just the assumption that a much smarter person could do a better job of it than we are doing?

The conception of competence as a range property has complementary attributes. It would not make paternalism so easy to justify, as the relativist view seems to do. We prize our powers to make decisions, come what may, even though others might do a better job. On this absolute understanding of competence we would retain these rights even if we encountered people so very bright that they would likely do a much better job than we are now doing, even assuming that they took our interests to heart. Of course, we would be at liberty to consult with them, and to ask them for their advice, but in the end it would be our decision whether to follow it. And if we come to grief because we reject the advice of people more intelligent than we are, then this is an eventuality for which we take full responsibility, without regret.

So far so good for the absolute view. But what considerations make it reasonable for us to insist on making key life decisions on our own? An adequate answer to this question cannot be given (if at all) in passing, but we can consider some of the standard candidates. First, no one else has the right to intervene, whether for good reasons or otherwise. Second, we learn—not only practical lessons but also what life is all about—from the mistakes we make, and if Big Brother keeps intervening to keep us out of harm's way, we cannot mature, improve, and deepen. Third, Big Brothers have proven to be not so wise after all, and certainly not consistently beneficent. In particular, it does not follow from the fact that one person is intellectually superior to another that the former would make decisions on behalf of the latter that would be better for the latter. Good decisions require not only insight but also compassion, sensitivity, maturity, and practicality—all of which may be lacking in an exceptionally smart person, as readers of this chapter no doubt know from personal experience.

Do these considerations, singly or in combination, justify our insistence on remaining free to err? The first asserts a right, but it does not provide the rationale for insisting on this right. Perhaps we assert a right against well-intentioned intervention because, in our own experience, we have done better than such intervenors, either personally or collectively. Perhaps in a brave new world of the cognitively enhanced (save for our small band of previously normal, now subnormal unenhanced ones), these rights seem less self-evident; perhaps they seem less to indicate sound political philosophy than flaws in judgment and character. Perhaps the second defense—that we learn by error—should be understood as our advice to the cognitively enhanced on what kind of intervention is most likely to benefit us. If we're right, they will grasp this and we will be permitted some opportunities to err, just as wise parents refrain from being overprotective while maintaining a discreet safety net under their young children. In this light, this second consideration counts as advice on how the cognitively enhanced should intervene, not as a defense against their doing so. The third consideration—the sorry record of those who insisted that they knew better what was good for adults who had the cognitive capacities that our minority retains in the new society of the cognitively-enhanced—fails for obvious reasons. These are not the bumbling do-gooders and bureaucrats of old, but greatly enhanced supermen who really are much smarter than we are. And even if, collectively, they are no more likely to exceed in non-cognitive dimensions of good decision-making, their intellectual superiority gives them a crucial advantage.

Before the age of cognitive enhancement, we "normals" are used to thinking that we generally do fairly well for ourselves. It is the moderately retarded—those who have enough capacity to formulate and assert preferences but who lack the mental equipment to guide their lives without coming to grief—who need help. But perhaps this sense of confidence is wishful thinking. We need only to look around us to see how much improvement there could be over the way that average, or even somewhat better than average people run things. Marriages fail, people do not save for their retirement, and voters elect manifestly inferior candidates. The recent flourishing of behavioral economics as a field research stems from abundant evidence of the gap between the ideal rationality of *homo economicus* and real human consumers and other decision-makers. If there were people much brighter than we, who had our interests at heart, things could go much better were they to make our decisions for us.

It might appear that we "normals" could retreat just a bit and still win the argument by claiming that the cognitive level of our newly-subnormal minority was and remains sufficient for us to know when we need help and advice from experts. We needn't know everything or be supreme geniuses to get by if we have knowledgeable geniuses to call upon for advice and help. In this view, our relative cognitive deficit vis-à-vis the newly enhanced does not render us incompetent. Indeed, precisely the opposite: the advent of techniques for enhancing cognition may have been denied to us, but it placed in our midst beings whose advice and assistance will prove to be more valuable than that of the accountants, marriage counselors, and psychotherapists we had been used to consulting. Like computers or the internet, the cognitively-enhanced thus enhance our own cognitive powers, even though our inherent cognitive abilities remain unchanged. We may be less clever than our newly-enhanced fellow-citizens, but we have sufficient cognitive capacity to manage our own affairs. If we mess things up, it will not be because of a lack of insight, or insufficient memory, or slow data processing—each a symptom of our cognitive inferiority. The problem is more likely to be arrogance or pride, if these vices result in our refusing to consult experts or to comply with their advice. Or perhaps we fail because we are rash, or immature, or self-destructive. We are just as prone to these vices as our cognitively-enhanced superiors. All of us, brilliant and dull alike, can be brought low through defects of character. The only advantage that our enhanced fellow-citizens have over us normals, according to this defense of civil liberties for the unenhanced, is that they need not seek out consultants. Assuming that we normals will get help when we need it and ask for it, our capacity to make good choices will remain in the same league as our smarter neighbors, and we need not cede any of our liberties to them in order to protect our own wellbeing.

This defense against paternalistic intervention by the cognitively-enhanced contains some truths (the unenhanced *would* have more expert experts to consult) but it does not succeed. If we always knew when we needed help or advice, then having experts around might suffice. Unfortunately, it takes insight to know when you don't know. Those who do not understand how little they understand are the most obvious of fools. The cognitively-enhanced would realize much sooner than we would that we were out of our depth and required their help. True, temperament is also a factor: some will gladly seek advice and follow it, while others spurn help at their peril. But these personality traits come into play only when we come to appreciate that we are in need of advice. If we are blissfully ignorant of the fact (when it is a fact) that we are ignorant, then it is pointless to invoke flaws of character in explaining our insistence of keeping our own counsel.

4. The Fairness and the Utility of Incompetence

The argument thus far stems from an initial distinction between two accounts of mental competence: a relativist view that likens our position vis-à-vis the cognitively enhanced to the position of the moderately retarded living among us; and a threshold view according to which the amount of cognitive capacity that most of us possess in the pre-enhancement age is sufficient for each sane adult to insist on a right to make key life decisions free of intervention from others. These seem to point to different justifications of the rights we assert in this, our current, pre-enhancement era, to make our most important decisions with no more help from others than we solicit. It is not clear that either could sustain this stance in an era in which most of our neighbors become cognitively enhanced. Thus far, neither seems to offer a secure foundation for a right to be left alone. But the worst is yet to come. Through further reflection on the social context in which ascriptions of mental competence are used to counter paternalism, a deeper problem comes into view. Liberty for the unenhanced would place a burden on their more clever fellow-citizens, one that might not be fair to them.[7]

To see this, let us recall the notion of mental competence as a range property. Some tasks can be handled equally well, or almost so, by people of widely divergent abilities. Grocery stores, for example, use bags that hold only so many products; the vast majority of people can walk away with two of these without difficulty. Building codes require that risers on stairs be no more than a certain height, again matching human capabilities at something like low-average capacity. Very strong people, or people with a long gait, can carry the grocery bags and climb the stairs, but, in ordinary circumstances,[8] not with noticeably less difficulty than average people. We make bags and staircases with these facts in mind. Indeed, much of our social environment is created to achieve some kind of desirable balance between utility—a multiplicity of tiny grocery bags would be a nuisance to everyone except tiny or very weak people, and the same is true for stairs with one-inch risers—and inclusion. By requiring only so much capacity, we make our society accessible to the vast majority of its members. We sacrifice some utility, especially for those with excess capability, i.e., talent that is not used because we place the bar so low. But efficiency is not our only goal.[9]

Something of the same story can be told about intellectual demands, too. The original idea behind Form 1040 of the United States Internal Revenue Service—an idea now lost in the mists of time, unfortunately—was that one did not have to be a genius or an accountant to use it to determine how much one owed by way of taxes. Directions on a power saw or even a bottle of pills are supposed to be simple enough for nearly

---

[7] The analysis that follows draws on Wikler, "Paternalism and the Mildly Retarded".

[8] People of average strength might struggle in carrying standard grocery bags if they have to carry them long distances (as an anonymous referee has pointed out) but this is the kind of circumstance not taken into account in deciding how big these bags should be.

[9] Occasionally we discover win-win compromises, such as curb cuts that make cities navigable for the wheelchair-bound without noticeably compromising the utility of curbs.

everyone to read them with sufficient comprehension to avoid injury. The sum of the outcomes of these attempts to balance utility for the majority with protection for the less-able yields a social definition of competence.

Seen in this light, both the relative and the absolute conceptions of competence capture part of the truth. At the lowest end of the spectrum of cognitive abilities, there is indeed an absolute threshold. Those incapable of language, for example, cannot comprehend the options between which they would have to choose. But there is considerable space above that line in which a person's status as competent or not depends on social arrangements. Those whose intellectual capacities put them in this zone could be made competent if society set its demands low enough. It is often observed that mildly or even moderately retarded people do not seem dull to themselves or others as long as they stay on the farm (rather: certain farms), but become so immediately when they move to the city. Here the relative difference between a dull or not-very-bright minority and the majority who are just below average, or better, becomes important, and as that majority arranges society to suit themselves, their less-bright peers become incompetent. When they do, then in respect to a host of tasks that are central to everyday living, everyone but the less-bright people are fully competent. Those who are rendered incompetent in this manner need supervision, and in order to protect them in that now-dangerous environment, their rights are taken away. Humane regimes strive to protect as much of their range of free choice as possible, consistent with the need to protect them from serious or irremediable harm (and to protect others), but there is no supposition that everyone has a natural, inalienable right to self-determination that would rule out all configurations of the social and physical environment that are disadvantageous to the less-talented. Those who are made incompetent, so that society can be organized by rules and other conventions that have great utility but require high ability, do not have the full status of free citizens, sovereign in their own affairs and sharing equally in general governance.

This observation does not quite settle the debate between the relative and the threshold views of intellectual competence, for it does not prove that competence is a range property in every task. Still, for a number of key decisions that adults must make to protect their own well-being, it seems undeniable that very able or very well-informed people can do much better than others. If they were asked to take control of those others' key life decisions, such as household budgeting or saving for retirement, they could do a better job (assuming of course that they had the interests of their less able or less well-informed fellow citizens at heart and that they did not suffer unduly from deficits in decision-making talents apart from intelligence).

5. When intelligence diverges

Robert Nozick posed the hypothetical question: what if a super-smart race or tribe arrived on the scene?[10] And this is our question, too, put to a different use. In my earlier paper, I was concerned with the notion of competence that played so important a role in determining which of our fellow humans are granted the status of free and equal citizens, as opposed to incompetents (with respect to specific tasks) for whom decisions must be made by a guardian. As we approach the day when science can make Nozick's hypothetical an actuality, the question becomes important all over again. Suppose that half, or two thirds, of the population moves into the passing lane in intellectual capacity, becoming geniuses (by current standards) and upping the ante in the requirements for civic participation? What becomes of the citizenship, the liberties, the status as equals, of those of us who are merely average? Or even those considered fairly clever by the standards of the *ancien regime*?

Before applying the foregoing discussion to this predicament, here are two observations in passing to link the imagined future of enhanced cognition to the present and the past:

- There are important disparities in cognitive functioning even today, in every country. In many cases these stem from different experience with respect to such determinants as nutrition, environmental pollution, and very different cultural and educational opportunities. These determinants do not track class differences precisely—which is why Harvard's students are brighter now that academic potential is the chief criterion for admission, rather than being a descendant of previous Harvard graduates—but they do have consequences for one's

---

[10] *Anarchy, State, and Utopia* (New York: Basic Books).

eventual placement in the socioeconomic hierarchy. Our concern over the advantages provided by superior education is the motivation for Head Start, the early-intervention program for less-privileged children. Absent a convincing argument that shows that postnatal IQ boosts for the privileged are more objectionable than prenatal IQ boosts for the privileged, the latter should be judged similarly. Good education for all is fine, but good education only for the well-to-do is not.

- As remarked earlier, Pearson was just wrong about egalitarianism's assumptions. It requires no claim, true or false as the case may be, that we all have approximately equal intellectual or other capacities. It is equality of civil status that we're after, and this is consistent with—even celebrates to some extent—the the evident fact of human differences. Why, then do egalitarians get so upset about allegations of innate differences in cognitive capacity? Because they are what *in*egalitarians and racists point to, to justify social class differences, to blame social miseries on the poor, and to deny learning opportunities to those who need them most. Eugenicists in the UK and US believed that the sufferings of the poor and the disadvantage of stigmatized racial and ethnic groups was a result of their inherited cognitive deficits; and for that reason society would do well to ensure that they reproduced less. Sterilization and worse were, in time, the regrettable result. Much recent political philosophy in the US and UK has called for different responses to misfortunes stemming from our free choices ("option luck") and those that just happen to us ("brute luck"); the latter, in this view, call for help at society's expense. For the eugenicists, it did not matter that the hereditarian explanation of the miseries of the lower classes invoked brute luck; that bad luck is what earned them their stigma. Though we would like to think that we live in a more enlightened age, we cannot know whether the cognitively enhanced, in the technologically-advanced society we are imagining, would regard their unenhanced, newly-subnormal brethren with kind concern or with contempt. As Thomas Scanlon noted in his "The Significance of Choice",[11] the right to make one's own choices is a

---

[11] Thomas Scanlon, "The Significance of Choice", The *Tanner Lectures on Human Values*, ed. Sterling M. McMurrin (Salt Lake City: University of Utah Press), 151–216, 1988.

badge of full and equal status in a society like ours. Even if the cognitively-enhanced intervened in the personal affairs of those of us who remained unenhanced, our social status could be undermined.

What, then, would be the effect of selective enhancement of intellectual capacity—that is, enhancement for some, but not all—for the social and political world that we "normals" would inhabit? Would it erode the foundations of egalitarianism, undermining the claims of many who now hold title as citizens to that equal status? Would those made or engineered to be born smart be within their rights to deprive the rest of us of our rights, presumably with humanitarian intent?

In a word: yes. Or, at least, that is what my earlier argument implies, so far as I can see. It would depend in part on circumstances and in part on moral issues:

- First: How many people would get the boost in intellectual capacity? If only a few do, nothing will or should change. But suppose it is a majority.
- Second: Would raising the intellectual bar over our heads (speaking of "we" as people like those writing and reading this chapter) have very substantial benefits for this new majority, while admitting of the possibility of protecting the rest of us through some form of guardianship?
- Third, it depends on our view of distributive justice. If we gave absolute priority to the worst-off, intellectually speaking, we would keep the bar low so that we would be equally competent relative the new intellectual elite. The tasks would be easy enough for us to handle them. Otherwise, if there would be much to gain (for most people, but not all) by raising the bar high, it looks like the arrangement that would most closely mirror our own would be a regime in which we would be excluded from equal citizenship.

That prospect is unpleasant to contemplate. Perhaps I've taken a wrong turn. Is there a threshold of competence that I have not sighted, one that justifies our claim to be autonomous beings, captains of our own fates, regardless of how well some newly-enhanced fellow citizens might do if made our guardians? Do I have the calculation of benefits and burdens wrong? Should we be eternally vigilant and suspicious of people who appoint themselves "guardians", profess humanitarian motives, and then take over our lives?

Or do the shoes just hurt because they would be on *our* feet?[12]

[12] The author is grateful to Dan Brock, Jonathan Glover, Nick Bostrom, Robin Hanson, Philippe Denney, and Michael Sandel for astute comments.

17

Enhancing Our Truth Orientation

Robin Hanson*

Abstract

Humans lie and deceive themselves, and often choose beliefs for reasons other than how closely those beliefs approximate truth. This is mainly why we disagree. Three future trends may reduce these epistemic vices. First, increased documentation and surveillance should make it harder to lie and self-deceive about the patterns of our lives. Second, speculative markets can create a relatively unbiased consensus on most debated topics in science, business, and policy. Third, brain modifications may allow our minds to be more transparent, so that lies and self-deception become harder to hide. In evaluating these trends, we should be wary of moral arrogance.

Self-deception has done us proud. Without it . . . we might still be running naked through the forest. . . . Self-deception was a splendid adaptation in a world populated by nomadic bands armed with sticks and stones. It is no longer such a good option in a world stocked with nuclear and biological weapons. . . . The most dangerous forms of self-deception are the collective ones. Patriotism, moral crusades, and religious fervor sweep across nations like plagues. (Smith, 2004)

People will hold an opinion because they want to keep the company of others who share the opinion, or because they think it is the respectable opinion, or because they have publicly expressed the opinion in the past and would be embarrassed by a "U-turn," or because the world would suit them better if the opinion were true. (Whyte, 2004)

For comments I thank Colleen Berndt, Nick Bostrom, Tyler Cowen, Hal Finney, Peter Kramer, Brett Paatsch, Julian Savulescu, Peter Singer, James Watson, Dan Wikler, and participants of the Transvision 2004 and the Oxford Uehiro Enhancing Humans 2004 conferences. I thank the Oxford Uehiro Center, the Center for Study of Public Choice, the Mercatus Center, and the International Foundation for Research in Experimental Economics for financial support.

* Department of Economics, George Mason University, November 2004 (revised June 2007).

Moral . . . opinions are often the result of self-interest, self-deception, historical and cultural accident, hidden class bias, and so on. (Daniels, 1979)

Introduction

Humans today have many epistemic virtues. We are clever animals who have discovered a vast division of labor, enabling our unprecedented and rapidly increasing power and understanding of science, industry, and more. But we also have many epistemic vices, such as using our knowledge to enable cruelty.

In particular, we often choose beliefs that are not the closest feasible approximation to the truth. By this I do not mean that we fail to spend all possible resources on obtaining or analyzing information. Instead, I mean that our beliefs are biased because we have motivations other than that of approximating truth while conserving resources (Mele, 2001). For example, because we like to think well of ourselves and our groups, we tend to overestimate our abilities and morality, exaggerate our influence, and take credit for our successes while blaming external factors for our failures (Giannetti, 1997).

This sort of self-deception is arguably the main reason humans disagree. It seems that honest truth-seeking agents should not knowingly disagree. Specifically, such agents should not be able to predict how others' future opinions will disagree with their own opinion about which of many possible worlds is the real one. Yet humans clearly do so disagree, especially on abstract topics in business, science, policy, and morality.

Apparently, beliefs are like clothes. In a harsh environment, we choose our clothes mainly to be functional, i.e., to keep us safe and comfortable. But when the weather is mild, we choose our clothes mainly for their appearance, i.e., to show our figure, our creativity, and our allegiances. Similarly, when the stakes are high we may mainly want accurate beliefs to help us make good decisions. But when a belief has few direct personal consequences, we in effect mainly care about the image it helps us to project.

Now admittedly, bias and self-deception do produce many personal and social benefits. For example, by over-estimating our ability we not only attract social allies, we also raise our self-esteem and happiness (Taylor, 1989), and motivate ourselves to excel (Kitcher, 1990). Depressed and mentally-ill people tend to be less self-deceived than others. Nevertheless, bias and self-deception seem to be morally wrong overall and especially dangerous in a world with technologies as powerful as nuclear weapons and genetic engineering.

We humans have been enhancing ourselves for many thousands of years, through nutrition, education, gadgets, and social institutions. In the future we may also directly and substantially change and augment our brains. What are the prospects that these changes will increase our truth-orientation, and decrease our bias and self-deception?

In this chapter, I review the basics of disagreement and self-deception, and then consider three general types of enhancements which may increase our truth-orientation: documentation, idea futures, and mental transparency. Finally, I warn against the danger of moral arrogance when evaluating these trends.

Disagreement

People disagree all the time, and always have. While many specific disagreements do not seem entirely honest, most people believe honest disagreements are both possible and common.

In his most cited paper, Nobel Prize winner Robert Aumann proved in 1976 a remarkable result on "agreeing to disagree." In technical terms, he showed that Bayesians with a common prior and common knowledge of their respective estimates of a random variable must have exactly the same estimates (Aumann, 1976). This result was provocative, but its assumptions seemed too strong to reflect much on human disagreement.

Aumann's result has since been greatly generalized, however. For example, agents need not know, and know that they know, and know that they know that they know, and so on forever with perfect confidence. Instead, agents need only be reasonably sure that they are mutually aware of their disagreement (Monderer and Samet, 1989). Instead of knowing the exact estimates they would each say next, the agents need only be aware of whether one of them thinks another's estimate will be higher or lower at some particular future date (Hanson, 2002).

In place of Bayesians, we need only agents who aspire to be Bayesian, even if they suffer severe computational limitations (Hanson, 2003b). And in place of common priors, the agents need only believe that the process that created their belief tendencies treated them similarly (Hanson, 2006). This analysis applies to any dispute that can be described in terms of which of many possible worlds is the real world. So agents can be uncertain about logical truths, via impossible possible worlds (Hintikka, 1975), and this analysis can include the morality of actions, especially when moral intuitions are used as evidence.

With these generalizations, this Aumann-initiated literature does now seem relevant to real human disagreements. In fact, it suggests that honest truth-seeking agents, i.e., who seek to minimize differences between their stated beliefs and the truth, should not knowingly disagree on business, policy, science, or morality. Of course the attentive reader need not yet be persuaded of this claim; space has limited me to quickly summarizing results described elsewhere (Cowen and Hanson, 2002), and which I will elaborate in an upcoming book.

If honest truth-seeking agents would not knowingly disagree, then how is it that humans do knowingly disagree, even when they are confident of their honesty? The obvious explanation is that humans do not seek only to believe the truth; they have other motivations influencing the choice of their beliefs, such as hope and self-respect (otherwise known as wishful-thinking and overconfidence).

Note that humans are not only surprisingly unaware of these other belief influences; they are often downright hostile to the suggestion that they are under such influences. Thus humans seem to be "self-deceived" about their non-truth-seeking belief motivations, and this fact can plausibly explain most human disagreement. That is, even though we usually consciously see ourselves as just trying to believe and say what is true, motivated biases keep us both from listening to others as we should, and from seeing this failing in ourselves.

Why self-deception?

To better understand what we are up against, let us first review the standard account of why humans evolved to be biased and self-deceived. This account could well contain errors, but it seems the place to start.

If we could easily believe one thing while we say another, there would be little need for self-deception. We do not, however, find it easy to say one thing and consciously believe another. It turns out that because of the way our brains are structured, we give off many unconscious clues about what we are consciously thinking. These include facial expressions, tone of voice, reaction time, and much more. These clues make it hard to deceive others about what we are thinking.

It seems that our brains evolved to deal this problem by unconsciously biasing our beliefs (Lockard and Paulhaus, 1988; Trivers, 2000). Instead of just pretending to think well of ourselves, in order to convince others to think well of us, we *honestly* think well of ourselves, even in the face of contrary evidence.

Of course it is not quite that simple. You can't lie about just one thing; you also have to lie about lying, and so on. So we also seem to have evolved to not much notice our tendencies to self-deceive, even though we are well aware of such tendencies in others. Even though we are intuitively skilled at social maneuvering, we find it hard to think explicitly about social strategizing, making social science a latecomer to the sciences. We also avoid being very obviously biased on topics that others might too easily check and challenge us on. Yet we maintain strong biases on topics, like patriotism, where others are likely to challenge us for not being biased enough.

How can we not know and yet be so skilled? It may be that parts of our unconscious mind are well aware of many of our deceptions, and it is only our conscious mind that is fooled. Our conscious minds may even be like the public relations department of a corporation, whose main purpose is to present a certain coherent image to the outside, and not to make key corporate policy decisions.

In any case, there are limits to our ability to self-deceive; we cannot just make ourselves believe anything we would like to believe. For example, we cannot very easily self-deceive about our recent overt actions or our direct perceptions; these are just too obvious to question. If I just punched you, I would have to admit it. But this still leaves much room for bias; I might still tell myself that "you asked for it."

Now let us consider three trends which might reduce this tendency toward self-deception.

Documentation

Humans have long worked to document their lives, inventing gadgets to aid in writing and recording, concepts and conventions to make what we say meaningful and comparable, and social institutions to let us coordinate in monitoring and verifying our documentation. It is harder to lie, and so to self-deceive, about documented events.

Once upon a time, you could believe that you were a faster runner than most, by focusing on that one time when you blazed through the woods. Standardized sporting races made it harder, but you could still think you've never seen anyone go faster than in that race you won. With the invention of the stopwatch, even that deception got harder. In general, standardized tests and contests make it harder for people to lie and self-deceive about their knowledge and skills.

Similarly, standardized accounting makes it harder for corporate officers to steal corporate assets, and for households to avoid paying taxes. Lab and field notebooks, and standardized procedures, make it harder for researchers to lie about their observations. Standardized formal models make it harder for theorists to hide the biased assumptions that lead to biased conclusions. And standardized statistical procedures make it harder to bias the inferences we draw from all this data.

The memory required for these records is tiny compared to the memory of a single human brain. Similarly, the computation needed to implement these procedures is tiny compared to the computational ability of a single human brain. Even so, these records and procedures have had a great influence, because of their relative "objectivity." That is, these records were stored in a form that was relatively hard for us to consciously or unconsciously manipulate.

The price of such external memory and computation has been falling rapidly over the last half century, roughly following "Moore's Law." It should continue to fall at a similar pace for many decades to come.[1] As such prices fall, we will be able to document far more of our lives, and to make far more standardized inferences.

---

[1] Moore's Law is roughly that computing power and memory become twice as cheap every two years.

Many lament, and some celebrate (Brin, 1998), a coming "surveillance society." Most web pages and email are already archived, and it is now feasible and cheap for individuals to make audio recordings of their entire lives. It will soon be feasible to make full video recordings as well. Add to this recordings by security cameras in stores and business, and most physical actions in public spaces may soon be a matter of public record. Private spaces will similarly be a matter of at least private record.[2]

Face recognition software will soon be sufficient to translate these recordings into a history of who was where when, and with whom. Speech recognition software will create searchable transcripts of everything said in public spaces. Cameras trained on eyes can also allow a record of who was looking where when. Simple visual processing should even be able to put our actions into standard categories such as sleeping, walking, talking, eating, etc.

Even more is possible if we regularly take standardized tests, or augment our records with indications of our subjective feelings. We might mark how happy we feel every hour, or how much we like each person we meet. Records will sometimes be faked, but redundant and independent sources should make faking hard. Even subjective records can be checked against body measurements, and cryptographic aids can prevent back-dating of records.

In addition, we will soon be able to fully record each person's DNA, and will learn more and more about how to interpret such records to predict individual behavior.

The net result is that it will be much harder to lie about, or to self-deceive about, who said what specific words, who spent how much time with whom, what percent of each person's time was spent in standardized categories, who is genetically similar to whom, and many other documentable facts.

Idea futures

Even massive documentation, however, does not obviously make it much harder to lie and self-deceive about abstract reasoning and conclusions. If

---

[2] Some hope that cryptography will let people work and play in complete anonymity by using virtual reality from secure rooms. Anonymous work would violate tax laws, however, and any correlation

you are biased in your reasons for preferring a political candidate, or for believing in a scientific theory, it seems hard to catch that bias just by looking at where you have been or what you have said.

For disputes that can eventually be resolved, it turns out that we have a social institution, feasible today, that is capable of eliminating much of this bias, producing relatively accurate unbiased estimates. That institution is idea futures, i.e., betting markets, also known as prediction markets or information markets (Wolfers and Zitzewitz, 2004; Hanson, 1999, 1995).

The basic idea is that people who have to put their money where their mouth is form beliefs in the equivalent of harsher weather, where they prefer more functional clothes. Those who know that they don't know tend to shut up, and those who don't know that they don't know lose their money and then shut up. Those who remain tend to know, and know that they know.

Decades of research on financial markets have shown that it is hard to find biases in market estimates. The few direct comparisons made so far have found markets to be at least as accurate as other institutions. Orange Juice futures improve on National Weather Service forecasts (Roll, 1984), horse race markets beat horse race experts (Figlewski, 1979), Oscar markets beat columnist forecasts (Pennock, Giles, and Nielsen, 2001), gas demand markets beat gas demand experts (Spencer, 2004), stock markets beat the official NASA panel at fingering the guilty company in the Challenger accident (Maloney and Mulherin, 2003), markets on economic statistics beat surveys of professional forecasters (Grkaynak and Wolfers, 2006), election markets beat national opinion polls (Berg, Nelson, and Rietz, 2001), and corporate sales markets beat official corporate forecasts (Chen and Plott, 1998).

Intentionally biasing these market estimates via trades turns out to be very difficult. Field observations have found that such attempts consistently fail, and controlled lab experiments have found no lasting effect on average prices or price accuracy from giving some traders such a manipulation incentive (Hanson, Oprea, and Porter, 2007). In fact, theoretical models suggest that manipulators are fundamentally no different from other noise

---

between your public and private persona would expose you, such as from your rhythm of speech or when you were sick or your connection was down.

traders, and so having more of them should on average increase price accuracy (Hanson and Oprea, 2004).

Today there are relatively few such markets. But this is largely because such markets are usually banned as illegal gambling. The same rapidly falling prices that are making documentation cheaper are also making these markets cheaper. In fact, it is possible to cheaply sustain billions of markets per person who trades in them (Hanson, 2003a). It is not entirely clear just how many topics are suitable for such market consensus, but it may be possible to apply similar methods to topics where no independent final judgment is possible (Prelec, 2004).

Once legal, or cheap enough to be widespread even if illegal, these markets can create unbiased consensus estimates on the observable policy consequences, on future scientific and moral consensus, and on much more. Having idea futures markets on most disputed topics could well change the character of conversation. Mass media might typically defer to market consensus on most disputed issues, just as business news now defers to stock prices. And pundits who dispute a market consensus might be expected to put their money where their mouth is. These markets could thus raise the cost of bias and self-deception in such debate, and offer the public precise continuously-updated consensus estimates, estimates that are consistent across a wide range of topics, and are relatively free of self-deception distortions.

Self-deception would remain

Even with far more documentation and market consensus, however, there would remain many topics where we can be biased and self-deceived.

Consider, for example, our level of interest and attachment in romantic and business relationships. Early in such relationships we tend to over-estimate how much we like our partners, and the chance we will remain together (Tennov, 1979). Late in such relationships, however, we tend to under-estimate these things. Both of these self-deceptions follow our biological interests; early on we want to convince others to invest in us, while later on we want them to think we will leave if not treated fairly.

Today we signal our interest and attachment in many ways, including in how we spend our time, attention, and money. Our ability to gauge levels of interest and attachment of partners and potential partners should improve with more documentation about their activities. Market estimates of relationship duration given various conditions should also help. Even so, a great deal of uncertainty would likely remain, and hence our desire to perceive and deceive should also remain.

Mental Transparency

What will happen if we can enhance our minds, not just via education, but also via more direct modification and augmentation of our brains? As we get smarter, more things will become obvious to us, and so there will be more topics on which we find it hard to self-deceive. But we will also have opinions on more topics, creating more opportunities for self-deception.

One tempting enhancement will be to better control the various subconscious clues we give off, so that we can lie more convincingly. We might put our facial expressions under more conscious control, for example, and use hidden internal speed improvements to help us fake reaction times.

Deception generally helps those who are trying to look like something they are not, at the expense of those who really are what others pretend to be. Such deception also generally hurts observers, who are trying to tell the difference between these other two types of people. Of these three groups, two have a common interest in preventing deception.

Those who really are what others pretend to be, and want it to show on their face, would try to convince others that they are not controlling facial expressions. So they might try to use brain scanners or brain modifications to give others the ability to see more directly inside their minds, in order to directly confirm their honesty (Glover, 1984). Once such mental transparency becomes possible, everyone might feel pressured to have and use it, if they did not want others to presume they were hiding something.

This situation would be similar to the way we now prefer to meet someone we need to trust in person rather than via teleconferencing, telecommuting, phone, or email; we subconsciously reveal more about ourselves in person. Also similar is the way corporations hire outside accounting firms to monitor their internal processes, and nations allow outside inspectors to monitor their elections and weapons.

It should be relatively easy to show people that our brains are not attached to hidden electronic devices. But it may be hard to let others see inside our brains, at least in a way that they could make much sense of what they see; our brains were not designed with this sort of transparency in mind. And even if we can let others make enough sense of things to figure out our current beliefs, that might just push our self-deception back to the process that produced those current beliefs.

To deal with self-deception in belief production, we might want to provide audit trails, giving more transparency about the origins of our beliefs. However this feature may be even harder to allow via small modifications of our evolved brains. There may thus be natural limits on how far our brain structure may allow this internal transparency trend to go.

On the other hand, these considerations might encourage efforts to more substantially reorganize our mental architecture. We might eventually expect such reorganization to also be attempted for other reasons, such as to allow a closer integration with other minds and computer aids.

On moral arrogance

While we may abstractly approve of the epistemic virtues that these changes would produce, we might also be uncomfortable with their sheer magnitude. How human are creatures with transparent minds, documented lives, and market induced agreement on most abstract topics? Could it really be good to create such creatures instead of creatures more like us? And if the end result of these trends seems repugnant, should we not enlist our moral fervor to push public policy to regulate such behavior?

It is hard to escape reflecting on and acting on our simple moral intuitions about such issues, at least regarding our own actions (such as what children we create). It is also tempting to use these same conclusions to regulate the behavior of others, including if possible that of our distant descendants (such as by trying to prevent the development of certain technologies). There are often good reasons to resist such temptations, however.

One reason often mentioned is a value of autonomy; lives seem more worth living when people make their own choices, independent of what actual choices they make. There is, however, a more important but rarely mentioned consideration: the risk of moral arrogance.

People ordinarily consider moral issues when choosing their actions, and typically estimate their own actions to be moral. So if you, based on your moral analysis, estimate that other people's behavior should be regulated and limited for moral reasons, then it seems that you estimate your moral judgment to be better than theirs. If so, the literature on the rationality of disagreement should make you pause.

Of course you need not pause if you have good reason to think they do not believe they are acting morally. In this case there is no disagreement; there is just your good fighting their evil. The same applies when you would likely also do what they would do. For example, if taxes were voluntary, then you might well not pay your taxes, even though you think society is better off when all are forced to pay taxes. These are largely questions of coordination, not moral disagreement.

Setting such cases aside, however, we are left with cases where you disapprove of their moral judgments. If it is possible for you to advise them before they act, and if they reject your advice, then you and they will soon find yourself in a position where you knowingly disagree with each other. And if you both see yourselves as just trying to believe moral truth, then if honest truth-seeking agents would not knowingly disagree, we must conclude that you or they are self-deceived about your moral analysis.

You might be tempted to believe that your moral analysis is better because you have more information. You may, after all, be a respected and learned academic who took years to consider such issues while consulting with similar colleagues. However, when a rational (i.e., truth-seeking) agent with little information disagrees with a self-deceived agent with much information, it is the rational agent who is more likely to be right.

The question is not who started the conversation knowing more, but rather who better learns by listening to others. Yes, by thinking too highly of their ability to analyze moral questions, people may take too little of your moral advice. But by thinking too highly of your own moral ability, you may offer too much moral advice. It is not obvious which bias is more severe.

You might argue that you are less likely to be self-deceived because you are a distant observer, with little direct interest in the actions in question. But such distance could tempt you to indulge general fantasies, instead of attending to important details. And what if the people you disagree with rely on the advice of other distant observers who disagree with you?

Perhaps your moral advice is based on the belief that most everyone, including yourself, is subject to a particular bias. For example, you might think most everyone is biased to quit school early, and so should be forced to stay in school. If true, this might be a reason to regulate behavior. But the question is why you are better positioned than they to evaluate such a claim. Those who reject your claim may, for example, see you as being in a position that makes you especially likely to be biased in favor of such a belief. You might, for example, be a teacher, or be beholden to a teacher union.

In general, you may point to particular indications suggesting that others are more biased than you, indications which do in fact correlate with who is more biased. But remember that those you disagree with can and do play the same game; humans are skilled at selectively finding reasons to dismiss others as more biased than they. Perhaps the safest rule is to avoid extreme positions, relative to the existing distribution of opinions, as these seem more likely to be the result of self-deception. But again we should beware of the human tendency to selectively apply such rules.

The warning to beware of our self-deception regarding our moral abilities would seem to apply with a special force to those who argue the virtues of self-deception. After all, does not the pro-self-deception side in a debate seem more likely to be self-deceived in this matter?

We should also be especially wary of moral arrogance regarding the moral behavior of our distant descendants, as those descendants will have a clear information advantage over us; we cannot listen to them as we could when arguing with a contemporary. Our descendants will know of our advice, and also of many other things we do not know. In addition, this chapter has suggested they may well have a stronger truth orientation than us.

Conclusion

I have briefly surveyed three trends which may cause our descendants to have a stronger truth-orientation that we do: more recording and standardized statistics on our lives, speculative markets in major disputed topics, and minds enhanced to allow more transparency. These three trends should reduce the epistemic vice of human self-deception, a vice that seems particularly dangerous in a world that differs so much from the environment to which those self-deceptions were adapted. A world with so much less self-deception and disagreement seems jarringly different from our world. Of course we are vastly different from our ancestors a hundred thousand years ago—our minds have been radically modified by education, culture, and civilization.

Even so, some may be tempted to reject such a truth-oriented future, regulating behavior to discourage it. Others may be tempted to regulate behavior to encourage a truth-orientation. Those who are so tempted should consider the risk of moral arrogance. How sure can they be that their moral judgment is better than the judgments of those they would regulate, especially the judgments of our better informed and more-truth-oriented descendants?

References

Aumann, R. (1976). 'Agreeing to Disagree', *The Annals of Statistics*, 4 (6), 1236–9.

Berg, J., Nelson, F., and Rietz, T. (2001). 'Accuracy and Forecast Standard Error of Prediction Markets'. Tech. rep., University of Iowa, College of Business Administration.

Brin, D. (1998). *Transparent Society*. Reading, Massachusetts: Addison-Wesley.

Chen, K.-Y., and Plott, C. R. (1998). 'Prediction markets and information aggregation mechanism: Experiments and application'. Tech. rep., California Institute of Technology.

Cowen, T., and Hanson, R. (2002). 'Are Disagreements Honest?'. Tech. rep., George Mason University Economics.

Daniels, N. (1979). 'Wide Reflective Equilibrium and Theory Acceptance in Ethics', *Journal of Philosophy*, 76 (5), 256–82.

Figlewski, S. (1979). 'Subjective Information and Market Efficiency in a Betting Market', *Journal of Political Economy*, 87 (1), 75–88.

Giannetti, E. (1997). *Lies We Live By—The Art of Self-Deception*. London: Bloomsbury.

Glover, J. (1984). *What Sort of People Should There Be?* New York: Penguin Books.

Grkaynak, R. S., and Wolfers, J. (2006). 'Macroeconomic Derivatives: An Initial Analysis of Market-Based Macro Forecasts, Uncertainty and Risk'. Tech. rep. 11929, NBER.

Hanson, R. (1995). 'Could Gambling Save Science? Encouraging an Honest Consensus', *Social Epistemology*, 9 (1), 3–33.

_____ (1999). 'Decision Markets', *IEEE Intelligent Systems*, 14 (3), 16–19.

_____ (2002). 'Disagreement is Unpredictable', *Economics Letters*, 77, 365–9.

_____ (2003a). 'Combinatorial Information Market Design', *Information Systems Frontiers* 5 (1), 105–19.

_____ (2003b). 'For Savvy Bayesian Wannabes, Are Disagreements Not About Information?', *Theory and Decision*, 54 (2), 105–23.

_____ (2006). 'Uncommon Priors Require Origin Disputes', *Theory and Decision*, 61 (4), 318–28.

_____ and Oprea, R. (2008). 'Manipulators Increase Information Market Accuracy', *Economica*, forthcoming.

_____ Oprea, R., and Porter, D. (2006). 'Information Aggregation and Manipulation in an Experimental Market', *Journal of Economic Behavior and Organization*, 60(4): 449–59.

Hintikka, J. (1975). 'Impossible Possible Worlds Vindicated', *Journal of Philosophical Logic*, 4, 475–84.

Kitcher, P. (1990). 'The Division of Cognitive Labor', *Journal of Philosophy*, 87 (1), 5–22.

Lockard, J., and Paulhaus, D. (eds.), (1988). *Self-Deception: An Adaptive Mechanism?* Englewood Cliffs, N. J.: Prentice Hall.

Maloney, M. T., and Mulherin, J. H. (2003). 'The complexity of price discovery in an efficient market: the stock market reaction to the Challenger crash', *Journal of Corporate Finance*, 9 (4), 453–79.

Mele, A. R. (2001). *Self-Deception Unmasked*. Princeton: Princeton University Press.

Monderer, D., and Samet, D. (1989). 'Approximating Common Knowledge with Common Beliefs', *Games and Economic Behavior*, 1, 170–90.

Pennock, D. M., Giles, C. L., and Nielsen, F. A. (2001). 'The Real Power of Artificial Markets', *Science*, 291, 987–8.

Prelec, D. (2004). 'A Bayesian truth serum for subjective data', *Science*, 306, 462–6.

Roll, R. (1984). 'Orange Juice and Weather', *American Economic Review*, 74 (5), 861–80.

Smith, D. L. (2004). *Why We Lie—The Evolutionary Roots of Deception and the Unconscious Mind*. New York: St. Martin's Press.

Spencer, J. (2004). 'New ICAP-Nymex Derivatives Have U.S. Gas Market's Number', *Wall Street Journal*, 4 Aug., p.1.

Taylor, S. (1989). *Positive Illusions: Creative Self-Deception and the Healthy Mind*. New York: Basic Books.

Tennov, D. (1979). *Love and Limerence*. Chelsea, MI: Scarborough House.

Trivers, R. (2000). 'The Elements of a Scientific Theory of Self-Deception'. In LeCroy, D., and Moller, P. (eds.), *Evolutionary Perspectives on Human Reproductive Behavior*, vol. 907, *Annals of the New York Academy of Sciences*.

Whyte, J. (2004). *Crimes Against Logic*. New York: McGraw Hill.

Wolfers, J., and Zitzewitz, E. (2004). 'Prediction Markets', *Journal of Economic Perspectives*, 18 (2), 107–26.

PART III
Enhancement as a Practical Challenge

18

The Wisdom of Nature: An Evolutionary Heuristic for Human Enhancement

*Nick Bostrom and Anders Sandberg**

Abstract

Human beings are a marvel of evolved complexity. Such systems can be difficult to enhance. When we manipulate complex evolved systems, which are poorly understood, our interventions often fail or backfire. It can appear as if there is a "wisdom of nature" which we ignore at our peril. Sometimes the belief in nature's wisdom—and corresponding doubts about the prudence of tampering with nature, especially human nature—manifest as diffusely moral objections against enhancement. Such objections may be expressed as intuitions about the superiority of the natural or the troublesomeness of hubris, or as an evaluative bias in favor of the status quo. This chapter explores the extent to which such prudence-derived anti-enhancement sentiments are justified. We develop a heuristic, inspired by the field of evolutionary medicine, for identifying promising human enhancement interventions. The heuristic incorporates the grains of truth contained in "nature knows best" attitudes while providing criteria for the special cases where we have reason to believe that it is feasible for us to improve on nature.

1. Introduction

1.1. The wisdom of nature, and the special problem of enhancement

We marvel at the complexity of the human organism, how its various parts have evolved to solve intricate problems: the eye to collect and pre-process

* Oxford Future of Humanity Institute, Faculty of Philosophy and James Martin 21st Century School, Oxford University. Forthcoming in *Enhancing Humans*, ed. Julian Savulescu and Nick Bostrom (Oxford: Oxford University Press)

visual information, the immune system to fight infection and cancer, the lungs to oxygenate the blood. The human brain—the focus of many of the most alluring proposed enhancements—is arguably the most complex thing in the known universe. Given how rudimentary is our understanding of the human organism, particularly the brain, how could we have any realistic hope of *enhancing* such a system?

To enhance even a system like a car or a motorcycle—whose complexity is trivial in comparison to that of the human organism—requires a fair bit of understanding of how the thing works. Isn't the challenge we face in trying to enhance human beings so difficult as to be hopelessly beyond our reach, at least until the biological sciences and the general level of human abilities have advanced vastly beyond their present state?

It is easier to see how *therapeutic* medicine should be feasible. Intuitively, the explanation would go as follows: Even a very excellently designed system will occasionally break. We might then be able to figure out what has broken, and how to fix it. This seems much less daunting than to take a very excellently designed, unbroken system, and enhance it beyond its normal functioning.

Yet we know that even therapeutic medicine is very difficult. It has been claimed that until circa 1900, medicine did more harm than good.[1] And various recent studies suggest that even much of contemporary medicine is ineffectual or outright harmful.[2] Iatrogenic deaths account for 2 to 4 percent of all deaths in the US (the third leading cause of death according to one accounting[3]) and may correspond to a loss of life expectancy by 6 to 12 months.[4] We are all familiar with nutritional advice, drugs, and therapies that were promoted by health authorities but later found to be damaging to health. In many cases, the initial recommendations were informed by large clinical trials. When even therapeutic medicine, based on fairly good data from large clinical trials, is so hard to get right, it seems that a prudent person has much reason to be wary of purported *enhancements*, especially as the case for such enhancements is often based on much weaker data. Evolution is a process powerful enough to have led to the development of systems—such as human brains—that are far more complex and capable than anything that human scientists or engineers have managed to design.

---

[1] McKeown and Lowe 1974.
[2] Newhouse and Group. 1993; Frech and Miller 1996; Kirsch, Moore, Scoboria, and Nicholls 2002.
[3] Starfield 2000.   [4] Bunker 2001.

Surely it would be foolish, absent strong supporting evidence, to suppose that we are currently likely to be able to do *better* than evolution, especially when so far we have not even managed to understand the systems that evolution has designed and when our attempts even just to repair what evolution has built so often misfire!

We believe that these informal considerations contain a grain of truth. Nonetheless, in many particular cases we believe it is practically feasible to improve human nature. The evolution heuristic is our explanation of why this is so. If the evolution heuristic works as we suggest, it shows that there is some validity to the widespread intuition that nature often knows best, especially in relation to proposals for human enhancement. But the heuristic also demonstrates that the validity of this intuition is limited, by revealing important exceptional cases in which we can hope to improve on nature using even our present or near-future science and technology.

The evolution heuristic might be useful for scientists working to develop enhancement technologies. It might also be useful in evaluating beliefs and arguments about the ethics of human enhancement. This is because intuitions about the wisdom of nature appear to play an important role in the cognitive ecology of many anti-enhancement advocates. While sophisticated bioconservatives (aware of the distinction between "is" and "ought") may not *explicitly* base their arguments on the alleged wisdom in nature, we believe that such intuitions influence their evaluation of the plausibility of various empirical assumptions and mid-level moral principles that are invoked in the enhancement discourse; just as the opinions and practical judgments of the pro-enhancement transhumanists look more plausible if one assumes that nature is generally unwise. Addressing such hidden empirical background assumptions may therefore help illuminate important questions in applied ethics.[5]

1.2. *The evolution heuristic*

The basic idea is simple. In order to decide whether we want to modify some aspect of a system, it is helpful to consider why the system has that aspect in the first place. Similarly, if we propose to introduce some new feature, we might ask why the system does not already possess it.

---

[5] On the role of mid-level principles in one area of applied ethics, see Beauchamp and Childress 1979.

The system of concern here is the human organism. The question why the human organism has a certain property can be answered on at least two different levels, ontogeny and phylogeny. Here the focus is on the phylogeny of the human organism.

We can conceive of a proposed enhancement as an ordered pair (a, A), where a is some specific intervention (e.g., the administration of a drug) and A is the trait that the intervention is intended to realize (e.g., improved memory consolidation). We define an enhancement as an intervention that causes either an improvement in the functioning of some subsystem (e.g. long-term memory) beyond its normal healthy state in some individual or the addition of a new capacity (e.g. magnetic sense).

On this definition, an enhancement is not necessarily desirable, either for the enhanced individual or for society. For instance, we might have no reason to value an enhancement of our sweat glands that increases their ability to produce perspiration in response to heat stimuli. In other instances, we might benefit from increased functionality or a new capacity, and yet not benefit from the enhancement because the intervention also causes unacceptable side-effects.[6] The evolution heuristic is a tool to help us think through whether some proposed enhancement is likely to yield a net benefit.

The starting point of the heuristic is to pose the *evolutionary optimality challenge*:

(EOC) If the proposed intervention would result in an enhancement, why have we not already evolved to be that way?

Suppose that we liken evolution to a surpassingly great engineer. (The *limitations* of this metaphor are part of what makes it useful for our purposes.) Using this metaphor, the EOC can be expressed as the question, "How could we realistically hope to improve on evolution's work?" We propose that there are three main categories of possible answers, which can be summarized as follows:

- *Changed tradeoffs.* Evolution "designed" the system for operation in one type of environment, but now we wish to deploy it in a very different type of environment. It is not surprising, then, that we might

---

[6] Which side-effects are acceptable depends, of course, on the benefits resulting from the enhancement, and these may vary between subjects depending on their goals, life plans, and circumstances.

be able to modify the system better to meet the demands imposed on it by the new environment. Making such modifications need not require engineering skills on a par with those of evolution: consider that it is much harder to design and build a car from scratch than it is to fit an existing car with a new set of wheels or make some other tweaks to improve functioning in some particular setting, such as icy roads. Similarly, the human organism, whilst initially "designed" for operation as a hunter-gatherer on the African savannah, must now function in the modern world. We may well be capable of making some enhancing tweaks and adjustments to the new environment even though our engineering talent does not remotely approach that of evolution.

- *Value discordance.* There is a discrepancy between the standards by which evolution measured the quality of her work, and the standards that we wish to apply. Even if evolution had managed to build the finest reproduction-and-survival machine imaginable, we may still have reason to change it because what we value is not primarily to be maximally effective inclusive-fitness optimizers. This discordance in objectives is an important source of answers to the EOC. It is not surprising that we can modify a system better to meet our goals, if these goals differ substantially from the ones that (metaphorically might be seen as having) guided evolution in designing the system the way she did. Again, this explanation does not presuppose that our engineering talent exceeds evolution's. Compare the case to that of a mediocre technician, who would never be able to design a car, let alone a good one; but who may well be capable of converting the latest BMW model into a crude rain-collecting device, thereby *enhancing* the system's functionality as a water collecting device.

- *Evolutionary restrictions.* We have access to various tools, materials, and techniques that were unavailable to evolution. Even if our engineering talent is far inferior to evolution's, we may nevertheless be able to achieve certain things that stumped evolution, thanks to these novel aids. We should be cautious in invoking this explanation, for evolution often managed to achieve with primitive means what we are unable to do with state-of-the-art technology. But in some cases one can show that it is practically impossible to create a certain feature without some particular tool—no matter how ingenious the engineer—while the same feature can be achieved by any dimwit given access to the right tool. In these special cases we might be able to overcome evolutionary restrictions.

In the following three sections, we will explore each of these categories of possible answers to the EOC in more detail, and show how they can help us decide whether or not to go ahead with various potential human enhancements.

Our ideas about enhancement in many ways parallel earlier work in evolutionary medicine. Evolutionary medicine is based on using evolutionary considerations to understand aspects of human health.[7] Hosts and parasites have adapted to one another, and analysis of the tradeoffs involved can reveal adaptations that contributed to fitness in the past but are maladaptive today, or symptoms that have been misdiagnosed as harmful but may actually aid recovery. Evolutionary medicine also helps explain the incidence of genetic diseases, which can be maintained in the population because of beneficial effects in historically normal environments. Another contribution of evolutionary medicine has been to draw attention to the fact that our modern environment may not always fit a biology designed for Pleistocene conditions, and how this mismatch can cause disease. These insights are recycled in our analysis of human enhancement.

Another strand of research relevant to our aims is evolutionary optimization theory, which seeks to determine the abilities and limitations of evolution in terms of producing efficient biological functions.[8] While, naively, evolution might be thought to maximize individual fitness (the expected lifetime number of surviving offspring), there are many contexts in which this simplification leads to error. Sometimes it is necessary to focus on the concept of inclusive fitness, which takes into account the effects of a genotype on the fitness of blood-relatives other than direct decedents. Sometimes a gene-centric perspective is needed, to account for phenomena such as segregation distortion and junk DNA.[9] There are also many other ways in which evolution routinely falls short of "optimality", some of which will be covered in later sections.

[7] Williams and Nesse 1991; Trevathan, Smith and McKenna 1999.
[8] Parker and Smith 1990.   [9] Dawkins 1976; Williams 1996/1966.

2. Changed tradeoffs

2.1. General remarks on tradeoffs

Evolutionary adaptation often involves striking a tradeoff between competing design criteria. Evolution has fine-tuned us for life in the ancestral environment, which, for the most part, was a life as a member of a hunter-gatherer tribe roaming the African savannah. Life in contemporary society differs in many ways from life in the environment of evolutionary adaptedness. Modern conditions are too recent for our species to have fully adapted to them, which means that the tradeoffs evolution struck may no longer be optimal today.

In evolutionary biology, the "environment of evolutionary adaptedness" (EEA) refers not to a particular time or place, but to the environment in which a species evolved and to which it is adapted.[10] It includes both inanimate and animate aspects of the environment, such as climate, vegetation, prey, predators, pathogens, and the social environment of conspecifics. We can also think of the EEA as the set of all evolutionary pressures faced by the ancestors of the species over recent evolutionary time—in the case of humans, at least 200,000 years.[11] Hunting, gathering of fruits and nuts, courtship, parasites, and hand-to-hand combat with wild animals and enemy tribes were elements of the EEA; speeding cars, high levels of trans fats, concrete ghettos, and tax return forms were not.

The import of this for the evolution heuristic is that even if the human organism were a wonderfully well-designed system for life in the EEA, it may not in all respects be well designed for life in contemporary society. If we can identify specific changes to our environment that have shifted the optimal tradeoff point between competing design desiderata in a certain direction, we may be able to find relatively easy interventions that could "retune" the tradeoff to a point that is closer to its present optimum. Such retuning interventions might be among the low-hanging fruits on the enhancement tree, fruits within reach even in the absence of super-advanced medical technology.

[10] Hagen 2002.   [11] Hagen 2002.

Proposed enhancements aiming to retune altered tradeoffs can often meet the EOC. The new trait that the enhancement gives us might have been maladaptive in the EEA even though it would be adaptive now. Alternatively, the new trait might be intrinsically associated with another trait that was maladaptive in the EEA but has become less disadvantageous (or even beneficial) in the modern environment, so that the terms of the tradeoff have shifted. In either case, the enhancement could be adaptive in the current environment without having been so in the EEA, which would explain why we do not have that trait, allowing us to meet the EOC.

We can roughly distinguish two ways in which tradeoffs can change: new *resources* may have become available that were absent, or available only at great cost, in the EEA; or, the *demands* placed on one of the subsystems of the human organism may have changed since we left the EEA. Let us consider these two possibilities in turn and look at some examples.

2.2. Resources

One of the main differences between human life today (for most people in developed countries) and life in the EEA is the abundant availability of food independently of place and season. In the state of nature, food is relatively scarce much of the time, making energy conservation paramount and forcing difficult energy expenditure tradeoffs between metabolically costly tissues, processes, and behaviors. As we shall see, increased access to nutrients suggests several promising enhancement opportunities. We have also gained access to important new non-dietary resources, including improved protection against physical threats, obstetric assistance, better temperature control, and increased availability of information. Let us examine how these new resources are relevant to potential enhancements of the brain and the immune system.

2.2.1. The brain   The human brain constitutes only 2 per cent of body mass yet accounts for about 20 per cent of total energy expenditure. Combined, the brain, heart, gastrointestinal tract, kidneys, and liver consume 70 per cent of basal metabolism. This forces tradeoffs between the size and capacity of these organs, and between allocation of time and energy to activities other than searching for food in greater quantity or quality.[12]

---

[12] Aiello, Bates and Joffe 2001; Fish and Lockwood 2003.

Unsurprisingly, we find that, in evolutionary lineages where nutritional demands are high and cognitive demands low (such as bats hunting in uncluttered environments), relative brain size is correspondingly smaller.[13] In humans, brain size correlates positively with cognitive capacity (. ≈ 0.33).[14]

Holding brain mass constant, a greater level of mental activity might also enable us to apply our brains more effectively to process information and solve problems. The brain, however, requires extra energy when we exert mental effort, reducing the normally tightly regulated blood glucose level by about 5 per cent (0.2 mmol/l) for short (<15 min) efforts and more for longer exertions.[15] Conversely, increasing blood glucose levels has been shown to improve cognitive performance in demanding tasks.[16]

The metabolic problem is exacerbated during prenatal and early childhood growth where brain development requires extra energy. Brain metabolism accounts for a staggering 60 per cent of total metabolism in newborns,[17] exacerbating the competitive situation between mother and child for nutritional resources—an unpleasant tradeoff.[18] Children with greater birth weight have a cognitive advantage.[19]

Another constraint on prenatal cerebral development is the size of the human birth canal (itself constrained by bipedalism), which historically placed severe constraints on the head size of newborns.[20] These constraints are partly obviated by modern obstetrics and the availability of caesarian section. One way of reducing head size at birth and perinatal energy demands would be to extend the period of postnatal maturation. However, delayed maturation was vastly riskier in the EEA than it is now.

What all this suggests is that cognitive enhancements might be possible if we can find interventions that recalibrate these legacy tradeoffs in ways that are more optimal in the contemporary world. For example, suppose we could discover interventions that moderately increased brain growth during gestation, or slightly prolonged the period of brain growth during infancy, or that triggered an increase in available mental energy. Applying the EOC to these hypothetical interventions, we get a green light. We can

---

[13] Niven 2005.   [14] McDaniel 2005.

[15] Scholey, Harper and Kennedy 2001; Fairclough and Houston 2004.

[16] Korol and Gold 1998; Manning, Stone, Korol and Gold 1998; Martin and Benton 1999; Meikle, Riby and Stollery 2005. Increasing oxygen levels (another requirement for metabolism) also improves cognition (Winder and Borrill 1998).

[17] Holliday 1986.   [18] Martin 1996.   [19] Matte 2001.   [20] Trevathan 1987.

see why these enhancements would have been maladaptive in the EEA, and why they may nevertheless have become entirely beneficial now that the underlying tradeoffs have changed as a result of the availability of new resources. If the "downside" of getting more mental energy is that we would burn more calories, many of us would pounce at the opportunity.

Not all cognitive enhancement interventions get an immediate green light from the above argument. Stimulants like caffeine and Modafinil enable increased wakefulness and control over sleep patterns.[21] But sleep serves various (poorly understood) functions other than to conserve energy.[22] If the explanation for why we do not sleep less than we do has to do with these other functions, then reducing sleep might well have more problematic side-effects than increasing the amount of calories we need to consume. For any particular intervention, such as the administration of some drug, we also of course need to consider the possibility of contingent side-effects, i.e. that the drug might have effects on the body other than simply retuning the target tradeoff.

2.2.2. The immune system   While the immune system serves an essential function by protecting us from infection and cancer, it also consumes significant amounts of energy.[23] Experiments have found direct energetic costs of immune activation.[24] In birds immune activation corresponded to a 29 per cent rise of resting metabolic rate[25] and in humans the rate increases by 13 per cent per degree centigrade of fever.[26] In addition, the protein synthesis demands of the immune system are sizeable yet prioritized, as evidenced by a 70 per cent increase in protein turnover in children during infection despite a condition of malnourishment.[27] One would expect the immune system to have evolved a level of activity that strikes a tradeoff between these and other requirements—a level optimized for life in the EEA but perhaps no longer ideal.

Such a tradeoff has been proposed as part of an explanation of the placebo effect.[28] The placebo effect is puzzling because it apparently involves getting something (accelerated recovery from disease or injury) for nothing (merely

---

[21] Caldwell 2001.   [22] Siegel 2005.   [23] McDade 2003.
[24] Demas, Chefer, Talan and Nelson 1997; Moret and Schmid-Hempel 2000; Ots, Kerimov, Ivankina, Ilyina and Horak 2001.
[25] Martin, Scheuerlein and Wikelski 2003.   [26] Elia 1992.
[27] Waterlow 1984; McDade 2003.   [28] Humphrey 2000.

having a belief). If the subjective experience of being treated causes a health-promoting response, why are we not always responding that way? Studies have shown that it is possible chemically to modulate the placebo response down[29] or up.[30]

One possible explanation is that mobilizing the placebo effect consumes resources, perhaps through activation of the immune system or other forms of physiological health investment. Also, to the extent that the placebo response reduces defensive reactions (such as pain, stiffness, and inflammation), it might increase our vulnerability to future injury and microbial assaults. If so, one might expect that natural selection would have made us such that the placebo response would be triggered by signals indicating that in the near future we will (a) recover from our current injury or disease (in which case there is no need to conserve resources to fight a drawn-out infection and less need to maintain defensive reactions), (b) have good access to nutrients (in which case, again, there is no need to conserve resources), and (c) be protected from external threats (in which case there is less need to keep resources in reserve for immediate action readiness). Consistent with this model, the evidence does indeed show that the healing system is activated not only by the expectation that we will get well soon but also by the impression that external circumstances are generally favorable. For example, social status,[31] success, having somebody looking after us,[32] sunshine, and regular meals might all indicate that we are in circumstances where it is optimal for the body to invest in healing and long-term health, and they do seem to prompt the body to do just that. By contrast, conflict,[33] stress, anxiety, uncertainty,[34] rejection, isolation, and despair appear to shift resources towards immediate readiness to face crises and away from building long-term health.

If this model of the placebo response is correct, several potential avenues of enhancement are worth exploring. One is that since physical safety and reliable access to food are much improved compared to the EEA, it might now be beneficial to invest more in biological processes that build long-term health than was usually optimal in the EEA. We might thus inquire whether the placebo effect and other evolved responses are flexible

---

[29] Sauro and Greenberg 2005.   [30] Colloca and Benedetti 2005.
[31] Sapolsky 2005.   [32] House, Landis and Umberson 1988.
[33] Kiecolt, Glaser, Cacioppo, MacCallum, Snydersmith, Kim and Malarkey 1997.
[34] McDade 2002.

enough to have adjusted the level of health investment to a level that is optimal under modern conditions. If not, we could benefit from an intervention that triggers a placebo-like response or otherwise increases the body's health investment.

However, while external stresses and resource constraints are reduced in the modern environment, the danger of auto-immune reactions remains. We would therefore have to be careful not to overshoot the target. It is possible that we would benefit from a *lower* baseline immune activity in some parts of the immune system since we are now less at risk of dying from infectious diseases. As an example, the hygiene theory of allergic diseases claims that the reduction in immunological challenge in particular from helminth parasites during early life increases the risk of allergic disease later in life.[35] If true, then a down-regulation of a particular dendritic cell subpopulation (DC2) sensitive to helminths, but causing allergic reactions, might be desirable. Alternatively, an up-regulation of regulatory (DCreg) cells that tend to be lost in unstimulated immune systems might be used to control the DC2 cells.

The evolution heuristic also leads us to consider other potential immune system enhancements. Even if the average activation level of our immune systems were still optimal in the modern era, we now possess more information (a new resource) about the detailed requirements in specific situations. We can use this information to override our bodies' natural response tendencies. For example, recipients of donated organs can benefit from immunosuppressant drugs. Conversely, a patient with early-stage cancer might be better off if her immune system could be induced to mount an immediate all-out assault on the incipient tumor instead of conserving resources for hypothetical future challenges.[36]

A more radical enhancement would be to improve DNA repair, which would reduce cancer-causing mutations and improve radiation resistance, at the price of increasing metabolic needs. The modification could be achieved through overexpression of existing DNA repair genes[37] or perhaps even by transgenic incorporation of the unique abilities of *Deinococcus radiodurans*.[38]

---

[35] Yazdanbakhsh, Kremsner and van Ree 2002; Maizels 2005.
[36] Boon and van Baren 2003; Dunn, Old and Schreiber 2004.
[37] Wood, Mitchell, Sgouros and Lindahl 2001.
[38] Battista, Earl and Park 1999; Venkateswaran, McFarlan, Ghosal, Minton, Vasilenko, Makarova, Wackett and Daly 2000.

Increased repair would have to be balanced with apoptosis and replacement of irreparably damaged cells (another energy cost). Until recently, increased DNA repair activity might have been too metabolically costly and mutation-prone for evolution to consider it a worthwhile bargain. One of the most well-studied pathways, the PARP-1 pathway, protects the genome from damage but requires so much energy that it can damage cells through energy depletion.[39]

Since the objective of the interventions suggested above is to restore health, one could argue that they should be regarded as therapeutic rather than enhancing. But these classifications are not necessarily incompatible. We could regard the interventions as therapeutic for the subsystems whose functioning has been deteriorated by disease, yet enhancing for the immune system, whose functioning is improved beyond its normal state.[40]

2.3. Demands

Just as we have many resources that were denied our hunter-gatherer ancestors, we also face a different set of demands than they did. This suggests further opportunities for enhancement.

Changes in demands on the human organism occur when old demands disappear or are reduced (e.g. less need for long treks to get food; hygienic surroundings reducing demands on the immune system), and when demands grow in strength or new demands arise (e.g. greater need to be able to concentrate on abstract material for long periods; new pathogens spreading in larger societies). The source and nature of a particular demand may also change. For instance, exercise is no longer necessary to gain sustenance, but is instead needed to maintain the body in good shape.

Many "diseases of civilization" are due to these changed demands. For example, our ancestors needed to exert themselves physically to secure adequate nutrition, whereas our easy access to abundant food can lead to obesity. People working indoors do not get the sun exposure that our ancestors had, leading to vitamin D deficiency;[41] yet we risk skin cancer when we expose pale skin to the sun during occasional recreational

---

[39] de Murcia and Shall 2000; Skaper 2003.

[40] In like manner, we can view vaccinations as both therapeutic (or more accurately, prophylactic) and as enhancing.

[41] Thomas, Lloyd-Jones, Thadhani, Shaw, Deraska, Kitch, Vamvakas, Dick, Prince and Finkelstein 1998.

activities. Rapid blood coagulation was beneficial in the past, when there was a high risk of wounding. The increased risk for cardiovascular problems and embolisms was an acceptable tradeoff. Today, the risk of wounding has sharply decreased, making the downsides relatively more important. Reducing coagulation, e.g. by taking low-dose aspirin, can be beneficial given these changed demands,[42] although we risk incidental side-effects such as stomach irritation.

While the change in demands can cause or exacerbate problems, it can also alleviate them. The recent emergence of the IT industry appears to have produced a refuge for people with Asperger's syndrome where their preference for structure and detail becomes a virtue and their problems with face-to-face communication less of a disadvantage.[43] Deliberate fitting of environments to human evolutionary adaptations and individual idiosyncrasies is a promising adjunct to direct human enhancement for improving human performance and wellbeing.

2.3.1. Literacy and numeracy   Intellectual capacity, or at least some specific forms of it, seem to have become more rewarded in contemporary society than they were in the EEA. There is a positive correlation in Western society between IQ and income.[44] Higher levels of general cognitive ability are important not just for highly demanding, high status jobs, but also for success in everyday life, such as being able to fill out forms, understand news, and maintain health. As society becomes more complex, these demands increase, placing people of low cognitive ability at a greater disadvantage.[45] While general cognitive ability may have been advantageous (and selected for) in our evolutionary past,[46, 47] numeracy and literacy represent more specific abilities whose utility has increased dramatically in recent times.

Before the invention of writing, the human brain faced no pressure to be literate. In the current age, however, literacy is in very high demand. Failing to meet this demand places an individual at a severe disadvantage

---

[42] Force 2002.   [43] Silberman 2001.

[44] Neisser, Boodoo, Bouchard, Boykin, Brody, Ceci, Halpern, Loehlin, Perloff, Sternberg and Urbina 1996; Gottfredson 1997; Bersaglieri, Sabeti, Patterson, Vanderploeg, Schaffner, Drake, Rhodes, Reich and Hirschhorn 2004.

[45] Gottfredson 1997; Gottfredson 2004.   [46] Gottfredson 2007.

[47] It should be noted that IQ correlates negatively with fertility in many modern societies (Udry 1978; Vancourt and Bean 1985; Vining, Bygren, Hattori, Nystrom and Tamura 1988). This might be an example of value discordance between human values and evolutionary fitness.

in modern society. Since writing is a relatively recent invention (3,500 BC), and since it is even more recently that written language has become such a dominant mode of communication, it is plausible that the human brain is not optimized for modern conditions. The fact that the neural machinery needed for writing and reading largely overlaps with that needed to produce and interpret oral communication means that the mismatch between evolved capacity and present demands is not as great as it might have been. Nevertheless, as the phenomenon of dyslexia demonstrates, it is possible to have deficits in language processing that are relatively specific to written language, possibly arising from minor variations in phonological processing.[48] Dyslexia also appears to be linked to enhanced or atypical visuospatial abilities.[49] These abilities might have been useful in the EEA, but today literacy is usually more important for achieving life goals. If our species had been using written language for a couple of million years and reproductive fitness had depended on literacy, dyslexia might have been much rarer than it is.

Modern society also places much greater demands on advanced numerical skills than we faced in the EEA. In hunter-gatherer societies, numeracy demands appear to have been limited to being able to count to five or ten.[50] In the modern world, one is at a major disadvantage if one cannot understand at least basic arithmetic. Many occupations require a grasp of statistics, calculus, geometry, or higher mathematics. Programming skills open up additional employment possibilities. Good logical and analytical skills create further opportunities in our information-dense, technology-mediated, and generally formalized modern society. These skills were much less useful in the Pleistocene.

The altered nature of the demands we face suggests opportunities for enhancement by readjusting tradeoffs that are no longer optimal. For example, number relations appear to be handled by brain circuits closely linked to spatial cognition of external objects, and affected by spatial attention abilities.[51] Hence enhancement of this type of spatial attention,[52] possibly at the expense of remote or peripheral attention, could be a useful enhancement. Similarly, enhancements in reading ability at the

---

[48] Goulandris, Snowling and Walker 2000.
[49] von Karolyi, Winner, Gray and Sherman 2003; Brunswick, Martin, Marzano and Savill 2007.
[50] Pica, Lemer, Izard and Dehaene 2004.
[51] McCord 2000; Hubbard, Piazza, Pinel and Dehaene 2005.   [52] Green and Bavelier 2006.

expense of the dyslexia-related visuospatial abilities might gain support from the EOC.

2.3.2. Concentration   The importance of being able to concentrate on abstract thinking and tasks with little sensory feedback has increased significantly in modern times relative to the importance of peripheral awareness. In the EEA, peripheral awareness was crucial for detecting predators and enemies, while an ability to exclude other stimuli had few applications. We may hence have evolved attention systems with a tendency to be too easily distracted in a modern setting. It has been suggested that ADHD is a form of "response-readiness" that was more adaptive in past environments.[53] Concentration enhancers may therefore be feasible and promising in modern settings, enabling users to meet high demands for sustained attention. Drugs such as metylphenidate (Ritalin) are already used to treat ADHD and occasionally also for enhancement purposes.[54]

2.3.3. Dietary preferences and fat storage   One tradeoff involving food availability relates to the question of how much nutrition the body should store in fatty deposits. If high-calorie foods are scarce and food availability highly variable, it is optimal for an individual to crave high-calorie foods and to store lots of energy in fat deposits as insurance against lean times. We still need an appetite today, and we still need fat deposits, but—at least in the developed world—they are much less important now than in the past. Many people's natural set-points of appetite and body fat are higher than optimal, leading to increased morbidity. In wealthy modern societies, where a Mars bar is never far away, the risks of obesity and diabetes outweigh the risk of under-nutrition,[55] and a sweet tooth is maladaptive.

This suggests that it might be possible to enhance human health by finding effective ways to down-regulate our cravings for fat and sugar, or by reducing the absorption and storage of these calories in fatty tissues. Such an enhancement might take various forms: nutritional advice, diet pills, artificial sweeteners, indigestible substances that taste like fat, weight-loss clubs, hypnotherapy, and, in the future, gene therapy. The evolution heuristic suggests that our natural proclivities to consume and store nutrients

---

[53] Jensen, Mrazek, Knapp, Steinberg, Pfeffer, Schowalter and Shapiro 1997.
[54] Farah, Illes, Cook-Deegan, Gardner, Kandel, King, Parens, Sahakian and Wolpe 2004.
[55] Fontaine, Redden, Wang, Westfall and Allison 2003.

might be a case where we could benefit from going against the wisdom of nature. Independent considerations and possibly further research would be needed to determine the most effective way of doing this, given that weight loss itself is a longevity risk factor[56] and that those who are mildly overweight have lower mortality than those who are underweight or obese.[57] Possibly an aversion to unhealthy foods and eating habits would be more effective and safer than a general down-regulation of appetite. The heuristic tells us only that there are no general "wisdom of nature" reasons to retain our current bodyweight set-points; it does not by itself tell us which approaches to changing them would be safest.

2.4. The interplay between resources and demands

The picture is complicated by the fact that some phenomena zigzag across the two subcategories of changed tradeoffs (resources and demands). Transport vehicles and machinery are new resources that reduce the demand for physical exertion. The effect is that most of us get less exercise in the course of our daily routines. Yet our bodies appear to be designed for physical activity, so a sedentary life causes a variety of health problems. New resources (gyms, exercise equipment, parks, jogging clubs) have been developed to help us overcome the problems of a sedentary lifestyle. But now a new demand arises: we need the energy and self-motivation to make use of these resources—a demand that many find it difficult to meet.

In a case like this, there are multiple potential intervention points where a change could result in an improvement of our lives. One approach would be to design our environment in such a way as to force us to be more physically active. Elevators could be removed, motor vehicles banned from certain areas, and so forth. Another approach would be to attempt to redesign our bodies so that they would not be dependent on frequent physical exertion to remain healthy. On this approach, we might try to develop pharmaceuticals that trigger effects in the body similar to those normally caused by exercise (such as the IGF-1/MGF signaling pathways, which are stimulated by exercise or muscle damage).[58] Yet another approach would be to attempt interventions that increase our energy and self-motivation, thereby making it easier for us to exercise on our own

---

[56] Gaesser 1999.   [57] Flegal, Graubard, Williamson and Gail 2005.
[58] Baldwin and Haddad 2002; Goldspink 2005.

initiative. For instance, there might be pharmaceuticals that would give us more energy or strengthen our willpower, or perhaps a habit of regular workouts instilled in childhood would carry over into adult life.

Whether any of these interventions will work, and, if so, which one would be the most effective and have the best balance of benefits over burdens, cannot be determined a priori. This is an empirical question, whose answer may depend on changing social circumstances, levels of technology, personal preferences, and other factors. One should note that it is not only biological interventions which can have undesirable side-effects. Removing elevators might cause some health benefits for people forced to climb the stairs, but it may also deny access for people with mobility impairments and cause unnecessary inconvenience to others. Encouraging high levels of physical activity in children might have overall health benefits but it might also lead to more injuries, more worn-out knees and hip joints later in life, and less time for non-physical activities.

Another illustration of the complex interplay between new resources and new demands is offered by the case of addictive drugs. Alcohol, heroin, and crack cocaine are comparatively novel resources. The availability of these resources create a new demand on the human organism: the ability to avoid becoming addicted to harmful drugs that hijack the brain's reward system. Individuals vary in how they metabolize these drugs and how their brains react to exposure. Again, the solution might be to develop new resources (e.g. detox clinics), temporary pharmacological interventions (methadone), permanent biological modifications (vaccines), educational initiatives (drug awareness programs), or social policies (criminalization). Alternatively, one might attempt to develop safer, non-addictive substitutes for harmful drugs.[59] There are many possible ways to defy or to work around the wisdom of nature.

3. Value discordance

3.1. General remarks on value discordance

We have discussed opportunities for enhancement arising from the changed tradeoffs we face in the modern world compared to those of the EEA. (A

---

[59] Nutt 2006.

great engineer built a system for use in a certain environment; we adapt it for use in a different environment.) In this section, we discuss another source of enhancement opportunities: the discordance between evolutionary fitness and human values. (A great engineer built a system that efficiently serves one purpose; we tinker with it to make it serve a different purpose.)

While our goals are not identical to those of evolution, there is considerable overlap. We value health, and health increases inclusive fitness. We value good eyesight, and good eyesight is useful for survival. We value musicality and artistic creativity, and these talents helped to attract mates in the EEA. If we are hoping to enhance some attribute for which the concordance in objectives is perfect, the present category will not give any help in meeting the EOC. We then either have to find an answer from one of the other categories or else suspect that what appears to be an easy enhancement will in fact come at a large hidden cost.

Whilst some of our traits are both valuable to us and conducive to fitness, many attributes that we value would either not have promoted inclusive fitness in our natural environment, or else would not have been fitness-promoting to a sufficient extent to result in a profile of traits that is optimal from the perspective of our own values. There is a plethora of capacities or characteristics to which we assign a value that exceeds the contribution these characteristics made to survival and reproduction.

One obvious example is contraceptive technology. Vasectomy, birth control pills, and other contraceptive methods enhance our control over our reproductive systems, severing the link between sex and reproduction. We may value such enhancements because they make family planning easier and increase choice. But evolution would frown on these practices. The great engineer would not regard the absence of an easy reproductive off-switch as a defect. When our goals differ from hers, it is unsurprising that we are able to modify her design in ways that make it better (by our lights) even if our design skills fall far short of hers.[60]

We can distinguish (at least) two distinct sources of such value discordance. The first is that the characteristics that would maximize an individual's inclusive fitness are nor always identical to the characteristics that would be best for her. The other is that the characteristics that would maximize

---

[60] Evolution might still have the last laugh if in the long run she redesigns our species to directly desire to have as many children as possible, or to have an aversion against contraceptives. Cultural "evolution" might beat biological evolution to the punch.

an individual's inclusive fitness are not always identical to those that would be best for society, or impersonally best. If our goal is to identify potential interventions that individuals would have prudential reasons for wanting, then we may perhaps set aside the second source of value discordance. If, however, we are interested in addressing ethical and public policy matters, then it is relevant to consider value discordance arising from either of these two sources. Let us consider each in turn.

3.2. Good for the individual

What characteristics promote individual well-being? There is a vast ethical and empirical literature on this question, which we shall not attempt to review here. For our purposes, it will suffice to list (Table 1) some candidate characteristics, ones which may with some plausibility be taken to be among those that contribute to individual well-being in a wide range of circumstances. This list is for illustration only. Other lists could be substituted without affecting the structure of our argument.[61]

Table 1. Some traits that may promote individual well-being

- Emotional well-being
- Freedom from severe or chronic pain
- Friendship and love
- Long-term memory
- Mathematical ability
- Awareness and consciousness
- Musicality
- Artistic appreciation and creativity
- Literary appreciation
- Confidence and self-esteem
- Healthy pleasures
- Mental energy
- Ability to concentrate
- Abstract thinking
- Longevity
- Social skills

---

[61] The items in the list need not be final goods. Characteristics that are mere *means* to more fundamental goods can be included. For example, even if one thinks that musicality or musical appreciation is not intrinsically good, one can still include them in the list if one believes that they tend—as a matter of empirical fact—to promote well-being (for example, by creating opportunities for enjoyment).

To illustrate the idea, take mathematical ability. Suppose that we believe that having greater mathematical ability would tend to make our lives go better—perhaps because it would give us competitive advantages in the job market, perhaps because appreciating mathematical beauty is a value in itself, or perhaps because we believe that mathematical ability is linked to other abilities that would increase our well-being. We then pose the EOC: Why has evolution not already endowed us with more mathematical ability than we have?

It is possible that answers to this EOC may be found in the other categories we discuss in this chapter (changed tradeoffs or evolutionary restrictions). Yet suppose that is not so. We may then appeal to an answer in the value discordance category. Even if greater mathematical capacity would have been maladaptive in the EEA and even if it would still be maladaptive today, it may nevertheless be good for us, because the good for humans is different from what maximizes our fitness.

But we are not yet done. What the evolution heuristic teaches us in this case is that we must expect that the intervention will have some effect that reduces fitness. If we cannot form any plausible idea of what sort of effect the intervention might produce that would reduce fitness, then we must suspect that the intervention will have important effects that we have not understood. That should give us pause. A fitness-reducing effect that we have not anticipated might be something very bad, such as a serious medical side-effect. The EOC hoists a warning flag. If, however, we can give a plausible account of why the proposed intervention to increase mathematical ability would reduce fitness, *and yet we judge this fitness-reducing effect as desirable or at least worth enduring for the sake of the benefit*, then we have met the EOC.

This does not guarantee that the enhancement will succeed. It is still possible that the intervention will fail to produce the desired result or that it would have some unforeseen side-effect. There might be more than one sufficient reason why evolution did not already make this intervention to enhance mathematical ability. But once we have identified at least one sufficient reason, the warning flag raised by the EOC comes down. We have shown that one potential reason for thinking that the enhancement will fail (the "wisdom of nature" reason) does not apply to the present case.

As an example, evolution has not optimized us for happiness and has instead led to a number of adaptations that cause psychological distress and frustration.[62] The "hedonic-treadmill" causes us quickly to adapt to positive experiences and to seek more, as goods we have gained become taken for granted as a new status quo.[63] Sexual jealousy, romantic heartaches, status envy, competitiveness, anxiety, boredom, sadness and despair may have been essential for survival and reproductive success in the EEA, but they take a toll in terms of human suffering and may substantially reduce our well-being. An intervention that caused an upward shift in hedonic set-point, or that down-regulated some of these negative emotions, would hence meet the EOC: we can see why the effect would have been maladaptive in the EEA, and yet believe that we would benefit from these effects because of a discordance between inclusive fitness and individual well-being.

3.3. Good for society

Many characteristics that promote individual well-being also promote the social good, but the two lists are unlikely to be identical. Table 2 lists some candidate traits that might contribute to the good of society.

As with the list for individual well-being, this one is for illustration only. One could create alternative lists for various related questions, such as traits that are good for humanity as a whole, or for sentient life, or for

Table 2. Some traits that may promote the social good

> • Extended altruism
> • Conscientiousness and honesty
> • Modesty and self-deprecation
> • Originality, inventiveness, and independent thinking
> • Civil courage
> • Knowledge and good judgment about public affairs
> • Empathy and compassion
> • Nurturing emotions and caring behavior
> • Just admiration and appreciation
> • Self-control, ability to control violent impulses
> • Strong sense of fairness
> • Lack of racial prejudice
> • Lack of tendency to abuse drugs
> • Taking joy in others' successes and flourishing
> • Useful forms of economic productivity
> • Healthy longevity

[62] Buss 2000.   [63] Diener, Suh, Lucas and Smith 1999.

a particular community, or traits that specifically help us become better moral agents. While the lists may overlap, they will likely disagree about some characteristics or their relative importance. The evolution heuristic can be applied using any such list as input.

To use such a list with the EOC, we proceed in the same way as with the "good for the individual" source of value discordance. For example, we might have a drug that appears to make those who take it more compassionate. This might seem like a good thing, but why has evolution not already made us more compassionate? Presumably, evolution could easily have produced an endogenous substance with similar effects to the drug; so the likely explanation is that a higher level of compassionateness would not have increased inclusive fitness in the EEA. We may press on and ask *why* it is that greater compassionateness would have been maladaptive in the EEA. One may surmise that such a trait would have been associated with evolutionary downsides—such as reduced ability credibly to threaten savage retaliation, a tendency to spare the lives of enemies allowing them to come back another day and reverse their defeat, an increased propensity to offer help to those in need beyond what is useful for reciprocity and social acceptance, and so forth. But these very effects, which would have made heightened compassionateness maladaptive for an individual in the EEA, are precisely the kinds of effects which we might believe would be beneficial for the common good today. We do not have to assume that the relevant trade-offs have changed since the EEA. Even in the EEA, it might have had net good effects for a local population of hunter-gatherers if one person was born with a mutation causing an unusually high level of compassionateness, even though that individual himself might have suffered a fitness penalty. If we accept these premises, then the hypothetical drug that increases compassionateness would pass the EOC. It would be a case where we have reason to think that the wisdom of nature has not achieved what would be best for society and that we could feasibly do better.

4. Evolutionary restrictions

4.1. General remarks on evolutionary restrictions

The final category of answers to the EOC focuses on the fact that there are certain limitations in what evolution can do. Using the "great engineer" metaphor, we may say that we can hope to achieve certain things with our ham-handed tinkering that stumped Evolution, because we have access to tools, materials, and techniques that the great ingenious engineer lacked.

Metaphors aside, we can identify several restrictions of evolution's ability to achieve fitness-maximizing phenotypes even in the EEA. These are important, because in some cases they will indicate clear limitations in the "wisdom of nature", and a fortiori cases where there is room for potentially easy improvements. At a high level of abstraction, we can divide these restrictions into three classes:

- *Fundamental inability*: evolution is fundamentally incapable of producing a trait A.
- *Entrapment in local optimum*: evolution is stuck in a local optimum that excludes trait A.
- *Evolutionary lag*: evolution of trait A takes so many generations that there has not yet been enough time for it to develop.

These three classes, which are discussed in more detail in the following three subsections, are not sharply separate. For example, one reason why a trait may take a vast number of generations to develop is that it requires escaping from one or more local optima. And given truly astronomical time scales, even some traits that we shall regard as fundamentally beyond evolution's reach might conceivably have evolved. However, the three classes are distinct enough to deserve individualized attention.

4.2. Fundamental inability

Biology is limited in what it can build. DNA can only code for proteins, which have to act on moieties in a water-based cellular environment using the relatively weak chemical forces that a protein can muster. This makes it very unlikely that any terrestrial organism could produce diamond, for instance, since the synthesis of diamondoid structures requires significant energy.[64] And while bacteria can produce microscopic metal crystals,[65] there is no way to unite them into contiguous metal. Hence evolution

---

[64] Adding a carbon dimer to a diamond surface using a nanotechnological tool would take more than 6.1 eV (Merkle and Freitas 2003), about 20 times more energy than is released by the ATP hydrolysis that powers most enzymatic actions.

[65] Klaus, Joerger, Olsson and Granqvist 1999.

cannot achieve diamond tooth enamel or a titanium skeleton, even if these traits would have improved fitness.

Examples can be multiplied. It is unlikely that evolution could have evolved high-performance silicon chips to augment neural computation, even though such augmentations might have provided important benefits. A theoretical design of artificial red blood cells has been published, calculating the performance of a potentially feasible physical structure for transporting oxygen and carbon dioxide in the blood.[66] This design, which is not limited by the materials and pressures that can be achieved using biology, would enable performance far outside the range of natural red blood cells.

Radical departures from nature are apt to raise a host of separate questions regarding biocompatibility and functional integration with evolved systems. But at least there is no mystery as to why we would not already have evolved these enhancements even if they would have increased inclusive fitness in the EEA.

Enhancements that evolution is fundamentally incapable of producing can therefore meet the EOC. When invoking "fundamental inability", it is important to determine that the inability does not pertain merely to the specific means one intends to use to effect the enhancement. If evolution would have been able to employ some different means to achieve the same effect, the challenge would remain to explain why evolution has not achieved the enhancement using that alternative route.

4.3. Entrapment in local optimum

Evolution sometimes gets stuck on solutions that are locally but not globally optimal. A locally optimal solution is one where any small change would make the solution worse, even if some big changes might make it better.

Being trapped in a local optimum is especially likely to account for failure to evolve polygenic traits that are adaptive only once fully developed and incur a fitness penalty in their intermediary stages of evolution. In some cases, the evolution of such traits may require an improbable coincidence of several simultaneous mutations that might simply not have occurred among our finite number of ancestors. A crafty genetic engineer may be able to solve some of the problems that were intractable to blind evolution.

---

[66] Freitas 1998.

A human engineer can think backwards, starting with a goal in mind, working out what genetic modifications are necessary for its attainment.

The human appendix, a vestigial remnant of the caecum in other mammals, whilst having some limited immunological function,[67] easily becomes infected. In the natural state appendicitis is a life-threatening condition, and is especially likely to occur at a young age. There is also evidence that surgical removal of the appendix reduces the risk of ulcerative colitis.[68] It appears that removal of the appendix would have increased fitness in the EEA. However, a *smaller* appendix increases the risk of appendicitis. Carriers of genes predisposing for small appendices have higher risks of appendicitis than non-carriers, and, presumably, lower fitness.[69] Therefore, unless evolution could find a way of doing away with the appendix entirely in one fell swoop, it might be unable to get rid of the organ; whence it remains. An intervention that safely and conveniently removed it might be an enhancement, increasing both fitness and quality of life.

Another source of evolutionary lock-in is antagonistic pleiotropy, referring to a situation in which a gene affects multiple traits in both beneficial and harmful ways. If one trait is strongly fitness-increasing and the other mildly fitness-decreasing, the overall effect is positive selection for the gene.[70] One example is the $\varepsilon 4$ allele of apolipoprotein E. Having one or two copies of the allele increases the risk of Alzheimer disease in middle age but lowers the incidence of childhood diarrhea and may protect cognitive development.[71] Antagonistic pleiotropy has also been discussed in relation to theories of ageing. The local optimum here is to retain the genes in question, but the global optimum would be to eliminate the antagonistic pleiotropy by evolving genes that specifically produced the beneficial traits without detrimental effects on other traits. Over longer timescales, evolution usually gets around antagonistic pleiotropy, for example by evolving modifier genes that counteract the negative effects,[72] but such developments can take a long time and in the meanwhile a species remains trapped in a local optimum.

[67] Fisher 2000.

[68] Koutroubakis and Vlachonikolis 2000; Andersson, Olaison, Tysk and Ekbom 2001.

[69] Nesse and Williams 1998.

[70] Leroi, Bartke, De Benedictis, Franceschi, Gartner, Gonos, Fedei, Kivisild, Lee, Kartaf-Ozer, Schumacher, Sikora, Slagboom, Tatar, Yashin, Vijg and Zwaan 2005.

[71] Oria, Patrick, Zhang, Lorntz, Costa, Brito, Barrett, Lima and Guerrant 2005.

[72] Hammerstein 1996.

Yet another way in which evolution can get locked into a suboptimal state is exemplified by the phenomenon of heterozygote advantage. This refers to the common situation where individuals who are heterozygous for a particular gene (i.e. have two different alleles of that gene) have an advantage over homozygote individuals (who have two identical copies of the gene). Heterozygote advantage is responsible for many cases of potentially harmful genes being maintained at a finite frequency in a population.

The classic example of heterozygote advantage is sickle-cell gene, where homozygote individuals suffer anemia while heterozygote individuals bene-fit from improved malaria resistance.[73] Heterozygotes have greater fitness than both types of homozygote (those lacking the sickle-cell allele and those having two copies of it). Balancing selection preserves the sickle-cell gene in populations (at a frequency that varies geographically with the prevalence of malaria). The "optimum" that evolution selects is one in which, by chance, some individuals will be born homozygous for the gene, resulting in sickle-cell anemia, a potentially fatal blood disease. The "ideal optimum"—everybody being heterozygous for the gene—is unattainable by natural selection because of Mendelian inheritance, which gives each child born to heterozygote parents a 25 per cent chance of being born homozygous for the sickle-cell allele.

Heterozygote advantage suggests an obvious enhancement opportunity. If possible, the variant allele could be removed and its gene product administered as medication. Alternatively, genetic screening could be used to guarantee heterozygosity, enabling us to reach the ideal optimum that eluded natural selection.

The phenomenon of heterozygote advantage points to potential enhancements beyond reducing susceptibility to diseases such as malaria and sickle-cell anemia. For instance, there is some indirect evidence that at least Type I Gaucher's Disease (and possibly other sphingolipid storage diseases) is linked to improved cognition, given the significantly higher proportion of sufferers in occupations correlated with high IQ.[74] This, and other circumstantial evidence, is used by the authors of the cited study to argue that heterozygote advantage can explain the high IQ test scores and the high prevalence of Type I Gaucher's Disease among Ashkenazi

[73] Allison 1954; Cavalli-Sforza and Bodmer 1999.
[74] Cochran, Hardy and Harpending 2006.

Jews. Should this prediction be borne out by finding an IQ advantage for heterozygote carriers of the diseases, it would suggest that screening to promote heterozygosity, or genetic interventions to induce it, would be viable forms of cognition enhancement that meet the EOC.

One other kind of evolutionary entrapment is worth noting here, that of an evolutionarily stable strategy (ESS), "a strategy such that, if all the members of a population adopt it, no mutant strategy can invade".[75] One way in which a species can become trapped in an ESS is through sexual selection. In order to be successful at wooing peahens, peacocks have to produce extravagant tails which serve to advertise the male's genetic quality. Only healthy peacocks can afford to produce and carry top-notch tails. It is adaptive for peahens to prefer to mate with peacocks that sport an impressive tail; and given this fact, it is also adaptive for peacocks to invest heavily in their plumage. It is likely that the species would have been better off if it had evolved some less costly way for males to signal fitness. Yet no individual peacock or peahen is able to defect from the ESS without thereby removing themselves from the gene pool. If there had been a United Nations of the peafowl, through which the birds could have adopted a coordinated millennium plan to overcome their species' vanity, the peacocks would surely soon be wearing a more casual outfit.

The concept of an ESS can be generalized to that of an evolutionarily stable state. A population is said to be in an evolutionarily stable state if its genetic composition is restored by selection after a disturbance, provided the disturbance is not too large.[76] Such a population can be genetically monomorphic or polymorphic. Thus, while ESS refers to a specific strategy that is stable if everybody adopts it, an evolutionary stable state can encompass a set of strategies whose distribution is stable under small perturbations. It has been suggested that the human population has been in a stable state in the EEA with regard to sociopathy, which can be seen as a defector strategy which can prosper when it is rare but becomes maladaptive when it is more common.[77]

Another way in which evolution can fail to produce solutions that are fitness-maximizing for organisms is intragenomic conflict, in which phenomena such as meiotic drive, transposons, homing endonuclease

---

[75] Smith 1982.   [76] Ibid.   [77] Mealey 1995.

genes, B-chromosomes, and plasmids result from natural selection among lower-level units such as individual genes.[78] In cases where we can identify intragenomic conflict as responsible for a suboptimal outcome, there is an opportunity for enhancement that can meet the EOC (provided we have the technological means to make the requisite interventions). Genes or traits that would not have evolved, or which would not have been stable against intragenomic competition, could be inserted, possibly supported by interventions removing some of the competing genetic elements.

4.4. Evolutionary lag

Evolution takes time—often, a long time. If conditions change rapidly, the genome will lag. Given that conditions for humanoid ancestors were quite variable—due to migration into new regions, climate change, social dynamics, advances in tool use, and adaptation in pathogens, parasites, predators, and prey—our species has never been perfectly adapted to its environment. Evolution is running up fitness slopes, but when the fitness landscape keeps changing under its feet, it may never reach a peak. Even if beneficial alleles or allele combinations exist, they may not have had the time to diffuse across human populations. For some proposed enhancements, evolutionary lag can therefore provide an answer to the EOC.

This source of answers to the EOC is related to the changed tradeoffs category, but with the difference that here we are focusing on ways in which even during the EEA we were not perfectly adapted to our environment. Even if we set aside the dramatic ways in which resources and demands have changed since the introduction of agriculture, there may still be instances of earlier evolutionary lags that have not yet been truncated and which may point to opportunities for enhancement.

There are many factors limiting the speed of evolution.[79] Some are inherent in the process itself, such as the mutation rate, the need for sufficient genetic diversity, and the constraint that selection can only encode a few bits into the genome per generation.[80] A recessive beneficial mutation will spread to an appreciable fraction of a fixed well-mixed population in time inversely proportional to its selective advantage. For

---

[78] Burt and Trivers 2006.   [79] Barton and Partridge 2000.   [80] Worden 1995.

example, if the mutation gives a 0.1 per cent increase in fitness, it will take 9,200 generations (230,000 years assuming 25 years per generation) to reach 50 per cent of the population from a starting level of 0.01 per cent. For a 10 per cent fitness-advantage, just 92 generations (2,300 years) are needed.[81] Population structure and especially low-population bottlenecks can accelerate the spread significantly.

In nature, the strength of selection for a trait is generally quite weak. A review of published studies[82] found the distribution of selection strengths across species to be exponential, with a small median magnitude: for most traits and in most systems directional selection is fairly weak. Selection via survival appears to be weaker than selection through mating success, making sexual selection a big factor. Quadratic selection gradients, indicating the "sharpness" of fitness peaks, were also found to be exponentially distributed and with small median. This implies that stabilizing selection (reducing genetic diversity once a population has reached a local fitness peak) is often fairly weak. Indirect selection (where trait fitness depends on another correlated trait) also appears to be playing only a minor role.[83] These results suggest that beneficial new traits are likely to spread slowly.

A population living in a heterogeneous or changeable environment may not be able to converge on a single fitness peak but will be spread out around it. This might reduce extinction risks for the lineage, since there will always be some individuals that are well adapted if the conditions change and the lineage will survive more easily than if a less dispersed population had to ascend the current gradient towards the top through a region of low survivability.

It is possible to detect empirically the presence of genetic variations under positive fitness pressure through their signatures.[84] These signatures range from multimillion-year timescale changes in gene sequence (mostly useful to point out ongoing or recurrent selection), to changes in genetic diversity caused by the rapid spread of a beneficial mutation in the past 250,000 years, to the differences between human populations which can

[81] Cavalli-Sforza and Bodmer 1999.
[82] Hoekstra, Hoekstra, Berrigan, Vignieri, Hoang, Hill, Beerli and Kingsolver 2001.
[83] Ibid.
[84] Sabeti, Schaffner, Fry, Lohmueller, Varilly, Shamovsky, Palma, Mikkelsen, Altshuler and Lander 2006.

indicate genetic selection over the last 50,000–75,000 years. Such long-term selection evidence is mainly useful for understanding the selection pressures in the EEA.

There is evidence for recent positive selection in humans.[85] Some of it may be in response to climate variations, producing a wide range of variation in salt-regulating genes in populations far from the equator.[86] Genes involved in brain development have also been shown to have been under strong positive selection with new variants emerging over the last 37,000 years[87] and 5,800 years.[88]

There is evidence that genes related to the brain have evolved more quickly in the human lineage than in other primates and rodents.[89] The rapid growth of the brain in the human lineage also suggests that its size must be controlled by relatively simple genetic mechanisms.[90] Despite this, it should be noted that the selection differential per generation for human brain weight during the Pleistocene was only 0.0004 per generation:[91] even under fast evolution brain size was limited by tradeoffs.

If we find a gene that has a desirable effect, and that evolved recently and has not yet spread far despite showing evidence of positive selection, interventions that insert it into the genome or mimic its effects would likely meet the EOC. A simple example would be lactose tolerance. While development of lactose intolerance is adaptive for mammals since it makes weaning easier, dairy products have stimulated selection for lactase in humans over the last 5,000–10,000 years.[92] This is so recent that there has not been time for the trait to diffuse to all human populations. (Populations that have domesticated cattle but do not have lactose tolerance instead make use of fermented milk or cheese.) Taking lactase pills enables lactose-intolerant people to digest lactose, widening the range of food they can enjoy. This enhancement clearly passes the EOC.

[85] Voight, Kudaravalli, Wen and Pritchard 2006.

[86] Thompson, Kuttab-Boulos, Witonsky, Yang, Roe and Di Rienzo 2004.

[87] Evans, Gilbert, Mekel-Bobrov, Vallender, Anderson, Vaez-Azizi, Tishkoff, Hudson and Lahn 2005.

[88] Mekel-Bobrov, Gilbert, Evans, Vallender, Anderson, Hudson, Tishkoff and Lahn 2005.

[89] Dorus, Vallender, Evans, Anderson, Gilbert, Mahowald, Wyckoff, Malcom and Lahn 2004.

[90] Roth and Dicke 2005.

[91] Cavalli-Sforza and Bodmer 1999, 692.

[92] Bersaglieri, Sabeti, Patterson, Vanderploeg, Schaffner, Drake, Rhodes, Reich and Hirschhorn 2004; Tishkoff, Reed, Ranciaro, Voight, Babbitt, Silverman, Powell, Mortensen, Hirbo, Osman, Ibrahim, Omar, Lema, Nyambo, Ghori, Bumpstead, Pritchard, Wray and Deloukas 2007.

5. Discussion

The evolution heuristic instructs us to consider, for an apparently attractive enhancement, why we have not already evolved the intended trait if it is really such a good idea. We called this question the Evolutionary Optimality Challenge, and we have described three broad categories of possible answers, and given some examples of particular enhancements for which it is possible to meet the EOC, and which, therefore, seem comparatively promising as intervention targets that may be feasible in the relatively near term and which may have on balance beneficial effects.

In general, when we pose the EOC for some particular proposed enhancement, we might discover one of several things:

1. Current ignorance prevents us from forming any plausible idea about the evolutionary factors at play.
2. We come up with a plausible idea about the relevant evolutionary factors, and this reveals that the proposed modification would likely not be a net benefit.
3. We come up with a plausible idea about the relevant evolutionary factors, and this reveals why we would not already have evolved to have the enhanced capacity even if it would be a net benefit.
4. We come up with several plausible but mutually inconsistent ideas about the relevant evolutionary factors.

The first possibility means that we have no clear idea about why, from a phylogenetic perspective, the trait that is the target of the proposed enhancement is the way it is. This should give us pause. If we do not understand why a very complex evolved system has a certain property, there is a considerable risk that something will go wrong if we try to modify it. The case might be one of those where nature does know best. Like an over-ambitious tinkerer with merely superficial understanding of what he is doing while he is making changes to the design of a master craftsman, the potential for damage is considerable and the chances of producing an all-things-considered improvement are small.

We are not claiming that it is always inadvisable to try an intervention when we have no adequate understanding of the subsystem we intend to enhance. We might have other sources of evidence that afford us sufficient assurance that the intervention will work and will not cause unacceptable side-effects, even without understanding the evolutionary functions involved. For example, we might have used the intervention many times before and found that it works well. Alternatively, we might have evidence from a closely analogous subsystem, such as an animal model, that suggests that the intervention should work in humans too. In such cases, the evolution heuristic delivers only a weak recommendation: that absent any good answer to the EOC, we should proceed only with great caution. In particular, we should be alert to the possibility that the proposed intervention will turn out to have significant (but perhaps subtle) side-effects.

The second possibility is that we succeed in developing a plausible understanding of the pertinent evolutionary factors, and, having done so, we find our initial hopes about the proposed modification undermined. None of the three categories we have described yields a satisfactory answer to the EOC: the relevant tradeoffs have not changed since the EOC, there is no relevant value discordance, and no evolutionary restriction would have prevented the modification from already having evolved by now. In this case we have strong reason for thinking that the enhancement intervention will fail or backfire. If we proceed, the wisdom of nature will bite us.

The fourth possibility is that we come up with two or more plausible but incompatible evolutionary accounts of the evolutionary factors at play. In this case, we can consider the implications of each of the different evolutionary accounts separately according to the above criteria. If all yield green lights, we are encouraged to proceed. If some of the evolutionary accounts yield green lights but others yield red lights, then we face a situation of uncertainty. We can use standard decision-theory to determine how to proceed—we can take a gamble if we feel that the balance of probabilities sufficiently favor the green lights; if not, we can attempt to acquire more information in order to reduce the uncertainty, or forgo the potential enhancement and try something else.

The evolution heuristic is not a rival method to the more obvious way of determining whether some enhancement intervention works: testing it in well-designed clinical trials. Instead, the heuristic is complementary. It helps us ask some useful questions. By posing the EOC, and carefully searching for and evaluating possible answers in each of the three categories we described, we can (a) identify promising candidate enhancement interventions, to be explored further in laboratory and clinical studies, and (b) better evaluate the likelihood that some intervention which has shown seemingly positive results in clinical studies will actually work as advertised and will not have unacceptable side-effects of a hidden, subtle, or long-term nature.

6. Conclusion

There is a widespread belief in some kind of "wisdom of nature". Many people prefer "natural" remedies, "natural" food supplements, and "natural" ways of improving human capacities such as training, diet, and grooming. "Unnatural" interventions are often viewed with suspicion, and this attitude seems to be especially pronounced in relation to unnatural ways of enhancing human capacities, which are viewed as unwise, short-sighted, and hubristic. We believe that such attitudes also exert an influence on beliefs about the kind of matters that arise in bioethical discussions of human enhancement.

While it is tempting to dismiss intuitions about the wisdom of nature as vulgar prejudice, we have suggested that these intuitions contain a grain of truth, especially as they pertain to human enhancement. We have attempted to explicate this grain of truth as the Evolutionary Optimality Challenge.

After posing this challenge, the evolution heuristic instructs us to examine three broad categories of potential ways of meeting the challenge: changed tradeoffs, value discordance, and evolutionary restrictions. These categories correspond to systematic limitations in the wisdom of nature idea. For some potential enhancement interventions, the challenge can be met with an answer from one of these categories; for other potential interventions, the challenge cannot be met. The latter interventions merit suspicion, and attempting them may indeed be unwise, short-sighted, and hubristic. The former interventions, in contrast, do not defy the wisdom of nature and have a better chance of working.

By understanding both the sense in which there is validity in the idea that nature is wise and the limits beyond which the idea ceases to be valid, we are in a better position to identify promising human enhancements and to evaluate the risk–benefit ratio of extant enhancements. If we are right in supposing that intuitions about the wisdom of nature exert an inarticulate influence on opinion in contemporary bioethics of human enhancement, then the evolution heuristic—while primarily a method for addressing empirical questions—may also help to inform our assessments of more normatively loaded items of dispute.[93]

References

Aiello, L. C., N. Bates, and T. Joffe. 2001. 'In defense of the Expensive Tissue Hypothesis'. In *Evolutionary Anatomy of the Primate Cerebral Cortex*. Falk, D. and K. R. Gibson (eds), Cambridge, UK: Cambridge University Press: 57–78.

Allison, A. C. 1954. 'Protection Afforded by Sickle Cell Trait Against Subtertian Malarial Infection', *British Medical Journal* 1: 290–4.

Andersson, R. E., G. Olaison, C. Tysk, and A. Ekbom. 2001. 'Appendectomy and protection against ulcerative colitis', *New England Journal of Medicine* 344(11): 808–14.

Baldwin, K. M. and F. Haddad. 2002. 'Skeletal muscle plasticity—Cellular and molecular responses to altered physical activity paradigms', *American Journal of Physical Medicine & Rehabilitation* 81(11): S40–S51.

Barton, N., and L. Partridge. 2000. 'Limits to natural selection', *Bioessays* 22(12): 1075–84.

Battista, J. R., A. M. Earl, and M. J. Park. 1999. 'Why is Deinococcus radiodurans so resistant to ionizing radiation?', *Trends in Microbiology* 7(9): 362–5.

Beauchamp, T. L., and J. F. Childress. 1979. *Principles of Biomedical Ethics*. New York and Oxford: Oxford University Press.

Bersaglieri, T., P. C. Sabeti, N. Patterson, T. Vanderploeg, S. F. Schaffner, J. A. Drake, M. Rhodes, D. E. Reich, and J. N. Hirschhorn. 2004. 'Genetic signatures of strong recent positive selection at the lactase gene', *American Journal of Human Genetics* 74(6): 1111–20.

Boon, T. and N. van Baren. 2003. 'Immunosurveillance against cancer and immunotherapy—synergy or antagonism?', *New England Journal of Medicine* 348(3): 252–4.

Brunswick, N., G. N. Martin, L. Marzano, and N. Savill. 2007. 'Visuo-spatial ability, handedness and developmental dyslexia: Just how sinister was Andy Warhol?' Presentation to the 25th European Workshop on Cognitive Neuropsychology, Italy 2007.

[93] For their comments, we are grateful to Rebecca Roache for helpful comments on an earlier draft of this paper, and to the audience at the *TransVision 2006* conference in Helsinki, Finland, for useful questions.

Bunker, J. P. 2001. 'The role of medical care in contributing to health improvements within societies', *Int. J. Epidemiol.* 30(6): 1260–3.

Burt, A., and R. L. Trivers. 2006. *Genes in Conflict: The Biology of Selfish Genetic Elements.* Harvard: Belknap Press.

Buss, D. M. 2000. 'The evolution of happiness', *American Psychologist* 55(1): 15–23.

Caldwell, J. A. 2001. 'Efficacy of stimulants for fatigue management: The effects of Provigil and Dexedrine on sleep-deprived aviators', *Fatigue in Transportation* (Part F): 19–37.

Cavalli-Sforza, L. L., and W. F. Bodmer. 1999. *The Genetics of Human Populations*, New York: Dover Publications.

Cochran, G., J. Hardy, and H. Harpending. 2006. 'Natural History of Ashkenazi Intelligence', *Journal of Biosocial Science* 38(5): 659–93.

Colloca, L., and F. Benedetti. 2005. 'Placebos and painkillers: is mind as real as matter?', *Nature Reviews Neuroscience* 6(7): 545–52.

Dawkins, R. 1976. *The Selfish Gene.* Oxford: Oxford University Press.

de Murcia, G., and S. Shall (eds.), 2000. *From DNA Damage and Stress Signaling to Cell Death: Poly ADP-Ribosylation Reactions.* Oxford: Oxford University Press.

Demas, G. E., V. Chefer, M. I. Talan, and R. J. Nelson. 1997. 'Metabolic costs of mounting an antigen-stimulated immune response in adult and aged C57BL/6J mice', *American Journal of Physiology—Regulatory Integrative and Comparative Physiology* 42(5): R1631–R7.

Diener, E., E. M. Suh, R. E. Lucas, and H. L. Smith. 1999. 'Subjective well-being: Three decades of progress', *Psychological Bulletin* 125(2): 276–302.

Dorus, S., E. J. Vallender, P. D. Evans, J. R. Anderson, S. L. Gilbert, M. Mahowald, G. J. Wyckoff, C. M. Malcom, and B. T. Lahn. 2004. 'Accelerated evolution of nervous system genes in the origin of Homo sapiens', *Cell* 119(7): 1027–40.

Dunn, G. P., L. J. Old, and R. D. Schreiber. 2004. 'The immunobiology of cancer immunosurveillance and immunoediting', *Immunity* 21(2): 137–48.

Elia, M. 1992. 'Organ and tissue contribution to metabolic rate', *Energy metabolism: tissue determinants and cellular corollaries.* McKinney, J. M. and H. N. Tucker (eds). New York: Raven, 61–79.

Evans, P. D., S. L. Gilbert, N. Mekel-Bobrov, E. J. Vallender, J. R. Anderson, L. M. Vaez-Azizi, S. A. Tishkoff, R. R. Hudson, and B. T. Lahn. 2005. 'Microcephalin, a gene regulating brain size, continues to evolve adaptively in humans', *Science* 309(5741): 1717–20.

Fairclough, S. H., and K. Houston. 2004. 'A metabolic measure of mental effort', *Biological Psychology* 66(2): 177–90.

Farah, M. J., J. Illes, R. Cook-Deegan, H. Gardner, E. Kandel, P. King, E. Parens, B. Sahakian, and P. R. Wolpe. 2004. 'Neurocognitive enhancement: what can we do and what should we do?', *Nature Reviews Neuroscience* 5(5): 421.

Fish, J. L., and C. A. Lockwood. 2003. 'Dietary constraints on encephalization in primates', *American Journal of Physical Anthropology* 120(2): 171–81.

Fisher, R. E. 2000. 'The primate appendix: A reassessment', *Anatomical Record* 261(6): 228–36.

Flegal, K. A., B. I. Graubard, D. F. Williamson, and M. H. H. Gail. 2005. 'Excess deaths associated with underweight, overweight, and obesity', *Jama—Journal of the American Medical Association* 293(15): 1861–7.

Fontaine, K. R., D. T. Redden, C. X. Wang, A. O. Westfall, and D. B. Allison. 2003. 'Years of life lost due to obesity', *Jama—Journal of the American Medical Association* 289(2): 187–93.

Force, U. S. P. S. T. 2002. 'Aspirin for the primary prevention of cardiovascular events: recommendation and rationale', *Annals of Internal Medicine* 136(2): 157–60.

Frech, H. E., and R. D. Miller. 1996. 'The Productivity of Health Care and Pharmaceuticals: An International Comparison'. UCLA Research Program in Pharmaceutical Economics and Policy 97–1. http://repositories.cdlib.org/pep/97-1/

Freitas, R. A., Jr. 1998. 'Exploratory Design in Medical Nanotechnology: A Mechanical Artificial Red Cell', *Artificial Cells, Blood Substitutes, and Immobilization Biotechnology* 26: 411–30.

Gaesser, G. A. 1999. 'Thinness and weight loss: beneficial or detrimental to longevity?', *Medicine and Science in Sports and Exercise* 31(8): 1118–28.

Goldspink, G. 2005. 'Mechanical signals, IGF-I gene splicing, and muscle adaptation', *Physiology* 20: 232–8.

Gottfredson, L. S. 1997. 'Why g matters: The complexity of everyday life', *Intelligence* 24(1): 79–132.

——— 2004. 'Life, death, and intelligence', *Journal of Cognitive Education and Psychology* 4(1): 23–46.

——— 2007. 'Innovation, fatal accidents, and the evolution of general intelligence'. In M. J. Roberts (ed.), *Integrating the mind: Domain general vesus domain specific process in higher cognition*, Hove: UK Psychology Press, 387–425.

Goulandris, N. K., M. J. Snowling, and I. Walker. 2000. 'Is dyslexia a form of specific language impairment? A comparison of dyslexic and language impaired children as adolescents', *Annals of Dyslexia* L: 103–20.

Green, C. S., and D. Bavelier. 2006. 'Enumeration versus multiple object tracking: the case of action video game players', *Cognition* 101(1): 217–45.

Hagen, E. H. 2002. 'What is the EEA?' (detailed answer), *Evolutionary Psychology FAQ*, retrieved 2 July, 2006, from http://www.anth.ucsb.edu/projects/human/epfaq/eea2.html.

Hammerstein, P. 1996. 'Darwinian adaptation, population genetics and the streetcar theory of evolution', *Journal of Mathematical Biology* 34(5–6): 511–32.

Hoekstra, H. E., J. M. Hoekstra, D. Berrigan, S. N. Vignieri, A. Hoang, C. E. Hill, P. Beerli, and J. G. Kingsolver. 2001. 'Strength and tempo of directional selection in the wild', *Proc. Natl. Acad. Sci. USA* 98(16): 9157–60.

Holliday, M. A. 1986. 'Body composition and energy needs during growth', *Human Growth: A Comprehensive Treatise*. Falkner, F. and J. M. Tanner (eds). New York: Plenum Press, 101–17.

House, J. S., K. R. Landis, and D. Umberson. 1988. 'Social relationships and health', *Science* 241(4865): 540–5.

Hubbard, E. M., M. Piazza, P. Pinel, and S. Dehaene. 2005. 'Interactions between number and space in parietal cortex', *Nature Reviews Neuroscience* 6(6): 435–48.

Humphrey, Nicholas, 2002. 'Great Expectations: The Evolutionary Psychology of Faith-healing and the Placebo Response'. In *Psychology at the Turn of Millennium*, vol. 2: *Social, Developmental, and Clinical Perspectives*. Hofsten, C. and L. Bäckman (eds). Hove: Psychology Press, 225–46.

Jensen, P. S., D. Mrazek, P. K. Knapp, L. Steinberg, C. Pfeffer, J. Schowalter, and T. Shapiro. 1997. 'Evolution and revolution in child psychiatry: ADHD as a disorder of adaptation', *Journal of the American Academy of Child and Adolescent Psychiatry* 36(12): 1672–9.

Kiecolt, J. K., R. Glaser, J. T. Cacioppo, R. C. MacCallum, M. Snydersmith, C. Kim, and W. B. Malarkey. 1997. 'Marital conflict in older adults: Endocrinological and immunological correlates', *Psychosomatic Medicine* 59(4): 339–49.

Kirsch, I., T. J. Moore, A. Scoboria, and S. S. Nicholls. 2002. 'The Emperor's New Drugs: An Analysis of Antidepressant Medication Data Submitted to the US Food and Drug Administration', *Prevention & Treatment*, 5.

Klaus, T., R. Joerger, E. Olsson, and C. G. Granqvist. 1999. 'Silver-based crystalline nanoparticles, microbially fabricated', *Proc. Natl. Acad. Sci. USA* 96(24): 13611–14.

Korol, D. L., and P. E. Gold. 1998. 'Glucose, memory, and aging', *American Journal of Clinical Nutrition* 67(4): 764S–71S.

Koutroubakis, I. E., and I. G. Vlachonikolis. 2000. 'Appendectomy and the development of ulcerative colitis: Results of a metaanalysis of published case-control studies', *American Journal of Gastroenterology* 95(1): 171–6.

Leroi, A. M., A. Bartke, G. De Benedictis, C. Franceschi, A. Gartner, E. S. Gonos, M. E. Fedei, T. Kivisild, S. Lee, N. Kartaf-Ozer, M. Schumacher, E. Sikora, E. Slagboom, M. Tatar, A. I. Yashin, J. Vijg, and B. Zwaan. 2005. 'What evidence is there for the existence of individual genes with antagonistic pleiotropic effects?' *Mechanisms of Ageing and Development* 126(8): 421–9.

Maizels, R. M. 2005. 'Infections and allergy—helminths, hygiene and host immune regulation', *Current Opinion in Immunology* 17(6): 656–61.

Manning, C. A., W. S. Stone, D. L. Korol, and P. E. Gold. 1998. 'Glucose enhancement of 24-h memory retrieval in healthy elderly humans', *Behavioural Brain Research* 93(1–2): 71–6.

Martin, L. B., 2nd, A. Scheuerlein, and M. Wikelski. 2003. 'Immune activity elevates energy expenditure of house sparrows: a link between direct and indirect costs?', *Proc. Biol. Sci.* 270(1511): 153–8.

Martin, P. Y., and D. Benton. 1999. 'The influence of a glucose drink on a demanding working memory task', *Physiology and Behavior* 67(1): 69–74.

Martin, R. D. 1996. 'Scaling of the mammalian brain: The maternal energy hypothesis', *News in Physiological Sciences* 11: 149–56.

Matte, T. D. 2001. 'Influence of variation in birth weight within normal range and within sibships on IQ at age 7 years: cohort study', *British Medical Journal* 323(7314): 310–14.

McCord, J. M. 2000. 'The evolution of free radicals and oxidative stress', *Am. J. Med.* 108(8): 652–9.

McDade, T. W. 2002. 'Status incongruity in Samoan youth: a biocultural analysis of culture change, stress, and immune function', *Medical Anthropology Quarterly* 16(2): 123–50.

———2003. 'Life History Theory and the Immune System: Steps Toward a Human Ecological Immunology', *Yearbook of Physical Anthropology* 46: 100–25.

McDaniel, M. A. 2005. 'Big-brained people are smarter: A meta-analysis of the relationship between in vivo brain volume and intelligence', *Intelligence* 33(4): 337–46.

McKeown, T., and C. R. Lowe. 1974. *An Introduction to Social Medicine*. Oxford: Blackwell Scientific.

Mealey, L. 1995. 'The Sociobiology of Sociopathy—an Integrated Evolutionary Model', *Behavioral and Brain Sciences* 18(3): 523–41.

Meikle, A., L. M. Riby, and B. Stollery. 2005. 'Memory processing and the glucose facilitation effect: the effects of stimulus difficulty and memory load', *Nutritional Neuroscience* 8(4): 227–32.

Mekel-Bobrov, N., S. L. Gilbert, P. D. Evans, E. J. Vallender, J. R. Anderson, R. R. Hudson, S. A. Tishkoff, and B. T. Lahn. 2005. 'Ongoing adaptive evolution of ASPM, a brain size determinant in Homo sapiens', *Science* 309(5741): 1720–2.

Merkle, R. C., and R. A. Freitas. 2003. 'Theoretical analysis of a carbon-carbon dimer placement tool for diamond mechanosynthesis', *Journal of Nanoscience and Nanotechnology* 3(4): 319–24.

Moret, Y., and P. Schmid-Hempel. 2000. 'Survival for immunity: the price of immune system activation for bumblebee workers', *Science* 290(5494): 1166–8.

Neisser, U., G. Boodoo, T. J. Bouchard, A. W. Boykin, N. Brody, S. J. Ceci, D. F. Halpern, J. C. Loehlin, R. Perloff, R. J. Sternberg, and S. Urbina. 1996. 'Intelligence: Knowns and unknowns', *American Psychologist* 51(2): 77–101.

Nesse, R. M., and G. C. Williams. 1998. 'Evolution and the origins of disease', *Scientific American* 279(5): 86–93.

Newhouse, J. P., and T. I. E. Group. 1993. *Free for All? Lessons from the RAND Health Insurance Experiment*. Cambridge, Mass.: Harvard University Press.

Niven, J. E. 2005. 'Brain evolution: Getting better all the time?', *Current Biology* 15(16): R624–R6.

Nutt, D. J. 2006. 'Alcohol alternatives—a goal for psychopharmacology?', *Journal of Psychopharmacology* 20(3): 318–20.

Oria, R. B., P. D. Patrick, H. Zhang, B. Lorntz, C. M. D. Costa, G. A. C. Brito, L. J. Barrett, A. A. M. Lima, and R. L. Guerrant. 2005. 'APOE4 protects the cognitive development in children with heavy diarrhea burdens in northeast Brazil', *Pediatric Research* 57(2): 310–16.

Ots, I., A. B. Kerimov, E. V. Ivankina, T. A. Ilyina, and P. Horak. 2001. 'Immune challenge affects basal metabolic activity in wintering great tits', *Proc. Biol. Sci.* 268(1472): 1175–81.

Parker, G. A. and J. M. Smith. 1990. 'Optimality Theory in Evolutionary Biology', *Nature* 348(6296): 27–33.

Pica, P., C. Lemer, V. Izard, and S. Dehaene. 2004. 'Exact and Approximate Arithmetic in an Amazonian Indigene Group', *Science* 306(5695): 499–503.

Roth, G., and U. Dicke. 2005. 'Evolution of the brain and intelligence', *Trends in Cognitive Sciences* 9(5): 250–7.

Sabeti, P. C., S. F. Schaffner, B. Fry, J. Lohmueller, P. Varilly, O. Shamovsky, A. Palma, T. S. Mikkelsen, D. Altshuler, and E. S. Lander. 2006. 'Positive natural selection in the human lineage', *Science* 312(5780): 1614–20.

Sapolsky, R. M. 2005. 'The influence of social hierarchy on primate health', *Science* 308(5722): 648–52.

Sauro, M. D., and R. P. Greenberg. 2005. 'Endogenous opiates and the placebo effect: a meta-analytic review', *Journal of Psychosomatic Research* 58(2): 115–20.

Scholey, A. B., S. Harper, and D. O. Kennedy. 2001. 'Cognitive demand and blood glucose', *Physiology and Behavior* 73(4): 585–92.

Siegel, J. M. 2005. 'Clues to the functions of mammalian sleep', *Nature* 437(7063): 1264–71.

Silberman, S. 2001. 'The Geek Syndrome', *Wired* 9(12).

Skaper, S. D. 2003. 'Poly(ADP-ribosyl)ation enzyme-1 as a target for neuroprotection in acute central nervous system injury', *Curr. Drug Targets, CNS Neurol. Disord.* 2(5): 279–91.

Smith, J. M. 1982. *Evolution and the Theory of Games.* Cambridge, UK: Cambridge University Press.

Starfield, B. 2000. 'Is US health really the best in the world?', *Jama—Journal of the American Medical Association* 284(4): 483–5.

Thomas, M. K., D. M. Lloyd-Jones, R. I. Thadhani, A. C. Shaw, D. J. Deraska, B. T. Kitch, E. C. Vamvakas, I. M. Dick, R. L. Prince, and J. S. Finkelstein. 1998. 'Hypovitaminosis D in medical inpatients', *New England Journal of Medicine* 338(12): 777–83.

Thompson, E. E., H. Kuttab-Boulos, D. Witonsky, L. Yang, B. A. Roe, and A. Di Rienzo. 2004. 'CYP3A variation and the evolution of salt-sensitivity variants', *American Journal of Human Genetics* 75(6): 1059–69.

Tishkoff, S. A., F. A. Reed, A. Ranciaro, B. F. Voight, C. C. Babbitt, J. S. Silverman, K. Powell, H. M. Mortensen, J. B. Hirbo, M. Osman, M. Ibrahim, S. A. Omar, G. Lema, T. B. Nyambo, J. Ghori, S. Bumpstead, J. K. Pritchard, G. A. Wray, and P. Deloukas. 2007. 'Convergent adaptation of human lactase persistence in Africa and Europe', *Nature Genetics* 39(1): 31–40.

Trevathan, W. 1987. *Human Birth: An Evolutionary Perspective.* New York: Aldine de Gruyter.

Trevathan, W. R., E. O. Smith, and J. J. McKenna (eds.), 1999. *Evolutionary Medicine.* Oxford: Oxford University Press.

Udry, J. R. 1978. 'Differential Fertility by Intelligence—Role of Birth Planning', *Social Biology* 25(1): 10–14.

Vancourt, M., and F. D. Bean. 1985. 'Intelligence and Fertility in the United States—1912–1982, *Intelligence* 9(1): 23–32.

Venkateswaran, A., S. C. McFarlan, D. Ghosal, K. W. Minton, A. Vasilenko, K. Makarova, L. P. Wackett, and M. J. Daly. 2000. 'Physiologic Determinants of Radiation Resistance in Deinococcus radiodurans', *Applied and Environmental Microbiology* 66(6): 2620–6.

Vining, D. R., L. Bygren, K. Hattori, S. Nystrom, and S. Tamura. 1988. 'IQ/Fertility Relationships in Japan and Sweden', *Personality and Individual Differences* 9(5): 931–2.

Voight, B. F., S. Kudaravalli, X. Q. Wen, and J. K. Pritchard. 2006. 'A map of recent positive selection in the human genome', *Plos Biology* 4(3): 446–58.

von Karolyi, C., E. Winner, W. Gray, and G. F. Sherman. 2003. 'Dyslexia linked to talent: Global visual-spatial ability', *Brain and Language* 85(3): 427–31.

Waterlow, J. C. 1984. 'Protein turnover with special reference to man', *Q. J. Exp. Physiol.* 69(3): 409–38.

Williams, G. C. 1996/1966. *Adaptation and Natural Selection*. Princeton, NJ: Princeton University Press.

——and R. M. Nesse. 1991. 'The Dawn of Darwinian Medicine', *Quarterly Review of Biology* 66(1): 1–22.

Winder, R., and J. Borrill. 1998. 'Fuels for memory: the role of oxygen and glucose in memory enhancement', *Psychopharmacology* 136(4): 349–56.

Wood, R. D., M. Mitchell, J. Sgouros, and T. Lindahl. 2001. 'Human DNA repair genes', *Science* 291(5507): 1284–9.

Worden, R. P. 1995. 'A Speed Limit for Evolution', *Journal of Theoretical Biology* 176(1): 137–52.

Yazdanbakhsh, M., P. G. Kremsner, and R. van Ree. 2002. 'Immunology—Allergy, parasites, and the hygiene hypothesis', *Science* 296(5567): 490–4.

Index